AMERICA'S

GREAT

DEPRESSION

BOOKS BY MURRAY N. ROTHBARD

The Panic of 1819
Power and Market
Man, Economy, and State

AMERICA'S

GREAT

DEPRESSION

by Murray N. Rothbard

NASH PUBLISHING, LOS ANGELES

This edition is sponsored by the INSTITUTE FOR
HUMANE STUDIES, INC., Menlo Park, California, which
was founded in 1961 as an independent center to encourage basic research and advanced study for the
strengthening of a free society. Through seminars, fellow-
ships, publications and other activities, the Institute seeks
to serve a worldwide community of scholars in education,
business and the professions, who are interested in broadening the knowledge and practice of the principles of
liberty.

Library of Congress Catalog Card Number: 70-179705
Standard Book Number: 8402-5003-7

Published simultaneously in the United States and
Canada by Nash Publishing Corporation,
9255 Sunset Boulevard, Los Angeles, California 90069.

Printed in the United States of America.

TO JOEY,
the indispensable framework

Acknowledgments

While the problem of 1929 has long been of interest to myself as well as most Americans, my attention was first specifically drawn to a study of the Great Depression when Mr. Leonard E. Read, President of the Foundation for Economic Education, asked me, some years ago, to prepare a brief paper on the subject. I am very grateful to Mr. Read for being, in this way, the sparkplug for the present book. Having written the article, I allowed the subject to remain dormant for several years, amid the press of other work. At that point, on the warm encouragement of Mr. Richard C. Cornuelle, now of the Foundation for Voluntary Welfare, I proceeded on the task of expansion to the present work, an expansion so far-reaching as to leave few traces of the original sketch. I owe a particular debt to the Earhart Foundation, without whose aid this study could never have been written.

My supreme debt is to Professor Ludwig von Mises, whose monumental theory of business cycles I have used to explain the causes of the otherwise mysterious 1929 depression. Of all Professor Mises' notable contributions to economic science, his business cycle theory is certainly one of the most significant. It is no exaggeration to say that any study of business cycles not based upon his theoretical foundation is bound to be a fruitless undertaking.

The responsibility for this work, of course, is entirely my own.

Table of Contents

Part III: THE GREAT DEPRESSION: 1929-1933

Introduction to the Second Edition

In the years that have elapsed since the publication of the first edition, the business cycle has re-emerged in the consciousness of economists. During the 1960's, we were again promised, as in the New Era of the 1920's, the abolition of the business cycle by Keynesian and other sophisticated policies of government. The substantial and marked recession which began around November, 1969, and from which at this writing we have not yet recovered, has been a salutary if harsh reminder that the cycle is still very much alive.

One feature of this current recession that has been particularly unpleasant and surprising is the fact that prices of consumer goods have continued to rise sharply throughout the recession. In the classic cycle, prices fall during recessions or depressions, and this decline in prices is the one welcome advantage that the consumer can reap from such periods of general gloom. In the present recession, however, even this advantage has been removed, and the consumer thus suffers a combination of the worst features of recession and inflation.

Neither the established Keynesian nor the contemporary "monetarist" schools anticipated or can provide a satisfactory explanation of this phenomenon of "inflationary recession." Yet the "Austrian" theory contained in this book not only explains this occurrence, but demonstrates that it is a general and universal tendency in recessions. For the essence of recession, as the Austrian theory shows, is a readjustment of the economy to liquidate the distortions imposed by the boom—in particular, the overexpansion of the "higher" orders of capital goods and the underinvestment in consumer goods industries. One of the ways by which the market redirects resources from the capital goods to the consumer goods sphere is by prices declining relatively in the former category and rising relatively in the latter category. Bankruptcies and relative price and wage contractions in the overblown and malinvested higher orders of capital goods will redirect land, labor, and capital resources into consumer goods and thereby re-establish the efficient responsiveness to consumer demands that is the normal condition of an unhampered market economy.

In short, the prices of consumer goods always tend to rise, relative to the prices of producer goods, during recessions. The reason that this phenomenon has not been noted before is that, in past recessions, prices have *generally fallen.* If, for example, consumer goods prices fall by 10 per cent and, say, cement prices fall by 20 per cent, no one worries about an "inflation" during the recession; but, actually, consumer goods prices in this case, too, have risen *relative to* the prices of producer goods. Prices in general fell during recessions because monetary and banking deflation used to be an invariable feature of economic contractions. But, in the last few decades, monetary deflation has been strictly prevented by governmental expansion of credit and bank reserves, and the phenomenon of an actual *decline* in the money supply has become at best a dim memory. The result of the government's abolition of deflation, however, is that general prices no longer fall, even in recessions. Consequently, the adjustment between consumer goods and capital goods that must take place during recessions, must now proceed without the merciful veil of deflation. Hence, the prices of consumer goods still rise relatively, but now, shorn of general deflation, they must rise absolutely and visibly as well. The government policy of stepping in to prevent monetary deflation, therefore, has deprived the public of the one great advantage of recessions: a falling cost of living. Government intervention against deflation has brought us the unwelcome phenomenon of inflationary recession.

Along with the renewed emphasis on business cycles, the late 1960's saw the emergence of the "monetarist" Chicago School, headed by Milton Friedman, as a significant competitor to the Keynesian emphasis on compensatory fiscal policy. While the Chicago approach provides a welcome return to the pre-Keynesian emphasis on the crucial role of money in business cycles, it is essentially no more than a recrudescence of the "purely monetary" theory of Irving Fisher and Sir Ralph Hawtrey during the 1910's and 1920's. Following the manner of the English classical economists of the nineteenth century, the monetarists rigidly separate the "price level" from the movement of individual prices; monetary forces supposedly determine the former while supply and demand for particular goods determine the latter. Hence, for the monetarists, monetary forces have no significant or systematic effect on the behavior of relative prices or in distorting the structure of production. Thus, while the monetarists see that a rise in the supply of money and credit will tend to raise the level of general prices, they ignore the fact that a recession is then required to eliminate the distortions and unsound investments of the preceding boom. Consequently, the monetarists have no causal theory of the business cycle; each stage of the cycle becomes an event unrelated to the following stage.

Furthermore, as in the case of Fisher and Hawtrey, the current monetarists uphold as an ethical and economic ideal the maintenance of a stable, constant price level. The essence of the cycle is supposed to be the rise and fall—the movements—of the price level. Since this level is determined by monetary forces, the monetarists hold that if the price level is kept constant by government policy, the business cycle will disappear. Friedman, for example, in his *A Monetary History of the United States, 1867-1960* (1963), emulates his mentors in lauding Benjamin Strong for keeping the wholesale price level stable during the 1920's. To the monetarists, the inflation of money and bank credit engineered by Strong led to no ill effects, no cycle of boom and bust; on the contrary, the Great Depression was caused by the tight money policy that ensued after Strong's death. Thus, while the Fisher-Chicago monetarists and the Austrians both focus on the vital role of money in the Great Depression as in other business cycles, the causal emphases and policy conclusions are diametrically opposed. To the Austrians, the monetary inflation of the 1920's set the stage inevitably for the depression, a depression which was further aggravated (and unsound investments maintained) by the Federal Reserve efforts to inflate further during the 1930's. The Chicagoans, on the other hand, seeing no causal factors at work generating recession out of preceding boom, hail the policy of the 1920's in keeping the price level stable and believe that the depression could have been quickly cured if only the Federal Reserve had inflated far more intensively during the depression.

The long-run tendency of the free market economy, un-hampered by monetary expansion, is a gently falling price level, falling as the productivity and output of goods and services continually increase. The Austrian policy of refraining at all times from monetary inflation would allow this tendency of the free market its head and thereby remove the disruptions of the business cycle. The Chicago goal of a constant price level, which can be achieved only by a continual expansion of money and credit, would, as in the 1920's, unwittingly generate the cycle of boom and bust that has proved so destructive for the past two centuries.

MURRAY N. ROTHBARD

New York, N.Y.
July, 1971

Introduction

The year 1929 stands as the great American trauma. Its shock impact on American thought has been enormous. The reasons for shock seem clear. Generally, depressions last a year or two; prices and credit contract sharply, unsound positions are liquidated, unemployment swells temporarily, and then rapid recovery ensues. The 1920-1921 experience repeated a familiar pattern, not only of such hardly noticeable recessions as 1899-1900 and 1910-1912, but also of such severe but brief crises as 1907-1908 and 1819-1821.[1] Yet the Great Depression that ignited in 1929 lasted, in effect, for eleven years.

In addition to its great duration, the 1929 depression stamped itself on the American mind by its heavy and continuing unemployment. While the intensity of falling prices and monetary contraction was not at all unprecedented, the intensity and duration of unemployment was new and shocking. The proportion of the American labor force that was unemployed had rarely reached 10 per cent at the deepest trough of previous depressions; yet it surpassed 20 per cent in 1931, and remained above 15 per cent until the advent of World War II.

If we use the commonly accepted dating methods and business-cycle methodology of the National Bureau of Economic Research, we shall be led astray in studying and interpreting the depression. Unfortunately, the Bureau early shifted its emphasis from the study of the qualitatively important periods of "prosperity" and "depression," to those of mere "expansion" and "contraction." In its dating methods, it picks out one month as the peak or trough, and thus breaks up all historical periods into expansions and contractions, lumping them all together as units in its averages, regardless of importance or severity. Thus, the long boom of the 1920's is hardly recognized by the Bureau— which highlights instead the barely noticeable recessions of

1

1923 and 1926. Furthermore, we may agree with the Bureau—and all other observers—that the Great Depression hit its trough in 1932-1933, but we should not allow an artificial methodology to prevent our realizing that the "boom" of 1933-1937 took place *within* a continuing depression. When unemployment remains over 15 per cent, it is folly to refer to the 1933-1937 period as "prosperity." It is still depression, even if slightly less intense than in 1933.[2]

The chief impact of the Great Depression on American thought was universal acceptance of the view that *"laissez-faire* capitalism" was to blame. The common opinion—among economists and the lay public alike—holds that "Unreconstructed Capitalism" prevailed during the 1920's, and that the tragic depression shows that old-fashioned *laissez-faire* can work no longer. It had always brought instability and depression during the nineteenth century; but now it was getting worse and becoming absolutely intolerable. The government must step in to stabilize the economy and iron out the business cycle. A vast army of people to this day consider capitalism almost permanently on trial. If the modern array of monetary-fiscal management and stabilizers cannot save capitalism from another severe depression, this large group will turn to socialism as the final answer. To them, another depression would be final proof that even a reformed and enlightened capitalism cannot prosper.

Yet, on closer analysis, the common reaction is by no means self-evident. It rests, in fact, on an unproven assumption—the assumption that business cycles in general, and depressions in particular, arise from the depths of the free-market, capitalist economy. Once assume that the business cycle stems from—is "endogenous" to—the free-market, and the common reaction seems plausible. And yet, the assumption is pure myth, resting not on proof but on simple faith. Karl Marx was one of the first to maintain that business crises stemmed from market processes. In the twentieth century, whatever their great positive differences, almost all economists—Mitchellians, Keynesians, Marxians, or whatnot—are convinced of this view. They may have conflicting causal theories to explain the phenomenon, or, like the Mitchellians, they may have no causal theory at all—but they are all convinced that business cycles spring from deep within the capitalist system.

Yet there is another and conflicting tradition of economic thought—now acknowledged by only a few economists, and by almost none of the public. This view holds that business cycles and depressions stem from disturbances generated in the market by *monetary intervention*. The monetary theory holds that money and credit-expansion, launched by the banking system, causes booms and busts. This doctrine was first advanced, in rudimentary form, by the Currency School of British classical economists in the early nineteenth century, and then fully developed by Ludwig von Mises and his followers in the twentieth. Although widely popular in early nineteenth century America and Britain, the Currency School thesis has been read out of business cycle theory and relegated to another compartment: "international trade theory." Nowadays, the monetary theory, when acknowledged at all, is scoffed at as over-simplified. And yet, neither simplicity nor single-cause explanation is a defect *per se* in science; on the contrary, other things being equal, science will prefer the simpler to the more complex explanation. And science is always searching for a unified "single cause" explanation of complex phenomena, and rejoices when it can be found. If a theory is incorrect, it must be combatted on its demerits only; it must not be simply accused of being monocausal or of relying on causes external to the free market. Perhaps, after all, the causes *are* external— exogenous, to the market! The only valid test is correctness of theoretical reasoning.

This book rests squarely on the Misesian interpretation of the business cycle.[3] The first part sets forth the theory and then refutes some prominent conflicting views. The theory itself is discussed relatively briefly, a full elaboration being available in other works. The implications of this theory for governmental policy are also elaborated—implications which run flatly counter to prevailing views. The second and third parts apply the theory to furnish an explanation of the causes of the 1929 depression in the United States. Note that I make no pretense of using the historical facts to "test" the truth of the theory. On the contrary, I contend that economic theories *cannot* be "tested" by historical or statistical fact. These historical facts are complex and cannot, like the controlled and isolable physical facts of the scientific laboratory, be used to test theory. There are always many causal factors impinging on each other to form historical facts. Only causal theories *a priori* to these facts can be used to isolate and identify the causal strands.[4] For example, suppose that the price of zinc rises over a certain time period. We may ask: why has it risen? We can only answer the question by employing various causal theories arrived at *prior* to our investigation. Thus, we know that the price might have risen from any one or a combination of these causes: an increase in demand for zinc; a reduction in its supply; a general increase in the supply of money and hence in monetary demand for all goods; a reduction in the general demand for money. How do we know which particular theory applies in these particular cases? Only by looking at the facts and seeing which theories are *applicable*. But whether or not a theory is applicable to a given case has no relevance whatever to its truth or falsity as a theory. It *neither confirms nor refutes* the thesis that a decrease in the supply of zinc will, *cet. par.,* raise the price, to find that this cut in supply actually occurred (or did not occur) in the period we may be investigating. The task of the economic historian, then, is to make the relevant applications of theory from the armory provided him by the economic theorist. The only *test* of a theory is the correctness of the premises and of the logical chain of reasoning.[5]

The currently dominant school of economic methodologists— the positivists—stand ready, in imitation of the physical scientists, to use false premises provided the conclusions prove sound upon testing. On the other hand, the institutionalists, who eternally search for more and more facts, virtually abjure theory altogether. Both are in error. Theory cannot emerge, Phoenix-like, from a cauldron of statistics; neither can statistics be used to test an economic theory.

The same considerations apply when gauging the results of political policies. Suppose a theory asserts that a certain policy will cure a depression. The government, obedient to the theory, puts the policy into effect. The depression is not cured. The critics and advocates of the theory now leap to the fore with interpretations. The critics say that failure proves the theory incorrect. The advocates say that the government erred in not pursuing the theory boldly enough, and that what is needed is stronger measures in the same direction. Now the point is that *empirically there is no possible way of deciding between them.*[6] Where is the empirical "test" to resolve the debate? How can the government rationally decide upon its next step? Clearly, the only possible way of resolving the issue is in the realm of pure theory—by examining the conflicting premises and chains of reasoning.

These methodological considerations chart the course of this book. The aim is to describe and highlight the causes of the 1929 depression in America. I do not intend to write a complete economic history of the period, and therefore there is no need to gather and collate all conceivable economic statistics. I shall only concentrate on the causal forces that first brought about, and then aggravated, the depression. I hope that this analysis will be useful to future economic historians of the 1920's and 1930's in constructing their syntheses.

It is generally overlooked that study of a business cycle should *not* simply be an investigation of the entire economic record of an era. The National Bureau of Economic Research, for example, treats the business cycle as an array of all economic activities during a certain period. Basing itself upon this assumption (and despite the Bureau's scorn of *a priori* theorizing, this is very much an unproven, *a priori* assumption), it studies the expansion-contraction statistics of all the time-series it can possibly accumulate. A National Bureau inquiry into a business cycle is, then, essentially a statistical history of the period. Adopting a Misesian, or Austrian, rather than the typically institutionalist methodology of the Bureau, however, the proper procedure becomes very different. The problem now becomes one of pinpointing the causal factors, tracing the chains of cause and effect, and isolating the cyclical strand from the complex economic world.

As an illustration, let us take the American economy during the 1920's. This economy was, in fact, a mixture of two very different, and basically conflicting, forces. On the one hand, America experienced a genuine prosperity, based on heavy savings and investment in highly productive capital. This great advance raised American living standards. On the other hand, we also suffered a credit-expansion, with resulting accumulation of *malinvested* capital, leading finally and *inevitably* to economic crisis. Here are two great economic forces—one that most people would agree to call "good," and the other "bad"—each separate, but interacting to form the final historical result. Price, production, and trade indices are the composite effects. We may well remember the errors of smugness and complacency that our economists, as well as financial and political leaders, committed during the great boom. Study of these errors might even chasten our current crop of economic soothsayers, who presume to foretell the future within a small, precise margin of error. And yet, we should not scoff unduly at the eulogists who composed paeans to our economic system as late as 1929. For, insofar as they had in mind the *first* strand—the genuine prosperity brought about by high saving and investment—they were correct. Where they erred gravely was in overlooking the second, sinister strand of credit expansion. This book concentrates on the cyclical aspects of the economy of the period—if you will, on the defective strand.

As in most historical studies, space limitations require confining oneself to a definite time period. This book deals with the period 1921-1933. The years 1921-1929 were the boom period preceding the Great Depression. Here we look for causal influences predating 1929, the ones responsible for the *onset* of the depression. The years 1929-1933 composed the historic contraction phase of the Great Depression, even by itself of unusual length and intensity. In this period, we shall unravel the aggravating causes that worsened and prolonged the crisis.

In any comprehensive study, of course, the 1933-1940 period would have to be included. It is, however, a period more familiar to us and one which has been more extensively studied.

The pre-1921 period also has some claim to our attention.

Many writers have seen the roots of the Great Depression in the inflation of World War I and of the post-war years, and in the allegedly inadequate liquidation of the 1920-1921 recession. However, sufficient liquidation does *not* require a monetary or price contraction back to pre-boom levels. We will therefore begin our treatment with the trough of the 1920-1921 cycle, in the fall of 1921, and see briefly how credit expansion began to distort production (and perhaps leave unsound positions unliquidated from the preceding boom) even at that early date. Comparisons will also be made between public policy and the relative durations of the 1920-1921 and the 1929-1933 depressions. We cannot go beyond that in studying the earlier period, and going further is not strictly necessary for our discussion.

One great spur to writing this book has been the truly remarkable dearth of study of the 1929 depression by economists. Very few books of substance have been specifically devoted to 1929, from any point of view. This book attempts to fill a gap by inquiring in detail into the causes of the 1929 depression from the standpoint of correct, praxeological economic theory.[7]

Part I

BUSINESS CYCLE THEORY

1

The Positive Theory of the Cycle

Study of business cycles must be based upon a satisfactory cycle theory. Gazing at sheafs of statistics without "pre-judgment" is futile. A cycle takes place in the economic world, and therefore a usable cycle theory *must* be integrated with general economic theory. And yet, remarkably, such integration, even attempted integration, is the exception, not the rule. Economics, in the last two decades, has fissured badly into a host of airtight compartments—each sphere hardly related to the others. Only in the theories of Schumpeter and Mises has cycle theory been integrated into general economics.[1]

The bulk of cycle specialists, who spurn any systematic integration as impossibly deductive and overly simplified, are thereby (wittingly or unwittingly) rejecting economics itself. For if one may forge a theory of the cycle with little or no relation to general economics, then general economics must be incorrect, failing as it does to account for such a vital economic phenomenon. For institutionalists—the pure data collectors—if not for others, this is a welcome conclusion. Even institutionalists, however, *must* use theory sometimes, in analysis and recommendation; in fact, they end by using a concoction of *ad hoc* hunches, insights, etc., plucked unsystematically from various theoretical gardens. Few, if any, economists have realized that the Mises theory of the trade cycle is not just another theory: that, in fact, it meshes closely with a general theory of the economic system.[2] The Mises theory *is*, in fact, the economic analysis of the necessary conse-

11

quences of *intervention* in the free market by bank credit expansion. Followers of the Misesian theory have often displayed excessive modesty in pressing its claims; they have widely protested that the theory is "only one of many possible explanations of business cycles," and that each cycle may fit a different causal theory. In this, as in so many other realms, eclecticism is misplaced. Since the Mises theory is the only one that stems from a general economic theory, it is the only one that can provide a correct explanation. Unless we are prepared to abandon general theory, we must reject all proposed explanations that do not mesh with general economics.

BUSINESS CYCLES AND BUSINESS FLUCTUATIONS

It is important, first, to distinguish between *business cycles* and ordinary *business fluctuations*. We live necessarily in a society of continual and unending change, change that can never be precisely charted in advance. People try to forecast and anticipate changes as best they can, but such forecasting can never be reduced to an exact science. Entrepreneurs are in the business of forecasting changes on the market, both for conditions of demand and of supply. The more successful ones make profits *pari passus* with their accuracy of judgment, while the unsuccessful forecasters fall by the wayside. As a result, the successful entrepreneurs on the free market will be the ones most adept at anticipating future business conditions. Yet, the forecasting can never be perfect, and entrepreneurs will continue to differ in the success of their judgments. If this were not so, no profits or losses would ever be made in business.

Changes, then, take place continually in all spheres of the economy. Consumer tastes shift; time preferences and consequent proportions of investment and consumption change; the labor force changes in quantity, quality, and location; natural resources are discovered and others are used up; technological changes alter production possibilities; vagaries of climate alter crops, etc. All these changes are typical features of any economic system. In fact, we could not truly conceive of a changeless society, in which everyone did exactly the same things day after day, and no economic data ever changed. And even if we could conceive of such a society, it is doubtful whether many people would wish to bring it about.

It is, therefore, absurd to expect every business activity to be "stabilized" as if these changes were not taking place. To stabilize and "iron out" these fluctuations would, in effect, eradicate any rational productive activity. To take a simple, hypothetical case, suppose that a community is visited every seven years by the seven-year locust. Every seven years, therefore, many people launch preparations to deal with the locusts: produce anti-locust equipment, hire trained locust specialists, etc. Obviously, every seven years there is a "boom" in the locust-fighting industry, which, happily, is "depressed" the other six years. Would it help or harm matters if everyone decided to "stabilize" the locust-fighting industry by insisting on producing the machinery evenly every year, only to have it rust and become obsolete? Must people be forced to build machines before they want them; or to hire people before they are needed; or, conversely, to delay building machines they want—all in the name of "stabilization"? If people desire more autos and fewer houses than formerly, should they be forced to keep buying houses and be prevented from buying the autos, all for the sake of stabilization? As Dr. F. A. Harper has stated:

This sort of business fluctuation runs all through our daily lives. There is a violent fluctuation, for instance, in the harvest of strawberries at different times during the year. Should we grow enough strawberries in greenhouses so as to stabilize that part of our economy throughout the year? [3]

We may, therefore, expect *specific* business fluctuations all the time. There is no need for any special "cycle theory" to account for them. They are simply the results of changes in economic data and are fully explained by economic theory. Many economists, however, attribute general business depression to "weaknesses" caused by a "depression in building" or a "farm depression." But declines in specific industries can never ignite a general depression. Shifts in data will cause increases in activity in one field, declines in another. There is nothing here to account for a *general* business depression—a phenomenon of the true "business cycle." Suppose, for example, that a shift in consumer tastes, and technologies, causes a shift in demand from farm products to other goods. It is pointless to say, as many people do, that a farm depression will ignite a general depression, because farmers will buy less goods, the people in industries selling to farmers will buy less, etc. This ignores the fact that people producing the *other* goods now favored by consumers will prosper; *their* demands will increase.

The problem of the business cycle is one of *general* boom and depression; it is not a problem of exploring specific industries and wondering what factors make each one of them relatively prosperous or depressed. Some economists—such as Warren and Pearson or Dewey and Dakin—have believed that there are no such things as general business fluctuations—that general movements are but the results of different cycles that take place, at different specific time-lengths, in the various economic activities. To the extent that such varying cycles (such as the 20-year "building cycle" or the seven-year locust cycle) may exist, however, they are irrelevant to a study of business cycles *in general* or to business depressions in particular. What we are trying to explain are *general* booms and busts in business.

In considering general movements in business, then, it is immediately evident that such movements must be transmitted through the general medium of exchange—money. Money forges the connecting link between all economic activities. If one price goes up and another down, we may conclude that demand has shifted from one industry to another; but if *all* prices move up or down together, some change must have occurred in the *monetary* sphere. Only changes in the demand for, and/or the supply of, money will cause general price changes. An increase in the supply of money, the demand for money remaining the same, will cause a fall in the purchasing power of each dollar, i.e. a general rise in prices; conversely, a drop in the money supply will cause a general decline in prices. On the other hand, an increase in the general demand for money, the supply remaining given, will bring about a rise in the purchasing power of the dollar (a general fall in prices); while a fall in demand will lead to a general rise in prices. Changes in prices in general, then, are determined by changes in the supply of and demand for money. The supply of money consists of the stock of money existing in the society. The demand for money is, in the final analysis, the willingness of people to hold cash balances, and this can be expressed as eagerness to acquire money in exchange, and as eagerness to retain money in cash balance. The supply of goods in the economy is one component in the social demand for money; an increased supply of goods will, *other things being equal,* increase the demand for money and therefore tend to lower prices. Demand for money will tend to be lower when the purchasing power of the money-unit is higher, for then each dollar is more effective in cash balance. Conversely, a lower purchasing power (higher prices) means that each dollar is less effective, and more dollars will be needed to carry on the same work.

The purchasing power of the dollar, then, will remain constant when the stock of, and demand for, money are in equilibrium with each other: i.e., when people are willing to hold in their cash balances the exact amount of money in existence. If the demand for money exceeds the stock, the purchasing power of money will rise until the demand is no longer excessive and the market is cleared; conversely, a demand lower than supply will lower the purchasing power of the dollar, i.e. raise prices.

Yet, fluctuations in general business, in the "money relation," do not by themselves provide the clue to the mysterious business cycle. It is true that any cycle in general business must be transmitted through this money relation: the relation between the stock of, and the demand for, money. But these changes in themselves explain little. If the money supply increases or demand falls, for example, prices will rise; but why should this generate a "business cycle"? Specifically, why should it bring about a depression? The early business cycle theorists were correct in focusing their attention on the *crisis* and *depression:* for these are the phases that puzzle and shock economists and laymen alike, and these are the phases that most need to be explained.

THE PROBLEM: THE CLUSTER OF ERROR

The explanation of depressions, then, will not be found by referring to specific or even general business fluctuations *per se.* The main problem that a theory of depression must explain is: *why is there a sudden general cluster of business errors?* This is the first question for any cycle theory. Business activity moves along nicely with most business firms making handsome profits. Suddenly, without warning, conditions change and the bulk of business firms are experiencing losses; they are suddenly revealed to have made grievous errors in forecasting.

A general review of entrepreneurship is now in order. Entrepreneurs are largely in the business of forecasting. They must invest and pay costs in the present, in the expectation of recouping a profit by sale either to consumers or to other entrepreneurs further down in the economy's structure of production. The better entrepreneurs, with better judgment in forecasting consumer or other producer demands, make profits; the inefficient entrepreneurs suffer losses. The market, therefore, provides a training ground for the reward and expansion of successful, far-sighted entrepreneurs and the weeding out of inefficient businessmen. As a rule only some businessmen suffer losses at any one time; the bulk either break even or earn profits. How, then, explain the curious phenomenon of the crisis when almost all entrepreneurs suffer sudden losses? In short, how did all the country's astute businessmen come to make such errors together, and why were they all suddenly revealed at this particular time? This is the great problem of cycle theory.

It is not legitimate to reply that sudden changes in the data are responsible. It is, after all, the business of entrepreneurs to forecast future changes, some of which are sudden. Why did their forecasts fail so abysmally?

Another common feature of the business cycle also calls for an explanation. It is the well-known fact that *capital-goods industries*

fluctuate more widely than do the consumer-goods industries.
The capital-goods industries—especially the industries supplying
raw materials, construction, and equipment to other industries
—expand much further in the boom, and are hit far more
severely in the depression.

A third feature of every boom that needs explaining is the
increase in the quantity of money in the economy. Conversely,
there is generally, though not universally, a fall in the money
supply during the depression.

THE EXPLANATION: BOOM AND DEPRESSION

In the purely free and unhampered market, there will be no
cluster of errors, since trained entrepreneurs will not all make
errors at the same time.[4] The "boom-bust" cycle is generated by
monetary intervention in the market, specifically bank credit expansion to business. Let us suppose an economy with a given
supply of money. Some of the money is spent in consumption;
the rest is saved and invested in a mighty structure of capital, in
various orders of production. The proportion of consumption to
saving or investment is determined by people's *time preferences*
—the degree to which they prefer present to future satisfactions.
The less they prefer them in the present, the lower will their time-
preference rate be, and the lower therefore will be the *pure
interest rate,* which is determined by the time preferences of the
individuals in society. A lower time-preference rate will be reflected in greater proportions of investment to consumption, a
lengthening of the structure of production, and a building-up of
capital. Higher time preferences, on the other hand, will be
reflected in higher pure interest rates and a lower proportion of
investment to consumption. The final market rates of interest
reflect the pure interest rate plus or minus entrepreneurial risk
and purchasing power components. Varying degrees of entrepreneurial risk bring about a *structure* of interest rates instead of
a single uniform one, and purchasing-power components reflect
changes in the purchasing power of the dollar, as well as in the
specific position of an entrepreneur in relation to price changes.

The crucial factor, however, is the pure interest rate. This interest rate first manifests itself in the "natural rate" or what is generally called the going "rate of profit." This going rate is reflected in the interest rate on the loan market, a rate which is determined by the going profit rate.[5]

Now what happens when banks print new money (whether as bank notes or bank deposits) and lend it to business? [6] The new money pours forth on the loan market and lowers the loan rate of interest. It *looks as if* the supply of saved funds for investment has increased, for the effect is the same: the supply of funds for investment apparently increases, and the interest rate is lowered. Businessmen, in short, are misled by the bank inflation into believing that the supply of saved funds is greater than it really is. Now, when saved funds increase, businessmen invest in "longer processes of production," i.e. the capital structure is lengthened, especially in the "higher orders" most remote from the consumer. Businessmen take their newly acquired funds and bid up the prices of capital and other producers' goods, and this stimulates a shift of investment from the "lower" (near the consumer) to the "higher" orders of production (furthest from the consumer)—from consumer goods to capital goods industries.[7]

If this were the effect of a genuine fall in time-preferences and increase in saving, all would be well and good, and the new lengthened structure of production could be indefinitely sustained. But this shift is the product of bank credit expansion. Soon the new money percolates downward from the business borrowers to the factors of production: in wages, rents, interest. Now, unless time preferences have changed, and there is no reason to think that they have, people will rush to spend the higher incomes in the *old* consumption/investment proportions. In short, people will rush to reestablish the old proportions, and demand will shift back from the higher to the lower orders. Capital goods industries will find that their investments have been in error: that what they thought profitable really fails for lack of demand by their entrepreneurial customers. Higher orders of production have turned out to be wasteful, and the malinvestment must be liquidated.

A favorite explanation of the crisis is that it stems from "under-consumption"—from a failure of consumer demand for goods at prices that could be profitable. But this runs contrary to the commonly known fact that it is *capital goods,* and not consumer goods, industries that really suffer in a depression. The failure is one of *entrepreneurial demand* for the higher order goods, and this in turn is caused by the shift of demand back to the old proportions.

In sum, businessmen were misled by bank credit inflation to invest too much in higher-order capital goods, which could only be prosperously sustained through lower time preferences and greater savings and investment; as soon as the inflation permeates to the mass of the people, the old consumption/investment proportion is reestablished, and business investments in the higher orders are seen to have been wasteful.[8] Businessmen were led to this error by the credit expansion and its tampering with the free-market rate of interest.

The "boom," then, is actually a period of wasteful misinvestment. It is the time when errors are made, due to bank credit's tampering with the free market. The "crisis" arrives when the consumers come to reestablish their desired proportions. The "depression" is actually the process by which the economy *adjusts* to the wastes and errors of the boom, and *reestablishes* efficient service of consumer desires. The adjustment process consists in rapid *liquidation* of the wasteful investments. Some of these will be abandoned altogether (like the Western ghost towns constructed in the boom of 1816-1818 and deserted during the Panic of 1819); others will be shifted to other uses. Always the principle will be not to mourn past errors, but to make most efficient use of the existing stock of capital. In sum, the free market tends to satisfy voluntarily-expressed consumer desires with maximum efficiency, and this includes the public's relative desires for present and future consumption. The inflationary boom hobbles this efficiency, and distorts the structure of production, which no longer serves consumers properly. The crisis signals the end of this inflationary distortion, and the depression is the process by which the economy returns to the efficient service of consumers. In short, and this is a highly important point to grasp, the depression *is* the "recovery" process, and the end of the depression heralds the return to normal, and to optimum efficiency. The depression, then, far from being an evil scourge, is the *necessary* and beneficial return of the economy to normal after the distortions imposed by the boom. The boom, then, *requires* a "bust."

Since it clearly takes very little time for the new money to filter down from business to factors of production, why don't all booms come quickly to an end? The reason is that the banks come to the rescue. Seeing factors bid away from them by consumer goods industries, finding their costs rising and themselves short of funds, the borrowing firms turn once again to the banks. If the banks expand credit further, they can again keep the borrowers afloat. The new money again pours into business, and they can again bid factors away from the consumer goods industries. In short, continually expanded bank credit can keep the borrowers one step ahead of consumer retribution. For this, we have seen, is what the crisis and depression are: the restoration by consumers of an efficient economy, and the ending of the distortions of the boom. Clearly, the greater the credit expansion and the longer it lasts, the longer will the boom last. The boom will end when bank credit expansion finally stops. Evidently, the longer the boom goes on the more wasteful the errors committed, and the longer and more severe will be the necessary depression readjustment.

Thus, bank credit expansion sets into motion the business cycle in all its phases—the inflationary boom, marked by expansion of the money supply and by malinvestment; the crisis, which arrives when credit expansion ceases and malinvestments become evident; and the depression recovery, the necessary adjustment process by which the economy returns to the most efficient ways of satisfying consumer desires.[9]

What, specifically, are the essential features of the depression-recovery phase? Wasteful projects, as we have said, must either be abandoned or used as best they can be. Inefficient firms, buoyed up by the artificial boom, must be liquidated or have their debts scaled down or be turned over to their creditors. Prices of producers' goods must fall, particularly in the higher orders of production—this includes capital goods, lands, and wage rates. Just as the boom was marked by a fall in the rate of interest, i.e. of price differentials between stages of production (the "natural rate" or going rate of profit) as well as the loan rate, so the depression-recovery consists of a rise in this interest-differential. In practice, this means a fall in the prices of the higher-order goods relative to prices in the consumer goods industries. Not only prices of particular machines must fall, but also the prices of whole aggregates of capital, e.g., stock market and real estate values. In fact, these values must fall more than the earnings from the assets, through reflecting the general rise in the rate of interest return.

Since factors must shift from the higher to the lower orders of production, there is inevitable "frictional" unemployment in a depression, but it need not be greater than unemployment attending any other large shift in production. In practice, unemployment will be aggravated by the numerous bankruptcies, and the large errors revealed, but it still need only be temporary. The speedier the adjustment, the more fleeting will the unemployment be. Unemployment will progress beyond the "frictional" stage and become really severe and lasting only if wage rates are kept artificially high and are prevented from falling. If wage rates are kept above the free-market level that clears the demand for and supply of labor, laborers will remain permanently unemployed. The greater the degree of discrepancy, the more severe will the unemployment be.

Secondary Features of Depression: Deflationary Credit Contraction

The above are the essential features of a depression. Other secondary features may also develop. There is no need, for example, for *deflation* (lowering of the money supply) during a depression. The depression phase begins with the end of inflation, and can proceed without any further changes from the side of money. Deflation has almost always set in, however. In the first place, the inflation took place as an expansion of bank credit; now, the financial difficulties and bankruptcies among borrowers cause banks to pull in their horns and contract credit.[10] Under the gold standard, banks have another reason for contracting credit—if they had ended inflation because of a gold drain to foreign countries. The threat of this drain forces them to contract their outstanding loans. Furthermore, the rash of business failures may cause questions to be raised about the banks; and banks, being inherently bankrupt anyway, can ill afford such questions.[11] Hence, the money supply will contract because of actual bank runs, and because banks will tighten their position in fear of such runs.

Another common secondary feature of depressions is *an increase in the demand for money*. This "scramble for liquidity" is the result of several factors: (1) people expect falling prices, due to the depression and deflation, and will therefore hold more money and spend less on goods, awaiting the price fall; (2) borrowers will try to pay off their debts, now being called by banks and by business creditors, by liquidating other assets in exchange for money; (3) the rash of business losses and bankruptcies makes businessmen cautious about investing until the liquidation process is over.

With the supply of money falling, and the demand for money increasing, *generally falling prices* are a consequent feature of most depressions. A general price fall, however, is caused by the secondary, rather than by the inherent, features of depressions. Almost all economists, even those who see that the depression-adjustment process should be permitted to function unhampered, take a very gloomy view of the secondary deflation and price fall, and assert that they unnecessarily aggravate the severity of depressions. This view, however, is incorrect. These processes not only do not aggravate the depression, they have positively beneficial effects.

There is, for example, no warrant whatever for the common hostility toward "hoarding." There is no criterion, first of all, to define "hoarding"; the charge inevitably boils down to mean that

A thinks that B is keeping more cash balances than A deems appropriate for B. Certainly there is no objective criterion to decide when an increase in cash balance becomes a "hoard." Secondly, we have seen that the demand for money increases as a result of certain needs and values of the people; in a depression, fears of business liquidation and expectations of price declines particularly spur this rise. By what standards can these valuations be called "illegitimate"? A general price fall is the way that an increase in the demand for money can be satisfied; for lower prices mean that the same total cash balances have greater effectiveness, greater "real" command over goods and services. In short, the desire for increased real cash balances has now been satisfied.

Furthermore, the demand for money will decline again as soon as the liquidation and adjustment processes are finished. For the completion of liquidation removes the uncertainties of impending bankruptcy and ends the borrowers' scramble for cash. A rapid unhampered fall in prices, both in general (adjusting to the changed money-relation), and particularly in goods of higher orders (adjusting to the malinvestments of the boom) will speedily end the realignment processes and remove expectations of further declines. Thus the sooner the various adjustments, primary and secondary, are carried out, the sooner will the demand for money fall once again. This, of course, is just one part of the general economic "return to normal."

Neither does the increased "hoarding" nor the fall of prices at all interfere with the primary depression-adjustment. The important feature of the primary adjustment is that the prices of producers' goods fall *more rapidly* than do consumer good prices (or, more accurately, that higher order prices fall more rapidly than do those of lower order goods); it does not interfere with the primary adjustment if all prices are falling to some degree. It is, moreover, a common myth among laymen and economists alike, that falling prices have a depressing effect on business. This is not necessarily true. What matters for business is not the general behavior of prices, but the price *differentials* between selling prices and costs (the "natural rate of interest").

If wage rates, for example, fall more rapidly than product prices, this stimulates business activity and employment.

Deflation of the money supply (*via* credit contraction) has fared as badly as hoarding in the eyes of economists. Even the Misesian theorists deplore deflation and have seen no benefits accruing from it.[12] Yet, deflationary credit contraction greatly *helps* to speed up the adjustment process, and hence the completion of business recovery, in ways as yet unrecognized. The adjustment consists, as we know, of a return to the desired consumption/saving pattern. Less adjustment is needed, however, if time preferences *themselves* change: *i.e.*, if savings increase and consumption relatively declines. In short, what can help a depression is not more consumption, but, on the contrary, less consumption and more *savings* (and, concomitantly, more investment). Falling prices encourage greater savings and decreased consumption by fostering an accounting illusion. Business accounting records the value of assets at their original cost. It is well known that general price increases distort the accounting record: what seems to be a large "profit" may only be just sufficient to replace the now higher-priced assets. During an inflation, therefore, business "profits" are greatly overstated, and consumption is greater than it would be if the accounting illusion were not operating—perhaps capital is even consumed without the individual's knowledge. In a time of deflation, the accounting illusion is reversed: what seem like losses and capital consumption, may actually mean profits for the firm, since assets now cost much less to be replaced. This overstatement of losses, however, restricts consumption and encourages saving; a man may merely think he is replacing capital, when he is actually making an added investment in the business.

Credit contraction will have another beneficial effect in promoting recovery. For bank credit expansion, we have seen, distorts the free market by lowering price differentials (the "natural rate of interest" or going rate of profit) on the market. Credit contraction, on the other hand, distorts the free market in the reverse direction. Deflationary credit contraction's first effect is to lower the money supply in the hands of business, particularly in the higher stages of production. This reduces the demand for factors in the higher stages, lowers factor prices and incomes, and increases price differentials and the interest rate. It *spurs* the shift of factors, in short, from the higher to the lower stages. But this means that credit contraction, when it follows upon credit expansion, speeds the market's adjustment process. Credit contraction returns the economy to free-market proportions much sooner than otherwise.

But, it may be objected, may not credit contraction over-compensate the errors of the boom and itself cause distortions that need correction? It is true that credit contraction may over-compensate, and, while contraction proceeds, it may cause interest rates to be higher than free-market levels, and investment lower than in the free market. But since contraction causes no positive *mal*-investments, it will not lead to any painful period of depression and adjustment. If businessmen are misled into thinking that *less* capital is available for investment than is really the case, no lasting damage in the form of wasted investments will ensue.[13] Furthermore, in the nature of things, credit contraction is severely limited—it cannot progress beyond the extent of the preceding inflation.[14] Credit *expansion* faces no such limit.

GOVERNMENT DEPRESSION POLICY: LAISSEZ-FAIRE

If government wishes to see a depression ended as quickly as possible, and the economy returned to normal prosperity, what course should it adopt? The first and clearest injunction is: *don't interfere with the market's adjustment process.* The more the government intervenes to delay the market's adjustment, the longer and more gruelling the depression will be, and the more difficult will be the road to complete recovery. Government hampering aggravates and perpetuates the depression. Yet, government depression policy has always (and would have even more today) aggravated the very evils it has loudly tried to cure. If, in fact, we list logically the various ways that government could *hamper* market adjustment, we will find that we have precisely listed the favorite "anti-depression" arsenal of government policy.

Thus, here are the ways the adjustment process can be hobbled:

(1) *Prevent or delay liquidation.* Lend money to shaky businesses, call on banks to lend further, etc.

(2) *Inflate further.* Further inflation blocks the necessary fall in prices, thus delaying adjustment and prolonging depression. Further credit expansion creates more malinvestments, which, in their turn, will have to be liquidated in some later depression. A government "easy money" policy prevents the market's return to the necessary higher interest rates.

(3) *Keep wage rates up.* Artificial maintenance of wage rates in a depression insures permanent mass unemployment. Furthermore, in a deflation, when prices are falling, keeping the same rate of money wages means that *real* wage rates have been pushed higher. In the face of falling business demand, this greatly aggravates the unemployment problem.

(4) *Keep prices up.* Keeping prices above their free-market levels will create unsalable surpluses, and prevent a return to prosperity.

(5) *Stimulate consumption and discourage saving.* We have seen that more saving and less consumption would speed recovery; more consumption and less saving aggravate the shortage of saved-capital even further. Government can encourage consumption by "food stamp plans" and relief payments. It can discourage savings and investment by higher taxes, particularly on the wealthy and on corporations and estates. As a matter of fact, any increase of taxes-and-government spending will discourage saving and investment and stimulate consumption, since government spending *is all consumption. Some* of the private funds would have been saved and invested; *all* of the government funds are consumed.[15] Any increase in the relative size of government in the economy, therefore, shifts the societal consumption/-investment ratio in favor of consumption, and prolongs the depression.

(6) *Subsidize unemployment.* Any subsidization of unemployment (via unemployment "insurance," relief, etc.) will prolong unemployment indefinitely, and delay the shift of workers to the fields where jobs are available.

These, then, are the measures which will delay the recovery process and aggravate the depression. Yet, they are the time-honored favorites of government policy, and, as we shall see, they were the policies adopted in the 1929-1933 depression, by a government known to many historians as a "laissez-faire" Administration.

Since deflation also speeds recovery, the government should encourage, rather than interfere with, a credit contraction. In a gold-standard economy, such as we had in 1929, blocking deflation has further unfortunate consequences. For a deflation increases the reserve ratios of the banking system, and generates more confidence in citizen and foreigner alike that the gold standard will be retained. Fear for the gold standard will precipitate the very bank runs that the government is anxious to avoid. There are other values in deflation, even in bank runs, which should not be overlooked. Banks should no more be exempt from paying their obligations than is any other business. Any interference with their comeuppance via bank runs will establish banks as a specially-privileged group, not obligated to pay their debts, and will lead to later inflations, credit expansions, and depressions. And if, as we contend, banks are inherently bankrupt and "runs" simply reveal that bankruptcy, it is beneficial for the economy for the banking system to be reformed, once and for all, by a thorough purge of the fractional-reserve banking system. Such a purge would bring home forcefully to the public the dangers of fractional-reserve banking, and, more than any academic theorizing, insure against such banking evils in the future.[16]

The most important canon of sound government policy in a depression, then, is to keep itself from interfering in the adjustment process. Can it do anything more positive to aid the adjustment? Some economists have advocated a government-decreed wage cut to spur employment, e.g., a 10 per cent across-the-board reduction. But free-market adjustment is the reverse of any "across-the-board" policy. Not all wages need to be cut; the degree of required adjustments of prices and wages differs from case to case, and can only be determined on the processes of the free and unhampered market.[17] Government intervention can only distort the market further.

There is one thing the government can do positively, however: it can drastically *lower* its relative role in the economy, slashing its own expenditures and taxes, particularly taxes that interfere with saving and investment. Reducing its tax-spending level will automatically shift the societal saving-investment/consumption ratio in favor of saving and investment, thus greatly lowering the time required for returning to a prosperous economy.[18] Reducing taxes that bear most heavily on savings and investment will further lower social time-preferences.[19] Furthermore, depression is a time of economic strain. Any reduction of taxes, or of any regulations interfering with the free-market, will stimulate healthy economic activity; any increase in taxes or other intervention will depress the economy further.

In sum, the proper governmental policy in a depression is strict *laissez-faire,* including stringent budget-slashing, and coupled perhaps with positive encouragement for credit contraction. For decades such a program has been labelled "ignorant," "reactionary," or "Neanderthal" by conventional economists. On the contrary, it is the policy clearly dictated by economic science to those who wish to end the depression as quickly and as cleanly as possible.[20]

It might be objected that depression only began when credit expansion ceased. Why shouldn't the government continue credit expansion indefinitely? In the first place, the longer the inflationary boom continues, the more painful and severe will be the necessary adjustment process, Secondly, the boom cannot continue indefinitely, because eventually the public awakens to the governmental policy of permanent inflation, and flees from money into goods, making its purchases while the dollar is worth more than it will be in future. The result will be a "runaway" or *hyper-inflation,* so familiar to history, and particularly to the modern world.[21] Hyperinflation, on any count, is far worse than any depression: it destroys the currency—the lifeblood of the economy; it ruins and shatters the middle class and all "fixed income groups"; it wreaks havoc unbounded. And furthermore, it leads finally to unemployment, and lower living standards, since there is little point in working when earned income depreciates by the hour. More time is spent hunting goods to buy. To avoid such a calamity, then, credit expansion must stop sometime, and this will bring a depression into being.

PREVENTING DEPRESSIONS

Preventing a depression is clearly better than having to suffer it. If the government's proper policy *during* a depression is *laissez-faire*, what should it do to prevent a depression from beginning? Obviously, since credit expansion necessarily sows the seeds of later depression, the proper course for the government is to stop any inflationary credit expansion from getting under way. This is not a very difficult injunction, for government's most important task is to *keep itself* from generating inflation. For government is an *inherently inflationary institution*, and consequently has almost always triggered, encouraged and directed the inflationary boom. Government is inherently inflationary because it has, over the centuries, acquired control over the monetary system. Having the power to print money (including the "printing" of bank deposits) gives it the power to tap a ready source of revenue. Inflation is a form of taxation, since the government can create new money out of thin air and use it to bid away resources from private individuals, who are barred by heavy penalty from similar "counterfeiting." Inflation therefore makes a pleasant substitute for taxation for the government officials and their favored groups, and it is a subtle substitute which the general public can easily—and can be encouraged to—overlook. The government can also pin the blame for the rising prices which are the inevitable consequence of inflation, upon the general public or some disliked segments of the public: e.g., business, speculators, foreigners. Only the unlikely adoption of sound economic doctrine could lead the public to pin the responsibility where it belongs: on the government itself.

Private banks, it is true, can themselves inflate the money supply by issuing more claims to standard money (whether gold or government paper) than they could possibly redeem. A bank deposit is equivalent to a warehouse-receipt for cash, a receipt which the bank pledges to redeem at any time the customer wishes to take his money out of the bank's vaults. The whole system of "fractional reserve banking" involves the issuance of receipts which cannot possibly be redeemed. But Mises has shown that, by themselves, private banks could not inflate the money supply by a great deal.[22] In the first place, each bank would find its newly-issued *uncovered,* or "pseudo," receipts (uncovered by cash) soon transferred to the clients of other banks, who would call on the bank for redemption. The narrower the clientele of each bank, then, the less scope for its issue of pseudo-receipts. All the banks could join together and agree to expand at the same rate, but such agreement would be difficult to achieve. Secondly, the banks would be limited by the degree to which the public used bank deposits or notes as against standard cash; and third, they would be limited by the confidence of the clients in their banks, which could be wrecked by runs at any time.

Instead of preventing inflation by prohibiting fractional-reserve banking as fraudulent, governments have uniformly moved in the opposite direction, and have step-by-step removed these free-market checks to bank credit expansion, at the same time putting themselves in a position to direct the inflation. In various ways, they have artificially bolstered public confidence in the banks, encouraged public use of paper and deposits instead of gold (finally outlawing gold), and shepherded all the banks under one roof so that they can all expand together. The main device for accomplishing these aims has been Central Banking, an institution which America finally acquired as the Federal Reserve System in 1913. Central Banking permitted the centralization and absorption of gold into government vaults, greatly enlarging the national base for credit expansion:[23] it also insured uniform action by the banks through basing their reserves on deposit accounts at the Central Bank instead of on gold. Upon establishment of a Central Bank, each private bank no longer gauges its policy according to its particular gold reserve; all banks are now tied together and regulated by Central Bank action. The Central

Bank, furthermore, by proclaiming its function to be a "lender of last resort" to banks in trouble, enormously increases public confidence in the banking system. For it is tacitly assumed by everyone that the government would never permit its own organ —the Central Bank—to fail. A Central Bank, even when on the gold standard, has little need to worry about demands for gold —from its own citizens. Only possible drains of gold to foreign countries (*i.e.,* by non-clients of the Central Bank) may cause worry.

The government assured Federal Reserve control over the banks by (1) granting to the FRB a monopoly over note issue; (2) compelling all the existing "national banks" to join the Federal Reserve System, and to keep all their legal reserves as deposits at the Federal Reserve;[24] and (3) fixing the minimum reserve-ratio of deposits at the Reserve to bank deposits (money owned by the public). The establishment of the FRS was furthermore inflationary in directly reducing existing reserve-ratio requirements.[25] The Reserve could then control the volume of money by governing two things: the volume of bank reserves, and the legal reserve requirements. The Reserve can govern the volume of bank reserves (in ways which will be explained below), and the government sets the legal ratio, but admittedly control over the money supply is not perfect, as banks can keep "excess reserves." Normally, however, reassured by the existence of a lender of last resort, and making profits by maximizing its assets and deposits, a bank will keep fully "loaned up" to its legal ratio.

While unregulated private banking would be checked within narrow limits and would be far less inflationary than Central Bank manipulation,[26] the clearest way of preventing inflation is to outlaw fractional-reserve banking, and to impose a 100 per cent gold-reserve to all notes and deposits. Bank cartels, for example, are not very likely under unregulated, or "free" banking, but they could nevertheless occur. Professor Mises, while recognizing the superior economic merits of 100 per cent gold money to free banking, prefers the latter because 100 per cent reserves would concede to the government control over banking, and government

could easily change these requirements to conform to its inflationist bias.[27] But a 100 per cent gold reserve requirement would
not be just another administrative control by government; it
would be part and parcel of the general libertarian legal prohibition against fraud. Everyone except absolute pacifists concedes
that violence against person and property should be outlawed,
and that agencies, operating under this general law, should
defend person and property against attack. Libertarians, advocates of *laissez-faire,* believe that "governments" should confine
themselves to being defense agencies only. Fraud is equivalent to
theft, for fraud is committed when one part of an exchange-
contract is deliberately not fulfilled after the other's property has
been taken. Banks that issue receipts to non-existent gold are
really committing fraud, because it is then impossible for all
property owners (of claims to gold) to claim their rightful
property. Therefore, prohibition of such practices would not
be an act of government *intervention* in the free market; it would
be part of the general legal *defense* of property against attack
which a free market requires. [28, 29]

What, then, was the proper government policy during the
1920's? What should government have done to prevent the crash?
Its best policy would have been to liquidate the Federal Reserve
System, and to erect a 100 per cent gold reserve money; failing
that, it should have liquidated the FRS and left private banks
unregulated, but subject to prompt, rigorous bankruptcy upon
failure to redeem their notes and deposits. Failing these drastic
measures, and given the existence of the Federal Reserve System,
what should its policy have been? The government should have
exercised full vigilance in not supporting or permitting any
inflationary credit expansion. We have seen that the Fed—the
Federal Reserve System—does not have complete control over
money because it cannot force banks to lend up to their reserves; but it *does* have absolute anti-inflationary control over
the banking system. For it does have the power to reduce bank
reserves at will, and thereby force the banks to cease inflating,
or even to contract if necessary. By lowering the volume of bank
reserves, and/or raising reserve requirements, the federal gov-

ernment, in the 1920's as well as today, has had the absolute power to prevent any increase in the total volume of money and credit. It is true that the FRS has no direct control over such money creators as savings banks, savings and loan associations, and life insurance companies, but any credit expansion from these sources could be offset by deflationary pressure upon the commercial banks. This is especially true because commercial bank deposits (1) form the monetary base for the credit extended by the other financial institutions, and (2) are the most actively circulating part of the money supply. Given the Federal Reserve System and its absolute power over the nation's money, the federal government, since 1913, must bear the complete responsibility for any inflation. The banks cannot inflate on their own; any credit expansion can only take place with the support and acquiescence of the federal government and its Federal Reserve authorities. The banks are virtual pawns of the government, and have been since 1913. Any guilt for credit expansion and the consequent depression must be borne by the federal government and by it alone.[30]

PROBLEMS IN THE MISESIAN THEORY OF THE TRADE CYCLE

The "Assumption" of Full Employment

Before proceeding to discuss alternative business cycle theories, several problems and time-honored misconceptions should be cleared up. Two standard misconceptions have already been refuted by Professor Mises: (1) that the Austrian theory "assumes" the previous existence of "full employment," and therefore does not apply if the credit expansion begins while there are unemployed factors; and (2) that the theory describes the boom as a period of "overinvestment." On the first point, the unemployed factors can either be labor or capital-goods. (There will always be unemployed, submarginal, *land* available.) Inflation will only put unemployed labor factors to work if their owners, though otherwise holding out for a higher real wage than the free market can provide, stupidly settle for a lower real wage if it is camouflaged in the form of a rise in the cost of living. As for idle capital goods, these may have been totally and hopelessly mal-invested in a previous boom (or at some other time) and hopelessly lost to profitable production for a long time or forever. A credit expansion may appear to render submarginal capital profitable once more, but this too will be *malinvestment,* and the now-greater error will be exposed when this boom is over. Thus, credit expansion generates the business cycle regardless of the existence of unemployed factors. Credit expansion in the midst of unemployment will create more distortions and malinvestments, delay recovery from the preceding boom, and make a more gruelling recovery necessary in the future. While it is true that the unemployed factors are not now diverted from more valuable uses as employed factors would be (since they were speculatively idle or malinvested instead of employed), the other complementary factors will be diverted into working with them, and these factors will be malinvested and wasted. Moreover, all the other distorting effects of credit expansion will still follow, and a depression will be necessary to correct the new distortion.[31]

"Overinvestment" or Malinvestment?

The second misconception, given currency by Haberler in his famous *Prosperity and Depression,* calls the Misesian picture of the boom an "overinvestment" theory.[32] Mises has brilliantly shown the error of this label. As Mises points out:

. . . additional investment is only possible to the extent that there is an additional supply of capital goods available. . . . The boom itself does not result in a restriction but rather in an increase in consumption, it does not procure more capital goods for new investment. The essence of the credit-expansion boom is not overinvestment, but investment in wrong lines, i.e., malinvestment on a scale for which the capital goods available do not suffice. Their projects are unrealizable on account of the insufficient supply of capital goods. . . . The unavoidable end of the credit expansion makes the faults committed visible. There are plants which cannot be utilized because the plants needed for the production of the complementary factors of production are lacking; plants the products of which cannot be sold because the consumers are more intent upon purchasing other goods which, however, are not produced in sufficient quantities. . . . The observer notices only the malinvestments which are visible and fails to recognize that these establishments are malinvestments only because of the fact that other plants—those required for the production of the complementary factors of productions and those required for the production of consumers' goods more urgently demanded by the public —are lacking. . . . The whole entrepreneurial class is, as it were, in the position of a master-builder [who] . . . overestimates the quantity of the available supply [of] materials . . . oversizes the groundwork . . . and only discovers later . . . that he lacks the material needed for the completion of the structure. It is obvious that our master-builder's fault was not over-investment, but an inappropriate [investment].[33]

Some critics have insisted that if the boom goes on long enough, these processes might finally be "completed." But this takes the metaphor too literally. The point is that credit expansion distorts investment by directing too much of the available capital into the higher orders of production, leaving too little for lower orders. The unhampered market assures that a complementary structure of capital is harmoniously developed; bank credit expansion hobbles the market and destroys the processes that bring about a balanced structure.[34] The longer the boom goes on, the greater the extent of the distortions and malinvestments.

Banks: Active or Passive?

During the early 1930's, there was a great deal of interest, in the United States and Great Britain, in Mises' theory of the trade cycle, an interest unfortunately nipped in the bud by the excitement surrounding the "Keynesian Revolution." The adherents had split on an important question; Mises asserting that the cycle is always generated by the interventionary banking system and his followers claiming that often banks might only err in being passive and not raising their interest charges quickly enough.[35] The followers held that for one reason or another the "natural rate" of interest might rise, and that the banks, which are after all not omniscient, may inadvertently cause the cycle by merely maintaining their old interest rate, now below the free market rate.

In defense of the Mises "anti-bank" position, we must first point out that the natural interest rate or "profit rate" does not suddenly increase because of vague improvements in "investment opportunities." The natural rate increases because time preferences increase.[36] But how can banks force market interest rates below the free-market rates? Only by *expanding their credit!* To avoid the business cycle, then, it is not necessary for the banks to be omniscient; they need only refrain from credit expansion. If they do so, their loans made out of their own capital will not expand the money supply but will simply take their place with other savings as one of the determinants of the free-market interest rate.[37]

Hayek believes that Mises' theory is somehow deficient because it is exogenous—because it holds that the generation of business cycles stems from interventionary acts rather than from acts of the market itself. This argument is difficult to fathom. Processes are either analyzed correctly or incorrectly; the only test of any analysis is its truth, not whether it is exogenous or endogenous. If the process is *really* exogenous, then the analysis should reveal this fact; the same holds true for endogenous processes. No particular virtue attaches to a theory because it is one or the other.

Recurrence of Cycles

Another common criticism asserts that Mises' theory may explain any *one* prosperity-depression cycle, but it fails to explain another familiar phenomenon of business cycles—their perpetual recurrence. Why does one cycle begin as the previous one ends? Yet Mises' theory *does* explain recurrence, and without requiring us to adopt the familiar but unproven hypothesis that cycles are "self-generating,"—that some mysterious processes within a cycle lead to another cycle without tending toward an equilibrium condition. The self-generating assumption violates the general law of the tendency of the economy toward an equilibrium, while, on the other hand, the Mises theory for the first time succeeds in integrating the theory of the business cycle into the whole structural design of economic theory. Recurrence stems from the fact that banks will always try to inflate credit if they can, and government will almost always back them up and spur them on. Bank profits derive mainly from credit expansion, so they will tend to inflate credit as much as they can until they are checked.[38] Government, too, is inherently inflationary. Banks are forced to halt their credit expansion because of the combined force of external and internal drains, and, during a deflation, the drains, and their fears of bankruptcy, force them to contract credit. When the storm has run its course and recovery has arrived, the banks and the government are free to inflate again, and they proceed to do so. Hence the continual recurrence of business cycles.

Gold Changes and the Cycle

On one important point of business cycle theory this writer is reluctantly forced to part company with Mises. In his *Human Action,* Mises first investigated the laws of a free market economy and then analyzed various forms of coercive intervention in the free market. He admits that he had considered relegating trade-cycle theory to the section on intervention, but then retained the discussion in the free-market part of the volume. He did so because he believed that a boom-bust cycle could also be generated by an increase in gold money, provided that the gold entered the loan market before all its price-raising effects had been completed. The potential range of such cyclical effects in practice, of course, is severely limited: the gold supply is limited by the fortunes of gold mining, and only a fraction of new gold enters the loan market before influencing prices and wage rates. Still, an important theoretical problem remains: can a boom-depression cycle of any degree be generated in a 100 per cent gold economy? Can a purely free market suffer from business cycles, however limited in extent?

One crucial distinction between a credit expansion and entry of new gold onto the loan market is that bank credit expansion *distorts* the market's reflection of the pattern of voluntary time preferences; the gold inflow *embodies changes* in the structure of voluntary time preferences. Setting aside any permanent shifts in income distribution caused by gold changes, time preferences may temporarily fall during the transition period before the effect of increased gold on the price system is completed. (On the other hand, time preferences may temporarily rise). The fall will cause a temporary increase in saved funds, an increase that will disappear once the effects of the new money on prices are completed. This is the case noted by Mises.

Here is an instance in which savings may be expected to increase first and then decline. There may certainly be other cases in which time preferences will change suddenly on the free market, first falling, then increasing. The latter change will undoubtedly cause a "crisis" and temporary readjustment to malinvestments, but these would be better termed irregular *fluctuations* than regular processes of the business cycle. Furthermore, entrepreneurs are trained to estimate changes and avoid error. They can handle irregular fluctuations, and certainly they should be able to cope with the results of an inflow of gold, results which are roughly predictable. They could not forecast the results of a credit expansion, because the credit expansion tampered with all their moorings, distorted interest rates and calculations of capital. No such tampering takes place when gold flows into the economy, and the normal forecasting ability of entrepreneurs is allowed full sway. We must, therefore, conclude that we cannot apply the "business cycle" label to any processes of the free market. Irregular fluctuations, in response to changing consumer tastes, resources, etc. will certainly occur, and sometimes there will be aggregate losses as a result. But the regular, systematic distortion that invariably ends in a cluster of business errors and depression—characteristic phenomena of the "business cycle"—can only flow from intervention of the banking system in the market.[39]

2

Keynesian Criticisms
of the Theory[1]

There are two standard Keynesian criticisms of the Mises cycle theory. One charge takes the followers of Mises to task for identifying *saving* and *investment*. Saving and investment, the Keynesians charge, are two entirely separate processes, performed by two sets of people with little or no link between them; the "classical" identification of saving and investment is therefore illegitimate. Savings "leak" out of the consumption-spending stream; investments pour in from some other phase of spending. The task of government in a depression, according to the Keynesians, is accordingly to stimulate investments and discourage savings, so that total spendings increase.

Savings and investment are indissolubly linked. It is impossible to encourage one and discourage the other. Aside from bank credit, investments can come from no other source than savings (and we have seen what happens when investments are financed by bank credit). Not only consumers save directly, but also consumers in their capacity as independent businessmen or as owners of corporations. But can't savings be "hoarded?" This, however, is an artificial and misleading way of putting the matter. Consider a man's possible allocation of his monetary assets:

He can (1) spend money on consumption; (2) spend on investment; (3) add to cash balance or subtract from previous cash balance. This is the sum of his alternatives. The Keynesians assume, most contrivedly, that he *first* decides how much to consume or not, calling this "not-consumption" *saving*, and *then* decides how much to invest and how much to "leak" into hoards. (This, of course, is neo-Keynesianism rather than pure Keynesian orthodoxy, which banishes hoarding from the living room, while readmitting it by the back door.) This is a highly artificial approach and confirms Sir Dennis Robertson's charge that the Keynesians are incapable of "visualizing more than two margins at once." [2] Clearly, our individual decides at one and the same stroke about allocating his income in the three different channels. Furthermore, he allocates between the various categories on the basis of two embracing utilities: *his time preferences* decide his allocation between consumption and investment (between spending on present vs. future consumption); *his utility of money* decides how much he will keep in his cash balance. In order to *invest* resources in the future, he must restrict his consumption and *save* funds. This restricting is his savings, and so saving and investment are always equivalent. The two terms may be used almost interchangeably.

These various individual valuations sum up to social time-preference ratios and social demand for money. If people's demand for cash balances increases, we do not call this "savings leaking into hoards"; we simply say that demand for money has increased. In the aggregate, total cash balances can only rise to the extent that the total supply of money rises, since the two are identical. But *real* cash balances can increase through a rise in the value of the dollar. If the value of the dollar is permitted to rise (prices are permitted to fall) without hindrance, no dislocations will be caused by this increased demand, and depressions will not be aggravated. The Keynesian doctrine artificially assumes that any increase (or decrease) in hoards will be matched by a corresponding fall (or rise) in invested funds. But this is not correct. The demand for money is completely unrelated to the time-preference proportions people might adopt; increased hoarding, therefore, could just as easily come out of reduced consumption as out of reduced investment. In short, the savings-investment/consumption proportions are determined by time preferences of individuals; the spending/cash balance proportion is determined by their demands for money.

THE LIQUIDITY "TRAP"

The ultimate weapon in the Keynesian arsenal of explanations of depressions is the "liquidity trap." This is not precisely a critique of the Mises theory, but it is the last line of Keynesian defense of their own inflationary "cures" for depression. Keynesians claim that "liquidity preference" (demand for money) may be so persistently high that the rate of interest could not fall low enough to stimulate investment sufficiently to raise the economy out of the depression. This statement assumes that the rate of interest is determined by "liquidity preference" instead of by time preference; and it also assumes again that the link between savings and investment is very tenuous indeed, only tentatively exerting itself *through* the rate of interest. But, on the contrary, it is not a question of saving and investment each being acted upon by the rate of interest; in fact, saving, investment, *and* the rate of interest are each and all *simultaneously* determined by individual time preferences on the market. Liquidity preference has nothing to do with this matter. Keynesians maintain that if the "speculative" demand for cash rises in a depression, this will raise the rate of interest. But this is not at all necessary. Increased hoarding can either come from funds formerly consumed, from funds formerly invested, or from a mixture of both that leaves the old consumption/investment proportion unchanged. *Unless* time preferences change, the last alternative will be the one adopted. Thus, the rate of interest depends solely on time preference, and not at all on "liquidity preference." In fact, if the increased hoards come mainly out of consumption, an increased demand for money will cause interest rates to *fall*— because time preferences have fallen.

In their stress on the liquidity trap as a potent factor in aggravating depression and perpetuating unemployment, the Keynesians make much fuss over the alleged fact that people, in a financial crisis, *expect* a rise in the rate of interest, and will therefore hoard money instead of purchasing bonds and contributing toward lower rates. It is this "speculative hoard" that constitutes the "liquidity trap," and is supposed to indicate the relation between liquidity preference and the interest rate. But the Keynesians are here misled by their superficial treatment of the interest rate as simply the price of loan contracts. The crucial interest rate, as we have indicated, is the *natural rate*—the "profit spread" on the market. Since loans are simply a form of investment, the rate on loans is but a pale reflection of the natural rate. What, then, does an expectation of rising interest rates really mean? It means that people expect increases in the rate of net return on the market, via wages and other producers' goods prices falling *faster* than do consumer goods' prices. But this needs no labyrinthine explanation; investors expect falling wages and other factor prices, and they are therefore holding off investing in factors until the fall occurs. But this is old-fashioned "classical" speculation on price changes. This expectation, far from being an *upsetting* element, actually *speeds up* the adjustment. Just as all speculation speeds up adjustment to the proper levels, so this expectation hastens the fall in wages and other factor prices, hastening the recovery, and permitting normal prosperity to return that much faster. Far from "speculative" hoarding being a bogy of depression, therefore, it is actually a welcome stimulant to more rapid recovery.[3]

Such intelligent neo-Keynesians as Modigliani concede that only an "infinite" liquidity preference (an unlimited demand for money) will block return to full-employment equilibrium in a free market.[4] But, as we have seen, heavy speculative demand for money speeds the adjustment process. Moreover, the demand for money could never be *infinite* because people must always continue consuming, on *some* level, regardless of their expectations. Since people must continue consuming, they must also continue producing, so that there can be adjustment and full-employment regardless of the degree of hoarding. The failure to juxtapose hoarding and *consuming* again stems from the Keynesian neglect of more than two margins at once and their erroneous belief that hoarding only reduces investment, not consumption.

In a brilliant article on Keynesianism and price-wage flexibility, Professor Hutt points out that:

No condition which even distinctly resembles infinite elasticity of demand for money assets has even been recognized, I believe, because general expectations have always envisaged either (a) the attainment in the not too distant future of some definite scale of prices, or (b) so gradual a decline of prices that no cumulative postponement of expenditure has seemed profitable.

But even if such an unlikely demand arose:

If one can seriously imagine [this situation] . . . with the aggregate real value of money assets being inflated, and prices being driven down catastrophically, then one may equally legitimately (and equally extravagantly) imagine continuous price coordination accompanying the emergence of such a position. We can conceive, that is, of prices falling rapidly, keeping pace with expectations of price changes, but never reaching zero, with full utilization of resources persisting all the way.[5]

WAGE RATES AND UNEMPLOYMENT

Sophisticated Keynesians now admit that the Keynesian theory of "underemployment equilibrium" does not really apply (as was first believed) to the free and unhampered market: that it assumes, in fact, that wage rates are *rigid downward*. "Classical" economists have always maintained that unemployment is caused precisely by wage rates not being allowed to fall freely; but in the Keynesian system this assumption has been buried in a mass of irrelevant equations. The assumption is there, nevertheless, and it is crucial.[6] The Keynesian prescription for unemployment rests on the persistence of a "money illusion" among workers, i.e., on the belief that while, through unions and government, they will keep money wage rates from falling, they will also accept a fall in *real* wage rates via higher prices. Governmental inflation, then, is supposed to eliminate unemployment by bringing about such a fall in real wage rates. In these times of ardent concentration on the cost-of-living index, such duplicity is impossible and we need not repeat here the various undesirable consequences of inflation.[7]

It is curious that even economists who subscribe to a general theory of prices, balk whenever the theory is logically applied to wages, the prices of labor services. Marginal productivity theory, for example, may be applied strictly to other factors; but, when wages are discussed, we suddenly read about "zones of indeterminacy" and "bargaining."[8] Similarly, most economists would readily admit that keeping the price of any good above the amount that would clear the market, will cause unsold surpluses to pile up. Yet, they are reluctant to admit this in the case of labor. If they claim that "labor" is a general good, and therefore that wage cuts will injure general purchasing power, it must first be replied that "general labor" is not sold on the market; that it is certain specific labor that is usually kept artificially high and that this labor will be unemployed. It is true, however, that the wider the extent of the artificially high wage rates, the more likely will mass unemployment be. If, for example, only a few crafts manage by union or government coercion to boost the wage rate in their fields above the free market rate, displaced workers will move into a poorer line of work, and find employment there. In that case, the remaining union workers have gained their wage increase at the expense of lower wage rates elsewhere and of a general misallocation of productive factors. The wider the extent of the rigid wages, however, the less opportunity there will be to move and the greater will be the extent and duration of the unemployment.

In a free market, wage rates will tend to adjust themselves so that there is no involuntary unemployment, i.e., so that all those desiring to work can find jobs. Generally, wage rates can only be kept above full-employment rates through coercion by government, unions, or both. Occasionally, however, the high wage rates are maintained by voluntary choice (although the choice is usually ignorant of the consequences) or by coercion supplemented by voluntary choice. It may happen, for example, that either business firms or the workers themselves may become persuaded that maintaining wage rates artificially high is their bounden duty. Such persuasion has actually been at the root of much of the unemployment of our time, and this was particularly true in the 1929 depression. Workers, for example, become persuaded of the great importance of preserving the *mystique* of the union: of union solidarity in "not crossing a picket line," or not undercutting union wage rates. Unions almost always reinforce this *mystique* with violence, but there is no gainsaying the breadth of its influence. To the extent that workers, both in and out of the union, feel bound by this *mystique,* to that extent will they *refuse* to bid wages downward even when they are unemployed. If they do that, then we must conclude that they are unemployed *voluntarily,* and that the way to end their unemployment is to convince them that the *mystique* of the union is morally absurd.[9] However, while these workers are unemployed voluntarily, as a consequence of their devotion to the union, it is highly likely that the workers do not fully realize the consequences of their ideas and actions. The mass of men are generally ignorant of economic truths. It is highly possible that once they discovered that their unemployment was the direct result of their devotion to union solidarity, much of this devotion would quickly wither away.

Both workers and businessmen may become persuaded by the mistaken idea that artificial propping of wage rates is beneficial. This factor played a great role in the 1929 depression. As early as the 1920's, "big" businessmen were swayed by "enlightened" and "progressive" ideas, one of which mistakenly held that American prosperity was *caused* by the payment of high wages (rates?) instead of the other way round. As if other countries had a lower standard of living because their businessmen stupidly refused to quadruple or quintuple their wage rates! By the time of the depression, then, businessmen were ripe for believing that lowering wage rates would cut "purchasing power" (consumption) and worsen the depression (a doctrine that the Keynesians later appropriated and embellished.) To the

extent that businessmen become convinced of this economic
error, they are responsible for unemployment, but responsible,
be it noted, not because they are acting "selfishly" and "greedily"
but precisely because they are trying to act "responsibly." Insofar
as government reinforces this conviction with cajolery and threat,
the government bears the primary guilt for unemployment.

What of the Keynesian argument, however, that a fall in
wage rates would *not* help cure unemployment because it
would slash purchasing power and therefore deprive industry
of needed demand for its products? This argument can be
answered on many levels. In the first place, as prices fall in a
depression, *real* wage rates are not only maintained but *increased*.
If this helps employment by raising purchasing power, why not
advocate drastic *increases* in money wage rates? Suppose the
government decreed, for example, a minimum wage law where
the minimum was triple the going wage rates? What would
happen? Why don't the Keynesians advocate such a measure?

It is clear that the effect of such a decree would be total mass
unemployment and a complete stoppage of the wheels of production. Unless . . . unless the money supply were increased to
permit employers to pay such sums, but in that case *real* wage
rates have not increased at all! Neither would it be an adequate
reply to say that this measure would "go too far" because wage
rates are *both* costs to entrepreneurs and incomes to workers.
The point is that the free market rate is precisely the one that
adjusts wages—costs *and* incomes—to the full-employment position. Any other wage rate distorts the economic situation.[10]

The Keynesian argument confuses wage *rates* with wage *incomes*—a common failing of the economic literature, which often
talks vaguely of "wages" without specifying rate or income.[11]
Actually, *wage income* equals *wage rate* multiplied by the
amount of time over which the income is earned. If the wage
rate is per hour, for example, wage rate will equal total wage
income divided by the total number of hours worked. But
then the total wage income depends on the number of hours
worked as well as on the wage rate. We are contending here
that a drop in the wage rate will lead to an *increase* in the

total number employed; if the total man-hours worked increases enough, it can also lead to an increase in the total wage bill, or payrolls. A fall in wage rate, then, does not necessarily lead to a fall in total wage incomes; in fact, it may do the opposite. At the very least, however, it *will* lead to an absorption of the unemployed, and this is the issue under discussion. As an illustration, suppose that we simplify matters (but not too drastically) and assume a fixed "wages fund" which employers can dispense to workers. Clearly, then, a reduced wage rate will permit the same payroll fund to be spread over a greater number of people. There is no reason to assume that total payroll will fall.

In actuality, there is no fixed fund for wages, but there is rather a fixed "capital fund" which business pays out to all factors of production. Ultimately, there is no return to capital goods, since their prices are all absorbed by wages and land rents (and interest, which, as the price of time, permeates the economy.) Therefore, what business as a whole has at any time is a fixed fund for wages, rents, and interest. Labor and land are perennial competitors. Since production functions are not fixed throughout the economy, a widespread reduction in wage rates would cause business to substitute labor for land, labor now being relatively more attractive vis à vis land than it was before. Consequently, aggregate payrolls would not be the *same;* they would *increase,* because of the substitution effect in favor of labor as against land. The aggregate demand for labor would therefore be "elastic." [12]

Suppose, however, that the highly improbable "worst" occurs, and the demand for labor turns out to be inelastic; i.e., total payrolls decline as a result of a cut in wage rates. What then? First, such inelasticity could only be due to businesses' holding off from investing in labor in expectation that wage rates will fall further. But the way to meet such speculation is to permit wage rates to fall as quickly and rapidly as possible. A quick fall to the free-market rate will demonstrate to businessmen that wage rates have fallen their maximum viable amount. Not only will this *not* lead business to wait further before investing in labor; it will stimulate business to hurry and invest before wage rates rise again. The popular tendency to regard speculation as a commanding force in its own right must be avoided; the more astute as forecasters and diviners of the economy the businessmen are, the more they will "speculate," and the more will their speculation spur rather than delay the natural equilibrating forces of the market. For any mistakes in speculation—selling or buying goods or services too fast or too soon—will directly injure the businessmen themselves. Speculation is *not* self-perpetuating; it depends wholly and ultimately on the underlying forces of natural supply and consumer demand, and it promotes adjustment to those forces. If businessmen overspeculate in inventory of a certain good, for example, the piling up of unsold stock will lead to losses and speedy correction. Similarly, if businessmen wait too long to purchase labor, labor "shortages" will develop and businessmen will quickly bid up wage rates to their "true" free-market rates. Entrepreneurs, we remember, are trained to forecast the market correctly; they only make mass errors when governmental or bank intervention distorts the "signals" of the market and misleads them on the true state of underlying supply and demand. There is no interventionary deception here; on the contrary, we are discussing a *return* to the free market after a previous intervention has been eliminated.

If a quick fall in wage rates ends and even reverses withholding of the purchase of labor, a slow, sluggish downward drift of wage rates will aggravate matters, because (a) it will perpetuate wages above free market levels and therefore perpetuate unemployment; and (b) it will stimulate withholding of labor purchases, thereby tending to aggravate the unemployment problem even further.

Secondly, whether or not such speculation takes place, there is still no reason why unemployment cannot be speedily eliminated. If workers do not hold out for a reserve price because of union pressure or persuasion, unemployment will disappear *even if* total payroll has declined.

The following diagram will illustrate this process: (see Figure 1). Quantity of Labor is on the horizontal axis; wage rate on the vertical. D_LD_L is the aggregate demand for Labor; IE is the total stock of labor in the society; that is, the total supply of labor seeking work. The supply of labor is represented by vertical line S_LS_L rather than by the usual forward-sloping supply curve, because we may abstain from any cutting of hours due to falling wage rates, and more important, because we are investigating the problem of *involuntary* unemployment rather than voluntary. Those who wish to cut back their hours, or quit working altogether when wage rates fall, can hardly be considered as posing an "unemployment problem" to society, and we can therefore omit them here.

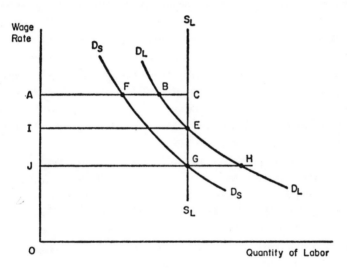

FIG. 1

Wage Rates and Unemployment

In a free market, the wage rate will be set by the intersection of the labor supply curve S_LS_L and the demand curve D_LD_L, or at point E or wage rate OI. The labor stock IE will be fully employed. Suppose, however, that because of coercion or persuasion, the wage rate is kept rigid so that it does not fall below OA. The supply of labor curve is now changed: it is now horizontal over AC, then rises vertically upward, CS_L. Instead of intersecting the demand for labor at point E the new supply of labor curve intersects it at point B. This equilibrium point now sets the minimum wage rate of OA, but only employs AB workers, leaving BC unemployed. Clearly, the remedy for the unemployment is to remove the artificial prop keeping the supply of labor curve at AC, and to permit wage rates to fall until full-employment equilibrium is reached.[13]

Now, the critic might ask: suppose there is not only speculation that will speed adjustment, but speculation that *overshoots* its mark. The "speculative demand for labor" can then be considered to be D_sD_s, purchasing less labor at every wage rate than the "true" demand curve requires. What happens? Not unemployment, but full employment at a lower wage rate, OJ. Now, as the wage rate falls *below* underlying market levels, the true demand for labor becomes ever greater than the supply of labor; at the new "equilibrium" wage the gap is equal to GH. The enormous pressure of this true demand leads entrepreneurs to see the gap, and they begin to bid up wage rates to overcome the resulting "shortage of labor." Speculation is self *correcting* rather than self aggravating, and wages are bid up to the underlying free-market wage OI.

If speculation presents no problems whatever and even helps matters when wage rates are permitted to fall freely, it accentuates the evils of unemployment as long as wages are maintained above free-market levels. Keeping wage rates up or only permitting them to fall sluggishly and reluctantly in a depression, sets up among businessmen the expectation that wage rates must *eventually* be allowed to fall. Such speculation lowers the aggregate demand curve for labor, say to D_sD_s. But with the supply curve of labor still maintained horizontally at AC, the equilibrium wage rate is pushed farther to the left at F, and the amount employed reduced to AF, the amount unemployed increased to FC.[14]

Thus, even if total payrolls decline, freely falling wage rates will always bring about a speedy end to involuntary unemployment. The Keynesian linkage of total employment with total monetary demand for products implicitly *assumes* rigid wage rates downward; it therefore cannot be used to criticize the policy of freely-falling wage rates. But even if full employment is maintained, will not the declining demand further depress business? There are two answers to this. In the first place, what has happened to the existing money supply? We are assuming throughout a given quantity of money existing in the society. This money has not disappeared. Neither, for that matter, has total monetary spending necessarily declined. If total payrolls have declined, something else has gone up: the total retained by entrepreneurs, or by investors, for example. In fact, given the total money supply, the total flow of monetary spending will *only decline if the social demand for money has increased.* In other words, if "hoarding" has increased. But an increase in hoarding, in total demand for money, is, as we have seen, no social calamity. In response to the needs and uncertainties of depression, people desire to increase their *real* cash balances, and they can only do so, with a given amount of total cash, by lowering prices. Hoarding, therefore, lowers prices all around, but need exert no depressing effect whatever upon business.[15] Business, as we have pointed out, depends for its profitability on price *differentials* between factor and selling prices not upon general price levels.[16] Decrease or increase in total monetary spending is, therefore, irrelevant to the general profitability of business.

Finally, there is the Keynesian argument that wage earners consume a greater proportion of their income than landlords or entrepreneurs, and therefore that a decreased total wage bill is a calamity because consumption will decline and savings increase. In the first place, this is not always accurate. It assumes (1) that the laborers are the relatively "poor" and the non-laborers the relative "rich," and (2) that the poor consume a greater proportion of their income than the rich. The first assumption is not necessarily correct. The President of General Motors is, after all, a "laborer," and so also is Mickey Mantle; on the other hand, there are a great many poor landlords, farmers, and retailers. Manipulating relations between wage earners and others is a very clumsy and ineffective way of manipulating relations between poor and rich (provided we desire any manipulation at all). The second assumption is often, but

not necessarily, true, as we have seen above. As we have also
seen, however, the empirical study of Lubell indicates that a
redistribution of income between rich and poor may not appreciably affect the social consumption/saving proportions. But
suppose that all these objections are waved aside for the moment,
and we concede for the sake of argument that a fall in total
payroll will shift the social proportion against consumption and
in favor of saving. What then? But this is precisely an effect that
we should highly prize. For, as we have seen, any shift in social
time preferences in favor of saving and against consumption, will
speed the advent of recovery, and decrease the need for a lengthy
period of depression-readjustment. Any such shift from consumption to savings will foster recovery. To the extent that
this dreaded fall in consumption *does* result from a cut in
wage rates, then, the depression will be cured that much more
rapidly.

A final note: The surplus "quantity of labor" caused by
artificially high wage rates is a surplus quantity of hours worked.
This can mean (1) actual unemployment of workers, and/or
(2) reduction in working time for employed workers. If a certain
number of labor-hours are surplus, workers can be discharged
outright, or many more can find their weekly working time
reduced and their payroll reduced accordingly. The latter scheme
is often advanced during a depression, and is called "spreading
the work." Actually, it simply spreads the unemployment. Instead of most workers being fully employed and others unemployed, all become *under*-employed. Universal adoption of this
proposal would render artificial wage maintenance absurd, because no one would be really benefitting from the high wage
rates. Of what use are continuing high *hourly* wage rates if
weekly wage rates are lower? The hour-reduction scheme, moreover, perpetuates underemployment. A mass of totally unemployed is liable to press severely on artificial wage rates, and
out-compete the employed workers. Securing a greater mass of
under-employed prevents such pressure—and this, indeed, is one
of the main reasons that unions favor the scheme. In many cases, of
course, the plea for shorter hours is accompanied by a call for

higher hourly wage rates to "keep weekly take-home pay the same"; this of course is a blatant demand for higher real wage rates, accompanied by reduced production and further unemployment as well.

Reduction of hours to "share the work" will also reduce everyone's real wage rate and the general standard of living, for production will not only be lower but undoubtedly far less efficient, and workers all less productive. This will further widen the gap between the artificially maintained wage rate and the free-market wage rate, and hence further aggravate the unemployment problem.

3

Some Alternative Explanations
of Depression: A Critique

Some economists are prepared to admit that the Austrian theory could "sometimes" account for cyclical booms and depressions, but add that other instances might be explained by different theories. Yet, as we have stated above, we believe this to be an error: we hold that the Austrian analysis is the *only* one that accounts for business cycles and their familiar phenomena. Specific crises can, indeed, be precipitated by other government action or intervention in the market. Thus, England suffered a crisis in its cotton textile industry when the American Civil War cut off its supply of raw cotton. A sharp increase in taxation may depress industry and the urge to invest and thereby precipitate a crisis. Or people may suddenly distrust banks and trigger a deflationary run on the banking system. Generally, however, bank runs only occur after a depression has already weakened confidence, and this was certainly true in 1929. These instances, of course, are not *cyclical* events but simple crises without preceding booms. They are always identifiable and create no mysteries about the underlying causes of the crises. When W. R. Scott investigated the business annals of the early modern centuries, he found such contemporary explanations of business crises as the following: famine, plague, seizure of bullion by Charles I, losses in war, bank runs, etc. It is the fact that no such obvious disaster can explain modern depressions that accounts

54

for the search for a deeper causal theory of 1929 and all other depressions. Among such theories, only Mises' can pass muster.[1]

GENERAL OVERPRODUCTION

"Overproduction" is one of the favorite explanations of depressions. It is based on the common-sense observation that the crisis is marked by unsold stocks of goods, excess capacity of plant, and unemployment of labor. Doesn't this mean that the "capitalist system" produces "too much" in the boom, until finally the giant productive plant outruns itself? Isn't the depression the period of rest, which permits the swollen industrial apparatus to wait until reduced business activity clears away the excess production and works off its excess inventory?

This explanation, popular or no, is arrant nonsense. Short of the Garden of Eden, there is no such thing as general "overproduction." As long as any "economic" desires remain unsatisfied, so long will production be needed and demanded. Certainly, this impossible point of universal satiation had not been reached in 1929. But, these theorists may object, "we do not claim that all desires have ceased. They still exist, but the people lack the money to exercise their demands." But *some* money still exists, even in the steepest deflation. Why can't this money be used to buy these "overproduced" goods? There is no reason why prices cannot fall low enough, in a free market, to clear the market and sell all the goods available.[2] If businessmen choose to keep prices up, they are simply speculating on an imminent rise in market prices; they are, in short, *voluntarily investing* in inventory. If they wish to sell their "surplus" stock, they need only cut their prices low enough to sell all of their product.[3] But won't they then suffer losses? Of course, but now the discussion has shifted to a different plane. We find no overproduction, we find now that the *selling prices* of products are *below* their cost of production. But since costs are determined by expected future selling prices, this means that costs were previously *bid too high* by entrepreneurs. The problem, then, is not one of "aggregate demand" or "overproduction," but one of cost-price differentials.

Why did entrepreneurs make the mistake of bidding costs higher than the selling prices turned out to warrant? The Austrian theory explains this cluster of error and the excessive bidding up of costs; the "overproduction" theory does not. In fact, there was overproduction of specific, not general, goods. The malinvestment caused by credit expansion diverted production into lines that turned out to be unprofitable (i.e., where selling prices were lower than costs) and away from lines where it would have been profitable. So there was *over*production of specific goods relative to consumer desires, and *under*production of other specific goods.

UNDERCONSUMPTION

The "underconsumption" theory is extremely popular, but it occupied the "underworld" of economics until rescued, in a sense, by Lord Keynes. It alleges that something happens during the boom—in some versions too much investment and too much production, in others too high a proportion of income going to upper-income groups—which causes consumer demand to be insufficient to buy up the goods produced. Hence, the crisis and depression. There are many fallacies involved in this theory. In the first place, as long as people exist, *some* level of consumption will persist. Even if people suddenly consume less and hoard instead, they must consume certain minimum amounts. Since hoarding cannot proceed so far as to eliminate consumption altogether, *some* level of consumption will be maintained, and therefore some monetary flow of consumer demand will persist. There is no reason why, in a free market, the prices of all the various factors of production, as well as the final prices of consumer goods, cannot adapt themselves to this desired level. Any losses, then, will be only temporary in shifting to the new consumption level. If they are anticipated there need be no losses at all.

Secondly, it is the entrepreneurs' business to anticipate consumer demand, and there is no reason why they cannot predict the consumer demand just as they make other predictions, and adjust the production structure to that prediction. The underconsumption theory cannot explain the cluster of errors in the crisis. Those who espouse this theory often maintain that production in the boom outruns consumer demand; but (1) since we are not in Nirvana, there will always be demand for further production, and (2) the unanswered question remains: why were costs bid so high that the product has become unprofitable at current selling prices? The productive machine expands because people want it so, because they desire higher standards of living in the future. It is therefore absurd to maintain that production could outrun consumer demand in general.

One common variant of the underconsumption theory traces the fatal flaw to an alleged shift of relative income to profits and to the higher-income brackets during a boom. Since the richer presumably consume less than the poor, the mass does not then have enough "purchasing-power" to buy back the expanded product. We have already seen that: (1) *marginally*, empirical research suggests a doubt about whether the rich consume less, and (2) there is not necessarily a shift from the poor to the rich during a boom. But even granting these assumptions, it must be remembered that: (a) entrepreneurs and the rich *also* consume, and (b) that savings constitute the demand for producers' goods. Savings, which go into investment, are therefore just as necessary to sustain the structure of production as consumption. Here we tend to be misled because national income accounting deals solely in *net* terms. Even "gross national product" is not *really* gross by any means; only gross durable investment is included, while gross inventory purchases are excluded. It is not true, as the underconsumptionists tend to assume, that capital is invested and then pours forth onto the market in the form of production, its work over and done. On the contrary, to sustain a higher standard of living, the production structure—the capital structure—must be *permanently* "lengthened." As more and more capital is added and maintained in civilized economies, more and more funds must be used just to maintain and replace the larger structure. This means higher gross savings, savings that must be sustained and invested in each higher stage of production. Thus, the retailers must continue buying from the wholesalers, the wholesalers from the jobbers, etc. Increased savings, then, are not wasted; they are, on the contrary, vital to the maintenance of civilized living standards.

Underconsumptionists assert that expanding production exerts a depressing secular effect on the economy because prices will tend to fall. But falling prices are not depressant; on the contrary, since falling prices due to increased investment and productivity are reflected in lower unit costs, profitability is not at all injured. Falling prices simply distribute the fruits of higher productivity to all the people. The natural course of economic development, then, barring inflation, is for prices to fall in response to increased capital and higher productivity. Money wage rates will also tend to fall, because of the increased work the given money supply is called upon to perform over a greater number of stages of production. But money wage rates will fall less than consumer goods prices, and as a result economic development brings about higher *real* wage rates and higher real incomes throughout the economy. Contrary to the underconsumption theory, a stable price level is not the norm, and inflating money and credit in order to keep the "price level" from falling can only lead to the disasters of the business cycle.[4]

If underconsumption were a valid explanation of any crisis, there would be depression in the consumer goods industries, where surpluses pile up, and at least relative prosperity in the producers' goods industries. Yet, it is generally admitted that it is the producers' not the consumers' goods industries that suffer most during a depression. Underconsumptionism cannot explain this phenomenon, while Mises' theory explains it precisely.[5,6] Every crisis is marked by *mal*investment and under-*saving*, not underconsumption.

THE ACCELERATION PRINCIPLE

There is only one way that the underconsumptionists can try to explain the problem of greater fluctuation in the producers' than the consumer goods' industries: the acceleration principle. The acceleration principle begins with the undeniable truth that all production is carried on for eventual consumption. It goes on to state that, not only does demand for producers' goods depend on consumption demand, but that this consumers' demand exerts a multiple leverage effect on investment, which it magnifies and accelerates. The demonstration of the principle begins inevitably with a hypothetical single firm or industry: assume, for example, that a firm is producing 100 units of a good per year, and that 10 machines of a certain type are needed in its production. And assume further that consumers demand and purchase these 100 units. Suppose further that the average life of the machine is 10 years. Then, in equilibrium, the firm buys 1 new machine each year to replace the one worn out. Now suppose that there is a 20 per cent increase in consumer demand for the firm's product. Consumers now wish to purchase 120 units. If we assume a fixed ratio of capital to output, it is now necessary for the firm to have 12 machines. It therefore buys 2 new machines this year, purchasing a total of 3 machines instead of 1. Thus, a 20 per cent increase in consumer demand has led to a 200 per cent increase in demand for the machine. *Hence,* say the accelerationists, a general increase in consumer demand in the economy will cause a greatly magnified increase in the demand for capital goods, a demand intensified in proportion to the *durability* of the capital. Clearly, the magnification effect is greater the more durable the capital good and the lower the level of its annual replacement demand.

Now, suppose that consumer demand remains at 120 units in the succeeding year. What happens now to the firm's demand for machines? There is no longer any need for firms to purchase any new machines beyond those necessary for replacement. Only 1 machine is still needed for replacement this year; therefore, the firm's total demand for machines will revert, from 3 the previous year, to 1 this year. Thus, an *unchanged* consumer demand will generate a 200 per cent *decline* in the demand for capital goods. Extending the principle again to the economy as a whole, a simple increase in consumer demand has generated far more intense fluctuations in the demand for fixed capital, first increasing it far more than proportionately, and then precipitating a serious decline. In this way, say the accelerationists, the increase of consumer demand in a boom leads to intense demand for capital goods. Then, as the increase in consumption tapers off, the lower rate of increase itself triggers a depression in the capital goods industries. In the depression, when consumer demand declines, the economy is left wtih the inevitable "excess capacity" created in the boom. The acceleration principle is rarely used to provide a full theory of the cycle; but it is very often used as one of the main elements in cycle theory, particularly accounting for the severe fluctuations in the capital-goods industries.

The seemingly plausible acceleration principle is actually a tissue of fallacies. We might first point out that the seemingly obvious pattern of one replacement per year assumes that 1 new machine has been *added* in each of the ten *previous* years; in short, it makes the highly dubious assumption that the firm has been expanding rapidly and continuously over the previous decade.[7] This is indeed a curious way of describing an *equilibrium* situation; it is also highly dubious to explain a *boom and depression* as only occurring *after* a decade of previous expansion. Certainly, it is just as likely that the firm bought all of its 10 machines at once—an assumption far more consonant with a current equilibrium situation for that firm. If that happened, then replacement demand by the firm would occur only once every decade. At first, this seems only to strengthen the acceleration principle. After all, the replacement-denominator is now that much less, and the intensified demand so much greater. But it is only strengthened on the surface. For everyone knows that, in real life, in the "normal" course of affairs, the economy in general does not experience zero demand for capital, punctuated by decennial bursts of investment. Overall, on the market, investment demand is more or less constant during near-stationary states. But if, overall, the market can iron out such rapid fluctuations, why can't it iron out the milder ones postulated in the standard version of the acceleration principle?

There is, moreover, an important fallacy at the very heart of the accelerationists' own example, a fallacy that has been uncovered by W. H. Hutt.[8] We have seen that consumer demand increases by 20 per cent—but why must the 2 extra machines be purchased in a year? What does the *year* have to do with it? If we analyze the matter closely, we find that the year is a purely arbitrary and irrelevant unit even within the terms of the example itself. We might just as well take a *week* as the time period. Then we would aver that consumer demand (which, after all, goes on continuously) increases 20 per cent over the first week, thus necessitating a 200 per cent increase in demand for machines in the first week (or even an *infinite* increase if replacement does not occur in the first week) followed by a 200 per cent (or infinite) decline in the next week, and stability thereafter. A week is never used by the accelerationists because the example would then clearly not apply to real life, which does not see such enormous fluctuations in the course of a couple of weeks, and the theory could certainly not then be used to explain the general business cycle. But a week is no more arbitrary than a year. In fact, the only non-arbitrary time-period to choose would be the life of the machine (e.g. 10 years).[9] Over a ten-year period, demand for machines had previously been 10 and in the current and succeeding decades will be 10 plus the extra 2, e.g. 12: in short, over the ten-year period, the demand for machines will increase *in precisely the same proportion* as the demand for consumer goods—and there is no magnification effect whatever. Since businesses buy and produce over planned periods covering the lives of their equipment, there is no reason to assume that the market will not plan production accordingly and smoothly, without the erratic fluctuations manufactured by the accelerationists' model. There is, in fact, no validity in saying that increased consumption *requires* increased production of machines immediately; on the contrary, it is increased saving and investment in machines, at points of time chosen by entrepreneurs strictly on the basis of expected profitability, that *permits* future increased production of consumer goods.[10]

There are other erroneous assumptions made by the acceleration principle. Its postulate of a fixed capital-output ratio, for example, ignores the ever-present possibility of substitution, more or less intensive working of different factors, etc. It also assumes that capital is finely divisible, ignoring the fact that investments are "lumpy," and made discontinuously, especially those in a fixed plant.

There is yet a far graver flaw—and a fatal one—in the acceleration principle, and it is reflected in the rigidity of the mechanical model. No mention whatever is made of the price system or of entrepreneurship. Considering the fact that all production on the market is run by entrepreneurs operating under the price system, this omission is amazing indeed. It is difficult to see how any economic theory can be taken seriously that completely omits the price system from its reckoning. A change in consumer demand will change the *prices* of consumer goods, yet such reactions are forgotten, and monetary and physical terms are hopelessly entwined by the theory without mentioning price changes. The extent to which any entrepreneur will invest in added production of a good depends on its *price relations*—on the differentials between its selling price and the prices of its factors of production. These price differentials are interrelated at each stage of production. If, for example, monetary consumer demand increases, it will reveal itself to producers of consumer goods through an increase in the price of the product. If the price differential between selling and buying prices is raised, production of this good will be stimulated. If factor prices rise faster than selling prices, production is curtailed, however, and there is no effect on production if the prices change *pari passus*. Ignoring prices in a discussion of production, then, renders a theory wholly invalid.

Apart from neglecting the price system, the principle's view of the entrepreneur is hopelessly mechanistic. The prime function of the entrepreneur is to *speculate,* to estimate the uncertain future by using his judgment. But the acceleration principle looks upon the entrepreneur as blindly and automatically *responding* to *present* data (i.e., data of the immediate past) rather than estimating future data. Once this point is stressed, it will be clear that entrepreneurs, in an unhampered economy, should be able to forecast the supposed slackening of demand and arrange their investments accordingly. If entrepreneurs can approximately forecast the alleged "acceleration principle," then the supposed slackening of investment demand, while leading to lower activity in those industries, need not be *depressive,* because it need not and would not engender losses among businessmen. Even if the remainder of the principle were conceded, therefore, it could only explain fluctuations, not depression—not the cluster of *errors* made by the entrepreneurs. If the accelerationists claim that the errors are precisely caused by entrepreneurial failure to forecast the change, we must ask, why the failure? In Mises' theory, entrepreneurs are prevented from forecasting correctly because of the tampering with market "signals" by government intervention. But here there is no government interference, the principle allegedly referring to the unhampered market. Furthermore, the principle is far easier to grasp than the Mises theory. There is nothing complex about it, and if it were true, then it would be obvious to all entrepreneurs that investment demand *would* fall off greatly in the following year. Theirs, and other people's, affairs would be arranged accordingly, and no general depression or heavy losses would ensue. Thus, the hypothetical investment in seven-year locust equipment may be very heavy for one or two years, and then fall off drastically in the next years. Yet this need engender no depression, since these changes would all be discounted and arranged in advance. This cannot be done as efficiently in other instances, but certainly entrepreneurs should be able to foresee the alleged effect. In fact, everyone should foresee it; and the entrepreneurs have achieved their present place precisely because of their predictive ability. The acceleration principle cannot account for entrepreneurial error.[11]

One of the most important fallacies of the acceleration principle is its wholly illegitimate leap from the single firm or industry to the overall economy. Its error is akin to those committed by the great bulk of Anglo-American economic theories: the concentration on only two areas—the single firm or industry, and the economy as a whole. Both these concentrations are fatally wrong, because they leave out the most important areas: the *interrelations* between the various parts of the economy. Only a *general* economic theory is valid—never a theoretical system based on either a partial or isolated case, or on holistic aggregates, or on a mixture of the two.[12] In the case of the acceleration principle, how did the 20 per cent increase in consumption of the firm's product come about? Generally a 20 per cent increase in consumption in one field, must signify a 20 per cent *reduction* of consumption somewhere else. In that case, of course, the leap from the individual to the aggregate is peculiarly wrong, since there is then no overall boom in consumption or investment. If the 20 per cent increase is to obtain over the whole economy, how is the increase to be financed? We cannot simply postulate an increase in consumption; the important question is: how can it be financed? What general changes are needed elsewhere to permit such an increase? These are questions that the accelerationists never face. Setting aside changes in the supply or demand for money for a moment, increased consumption can only come about through a *decrease* in saving and investment. But if aggregate saving and investment must *decrease* in order to permit an aggregate increase in consumption, then investment *cannot* increase in response to rising consumption; on the contrary, *it must decline*. The acceleration principle never faces this problem because it is profoundly ignorant of economics—the study of the working of the means-ends principle in human affairs. Short of Nirvana, all resources are scarce, and these resources must be allocated to the uses most urgently demanded by all individuals in the society. This is the unique economic problem, and it means that to gain a good of greater value, some other good of lesser value to individuals must be given up. Greater aggregate present consumption can only be acquired through lowered aggregate savings and investment. In short, people choose between present and future consumption, and can only increase present consumption at the expense of future, or *vice versa*. But the acceleration principle neglects the economic problem completely and disastrously.

The only way that investment can rise together with consumption is through inflationary credit expansion—and the accelerationists will often briefly allude to this prerequisite. But this admission destroys the entire theory. It means, first, that the acceleration principle could not possibly operate on the free market:

that, if it exists at all, it must be attributed to government rather than to the working of *laissez-faire* capitalism. But even granting the necessity of credit expansion cannot save the principle. For the example offered by the acceleration principle deals in physical, real terms. It postulates an increased production of units in response to increased demand. But if the increased demand is purely monetary, then prices, both of consumer and capital goods, can simply rise without any change in physical production—and there is no acceleration effect at all. In short, there might be a 20 per cent rise in money supply, leading to a 20 per cent rise in consumption and in investment—indeed in *all* quantities—but *real* quantities and price relations need not change, and there is no magnification of investment, in real or monetary terms. The same applies, incidentally, if the monetary increase in investment or consumption comes from dishoarding rather than monetary expansion.

It might be objected that inflation does not and cannot increase all quantities proportionately, and that this is its chief characteristic. Precisely so. But proceed along these lines, and we are back squarely and firmly in the Austrian theory of the trade cycle—and the acceleration principle has been irretrievably lost. The Austrian theory deals precisely with the distortions of market adjustment to consumption/investment proportions, brought about by inflationary credit expansion.[13] Thus, the accelerationists maintain, in effect, that the entrepreneurs are lured by increased consumption to overexpand durable investments. But the Austrian theory demonstrates that, due to the effect of inflation on prices, even credit expansion can only cause *mal*investment, not "overinvestment." Entrepreneurs will overinvest in the higher stages, and underinvest in the lower stages, of production. Total investment is limited by the total supply of savings available, and a general increase in consumption signifies a *decrease* in saving and therefore a *decline* in total investment (and not an increase or even magnified increase, as the Acceleration Principle claims).[14] Furthermore, the Austrian theory shows that the cluster of entrepreneurial error is caused by the inflationary distortion of market interest rates.[15]

DEARTH OF "INVESTMENT OPPORTUNITIES"

A very common tendency among economists is to attribute depression to a dearth, or "saturation," of "investment opportunities." Investment opportunities open themselves up during the boom and are exploited accordingly. After a while, however, these opportunities disappear, and hence depression succeeds the boom. The depression continues until opportunities for investment reappear. What gives rise to these alleged "opportunities"? Typical are the causal factors listed in a famous article by Professor Hansen, who attributed the depression of the 1930's to a dearth of investment opportunities caused by an insufficient rate of population growth, the lack of new resources, and inadequate technical innovation.[16] The importance of this doctrine goes far beyond Hansen's "stagnation" theory—that these factors would behave in the future so as to cause a permanent tendency toward depression. For the "refuters" of the stagnation theory tacitly accepted Hansen's causal theory and simply argued empirically that these factors would be stronger than Hansen had believed.[17] Rarely have the causal connections themselves been challenged. The doctrine has been widely assumed without being carefully supported.

Whence come these causal categories? A close look will show their derivation from the equilibrium conditions of the Walrasian system which assumes a constant and evenly rotating economy, with tastes, technological knowledge, and resources considered given. Changes can only occur if one or more of these givens change. If new net investment is considered the key to depression or prosperity, then, knowing that new investment is zero in equilibrium (i.e., there is only enough investment to replace and maintain capital), it is easy to conclude that only changes in the ultimate givens can lead to new investment. Population and natural resources both fall under the Walrasian "resource" category. Hansen's important omission, of course, is *tastes*. The omission of tastes is enough to shatter the entire scheme. For it is *time preferences* (the "tastes" of the society for present *vis à vis* future consumption) that determines the amount that individuals will save and invest. Omitting time preferences leaves out the essential determinant of saving and investment.

New natural resources, a relatively unimportant item, is rarely stressed. We used to hear about the baleful effects on the "closing of the frontier" of open land, but this frontier closed long before the 1930's with no ill effects.[18] Actually, physical space by itself provides no assurance of profitable investment opportunities. Population growth is often considered an important factor making for prosperity or depression, but it is difficult to see why. If population is below the optimum (maximum real income per capita), its further growth permits investment to increase productivity by extending the division of labor. But this can only be done through greater investment. There is no way, however, that population growth can stimulate *investment,* and this is the issue at hand. One thesis holds that increased population growth stimulates demand for residential construction. But demand stems from purchasing power, which in turn stems ultimately from production, and an increase in babies may run up against inability to produce enough goods to demand the new houses effectively. But even if more construction is demanded, this will simply *reduce* consumption demand in other areas of the economy. If total consumption increases due to population growth (and there is no particular reason why it should), it will cause a *decline* in saved and invested funds rather than the reverse.

Technology is perhaps the most emphatically stressed of these alleged causal factors. Schumpeter's cycle theory has led many economists to stress the importance of technological innovation, particularly in great new industries; and thus we hear about the Railroad Boom or the Automobile Boom. Some great technological innovation is made, a field for investment opens up, and a boom is at hand. Full exploitation of this field finally exhausts the boom, and depression sets in. The fallacy involved here is neglect of the fact that technology, while vitally important, is only *indirectly,* and not directly, involved in an investment. At this point, we see again why the conditions of Misesian rather than Walrasian equilibrium should have been employed. Austrian theory teaches us that investment is always *less* than the maximum amount that could possibly exploit existing technology. Therefore, the "state of technical knowledge" is not really a limiting condition to investment. We can see the truth of this by simply looking about us; in every field, in every possible line of investment, there are always *some* firms which are *not* using the latest possible equipment, which are still using older methods. This fact indicates that there is a narrower limit on investment than technological knowledge. The backward countries may send engineers aplenty to absorb "American know-how"; but this will not bring these countries the great amount of investment needed to raise their standard of living appreciably. What they need, in short, is *saving:* this is the factor limiting investment.[19] And saving, in turn, is limited by time preference: the preference for present over future consumption. Investment always takes place by a lengthening of the processes of production, since the shorter productive processes are the first to be developed. The longer processes remaining untapped are more productive, but they are not exploited because of the limitations of time-preference. There is, for example, no investment in better and new machines because not enough saving is available.

Even if all existing technology were exploited, there would *still* be unlimited opportunities for investment, since there would still not be satiation of wants. Even if better steel mills, better factories, could not be built, *more* of them could always be built, to produce more of the presently produced consumer goods. New technology improves productivity, but is not essential for creating investment opportunities; these *always* exist, and are only limited by time preferences and available saving. The more saving, the more investment there will be to satisfy those desires not now fulfilled.

Just as in the case of the acceleration principle, the fallacy of the "investment opportunity" approach is revealed by its complete neglect of the price system. Once again, price and cost have disappeared. Actually, the trouble in a depression comes from *costs* being greater than the *prices* obtained from sale of capital goods; with costs greater than selling prices, businessmen are naturally reluctant to invest in losing concerns. The problem, then, is the rigidity of costs. In a free market, prices determine costs and not *vice versa,* so that reduced final prices will also lower the prices of productive factors—thereby lowering the costs of production. The failure of "investment opportunity" in the crisis stems from the overbidding of costs in the boom, now revealed in the crisis to be too high relative to selling prices. This erroneous over-bidding was generated by the inflationary credit expansion of the boom period. The way to retrieve investment opportunities in a depression, then, is to permit costs—factor prices—to fall rapidly, thus reestablishing profitable price-differentials, particularly in the capital goods industries. In short, wage rates, which constitute the great bulk of factor costs, should fall freely and rapidly to restore investment opportunities. This is equivalent to the reestablishment of higher price-differentials—higher natural interest rates—on the market. Thus, the Austrian approach explains the problem of investment opportunities, and other theories are fallacious or irrelevant.

Equally irrelevant is all discussion in terms of specific industries —an approach very similar to the technological opportunity doctrine. Often it is maintained that a certain industry—say construction or autos—was particularly prosperous in the boom, and that the depression occurred because of depressed conditions in that particular industry. This, however, confuses simple specific business *fluctuations* with general business *cycles.* Declines in one or several industries are offset by expansion in others, as demand shifts from one field to another. Therefore, attention to particular industries can *never* explain booms or depressions in general business—especially in a multi-industry country like the United States.[20] It is, for example, irrelevant whether or not the construction industry experiences a "long cycle" of twenty-odd years.

SCHUMPETER'S BUSINESS CYCLE THEORY

Joseph Schumpeter's cycle theory is notable for being the only doctrine, apart from the Austrian, to be grounded on, and integrated with, general economic theory.[21] Unfortunately it was grounded on Walrasian, rather than Austrian, general economics, and was thus doomed from the start. The unique Schumpeterian element in discussing equilibrium is his postulate of a zero rate of interest. Schumpeter, like Hansen, discards consumer tastes as an active element and also dispenses with new resources. With time preference ignored, interest rate becomes zero in equilibrium, and its positive value in the real world becomes solely a reflection of positive profits, which in turn are due to the only possible element of change remaining: technological innovations. These innovations are financed, Schumpeter maintains, by bank credit expansion, and thus Schumpeter at least concedes the vital link of bank credit expansion in generating the boom and depression, although he pays it little actual attention. Innovations cluster in some specific industry, and this generates the boom. The boom ends as the innovatory investments exhaust themselves, and their resulting increased output pours forth on the market to disrupt the older firms and industries. The ending of the cluster, accompanied by the sudden difficulties faced by the old firms, and a generally increased risk of failure, bring about the depression, which ends as the old and new firms finally adapt themselves to the new situation.

There are several fallacies in this approach:

1. There is no explanation offered on the lack of accurate forecasting by both the old and new firms. Why were not the difficulties expected and discounted? [22]

2. In reality, it may take a long time for a cluster of innovations in a new industry to develop, and yet it may take a relatively short time for the output of that industry to increase as a result of the innovations. Yet the theory must assume that output increases after the cluster has done its work; otherwise, there is no boom nor bust.

3. As we have seen above, time preferences and interest are ignored, and also ignored is the fact that saving and *not* technology is the factor limiting investment.[23] Hence, investment financed by bank credit need not be directed into innovations, but can also finance greater investment in already-known processes.

4. The theory postulates a periodic cluster of innovations in the boom periods. But there is no reasoning advanced to account for such an odd cluster. On the contrary, innovations, technological advance, take place continually, and in most, not just a few, firms. A cluster of innovations implies, furthermore, a *periodic cluster of entrepreneurial ability,* and this assumption is clearly unwarranted. And insofar as innovation is a regular business procedure of research and development, rents from innovations will accrue to the research and development departments of firms, rather than as entrepreneurial profits.[24]

5. Schumpeter's view of entrepreneurship—usually acclaimed as his greatest contribution—is extremely narrow and one-sided. He sees entrepreneurship as solely the making of innovations, setting up new firms to innovate, etc. Actually, entrepreneurs are continually at work, *always adjusting* to uncertain future demand and supply conditions, including the effects of innovations.[25]

In his later version, Schumpeter recognized that different specific innovations generating cycles would have different "periods of gestation" for exploiting their opportunities until new output had increased to its fullest extent. Hence, he modified his theory by postulating an economy of *three* separate, and interacting, cycles: roughly one of about three years, one of nine years, and one of 55 years. But the postulate of multi-cycles breaks down any theory of a general business cycle. All economic processes interact on the market, and all processes mesh together. A cycle takes place over the entire economy, the boom and depression each being *general.* The price system integrates and interrelates all activities, and there is neither warrant nor relevance for assuming hermetically-sealed "cycles," each running concurrently and adding to each other to form some resultant of business activity. The multicycle scheme, then, is a complete retreat from the original Schumpeterian model, and itself adds grievous fallacies to the original.[26]

Qualitative Credit Doctrines

Of the theories discussed so far, only the Austrian or Misesian sees anything wrong in the boom. The other theories hail the boom, and see the depression as an unpleasant reversal of previous prosperity. The Austrian and Schumpeterian doctrines see the depression as the inevitable result of processes launched in the boom. But while Schumpeter considers "secondary wave" deflation unfortunate and unsettling, he sees the boom-bust of his pure model as the necessary price to be paid for capitalist economic development. Only the Austrian theory, therefore, holds the inflationary boom to be wholly unfortunate and sees the full depression as necessary to eliminate distortions introduced by the boom. Various "qualitative credit" schools, however, also see the depression as inevitably generated by an inflationary boom. They agree with the Austrians, therefore, that booms should be prevented before they begin, and that the liquidation process of depression should be allowed to proceed unhampered. They differ considerably, however, on the causal analysis, and the specific ways that the boom and depression can be prevented.

The most venerable wing of qualitative credit theory is the old Banking School doctrine, prominent in the nineteenth century and indeed until the 1930's. This is the old-fashioned "sound banking" tradition, prominent in older money-and-banking textbooks, and spearheaded during the 1920's by two eminent economists: Dr. Benjamin M. Anderson of the Chase National Bank, and Dr. H. Parker Willis of the Columbia University Department of Banking, and editor of the *Journal of Commerce*. This school of thought, now very much in decline, holds that bank credit expansion only generates inflation when directed into the wrong lines, i.e., in assets other than self-liquidating short-term credit matched by "real goods," loaned to borrowers of impeccable credit standing. Bank credit expansion in such assets is held not to be inflationary, since it is then allegedly responsive solely to the legitimate "needs of business," the money supply rising with increased production, and falling again as goods are sold. All

other types of loans: whether in long-term credit, real estate, stock market, or to shaky borrowers, are considered inflationary, and create a boom-bust situation, the depression being necessary to liquidate the wasteful inflation of the boom. Since the bank loans of the 1920's were extended largely in assets considered unsound by the Banking School, these theorists joined the "Austrians" in opposing the bank credit inflation of the 1920's and in warning of impending depression.

The emphasis of the Banking School, however, is invalid. The important aspect of bank credit expansion is the *quantity* of new money thrown into business lending, and not at all the *type* of business loans that are made. Short-term, "self-liquidating" loans are just as inflationary as long-term loans. Credit needs of business, on the other hand, can be financed by borrowing from voluntary savings; there is no good reason why short-term loans in particular should be financed by bank inflation. Banks do not simply passively await business firms demanding loans; these very demands vary inversely to the rate of interest that the banks charge. The crucial point is the injection of new money into business firms; regardless of the type of business loan made, this money will then seep into the economy, with the effects described in the Austrian analysis. The irrelevance of the *type* of loan may be seen from the fact that business firms, if they wish to finance long-term investment, can finance it *indirectly* from the banks just as effectively as from direct loans. A firm may simply cease using its own funds for financing short-term inventory, and instead borrow the funds from the banks. The funds released by this borrowing can then be used to make long-term investments. It is impossible for banks to prevent their funds being used indirectly in this manner. All credit is interrelated on the market, and there is no way that the various types of credit can be hermetically sealed from each other.[27] And even if there were, it would make no economic sense to do so.

In short, the "self-liquidating" loan is just as inflationary as any other type of loan, and the only merit of this theory is the indirect one of quantitatively limiting the lending of banks that cannot find as many such loans as they would like. This loan does not even have the merit of speedier retirement, since short-term loans can and are renewed or reloaned elsewhere, thus perpetuating the loan for as long a time as any "long-term" loan. This emphasis of the Banking School weakened its salutary effect in the 1920's, for it served to aggravate the general over-emphasis on *types* of loans—in particular the stock market—as against the quantity of money outstanding.

More dangerous than the Banking School in this qualitative emphasis are those observers who pick out some type of credit as being particularly grievous. Whereas the Banking School opposed a quantitative inflation that went into any but stringently self-liquidating assets, other observers care not at all about quantity, but only about some particular type of asset—e.g., real estate or the stock market. The stock market was a particular whipping-boy in the 1920's and many theorists called for restriction on stock loans in contrast to "legitimate" business loans. A popular theory accused the stock market of "absorbing" capital credit that would otherwise have gone to "legitimate" industrial or farm needs. "Wall Street" had been a popular scapegoat since the days of the Populists, and since Thorstein Veblen had legitimated a fallacious distinction between "finance" and "industry."

The "absorption of capital" argument is now in decline, but there are still many economists who single out the stock market for attack. Clearly, the stock market is a channel for invest-ing in industry. If A buys a new security issue, then the funds are directly invested; if he buys an old share, then (1) the increased price of stock will encourage the firm to float further stock issues, and (2) the funds will then be transferred to the seller B, who in turn will consume or directly invest the funds. If the money is directly invested by B, then once again the stock market has channelled savings into investment. If B consumes the money, then his consumption or dissaving just offsets A's saving, and no aggregate net saving has occurred.

Much concern was expressed in the 1920's over brokers' loans, and the increased quantity of loans to brokers was taken as proof of credit absorption in the stock market. But a broker only *needs* a loan when his client calls on him for cash after selling his stock;

otherwise, the broker will keep an open book account with no need for cash. But when the client needs cash he sells his stock and gets out of the market. Hence, the higher the volume of brokers' loans from banks, the greater the degree that funds are *leaving* the stock market rather than entering it. In the 1920's the high volume of brokers' loans indicated the great degree to which industry was using the stock market as a channel to acquire saved funds for investment.[28]

The often marked fluctuations of the stock market in a boom and depression should not be surprising. We have seen the Austrian analysis demonstrate that greater fluctuations will occur in the capital goods industries. Stocks, however, are *units of title to masses of capital goods.* Just as capital goods' prices tend to rise in a boom, so will the prices of titles of ownership to masses of capital.[29] The fall in the interest rate due to credit expansion raises the capital value of stocks, and this increase is reinforced both by the actual and the prospective rise in business earnings. The discounting of higher prospective earnings in the boom will naturally tend to raise stock prices further than most other prices. The stock market, therefore, is not really an independent element, separate from or actually disturbing, the industrial system. On the contrary, the stock market tends to reflect the "real" developments in the business world. Those stock market traders who protested during the late 1920's that their boom simply reflected their "investment in America" did not deserve the bitter comments of later critics; their error was the universal one of believing that the boom of the 1920's was natural and perpetual, and not an artificially-induced prelude to disaster. This mistake was hardly unique to the stock market.

Another favorite whipping-boy during recent booms, has been *installment credit to consumers.* It has been charged that installment loans to consumers are somehow uniquely inflationary and unsound. Yet the reverse is true. Installment credit is no more inflationary than any other loan, and it does far less harm than business loans (including the supposedly "sound" ones) because it does not lead to the boom-bust cycle. The Mises analysis of the business cycle traces causation back to inflationary expansion of credit *to business* on the loan market. It is the expansion of credit to business that over-stimulates investment in the higher orders, misleads business about the amount of savings available, etc. But loans to *consumers, qua* consumers, have no ill effects. Since they stimulate consumption rather than business spending, they do not set a boom-bust cycle into motion. There is less to worry about in such loans, strangely enough, than in any other.

OVEROPTIMISM AND OVERPESSIMISM

Another popular theory attributes business cycles to alternating psychological waves of "overoptimism" and "overpessimism." This view neglects the fact that the market is geared to reward correct forecasting and penalize poor forecasting. Entrepreneurs do not have to rely on their own psychology; they can always refer their actions to the objective tests of profit and loss. Profits indicate that their decisions have borne out well; losses indicate that they have made grave mistakes. These objective market tests check any psychological errors that may be made. Furthermore, the successful entrepreneurs on the market will be precisely those, over the years, who are best equipped to make correct forecasts and use good judgment in analyzing market conditions. Under these conditions, it is absurd to suppose that the entire mass of entrepreneurs will make such errors, *unless* objective facts of the market are distorted over a considerable period of time. Such distortion will hobble the objective "signals" of the market and mislead the great bulk of entrepreneurs. This is the distortion explained by Mises' theory of the cycle. The prevailing optimism is not the cause of the boom; it is the reflection of events that seem to offer boundless prosperity. There is, furthermore, no reason for general over-optimism to shift suddenly to overpessimism; in fact, as Schumpeter has pointed out (and this was certainly true after 1929) businessmen usually persist in dogged and unwarranted optimism for quite a while after a depression breaks out.[30] Business psychology is, therefore, derivative from, rather than causal to, the objective business situation.

Economic expectations are therefore self-*correcting*, not self-aggravating. As Professor Bassie has pointed out:

The businessman may expect a decline, and he may cut his inventories, but he will produce enough to fill the orders he receives; and as soon as the expectations of a decline prove to be mistaken, he will again rebuild his inventories . . . the whole psychological theory of the business cycle appears to be hardly more than an inversion of the real causal sequence. Expectations more nearly derive from objective conditions than produce them. The businessman both expands and expects that his expansion will be profitable because the conditions he sees justifies the expansion . . . It is not the wave of optimism that makes times good. Good times are almost bound to bring a wave of optimism with them. On the other hand, when the decline comes, it comes not because anyone loses confidence, but because the basic economic forces are changing. Once let the real support for the boom collapse, and all the optimism bred through years of prosperity will not hold the line. Typically, confidence tends to hold up after a downturn has set in.[31]

Part II

THE INFLATIONARY
BOOM: 1921-1929

4

The Inflationary Factors

Most writers on the 1929 depression make the same grave mistake that plagues economic studies in general—the use of historical statistics to "test" the validity of economic theory. We have tried to indicate that this is a radically defective methodology for economic science, and that theory can only be confirmed or refuted on prior grounds. Empirical fact enters into the theory, but only at the level of basic axioms and without relation to the common historical-statistical "facts" used by present-day economists. The reader will have to go elsewhere—notably to the works of Mises, Hayek, and Robbins—for an elaboration and defense of this epistemology. Suffice it to say here that statistics can prove nothing because they reflect the operation of numerous causal forces. To "refute" the Austrian theory of the inception of the boom because interest rates might not have been lowered in a certain instance, for example, is beside the mark. It simply means that other forces—perhaps an increase in risk, perhaps expectation of rising prices—were strong enough to raise interest rates. But the Austrian analysis of the business cycle continues to operate regardless of the effects of other forces. For the important thing is that interest rates *are lower than they would have been without the credit expansion.* From theoretical analysis we know that this is the effect of every credit expansion by the banks; but statistically we are helpless—we cannot use statistics to estimate *what* the interest rate *would have been.* Statistics can only record past events; they cannot describe possible but unrealized events.

Similarly, the designation of the 1920's as a period of inflationary boom may trouble those who think of inflation as a rise
in prices. Prices generally remained stable and even fell slightly
over the period. But we must realize that two great forces were
at work on prices during the 1920's—the monetary inflation
which propelled prices upward and the increase in productivity
which lowered costs and prices. In a purely free market society,
increasing productivity will increase the supply of goods and
lower costs and prices, spreading the fruits of a higher standard
of living to all consumers. But this tendency was offset by the
monetary inflation which served to stabilize prices. Such stabilization was and is a goal desired by many, but it (a) prevented the
fruits of a higher standard of living from being diffused as widely
as it would have been in a free market; and (b) generated the
boom and depression of the business cycle. For a hallmark of
the inflationary boom is that prices are higher *than they would
have been* in a free and unhampered market. Once again, statistics
cannot discover the causal process at work.

If we were writing an economic history of the 1921-1933 period,
our task would be to try to isolate and explain all the causal
threads in the fabric of statistical and other historical events. We
would analyze various prices, for example, to identify the effects
of credit expansion on the one hand and of increased productivity on the other. And we would try to trace the processes of
the business cycle, along with all the other changing economic
forces (such as shifts in the demand for agricultural products, for
new industries, etc.) that impinged on productive activity. But
our task in this book is much more modest: it is to pinpoint the
specifically cyclical forces at work, to show how the cycle was
generated and perpetuated during the boom, and how the adjustment process was hampered and the depression thereby aggravated. Since government and its controlled banking system are
wholly responsible for the boom (and thereby for generating the
subsequent depression) and since government is largely responsible for aggravating the depression, we must necessarily concentrate on these acts of government intervention in the economy.
An unhampered market would not generate booms and depres-

sions, and, if confronted by a depression brought about by prior intervention, it would speedily eliminate the depression and particularly eradicate unemployment. Our concern, therefore, is not so much with studying the market, as with studying the actions of the culprit responsible for generating and intensifying the depression—government.

THE DEFINITION OF THE MONEY SUPPLY

Money is the general medium of exchange. On this basis, economists have generally defined money as the supply of basic currency and demand deposits at the commercial banks. These have been the means of payment: either gold or paper money (in the United States largely Federal Reserve Notes), or deposits subject to check at the commercial banks. Yet, this is really an inadequate definition. *De jure,* only gold during the 1920's and now only such government paper as Federal Reserve Notes have been standard or legal tender. Demand deposits only function as money because they are considered perfect *money-substitutes,* i.e., they readily take the place of money, at par. Since each holder believes that he can convert his demand deposit into legal tender at par, these deposits circulate as the unchallenged equivalent to cash, and are as good as money proper for making payments. Let confidence in a bank disappear, however, and a bank fail, and its demand deposit will no longer be considered equivalent to money. The distinguishing feature of a money-substitute, therefore, is that people believe it can be converted at par into money at any time on demand. But on this definition, demand deposits are by no means the only—although the most-important—money-substitute. They are not the only constituents of the money supply in the broader sense.[1]

In recent years, more and more economists have begun to include time deposits in banks in their definition of the money supply. For a time deposit is also convertible into money at par on demand, and is therefore worthy of the status of money. Opponents argue (1) that a bank may legally require a 30-day wait before redeeming the deposit in cash, and therefore the deposit is not strictly convertible *on demand* and (2) that a time deposit is not a true means of payment, because it is not easily transferred: a check cannot be written on it, and the owner must present his passbook to make a withdrawal. Yet these are unimportant considerations. For, in reality, the 30-day notice is a dead letter; it is practically never imposed, and, if it were, there would undoubtedly be a prompt and devastating run on the bank.[2] Everyone acts as if his time deposits were redeemable on demand, and the banks pay out their deposits in the same way they redeem demand deposits. The necessity for personal withdrawal is merely a technicality; it may take a little longer to go down to the bank and withdraw the cash than to pay by check, but the essence of the process is the same. In both cases, a deposit at the bank is the source of monetary payment.[3] A further suggested distinction is that banks pay interest on time, but not on demand, deposits and that money must be non-interest-bearing. But this overlooks the fact that banks *did* pay interest on demand deposits during the period we are investigating, and continued to do so until the practice was outlawed in 1933.[4] Naturally, higher interest was paid on time accounts to induce depositors to shift to the account requiring less reserve.[5] This process has led some economists to distinguish between time deposits at commercial banks from those at mutual savings banks, since commercial banks are the ones that profit directly from the shift. Yet, mutual savings banks also profit when a demand depositor withdraws his account at a bank and shifts to the savings bank. There is therefore no real difference between the categories of time deposits; both are accepted as money-substitutes and, in both cases, outstanding deposits redeemable *de facto* on demand are many times the cash remaining in the vault, the rest representing loans and investments which have gone to swell the money supply.

To illustrate the way a savings bank swells the money supply, suppose that Jones transfers his money from a checking account at a commercial bank to a savings bank, writing a check for $1000 to his savings account. As far as Jones is concerned, he simply has $1000 in a savings bank instead of in a checking account at a commercial bank. But the savings bank now itself owns $1000 in the checking account of a commercial bank and uses this money to lend to or invest in business enterprises. The result is that there are now $2000 of effective money supply where there was only $1000 before—$1000 held as a savings deposit and another $1000 loaned out to industry. Hence, in any inventory of the money supply, the total of time deposits, in savings as well as in commercial banks, should be added to the total of demand deposits.[6]

But if we concede the inclusion of time deposits in the money supply, even broader vistas are opened to view. For then all claims convertible into cash on demand constitute a part of the money supply, and swell the money supply whenever cash reserves are less than 100 per cent. In that case, the shares of savings-and-loan associations (known in the 1920's as building-and-loan associations), the shares and savings deposits of credit unions, *and* the cash surrender liabilities of life insurance companies must also form part of the total supply of money.

Savings and loan associations are readily seen as contributing to the money supply; they differ from savings banks (apart from their concentration on mortgage loans) only in being financed by shares of stock rather than by deposits. But these "shares" are redeemable at par in cash on demand (any required notice being a dead letter) and therefore must be considered part of the money supply. Savings-and-loan associations grew at a great pace during the 1920's. Credit unions are also financed largely by redeemable shares; they were of negligible importance during the period of the inflationary boom, their assets totalling only $35 million in 1929. It might be noted, however, that they practically began operations in 1921, with the encouragement of Boston philanthropist Edward Filene.

Life insurance surrender liabilities are our most controversial suggestion. It cannot be doubted, however, that they can supposedly be redeemed at par on demand, and must therefore, according to our principles, be included in the total supply of money. The chief differences, for our purposes, between these liabilities and others listed above are that the policy-holder is discouraged by all manner of propaganda from cashing in his claims, and that the life insurance company keeps almost none of its assets in cash—roughly between one and two per cent. The cash surrender liabilities may be approximated statistically by the total policy reserves of life insurance companies, less policy loans outstanding, for policies on which money has been borrowed from the insurance company by the policy holder are not subject to immediate withdrawal.[7] Cash surrender values of life insurance companies grew rapidly during the 1920's.

It is true that, of these constituents of the money supply, demand deposits are the most easily transferred and therefore are the ones most readily used to make payments. But this is a question of form; just as gold bars were no less money than gold coins, yet were used for fewer transactions. People keep their more active accounts in demand deposits, and their less active balances in time, savings, etc. accounts; yet they may always shift quickly, and on demand, from one such account to another.

INFLATION OF THE MONEY SUPPLY, 1921-1929

— It is generally acknowledged that the great boom of the 1920's began around July, 1921, after a year or more of sharp recession, and ended about July, 1929. Production and business activity began to decline in July, 1929 although the famous stock market crash came in October of that year. Table 1 depicts the *total money supply* of the country, beginning with $45.3 billion on June 30, 1921 and reckoning the total, along with its major constituents, roughly semiannually thereafter.[8] Over the entire period of the boom, we find that the money supply increased by $28.0 billion, a 61.8 per cent increase over the eight-year period. This is an average annual increase of 7.7 per cent, a very sizable degree of inflation. Total bank deposits increased by 51.1 per cent, savings and loan shares by 224.3 per cent, and net life insurance policy reserves by 113.8 per cent. The major increases took place in 1922-1923, late 1924, late 1925, and late 1927. The abrupt leveling off occurred precisely when we would expect—in the first half of 1929, when bank deposits declined and the total money supply remained almost constant.

To generate the business cycle, inflation must take place via loans to business, and the 1920's fit the specifications. *No* expansion took place in currency in circulation, which totalled $3.68 billion at the beginning, and $3.64 billion at the end, of the period. The entire monetary expansion took place in money-substitutes, which are products of credit expansion. Only a negligible amount of this expansion resulted from purchases of government securities: the vast bulk represented private loans and investments. (An "investment" in a corporate security is, economically, just as much a *loan* to business as the more short-term credits labelled "loans" in bank statements.) U.S. government securities held by banks rose from $4.33 billion to $5.50 billion over the period, while total government securities held by life insurance companies actually fell from $1.39 to $1.36 billion. The loans of savings and loan associations are almost all in private real estate, and not in government obligations. Thus, only one billion dollars of the new money was not cycle-generating and represented investments in government securities; almost all of this negligible increase occurred in the early years, 1921-1923.

The other non-cycle-generating form of bank loan is consumer credit; but the increase in bank loans to consumers during the 1920's amounted to a few hundred million dollars at most; the bulk of consumer credit was extended by nonmonetary institutions.[9]

As we have seen, inflation is not precisely the increase in total money supply; it is the increase in money supply *not consisting in,* i.e., not covered by, an increase in gold, the standard commodity money. In discussions of the 1920's a great deal is said about the "gold inflation," implying that the monetary expansion was simply the natural result of an increased supply of gold in America. The increase in total gold in Federal and Treasury reserves, however, was only $1.16 billion from 1921-1929. This covers only a negligible portion of the total monetary expansion —the inflation of dollars.

Specifically, the following table compares total dollar claims issued by the U.S. government, its controlled banking system, and the other monetary institutions (the total supply of money)

TABLE 1

Total Money Supply of the United States, 1921-29 *

(in billions of dollars)

Date	Currency Outside Banks	Demand Deposits Adjusted	Time Deposits	Total Deposits Adjusted and Currency Outside Banks	Savings and Loan Capital	Life Insurance Net Policy Reserves	Total Money Supply	Per Cent Annual Change From Previous
	(1)	(2)	(3)	(4)	(5)	(6)	(7)	(8)
1921—Je. 30	3.68	17.11	16.58	37.79	1.85	5.66	45.30	.....
1922—Je. 30	3.35	18.04	17.44	39.00	2.08	6.08	47.16	4.1
1923—Je. 30	3.74	18.96	19.72	42.75	2.42	6.62	51.79	9.8
1923—Dec. 31	3.73	19.14	20.38	43.50	2.63	6.93	53.06	4.9
1924—Je. 30	3.65	19.41	21.26	44.51	2.89	7.27	54.67	6.1
1924—Dec. 31	3.70	20.90	22.23	47.08	3.15	7.62	57.85	11.6
1925—Je. 30	3.57	21.38	23.19	48.32	3.48	8.06	59.86	7.1
1925—Dec. 31	3.77	22.29	23.92	50.30	3.81	8.48	62.59	9.2
1926—Je. 30	3.60	22.00	24.74	50.57	4.09	8.96	63.62	3.3
1926—Dec. 31	3.83	21.72	25.33	51.12	4.38	9.46	64.96	4.2
1927—Je. 30	3.56	21.98	26.46	52.23	4.70	9.98	66.91	6.0
1927—Dec. 31	3.70	22.73	27.37	54.08	5.03	10.50	69.61	8.1
1928—Je. 30	3.62	22.26	28.53	54.68	5.39	11.05	71.12	4.4
1928—Dec. 31	3.59	23.08	28.68	55.64	5.76	11.60	73.00	5.2
1929—Je. 30	3.64	22.54	28.61	55.17	6.00	12.09	73.26	0.7

* Column 1, *currency outside the banks*, includes gold coins, Treasury currency, Federal Reserve Notes, and various minor currencies; currency held by the banks is, as usual, excluded because it is used as a *reserve* against part of the outstanding money supply. Column 3, *time deposits*, includes accounts at the commercial and savings banks and at the Postal Savings System. Column 4 totals the above three plus the negligible amount of U.S. Government deposits, to give total deposits and outside currency. Column 5 is the share capital of savings and loan associations, Column 6 the policy reserves less policy loans of life insurance companies. Column 7 is the *total money supply*, adding Columns 4, 5, and 6. Column 8 gives the percentage annual change of Column 7 from the preceding date. Currency and deposit statistics can be found in Board of Governors of Federal Reserve System, *Banking and Monetary Statistics* (Washington, D.C.: Federal Reserve Board, 1943), pp. 34 and *passim*. Savings and loan data are available in *Historical Statistics of the U.S., 1789-1945* (Washington, D.C.: U.S. Dept. of Commerce, 1949), p. 175, and life insurance data in the *Life Insurance Year Book*.

with the total holdings of gold reserve in the central bank (the total supply of the gold which could be used to sustain the pledges to redeem dollars on demand). The absolute difference between total dollars and total value of gold on reserve equals the amount of "counterfeit" warehouse receipts to gold that were issued and the degree to which the banking system was effectively, though not *de jure,* bankrupt. These amounts are compared for the beginning and end of the boom period.

TABLE 2

TOTAL DOLLARS AND TOTAL GOLD RESERVES *
(billions of dollars)

	Total Dollar Claims	Total Gold Reserve	Total Uncovered Dollars
June, 1921	44.7	2.6	42.1
June, 1929	71.8	3.0	68.8

* "Total dollar claims" is the "total money supply" of Table 1 minus that portion of currency outstanding that does *not* constitute dollar claims against the gold reserve: i.e., gold coin, gold certificates, silver dollars, and silver certificates. "Total gold reserve" is the official figure for gold reserve *minus* the value of gold certificates outstanding, and equals official "total reserves" of the Federal Reserve Banks. Since gold certificates were bound and acknowledged to be covered by 100 per cent gold backing, this amount is excluded from our reserves for dollar claims, and similarly, gold certificates are here excluded from the "dollar" total. Standard silver and claims to standard silver were excluded as not being claims to gold, and gold coin *is* gold and a claim to gold. See *Banking and Monetary Statistics* (Washington, D.C.: Federal Reserve System, 1943), pp. 544-545, 409, 346-348.

The total of uncovered, or "counterfeited," dollars increased from $42.1 to $68.8 billion in the eight-year period, an increase of 63.4 per cent contrasting to an increase of 15 per cent in the gold reserve. Thus, we see that this corrected measure of inflation yields an even higher estimate than before we considered the gold inflow. The gold inflow cannot, therefore, excuse any part of the inflation.

GENERATING THE INFLATION, I: RESERVE REQUIREMENTS

What factors were responsible for the 63 per cent inflation of the money supply during the 1920's? With currency in circulation not increasing at all, the entire expansion occurred in bank deposits and other monetary credit. The most important element in the money supply is the commercial bank credit base. For while savings banks, saving and loan associations, and life insurance companies can swell the money supply, they can only do so upon the foundation provided by the deposits of the commercial banking system. The liabilities of the other financial institutions are redeemable in commercial bank deposits as well as in currency, and all these institutions keep their reserves in the commercial banks, which therefore serve as a credit base for the other money-creators.[10] Proper federal policy, then, would be to tighten monetary restrictions on commercial banks in order to offset credit expansion in the other areas; failing, that is, the more radical reform of subjecting all of these institutions to the 100 per cent cash reserve requirement.[11]

What factors, then, were responsible for the expansion of commercial bank credit? Since banks were and are required to keep a minimum percentage of reserves to their deposits, there are three possible factors—(a) a lowering in reserve requirements, (b) an increase in total reserves, and (c) a using up of reserves that were previously over the minimum legal requirement.

On the problem of excess reserves, there are unfortunately no statistics available for before 1929. However, it is generally known that excess reserves were almost nonexistent before the Great Depression, as banks tried to keep fully loaned up to their legal requirements. The 1929 data bear out this judgment.[12] We can safely dismiss any possibility that resources for the inflation came from using up previously excessive reserves.

We can therefore turn to the other two factors. Any lowering of reserve requirements would clearly create excess reserves, and thereby invite multiple bank credit inflation. During the 1920's, however, member bank reserve requirements were fixed by statute as follows: 13 per cent (reserves to demand deposits) at Central

Reserve City Banks (those in New York City and Chicago); 10 per cent at Reserve City banks; and 7 per cent at Country banks. Time deposits at member banks only required a reserve of 3 per cent, regardless of the category of bank. These ratios did not change at all. However, reserve requirements need not only change in the minimum ratios; any *shifts* in deposits from one category to another are important. Thus, if there were any great shift in deposits from New York to country banks, the lower reserve requirements in rural areas would permit a considerable net overall inflation. In short, a shift in money from one type of bank to another or from demand to time deposits or *vice versa* changes the *effective* aggregate reserve requirements in the economy. We must therefore investigate possible changes in *effective* reserve requirements during the 1920's.

Within the class of member bank demand deposits, the important categories, for legal reasons, are geographical. A shift from country to New York and Chicago banks raises effective reserve requirements and limits monetary expansion; the opposite shift lowers requirements and promotes inflation. Table 3 presents the total member bank demand deposits in the various areas in June, 1921 and in June, 1929, and the percentage which each area bore to total demand deposits at each date.

TABLE 3

MEMBER BANK DEMAND DEPOSITS *

Date	Central Reserve City	Reserve City	Country	Total
	(in billions of dollars)			
June 30, 1921	5.01	4.40	4.88	14.29
June 30, 1929	6.87	6.17	5.96	19.01
	(in percentages)			
June 30, 1921	35.7	30.8	34.2	100.0
June 29, 1929	36.1	32.5	31.4	100.0

* *Banking and Monetary Statistics* (Washington, D.C.: Federal Reserve Board, 1943), pp. 73, 81, 87, 93, 99. These deposits are the official "U.S. Government" plus "other demand" deposits. They are roughly equal to "net demand deposits." "Demand deposits adjusted" are a better indication of the money supply and are the figures we generally use, but they are not available for geographic categories.

We see that the percentage of demand deposits at the country banks declined during the twenties, from 34.2 to 31.4, while the percentage at urban banks increased, in both categories. Thus, the shift in *effective* reserve requirements was *anti*-inflationary, since the urban banks had higher legal requirements than the country banks. Clearly, no inflationary impetus came from geographical shifts in demand deposits.

What of the relation between member and *non*-member bank deposits? In June, 1921, member banks had 72.6 per cent of total demand deposits; eight years later they had 72.5 per cent of the total. Thus, the relative importance of member and non-member banks remained stable over the period, and both types expanded in about the same proportion.[13]

The relation between *demand* and *time* deposits offers a more fruitful field for investigation. Table 4 compares total demand and time deposits:

TABLE 4

DEMAND AND TIME DEPOSITS
(in billions of dollars)

Date	Demand Deposits	Time Deposits	Per Cent Demand Deposits of Total
June 30, 1921	17.5	16.6	51.3
June 29, 1929	22.9	28.6	44.5

Thus, we see that the 1920's saw a significant shift in the relative importance of demand and time deposits: demand deposits were 51.3 per cent of total deposits in 1921, but had declined to 44.5 per cent by 1929. The relative expansion of time deposits signified an important *lowering* of effective reserve requirements for American banks: for demand deposits required roughly 10 per cent reserve backing, while time deposits needed only 3 per cent reserve. The relative shift from demand to time deposits, therefore, was an important factor in permitting the great monetary inflation of the 1920's. While demand deposits increased 30.8 per cent from 1921 to 1929, time deposits increased by no less than 72.3 per cent!

Time deposits, during this period, consisted of deposits at commercial banks and at mutual savings banks. Mutual savings banks keep only time deposits, while commercial banks, of course, also provide the nation's supply of demand deposits. If we wish to ask to what extent this shift from demand to time deposits was *deliberate,* we may gauge the answer by considering the degree of expansion of time deposits at commercial banks. For it is the commercial banks who gain directly by inducing their customers to shift from demand to time accounts, thereby reducing the amount of required reserves and freeing their reserves for further multiple credit expansion. In the first place, time deposits at commercial banks were about twice the amount held at mutual savings banks. And further, commercial banks expanded their time deposits by 79.8 per cent during this period, while savings banks expanded theirs by only 61.8 per cent. Clearly, commercial banks were the leaders in the shift to time deposits.

This growth in time deposits was not accidental. Before the establishment of the Federal Reserve System, national banks were not legally permitted to pay interest on time deposits, and so this category was confined to the less important state banks and savings banks. The Federal Reserve Act permitted the national banks to pay interest on time deposits. Moreover, before establishment of the Federal Reserve System, banks had been required to keep the same minimum reserve against time as against demand deposits. While the Federal Reserve Act cut the required reserve ratio roughly in half, it reduced required reserves against time deposits to 5 per cent and, in 1917, to 3 per cent. This was surely an open invitation to the banks to do their best to shift deposits from the demand to the time category.

During the 1920's, time deposits increased most in precisely those areas where they were most active and least likely to be misconstrued as idle "savings." Table 5 presents the record of the various categories of time deposits.

TABLE 5

TIME DEPOSITS
(in billions of dollars)

Date	Savings Banks	All Commercial Banks	Member Banks	Central Reserve City Banks	Reserve City Banks	Country Banks
		(in billions of dollars)				
June 30, 1921	5.5	10.9	6.3	.4	2.1	3.8
June 29, 1929	8.9	19.6	13.1	2.2	4.8	6.8

The least active time accounts are in savings banks, the most active in the large city commercial banks. Bearing this in mind, here are the increases over the period in the various categories:

Savings Banks	61.8%
Commercial Banks	79.8
Member Banks	107.9
Country Banks	78.9
Reserve City Banks	128.6
Central Reserve City Banks	450.0

Thus, we see that, unerringly, the most active categories of time deposits were precisely the ones that increased the most in the 1920's, and that this correlation holds for each category. The most active—the Central Reserve City accounts—increased by 450 per cent.[14]

GENERATING THE INFLATION, II: TOTAL RESERVES

Two influences may generate bank inflation—a change in effective reserve requirements and a change in total bank reserves at the Federal Reserve Bank. The relative strength of these two factors in the 1920's may be gauged by Table 6.

TABLE 6 *

MEMBER BANK RESERVES AND DEPOSITS

Date	Reserves Member Bank	Member Bank Deposits	Reserve Ratio
	(in billions of dollars)		
June 30, 1921	1.60	18.6	11.6 : 1
June 30, 1925	2.17	25.5	11.7 : 1
June 29, 1929	2.36	29.4	12.5 : 1

* Column 1 is the total legal member bank reserves at the Fed, excluding vault cash (which remained steady at about $500 million throughout). Column 2 is member bank deposits, demand and time. Column 3 is the ratio of deposits to reserves.

Clearly, the first four years of this period was a time of greater monetary expansion than the second four. The member bank contribution to the money supply increased by $6.9 billion, or 37.1 per cent, in the first half of our period, but only by $3.9 billion or 15.3 per cent in the second half. Evidently, the expansion in the first four years was financed exclusively out of total reserves, since the reserve ratio remained roughly stable at about 11.5 : 1. Total reserves expanded by 35.6 per cent from 1921 to 1925, and member bank deposits rose by 37.1 per cent. In the later four years, reserves expanded by only 8.7 per cent, while deposits rose by 15.3 per cent. This discrepancy was made up by an increase in the reserve ratio from 11.7 : 1 to 12.5 : 1, so that each dollar of reserve carried more dollars in deposits. We may judge how important shifts in reserve requirements were over the period by multiplying the final reserve figure, $2.36 billion, by 11.6, the original ratio of deposits to reserves. The result is $27.4 billion. Thus, of the $29.4 billion in member bank deposits in June, 1929, $27.4 billion may be accounted for by total reserves, while the remaining $2.0 billion may be explained by the shift in reserves. In short, a shift in reserves accounts for $2.0 billion out of the $10.8 billion increase, or 18.5 per cent. The remaining 81.5 per cent of the inflation was due to the increase in total reserves.

Thus, the prime factor in generating the inflation of the 1920's was the increase in total bank reserves: this generated the expansion of the member banks and of the non-member banks, which keep their reserves as deposits with the member banks. It was the 47.5 per cent increase in total reserves (from $1.60 billion to $2.36 billion) that primarily accounted for the 62 per cent increase in the total money supply (from $45.3 to $73.3 billion). A mere $760 million increase in reserves was so powerful because of the nature of our governmentally-controlled banking system. It could roughly generate a $28 billion increase in the money supply.

What then caused the increase in total reserves? The answer to this question must be the chief object of our quest for factors responsible for the inflationary boom. We may list the well-known "factors of increase and decrease" of total reserves, but with special attention to whether or not they can be *controlled* or must be *uncontrolled* by the Federal Reserve or Treasury authorities. The uncontrolled forces emanate from the public at large, the controlled stem from the government.

There are ten factors of increase and decrease of bank reserves.

(1) *Monetary gold stock.* This is, actually, the only *uncontrolled factor of increase*—an increase in this factor increases total reserves to the same extent. When someone deposits gold in a commercial bank (as he could freely do in the 1920's), the bank deposits it at the Federal Reserve Bank and adds to its reserves there by that amount. While some gold inflows and outflows were domestic, the vast bulk were foreign transactions. A decrease in monetary gold stock causes an equivalent decrease in bank reserves. Its behavior is uncontrolled—decided by the public—although in the long run, Federal policies influence its movement.

(2) *Federal Reserve assets purchased.* This is the preeminent *controlled factor of increase* and is wholly under the control of the Federal Reserve authorities. Whenever the Federal Reserve purchases an asset, whatever that asset may be, it can purchase either from the banks or from the public. If it purchases the asset from a (member) bank, it buys the asset and, in exchange, grants the bank an increase in its reserve. Reserves have clearly increased to the same extent as Federal Reserve assets. If, on

the other hand, the Federal Reserve buys the asset from a member of the public, it gives a check on itself to the individual seller. The individual takes the check and deposits it with his bank, thus giving his bank an increase in reserves equivalent to the increase in Reserve assets. (If the seller decides to take currency instead of deposits, then this factor is exactly offset by an increase in money in circulation outside the banks—a *factor of decrease.*)

Gold is not included among these assets; it was listed in the first category (Monetary Gold Stock) and is generally deposited in, rather than purchased by, the Federal Reserve Banks. The major assets purchased are *Bills Bought* and *U.S. Government Securities.* U.S. Government Securities are perhaps the most publicized field of "open-market operations"; Federal Reserve purchases add to bank reserves and sales diminish them. Bills Bought were *acceptance paper* which the Federal Reserve bought outright in a policy of subsidy that practically created this type of paper *de novo* in the United States. Some writers treat Bills Bought as an uncontrolled factor, because the Federal Reserve announced a rate at which it would buy all acceptances presented to it. No law, however, compelled it to adopt this policy of unlimited purchase; it therefore must be counted as a pure creation of Federal Reserve policy and under its control.

(3) *Bills Discounted by the Federal Reserve.* These bills are not purchased, but represent *loans* to the member banks. They are rediscounted bills, and advances to banks on their IOU's. Clearly a factor of increase, they are not as welcome to banks as are other ways of increasing reserves, because they must be repaid to the System; yet, while they remain outstanding, they provide reserves as effectively as any other type of asset. Bills Discounted, in fact, can be loaned precisely and rapidly to those banks that are in distress, and are therefore a powerful and effective means of shoring up banks in trouble. Writers generally classify Bills Discounted as uncontrolled, because the Federal Reserve always stands ready to lend to banks on their eligible assets as collateral, and will lend almost unlimited amounts at a given rate. It is true, of course, that the Federal Reserve fixes this *rediscount rate,* and at a lower rate when stimulating bank borrowing,

but this is often held to be the only way that the System can
control this factor. But the Federal Reserve Act does not *compel,*
it only authorizes, the Federal Reserve to lend to member banks.
If the authorities want to exercise an inflationary role as "lender of
last resort" to banks in trouble, it chooses to do so by itself. If it
wanted, it could simply refuse to lend to banks at any time. Any
expansion of Bills Discounted, then, must be attributed to the
will of the Federal Reserve authorities.

On the other hand, member banks themselves have largely controlled the speed of *repayment* of Reserve loans. When the banks
are more prosperous, they generally reduce their indebtedness to
the Federal Reserve. The authorities *could* compel more rapid
repayment, but they have decided to lend freely to banks and
to influence banks by changing its rediscount charges.

To separate controlled from uncontrolled factors as best we
can, therefore, we are taking the rather drastic step of considering
any *expansion* of Bills Discounted as *controlled* by the government, and any *reduction* as being *uncontrolled,* and determined
by the banks. Of course, repayments will be partly governed by
the amount of previous debt, but this seems to be the most
reasonable division. We must take this step, therefore, even
though it complicates the historical record. Thus, if Bills Discounted increase by $200 million over some three-year period, we
may call this a controlled increase of $200 million, if we consider
only this overall record. On the other hand, if we break down
the record from year to year, it may be that Bills Discounted
first increased by $500 million, then were reduced by $400 million,
and then increased again by $100 million the final year. When we
consider a year-to-year basis, then, controlled increase of reserves
for the three years was $600 million and uncontrolled decrease
was $400 million. The finer we break down the record, there-
fore, the greater the extent both of controlled increases by the
government, and of uncontrolled declines prompted by the banks.
Perhaps the best way of resolving this problem is to break down
the record to the most significant periods. It would be far simpler
to lump all Bills Discounted as controlled and let it go at that,
but this would distort the historical record intolerably; thus, in

the early 1920's it would give the Federal Reserve an undeserved accolade for reducing member bank debts when this reduction was largely accomplished by the banks themselves.

We may therefore divide Bills Discounted into: New Bills Discounted (controlled factor of increase) and Bills Repaid (uncontrolled factor of decrease).

(4) *Other Federal Reserve Credit.* This is largely "float," or checks on banks remaining temporarily uncollected by the Federal Reserve. This is an interest-free form of lending to banks and is therefore a factor of increase wholly controlled by the Federal Reserve. Its importance was negligible in the 1920's.

(5) *Money in Circulation Outside the Banks.* This is the main factor of decrease—an increase in this item decreases total reserves to the same extent. This is the total currency in the hands of the public and is determined wholly by the relative place people wish to accord paper money as against bank deposits. It is therefore an uncontrolled factor, decided by the public.

(6) *Treasury Currency Outstanding.* Any increase in Treasury currency outstanding is deposited with the Federal Reserve in the Treasury's deposit account. As it is spent on government expenditures, the money tends to flow back into commercial bank reserves. Treasury currency is therefore a factor of increase, and is controlled by the Treasury (or by Federal statute). Its most important element is silver certificates backed 100 per cent by silver bullion and silver dollars.

(7) *Treasury Cash Holdings.* Any increase in Treasury cash holdings represents a shift from bank reserves, while a decline in Treasury cash is spent in the economy and tends to increase reserves. It is therefore a factor of decrease and is controlled by the Treasury.

(8) *Treasury Deposits at the Federal Reserve.* This factor is very similar to Treasury cash holdings; an increase in deposits at the Reserve represents a shift from bank reserves, while a decrease means that more money is added to the economy and swells bank reserves. This is, therefore, a factor of decrease controlled by the Treasury.

(9) *Non-member Bank Deposits at the Federal Reserve.* This

factor acts very similarly to Treasury deposits at the Federal Reserve. An increase in non-member bank deposits lowers member bank reserves, for they represent shifts from member banks to these other accounts. A decline will increase member bank reserves. These deposits are mainly made by non-member banks, and by foreign governments and banks. They are a factor of decrease, but uncontrolled by the government.

(10) *Unexpended Capital Funds of the Federal Reserve.* They are capital funds of the Federal Reserve not yet expended in assets (largely bank premises and expenses of operation). This capital is drawn from commercial banks, and, therefore, if unexpended, is a withdrawal of reserves. This is almost always a negligible item; it is clearly under the control of the Federal Reserve authorities.

Summing up, the following are the factors of change of member bank reserves: [15]

Factors of Increase

Monetary Gold Stock..uncontrolled
Federal Reserve Assets Purchased ....controlled
    Bills Bought
    U.S. Government Securities
New Bills Discounted .... controlled
Other Federal Reserve Credit ....controlled
Treasury Currency Outstanding ....controlled

Factors of Decrease

Outside Money in Circulation ....uncontrolled
Treasury Cash Holdings ....controlled
Treasury Deposits at the Federal Reserve ....controlled
Unexpended Capital Funds of the Federal Reserve ....controlled
Non-member Bank Deposits at the Federal
    Reserve ....uncontrolled
Bills Repaid ....uncontrolled

An overall survey of the entire 1921-1929 period does not give an accurate picture of the broad forces behind the movements in total reserves. For while total reserves continued to increase, there were continual fluctuations within the various categories, with some increasing and other decreasing in any one period and different factors predominating at different times. Tables 6 and 7 depict the forces causing changes in total reserves during the 1920's. Table 6 breaks down 1921-1929 into twelve sub periods, shows the changes in each causal factor, and the consequent changes in member bank reserves, for each sub period. Table 7 transforms the data of Table 6 into per-month figures, thus enabling comparison of the relative *rates* of change for the various periods.

Member bank reserves totalled $1604 million on June 30, 1921, and reached $2356 million eight years later. Over the twelve subperiods, uncontrolled reserves *declined* by $1.04 billion, while controlled reserves *increased* by $1.79 billion. By themselves, then, uncontrolled factors were deflationary; the inflation was clearly precipitated deliberately by the Federal Reserve. The plea that the 1920's was simply a "gold inflation" that the Federal Reserve did not counter actively is finally exploded. Gold was never the major problem, and in not one subperiod did it provide the crucial factor in increasing reserves.

In the twelve subperiods, uncontrolled factors declined seven times and increased five times. Controlled factors, on the other hand, rose in eight periods and declined in four. Of the controlled factors, Bills Bought played a vital role in changing reserves in nine periods, Government Securities in seven, Bills Discounted in five, and Treasury Currency in three (the first three). If we add up, regardless of arithmetic sign, the total impact of each controlled factor on reserves over the twelve periods, we find Government Securities in the lead (with $2.24 billion), Bills Bought slightly behind ($2.16 billion) and New Discounts behind that ($1.54 billion).

At the start of the eight-year period, Bills Discounted totalled $1.75 billion, Bills Bought were $40 million, U. S. Government Securities held were $259 million, Treasury Currency Outstanding totalled $1.75 billion, Monetary Gold Stock was $3.00 billion, and Money in Circulation was $4.62 billion.

TABLE 7

Changes in Reserves and Causal Factors, Over Twelve Periods, 1921-1929
(in millions of dollars)

Factors	I June 1921-July 1922	II July 1922-Dec. 1922	III Dec. 1922-Oct. 1923	IV Oct. 1923-June 1924	V June 1924-Nov. 1924	VI Nov. 1924-Nov. 1925	VII Nov. 1925-Oct. 1926	VIII Oct. 1926-July 1927	IX July 1927-Dec. 1927	X Dec. 1927-July 1928	XI July 1928-Dec. 1928	XII Dec. 1928-June 1929
Federal Reserve Credit	—996	305	—186	—388	355	235	—60	—268	562	—222	376	—409
Bills Discounted	—1345	212	266	—550	—92	446	2	—248	140	449	25	—19
Bills Bought	100	132	—67	—168	277	45	—36	—151	220	—230	327	—407
U.S. Government Securities	278	—101	—344	339	153	—242	—41	91	225	—402	13	—12
Other Credit	—28	62	—40	—9	17	—14	14	39	—22	—39	10	30
Treasury Currency	115	93	47	14	5	—43	9	13	3	—2	8	7
Treasury Cash	—43	16	2	4	0	5	—2	13	—4	7	—1	—2
Treasury Deposits	—16	48	—29	—3	6	—2	0	14	7	—6	1	—13
Unexpended Capital Funds of the Federal Reserve	56	6	—6	21	3	—15	—20	—3	—5	—28	—19	—26
Monetary Gold Stock	554	100	238	321	39	—130	76	107	—201	—266	28	183
Money in Circulation	487	—393	—112	80	—203	8	23	175	—157	302	—272	227
Other Deposits	1	—2	6	0	—6	—4	1	4	2	—3	2	—1
Controlled Reserve	462	468	—171	198	461	180	—74	16	564	—251	364	—423
Uncontrolled Reserve	—303	—295	132	—149	—262	—126	100	38	—356	33	—242	390
Member Bank Reserve	157	173	—39	49	199	54	26	54	210	—220	122	—33

TABLE 8

PER MONTH CHANGES IN RESERVES AND CAUSAL FACTORS, OVER TWELVE PERIODS, 1921-1929

(in millions of dollars)

Factors	I June 1921-July 1922	II July 1922-Dec. 1922	III Dec. 1922-Oct. 1923	IV Oct. 1923-June 1924	V June 1924-Nov. 1924	VI Nov. 1924-Nov. 1925	VII Nov. 1925-Oct. 1926	VIII Oct. 1926-July 1927	IX July 1927-Dec. 1927	X Dec. 1927-July 1928	XI July 1928-Dec. 1928	XII Dec. 1928-June 1929
Federal Reserve Credit	—76.6	61.0	—18.6	—48.5	71.0	2.0	—5.5	—29.8	112.4	—31.7	75.2	—68.2
Bills Discounted	—103.5	42.4	26.6	—68.8	—18.4	37.2	0.2	—27.6	28.0	64.1	5.0	—3.2
Bills Bought	7.7	26.4	—6.7	—21.0	55.4	3.8	—3.3	—16.8	44.0	—32.9	65.4	—67.8
U.S. Government Securities	21.4	—20.2	—34.4	42.4	30.6	—20.2	—3.7	10.1	45.0	—57.4	2.6	—2.0
Other Credit	—2.2	12.4	—4.0	—1.1	3.4	—1.2	1.3	4.3	—4.4	—5.6	2.0	5.0
Treasury Currency	8.8	18.6	4.7	1.8	1.0	—3.6	0.8	1.4	0.6	—0.3	1.6	1.2
Treasury Cash	—4.0	3.2	0.2	0.5	0	0.4	—0.2	1.4	—0.8	1.0	—0.2	—0.3
Treasury Deposits	—1.2	9.6	—2.9	—0.4	1.2	—0.2	0	1.5	1.4	—0.9	0.2	—2.2
Unexpended Capital Funds of the Federal Reserve	4.3	1.2	—0.6	2.6	0.6	—1.2	—1.8	—0.3	—1.0	—4.0	—3.8	—4.3
Monetary Gold Stock	42.6	20.0	23.8	40.1	7.8	—10.8	6.9	11.9	—40.2	—38.0	5.6	30.5
Money in Circulation	37.5	—78.6	—11.2	10.0	—40.6	0.7	2.1	19.4	—31.4	43.1	—54.2	37.8
Other Deposits	0	0.4	0.6	0	—1.2	—0.3	0.1	0.4	—0.4	—0.4	0.4	—0.2
Contolled Reserve	35.5	93.6	—17.1	24.8	92.2	15.0	—6.7	1.8	112.8	—37.3	72.8	—70.5
Uncontrolled Reserve	—23.3	—59.0	13.2	—18.6	—52.4	—10.5	9.1	4.2	—71.2	4.7	—48.4	65.0
Member Bank Reserve	12.1	34.6	—3.9	6.1	39.8	4.5	2.4	6.0	42.0	—32.6	24.4	—5.5

Tables 6 and 7 are organized as follows: Bills Discounted, Bills Bought, Government Securities held by the Federal Reserve and Other Credit constitute Federal Reserve Credit. Changes in Federal Reserve Credit (except for net *reductions* in Bills Discounted), plus changes in Treasury Currency, Treasury Cash, Treasury Deposits at the Federal Reserve, and Unexpended Capital Funds of the Reserve constitute the *controlled* changes in member bank reserves. Changes in Monetary Gold Stock, Money in Circulation, and Other Deposits at the Federal Reserve constitute the *uncontrolled* changes, and the resultant effect constitutes the changes in bank reserves. The arithmetic signs of the actual changes of *factors of decrease* are reversed to accord with their effects on reserves; thus, a reduction of $165 million in Money in Circulation from 1921-1929 is listed in the table as a change of *plus* 165 on reserves.

Any division into historical periods is to a degree arbitrary. Yet the divisions of Tables 6 and 7 were chosen because the author believes they accord best with the most significant subperiods of the 1920's, subperiods which differ too much to be adequately reflected in any overall assessment. The following are the unique characteristics of each of these subperiods.

I. June 1921—July 1922 (dates are all end-of-the-month). Bills Discounted, which had been falling since 1920, continued a precipitate decline, from $1751 million in June 1921 to a bottom of $397 million in August 1922. Total Reserve Credit also fell to reach a bottom in July 1922, as did Money in Circulation, which reached its bottom in July 1922. July was therefore chosen as the terminal month.

II. July 1922—December 1922. Total Reserve Credit climbed upward sharply, hitting a peak in December, as did total reserves. Bills Discounted reached a peak in November.

III. December 1922—October 1923. Bills Discounted continued to climb, reaching a peak in October. In the meanwhile, U.S. Government Securities fell sharply to reach a trough of 92 million in October, a trough for the whole period.

IV. October 1923—June 1924. Bills Bought fell abruptly, to reach a trough in July. Total Reserve Credit reached a trough in June.

V. June 1924—November 1924. Bills Discounted, which had been falling since October 1923, continued to fall, reaching bottom in November 1924. U.S. Government Securities climbed to a peak in the same month. The Monetary Gold Stock also reached a peak in November 1924. Bills Bought climbed to a peak in December 1924, as did total Reserve Credit and total reserves.

VI. November 1924—November 1925. Bills Discounted climbed again to a peak in November. U.S. Securities fell to a trough in October, and total Reserve Credit reached a peak in December.

VII. November 1925—October 1926. U.S. Government Securities reached a trough in October, and Bills Discounted a peak in the same month. Clearly, both items milled around during this period.

VIII. October 1926—July 1927. Bills Bought fell to a trough in July, and Bills Discounted reached a trough in August. Total Reserve Credit reached its trough in May.

IX. July 1927—December 1927. U.S. Government Securities climbed to a peak in December, as did Bills Discounted, total Reserve Credit, and total reserves.

X. December 1927—July 1928. Bills Bought fell to a low in July, as did U.S. Government Securities, total Reserve Credit, and total reserves. Bills Discounted climbed to a peak in August.

XI. July 1928—December 1928. Bills Bought reached a peak in December, as did total reserves, while Bills Discounted and Reserve Credit reached a peak in November.

XII. December 1928—June 1929. Concludes the period under study.

Using these subperiods and their changes, we may now analyze precisely the course of the monetary inflation in the 1920's.

In Period I (June 1921—July 1922) a superficial glance would lead one to believe that the main inflationary factor was the heavy gold inflow, and that the Federal Reserve simply did not offset this influx sufficiently. A deeper analysis, however, shows that the banks paid off their loans at such a rapid rate that uncontrolled factors *fell* by $303 million. If the government had remained completely passive, therefore, member bank reserves would have declined by $303 million. Instead, the government actively pumped in $462 million of new reserves, yielding a net increase of $157 million. (Subtraction differences come from rounding.) The major channels of this increase were purchase of U.S. Government Securities ($278 million), Treasury currency ($115 million), and Bills Bought ($100 million).

Period II (July 1922—December 1922) saw a rapid acceleration of the inflation of reserves. Increasing at an average rate of $12 million per month in Period I, reserves now increased at a rate of $35 million per month. Once again, uncontrolled factors *declined,* by $295 million, but they were more than offset by increases in controlled reserves pumped into the economy. These consisted of Bills Discounted ($212 million), Bills Bought ($132 million), and Treasury Currency ($93 million).

Periods III and IV (December 1922—June 1924) saw the inflation come roughly to a halt. Reserves actually fell slightly (by $4 million per month) in Period III (December 1922—October 1923), and rose only slightly (by $6 million per month) in Period IV. Simultaneously, bank deposits remained about level, member bank demand deposits staying at about $13.5 billion. Total deposits and total money supply, however, rose more in this period, with banks shifting to time deposits to permit increases. (Demand deposits rose by $450 million from June 1923 to June 1924, but time deposits rose by $1.5 billion). Total money supply rose by $3 billion. The economy responded to the slowdown of inflation by entering upon a mild minor recession, from May 1923 to July 1924.

The slight fall in reserves during Period III was brought about by selling U.S. Government Securities (—$344 million) and reducing the amount of bills held (—$67 million). This, indeed, was a positive decline, more than offsetting uncontrolled factors, which had increased by $132 million. The decline in reserves would have been even more effective, if the Federal Reserve had not increased its discounts ($266 million) and Treasury currency had not increased ($47 million).

Period IV (October 1923—June 1924), however, began to repeat the pattern of Period I and resume the march of inflation. Uncontrolled factors this time fell by $149 million, but they were more than offset by a controlled increase of $198 million, led by the heavy purchase of government securities ($339 million)—the heaviest average monthly buying spree yet seen in the 1920's ($42.4 million).

Period V was the most rapid reserve inflation to date, over-reaching the previous peak of late 1922. Reserves increased by $39.8 million per month. Once again, the inflation was deliberate, uncontrolled factors declining by $262 million, but offset by a deliberate increase of $461 million. The critical factors of inflation were Bills Bought ($277 million) and U.S. Securities ($153 million).

The pace of inflation was greatly slowed in the next three periods, but continued nevertheless. From December 31, 1924 to June 30, 1927, reserves increased by $750 million; demand deposits adjusted, of all banks, rose by $1.1 billion. But *time* deposits rose by $4.3 billion during the same period, underscoring the banks' ability to induce customers to shift from demand to time deposits, while savings and loan shares and life-insurance reserves rose by another $4.3 billion. In 1926 there was a decided slowing down of the rate of inflation of the money supply, and this led to another mild economic recession during 1926 and 1927.

In Period VI (November 1924—November 1925), a tendency of uncontrolled reserves to decline was again more than offset by an increase in *controlled* reserves; these were Bills Discounted ($446 million) and Bills Bought ($45 million). Period VII (November 1925—October 1926) was the first time after Period III that uncontrolled factors acted to *increase* reserves. But, in contrast, this time, the Federal Reserve failed to offset these factors sufficiently, although the degree of inflation was very slight (only $2.4 million per month). In Period VIII (October 1926—July 1927), the degree of inflation was still small, but,

ominously, the Federal Reserve stoked the fires of inflation rather
than checked them; controlled factors increased, as did the uncontrolled. The culprits this time were the U.S. Government's ($91
million) and Other Credit ($30 million).

Period IX (July 1927—December 1927), was another period of
accelerated and heavy inflation, surpassing the previous peaks
of latter 1922 and 1924. The per-monthly reserve increase in
latter 1927 was $42.0 million. Once again, uncontrolled factors
declined, but were more than offset by a very large increase in
controlled reserves, emanating from Bills Bought ($220 million),
U.S. Governments ($225 million), and Bills Discounted ($140
million).

Period X was the sharpest deflationary period (in *reserves*) in
the 1920's. Uncontrolled factors rose, but were more than offset
by a controlled decrease. Bills Discounted rose ($409 million),
but the deflationary lead was taken by U.S. Governments (—$402
million) and Bills Bought (—$230 million). The decline of over
$200 millions in reserves generated a decline of about $600
million in member bank demand deposits. Time deposits rose
by over $1 billion, however, and life insurance reserves by $550
million, so that the total money supply rose substantially, by
$1.5 billion, from the end of 1927 to mid-1928.

With the boom now well advanced in years, and developing
momentum, it was imperative for the Fed to accelerate its
deflationary pressure, if a great depression was to be avoided. The
deflation of reserves in the first half of 1928, as we have seen, was
not even sufficient to offset the shift to time deposits and the
other factors increasing the money supply. Yet, disastrously,
the Fed resumed its inflationary course in latter 1928. In Period
XI, a tendency of uncontrolled reserves to decrease, was offset by
a positive and deliberate increase ($364 million of controlled re-
serves, against—$122 million of uncontrolled). The culprit in
this program was Bills Bought, which increased by $327 million,
while all the other reserve assets were only increasing slightly.
Of all the periods of the 1920's, Period XI saw the sharpest
average monthly rise in Bills Bought ($65.4 million).

In the final Period XII, the tide, at last, definitely and sharply turned. Uncontrolled factors *increased* by $390 million, but were offset by no less than a $423 million decrease in controlled reserves, consisting almost wholly of a reduction of $407 million in bills bought. Total reserves fell by $33 million. Member bank demand deposits, which also reached a peak in December, 1928, fell by about $180 million. Total demand deposits fell by $540 million.

So far, we have seen no reason why this deflation should have had any greater effect than the deflation of Period X. Indeed, total reserves fell by only $33 million as against $228 million in the former period. Member bank deposits fell by less ($180 million as against $450 million), and total demand deposits fell by about the same amount ($540 million against $470 million). The crucial difference, however, is this: in Period X time deposits rose by $1.1 billion, insuring a rise in the nation's total currency and deposits of $600 million. But in Period XII, time deposits, far from rising, actually fell by $70 million. Total deposits, therefore, fell by $510 million, while the total money supply rose very slightly, impelled by continued growth in life insurance reserves. Time deposits no longer came to the rescue, as in 1923 and 1928, and total money supply rose only from $73.00 billion at the end of 1928, to $73.26 billion in mid-1929. For the first time since June 1921, the money supply stopped increasing, and remained virtually constant. The great boom of the 1920's was now over, and the Great Depression had begun. The country, however, did not really discover the change until the stock market finally crashed in October.

TREASURY CURRENCY

An increase in Treasury currency played a considerable role in the inflation in the early years from 1921-1923. It is unusual for Treasury currency to change considerably, as we see from its behavior over the rest of the 1921-1929 period. The surprising increase in 1921-1923 consisted almost exclusively of *silver certificates,* representing silver bullion held in the Treasury at 100 per cent of its value. (Of the $225 million increase in Treasury currency during Periods I-III, $211 million was silver certificates.) In 1918, the Pittman Act had permitted the United States government to sell silver to Britain as a wartime measure, and the silver stock of the Treasury, as well as the silver certificates based 100 per cent upon them, was reduced as a consequence. In May, 1920, however, in accordance with its obligation under the Act to buy silver bullion at the inflated price of one dollar per ounce until its stock had been replenished, the Treasury began to buy silver bullion, and this subsidy to domestic silver miners swelled bank reserves. This silver purchase policy effectively ended by mid-1923. The Treasury was forced to embark upon the silver purchase program by the terms of the Pittman Act of 1918, the responsibility of the Wilson Administration. The Harding Administration, however, could have repealed the Pittman Act if it had had the desire to do so. It must therefore bear its share of the blame for the silver purchase policy.[16]

BILLS DISCOUNTED

We have seen the important role played by discounted bills in spurring the inflation. In 1923, 1925 and 1928, bills discounted came to the rescue of the banks at periods when the Fed was trying to exert anti-inflationary pressure by selling government securities, and, in 1923 and 1928 at least, reducing its holding of acceptances. In each instance, bills discounted was responsible for continuing the inflationary surge. The main trouble lay in the Federal Reserve's assumption of the role of "lender of last resort," more or less passively waiting to grant discounts to any banks that apply. But this was a policy adopted by the Fed, and it could have been changed at any time. The Fed allowed itself to affect discounts merely by setting and changing its rediscount rate.

The bulk of discounts consisted of rediscounted business paper (including commercial, agricultural and industrial), and advances to banks on their promissory notes secured by U.S. government securities as collateral. When our period began, maximum legal maturity on discounts was 90 days, except for agricultural paper, which could be discounted for six months. In March 1923, Congress extended the special privilege to agricultural paper to nine months, and the Fed was also granted authority to rediscount agricultural paper held by the newly-established Federal Intermediate Credit Banks. More important, the FRB changed its original idea of making careful credit analyses of the original borrowers, and instead relied on the apparent solvency of the discounting banks, or else directly bailed out banks in distress.[17] This relaxation permitted a greater quantitative level of rediscounts.

If the Federal Reserve induced changes in discounts through the rediscount rate, it should certainly have always set it at a "penalty rate," i.e., high enough so that the banks would lose money by borrowing from it. If a bank earns 5 per cent on its loan or investment, for example, and the Reserve sets its rediscount rate above that, say at 8 per cent, then a bank will only borrow in the direst emergency when it desperately needs reserves. On the other hand, if the rediscount rate is set *below* the market, the bank can make a pleasant career out of borrowing, say, at 4 per cent and relending the money at 5 per cent. To discourage bank discounting, then, a permanent penalty rate above the market is essential. There was considerable opinion in the early 1920's that the FRB should maintain penalty rates in accord with British central banking tradition, but unfortunately the proponents only wanted rates above the lowest-yielding loans —prime commercial paper. Such a penalty rate would have been rather ineffectual, since the banks could still profit by discounting and relending to their riskier borrowers. A truly effective penalty rate would keep the rediscount rate above the rates of *all* bank loans.

Opinions clashed within the government in the early years on proposals for a mild penalty rate above prime commercial paper. The three main centers of monetary power were the Treasury, the Federal Reserve Board, and the New York Federal Reserve Bank, the latter two institutions clashing over power and policy throughout our period. At first, the Federal Reserve leaders favored penalty rates, and the Treasury was opposed: thus, the annual Federal Reserve Board report of 1920 promised establishment of the high rates.[18] By mid-1921, however, the Federal Reserve began to weaken, with Governor W. P. G. Harding, Chairman of the Federal Reserve Board, shifting his views—largely for political reasons. Benjamin Strong, very powerful Governor of the Federal Reserve Bank of New York, also changed his mind at about the same time, and, as a result, penalty rates were doomed, and were no longer an issue from that point on.

Another problem of discount policy was whether the Federal Reserve should lend *continuously* to banks or only in emergencies.[19] While anti-inflationists must frown on either policy, certainly a policy of continuous lending is more inflationary, since it stokes the fires of monetary expansion continuously. The original theory of the Federal Reserve was to promote continuous credit, but for a while in the early 1920's, the Reserve shifted to favoring emergency credit only. Indeed, in an October, 1922 conference, FRB authorities approved the proposal of New York Federal Reserve Bank official, Pierre Jay, that the Federal Reserve should only supply seasonal and emergency credit and currency, and that even this should be restrained by the necessity of preventing credit inflation. By early 1924, however, the Federal Reserve abandoned this doctrine, and its Annual Report of 1923 supported the following disastrous policy:

The Federal Reserve banks are the . . . source to which the member banks turn when the demands of the business community have outrun their own unaided resources. The Federal reserve supplies the needed additions to credit in times of business expansion and takes up the slack in times of business recession.[20]

If the Federal Reserve is to extend credit during a boom *and* during a depression, it follows quite clearly that the Reserve's policy was frankly to promote continuous and permanent inflation.

Finally, in early 1926, Pierre Jay himself repudiated his own doctrine, and the "emergency" theory was now dead as a dodo.

Not only did the FRB, throughout the 1920's, keep rediscount rates below the market and lend continuously; it also kept delaying much needed raises in the rediscount rate. Thus, in 1923 and in 1925 the Fed sabotaged its own attempts to restrict credit by failing to raise the rediscount rate until too late, and it also failed to raise the rate sufficiently in 1928 and 1929.[21] One of the reasons for this failure was the Federal Reserve's consistent desire to supply "adequate" credit to business, and its fear of penalizing "legitimate business" through raising rates of interest. As soon as the Fed was established, in fact, Secretary of the Treasury William G. McAdoo trumpeted the policy which the Federal Reserve was to continue pursuing throughout the 1920's and during the Great Depression:

The primary purpose of the Federal Reserve Act was to alter and strengthen our banking system that the enlarged credit resources demanded by the needs of business and agricultural enterprises will come almost automatically into existence and at rates of interest low enough to stimulate, protect and prosper all kinds of legitimate business.[22]

Thus did America embark on its disastrous twentieth century policy of inflation and subsequent depression—via a stimulation of legalized counterfeiting for special privilege conferred by government on favored business and farm enterprises.

As early as 1915 and 1916, various Board Governors had urged banks to discount from the Federal Reserve and extend credit, and Comptroller John Skelton Williams urged farmers to borrow and hold their crops for a higher price. This policy was continued in full force after the war. The inflation of the 1920's began, in fact, with an announcement by the FRB (Federal Reserve Board) in July, 1921, that it would extend further credits for harvesting and marketing in whatever amounts were legitimately required. And, beginning in 1921, Secretary of Treasury Andrew Mellon was privately urging the Fed that business be stimulated, and discount rates reduced; the records indicate that his advice was heeded to the full. Governor James, of the FRB, declared to his colleagues in 1926 that the "very purpose" of the Federal Reserve System "was to be of service to the agriculture, industry and commerce of the nation," and no one was apparently disposed to contradict him.

Also in 1926, Dr. Oliver M. W. Sprague, economist and influential advisor to the Federal Reserve System, prophesied no immediate advances in the rediscount rate, because business had naturally been assuming since 1921 that plenty of Federal Reserve credit would always be available. Business, of course, could not be let down.[23] The Federal Reserve's very weak discount policy in 1928 and 1929 was caused by its fear that a higher interest rate would no longer "accommodate" business sufficiently.

An inflationary, low discount rate, policy was a prominent and important feature of the Harding and Coolidge Administrations. Even before taking office, President Harding had urged reduction of interest rates, and he repeatedly announced his intention of reducing discount rates after he became President. And President Coolidge, in a famous pre-election speech on October 22, 1924, declared that "It has been the policy of this Administration to reduce discount rates," and promised to keep them low. Both Presidents appointed FRB members who favored this policy.[24] Eugene Meyer, chairman of the War Finance Corporation, warned the banks that by advertising that they do not discount with this farm-loan agency, they were being "injurious to the public interest." [25] While such men as the head of the Merchants' Association of New York warned Coolidge about Federal Reserve credit to farmers, others pressed for more inflation: a Nebraska congressman proposed loans in new Treasury Notes at one-half per cent to farmers, Senator Magnus Johnson urged a maximum rediscount rate of 2 per cent, and the National Farmer-Labor Party called for the nationalization of all banking. Driven by their general desire to provide cheap and abundant credit to industry, as well as their policy (as we shall see below) of helping Britain avoid the consequences of its own monetary policies, the Federal Reserve sought constantly to avoid raising discount rates. In latter 1928 and 1929, with the need clearly evident, the FRB took refuge in the dangerous qualitative doctrine of "moral suasion." Moral suasion was an attempt to keep credit abundant to "legitimate" industry, while denying it to "illegitimate" stock market speculators. As we have seen, such attempts to segregate credit markets were inevitably self defeating, and were mischievous in placing different ethical tags on equally legitimate forms of business activity.

Moral suasion emerged in the famous February, 1929 letter of the FRB to the various Federal Reserve Banks, warning them that member banks were beyond their rights in making speculative loans, and advising restraint of Federal Reserve credit speculation, while maintaining credit to commerce and business. This step was taken in evasive response to persistent urging by the New York Federal Reserve Bank to raise the rediscount rate from 5 to 6 per cent, a feeble enough step that was delayed until the latter part of 1929. Whereas, the New York Bank was the more inflationary organ in 1927 (as we shall see below), after that the New York Bank pursued a far more sensible policy: general credit restraint, e.g. raising the rediscount rate, while the Federal Reserve Board fell prey to qualitative credit fallacies at a peculiarly dangerous period—1929. The FRB went so far as to tell the New York Bank to lend freely and abundantly for commercial purposes.[26] The late Benjamin Strong had always held that it was impossible to earmark bank loans, and that the problem was quantitative and not qualitative. The New York Bank continued to stress this view, and refused to follow the FRB directive, repeating that it should not concern itself with bank loans, but rather with bank reserves and deposits.[27] The refusal of the New York Bank to follow the FRB directive of moral suasion finally drew a letter from the FRB on May 1, listing certain New York member banks that were borrowing continuously from the Federal Reserve, and were also carrying "too many" stock loans, and requesting that the New York Bank deal with them accordingly. On May 11, the New York Bank flatly refused, reiterating that banks have a right to make stock loans, and that there was no way to determine which loans were speculative. By June 1, the FRB succumbed, and dropped its policy of moral suasion. It did not raise the rediscount rate until August, however.[28]

Apart from the actions of the New York Bank, the policy of moral suasion failed, even on its own terms, for non-bank lenders used their bank-derived funds to replace bank lenders in the stock market. This inevitable result surprised and bewildered the qualitativists, and the stock-market boom continued merrily onward.[29]

While stock market loans are no worse than any other form of loan, and moral suasion was a fallacious evasion of the need for *quantitative* restriction, any *special* governmental support for a certain type of loan is important in two ways: (1) government encouragement of one type of loan is apt to swell the overall *quantity* of bank loans; and (2) it will certainly overstimulate the particular loan and add to its readjustment difficulties in the depression phase. We must therefore examine the important instances of particular governmental stimulation to the stock market in the 1920's. While not as important as the increase in reserves and the money supply, this special aid served to spur the quantitative increase, and also created particular distortions in the stock market which caused greater troubles in the depression.

One important aid to stock market inflation was the FRS policy of keeping call loan rates (on bank loans to the stock market) particularly low. Before the establishment of the Federal Reserve System, the call rate frequently rose far above 100 per cent; but since its inception, the call rate never rose above 30 per cent, and very rarely above 10 per cent.[30] The call rates were controlled at these low levels by the New York Federal Reserve Bank, in close cooperation with, and at the advice of, a Money Committee of the New York Stock Exchange. The New York Fed also loaned consistently to Wall Street banks for the purpose of regulating the call rate.

Another important means of encouraging the stock market boom was a rash of cheering public statements, designed to spur on the boom whenever it showed signs of flagging. President Coolidge and Secretary of Treasury Mellon in this way acted as the leading "capeadores of Wall Street." [31] Thus, when the emerging stock market boom began to flag in January, 1927, Secretary Mellon drove it onward. The subsequent spurt in February levelled off in March, whereupon Mellon announced the Treasury's intention to refinance the 4¼ per cent Liberty Bonds into 3½ per cent notes the next November. He predicted lower interest **rates** (accurately, due to the subsequent monetary inflation) and urged low rates upon the market. The announcement drove stock prices up again during March. The boom again began to weaken in the latter part of March, whereupon Mellon once more promised continued low rediscount rates and pictured a primrose path of easy money. He said, "There is an abundant supply of easy money which should take care of any contingencies that might arise." Stocks continued upward again, but slumped slightly during June. This time President Coolidge came to the rescue, urging optimism upon one and all. Again the market rallied strongly, only to react badly in August when Coolidge announced he did not choose to run again. After a further rally and subsequent recession in October, Coolidge once more stepped into the breach with a highly optimistic statement. Further optimistic statements by Mellon and Coolidge trumpeting the "new era" of permanent prosperity repeatedly injected tonics into the market. The New York *Times* declared on November 16 that Washington was the source of most bullish news and noted the growing "impression that Washington may be depended upon to furnish a fresh impetus for the stock market."

BILLS BOUGHT—ACCEPTANCES

Tables 6 and 7 show the enormous importance of Bills Bought in the 1920's. While purchase of U.S. securities has received more publicity, bills bought was at least as important and indeed more important than discounts. Bills bought led the inflationary parade of Reserve credit in 1921 and 1922, was considerably more important than securities in the 1924 inflationary spurt, and equally important in the 1927 spurt. Furthermore, bills bought alone continued the inflationary stimulus in the fatal last half of 1928.

These bills bought were all *acceptances* (and almost all *bankers' acceptances*), and the Federal Reserve policy on acceptances was undoubtedly the most curious, and the most indefensible, of the whole catalog of Federal Reserve policies. As in the case of securities, acceptances were purchased on the open-market, and thus provided reserves to banks outright with no obligation to repay (as in discounting). Yet while the FRS preserved its freedom of action in buying or selling U.S. securities, it tied its own hands on acceptances. It insisted on setting a very low rate on acceptances, thus subsidizing and indeed literally *creating* the whole acceptance market in this country, and then pledging itself to buy all the bills offered at that cheap rate.[32] The Federal Reserve thus arbitrarily created and subsidized an artificial acceptance market in the United States and bought whatever was offered to it at an artificially cheap rate. This was an inexcusable policy on two counts —its highly inflationary consequences, and its grant of special privilege to a small group at the expense of the general public.

In contrast to Europe, where acceptances had long been a widely used form of paper, the very narrow market for them in this country, and its subsidization by the FRS, led to the Reserve's becoming the predominant buyer of acceptances.[33] It was a completely Federal Reserve-made market, and used only in international trade, or in purely foreign transactions. In 1928 and 1929, banks avoided borrowing from the Fed by making acceptance loans instead of straight loans, thus taking advantage of the FRS market and cheap acceptance rates. When the Federal Reserve bought the acceptance, the bank now acquired a reserve less expensively than by discounting, and without having to repay. Hence the inflationary role of acceptances in 1929 and its sabotaging of other Federal Reserve attempts to restrain credit.

In addition to acceptances held by the FRS on its own account, it also bought a large amount of acceptances as agent for foreign Central Banks. Moreover, the Reserve's buying rate on acceptances for foreign account was *lower* than for its own, thus subsidizing these foreign governmental purchases all the more. These holdings were not included in "bills bought," but they were endorsed by the FRS, and, in times of crisis, such endorsement could become a liability of the Federal Reserve; it did in 1931. The Reserve's acceptances were purchased from member banks, non-member banks, and private acceptances houses—with the bills for foreign account bought *entirely* from the private dealers.[34]

The first big investment in acceptances came in 1922, coinciding with the FRB's allowing the New York Reserve Bank to control acceptance policy. Federal Reserve holdings rose from $75 million in January to $272 million in December of that year. Despite the fact that the Federal Reserve kept its buying rate on acceptances below its rediscount rate, Paul Warburg, America's leading acceptance banker and one of the founders of the Federal Reserve System, demanded still lower buying rates on acceptances.[35] Undersecretary of the Treasury Gilbert, on the other hand, was opposed to the specially privileged acceptance rates, but the Federal Reserve continued its policy of subsidy, directed largely by the New York Bank.[36] It was, indeed, only in the first half of 1929 that the Federal Reserve partially abandoned its subsidizing, and at least pushed its buying rate on acceptances above the rediscount rate, thereby causing a sharp reduction in its acceptance holdings. In fact, the decline in acceptances was almost the sole factor in the decline of reserves in 1929 that brought the great inflation of the 1920's to its end.

Why did the Federal Reserve newly create and outrageously subsidize the acceptance market in this country? The only really plausible reason seems to center around the role played by Paul M. Warburg, former German investment banker who came to America to become a partner of Kuhn, Loeb and Co., and be one of the founders of the Federal Reserve System. Warburg worked for years to bring the rather dubious blessings of central banking to the hitherto backward United States. After the war and during the 1920's, Warburg continued to be chairman of the highly influential Federal Advisory Council, a statutory group of bankers advising the Federal Reserve System. Warburg, it appears, was a principal beneficiary of the Federal Reserve's pampering of the acceptance market. From its inception in 1920, Warburg was Chairman of the Board of the International Acceptance Bank of New York, the world's largest acceptance bank. He also became a director of the important Westinghouse Acceptance Bank and of several other acceptance houses, and was the chief founder and Chairman of the Executive Committee of the American Acceptance Council, a trade association organized in 1919. Surely, Warburg's leading role in the Federal Reserve System was not unconnected with his reaping the lion's share of benefits from its acceptance policy.

And certainly, there is hardly any other way adequately to explain the adoption of this curious program. Indeed, Warburg himself proclaimed the success of his influence in persuading the Federal Reserve to loosen eligibility rules for purchase of acceptances, and to establish subsidized rates at which the Federal Reserve bought all acceptances offered.[37] And finally, Warburg was a very close friend of Benjamin Strong, powerful ruler of the New York Bank which engaged in the subsidy policy.[38]

The Federal government progressively widened the scope of the acceptance market from the very inception of the Federal Reserve Act. Before then, national banks had been prohibited from purchasing acceptances. After the Act, banks were permitted to buy foreign trade acceptances up to a limit of 50 per cent of a bank's capital and surplus. Subsequent amendments raised the limit to 100 per cent of capital and surplus, and then 150 per cent, and allowed other types of acceptances—"dollar exchange," and domestic acceptances. Furthermore, English acceptance practice had been strictly limited to documentary exchange, representing definite movements of goods. The Federal Reserve Board at first tried to limit acceptance to such exchanges, but in 1923 it succumbed to the pressure of the New York Reserve Bank and permitted "finance bills" without documents. Wider powers were also granted to the New York and other Reserve Banks in 1921 and 1922 to purchase *purely foreign* acceptances, and their permissible maturity was raised from three to six months. In 1923, as part of the agricultural credit program, the Fed was permitted to rediscount agricultural-based acceptances up to six months.[39] In 1927, bills were made eligible even if drawn *after* the goods had been moved.[40]

With the rules relaxed, purely foreign acceptances, representing goods stored in or shipped between foreign points, rose from nothing to the leading role in Federal Reserve acceptance holdings during the crucial 1928-1929 period. Foreign acceptance purchases played a large part, especially in the latter half of 1928, in frustrating all attempts to check the boom. Previous credit restrictions had been on the way to ending the inflationary boom in 1928. But in August, the Federal Reserve deliberately reversed its tight money policy on the acceptance market, and the Board authorized the Federal Reserve Banks to buy heavily in order to accommodate credit needs.[41] The reasons for this unfortunate reversal were largely general: the political pressure for easier credit in an election year, and the fear of repercussions on Europe of high interest rates in the United States, played the leading roles. But there was also a more specific cause connected with the foreign acceptance market.

In contrast to older types of acceptance, the purely foreign acceptances were bills representing stored goods *awaiting* sale, rather than goods in transit between specific buyers and sellers.[42] The bulk was used to finance the storage of unsold goods in Central Europe, particularly Germany.[43] How did this increase in the holding of German acceptances come about? As the result of a spectacular American boom in foreign loans, financed by new issues of foreign bonds. This boom flourished from 1924 on, reaching a peak in mid-1928. It was the direct reflection of American credit expansion, and particularly of the low interest rates generated by that expansion. As we shall see further below, this result was deliberately fostered by the Federal Reserve authorities. Germany was one of the leading borrowers on the American market during the boom. Germany was undoubtedly short of capital, bereft as she was by the war and then by her ruinous inflation, culminating in late 1923. However, the German bonds floated in the United States did not, as most people thought, rebuild German capital. For these loans were largely extended to German local and state *governments*, and not to private German business. The loans made capital even *scarcer* in Germany, for the local governments were now able to compete even more strongly with private business for factors of production.[44] To their great credit, many German authorities, and especially Dr. Hjalmar Schacht, head of the Reichsbank, understood the unsoundness of these loans, and they together with the American Reparations Agent, Mr. S. Parker Gilbert, urged the New York banking community to stop lending to German local governments.[45] But American investment bankers, lured by the large commissions on foreign government loans, sent hundreds of agents abroad to urge prospective borrowers to float loans on the American market. They centered their attention on Germany.[46]

The tide of foreign lending turned sharply after mid-1928. Rising interest rates in the United States, combined with the steep stock-exchange boom, diverted funds from foreign bonds to domestic stocks. German economic difficulties aggravated the slump in foreign lending in late 1928 and 1929. In consequence, German banks, finding their clients unable to float new bonds in the United States, obtained loans in the form of acceptance credits from the New York Reserve Bank, to cover the cost of carrying unsold stocks of cotton, copper, flour, and other commodities in German warehouses.[47] Those American banks that served as agents of foreign banks sold great quantities of foreign (largely German) acceptances to other American banks and to the FRS.[48] This explains the rise in Reserve holdings of German acceptances.

Other acceptances flourishing in 1928 and 1929 represented domestic cotton and wheat awaiting export, and exchange bills providing dollars to South America. In early 1929, there was also a rash of acceptances based on the import of sugar from Cuba, in anticipation of a heavier American tariff on sugar.[49]

Not only did the Federal Reserve—in effect the New York Bank—subsidize the acceptance market, it also confined its subsidizing to a few large acceptance houses. It refused to buy any acceptances directly from business, insisting on buying them from acceptance dealers as intermediaries—thus deliberately subsidizing the dealers. Further, it only bought acceptances from the few dealers with a capital of one million dollars and over. Another special privilege was the Federal Reserve's increasing purchase of acceptances under *repurchase* agreements. In this procedure, the New York Bank agreed to buy acceptances from a few large and recognized acceptance dealers who had the option to buy them back in 15 days at a currently fixed price. Repurchase agreements varied from one-tenth to almost two-thirds of acceptance holdings.[50] All this tends to confirm our hypothesis of the Warburg role.

In short, the Federal Reserve granted virtual call loans to the ac-

ceptance dealers, as well as unrestricted access at subsidized rates—
and accorded these privileges to dealers who were not, of course,
members of the Federal Reserve System. In fact, as unincorporated
private bankers, the dealers did not even make public reports.
So curiously jealous was the New York Bank of the secrecy of
its favorites, that it arrogantly refused to give a Congressional
investigating committee either a list of the acceptance dealers
from whom it had bought bills, or a breakdown of foreign acceptances by countries. The officials of the New York Bank were
not cited for contempt by the committee.[51]

U.S. Government Securities

Member bank reserves increased during the 1920's largely in
three great surges—one in 1922, one in 1924, and the third in
the latter half of 1927. In each of these surges, Federal Reserve
purchases of government securities played a leading role. "Open-
market" purchases and sales of government securities only emerged
as a crucial factor in Federal Reserve monetary control during the
1920's. The process began when the Federal Reserve tripled its
stock of government securities from November, 1921 to June,
1922 (its holdings totalling $193 million at the end of October,
and $603 million at the end of the following May). It did so, not
to make money easier and inflate the money supply, these rela-
tionships being little understood at the time, but simply in order
to add to Federal Reserve earnings. The inflationary result of
these purchases came as an unexpected consequence.[52] It was a
lesson that was appreciatively learned and used from then on.

If the Reserve authorities had been innocent of the *consequences* of their inflationary policy in 1922, they were not innocent
of intent. For there is every evidence that the inflationary result
was most welcome to the Federal Reserve. Inflation seemed justified as a means of promoting recovery from the 1920-1921 slump,
to increase production and relieve unemployment. Governor
Adolph Miller, of the Federal Reserve Board, who staunchly
opposed the later inflationary policies, defended the 1922 inflation in Congressional hearings. Typical of Federal Reserve opinion

at this time was the subsequent apologia of Professor Reed, who complacently wrote that bank credit "was being productively employed and that goods were being prepared for the consumer at least as rapidly as his money income was expanding." [53]

Open-market policy was then well launched, and played a major role in the 1924 and 1927 inflationary spurts and therefore in the overall inflation of the 1920's.

The individual Reserve Banks at first bought the securities on their own initiative, and this decentralized policy was resented by the Treasury. On the initiative of the Treasury, and seconded by Benjamin Strong, the Governors of the various Reserve Banks formed an Open-Market Committee to coordinate Reserve purchases and sales. The Committee was established in June, 1922. In April, 1923, however, this Governors' Committee was dissolved and a new Open-Market Investment Committee was appointed by the Federal Reserve Board. Originally, this was a coup by the Board to exert leadership over open-market policy in place of the growing power of Strong, Governor of the New York Bank. Strong was ill throughout 1923, and it was during that year that the Board managed to sell most of the FRB holdings of government securities. As soon as he returned to work in November, however, Strong, as chairman of the Open-Market Investment Committee, urged purchases of securities without hesitation should there be even a threat of business recession.

As a result of Strong's new accession to power, the Federal Reserve resumed within two months a heavy purchase of governments, and the economy was well launched on its dangerous inflationary path. As Strong's admiring biographer puts it: "This time the Federal Reserve knew what it was doing, and its purchases were not earnings but for broad policy purposes," i.e., for inflation. Ironically, Benjamin Strong had now emerged as more powerful than ever, and in fact from that time until his retirement, the FRS's open-market policy was virtually controlled by Governor Strong.[54] One of Strong's first control devices was to establish a "Special System Investment Account," under which, as in the case of acceptances, Reserve purchases of governments were made largely by the New York Bank, which then distributed them *pro rata* to those other Reserve Banks that wanted the securities.

Another new and important feature of the 1920's was the maintenance of a large volume of floating, short-term government debt. Before the war, almost all of the U.S. debt had been funded into long-term bonds. During the war, the Treasury issued a myriad of short-term bills, only partially funded at a later date. From 1922 on, one half to one billion dollars of short-term Treasury debt remained outstanding in the banks, and had to be periodically refinanced. Member banks were encouraged to carry as much of these securities as possible: the Treasury kept deposits in the banks, and they could borrow from the Federal Reserve, using the certificates as collateral. Federal open-market purchases also helped make a market in government securities at low interest rates. As a result, banks held more government debt in 1928 than they had held during the war! Thus the Federal Reserve, by employing various means to bolster the market for Federal floating debt, added to the impetus for inflation.[55]

5

The Development of the Inflation

We have seen how the leading factors in the changing of reserves played their roles during the boom of the 1920's. Treasury currency played a considerable part in the early years, due to the silver purchase policy inherited from the Wilson Administration. Bills discounted were deliberately spurred throughout the period by the Federal Reserve's violation of central banking tradition in keeping rediscount rates below the market. Acceptances were subsidized outrageously, with the Federal Reserve deliberately keeping acceptance rates very low and buying all the acceptances offered at this cheap rate by the few leading acceptance houses. Open-market purchase of government securities began as a means of adding to the earning assets of the Federal Reserve Banks, but was quickly continued as a means of promoting monetary expansion. We may now turn from the *anatomy* of the inflation of the 1920's, to a *genetic* discussion of the actual course of the boom, including an investigation of some of the reasons for the inflationary policy.

FOREIGN LENDING

The first inflationary spurt, in late 1921 and early 1922—the beginning of the boom—was led, as we can see in Table 7, by Federal Reserve purchases of government securities. Premeditated or not, the effect was welcome. Inflation was promoted by a desire to speed recovery from the 1920-1921 recession. In July,

1921, the Federal Reserve announced that it would extend further credits for harvesting and agricultural marketing, up to whatever amounts were legitimately required. Soon, Secretary Mellon was privately proposing that business be further stimulated by cheap money.[1]

Another motive for inflation was one we shall see recurring as a constant and crucial factor in the 1920's: a desire to help foreign governments and American exporters (particularly farmers). The process worked as follows: inflation and cheap credit in the United States stimulated the floating of foreign loans in the U.S. One of Benjamin Strong's major motives for open-market purchases in 1921-1922 was to stimulate foreign lending. Inflation also helped to check the inflow of gold from Europe and abroad, an inflow caused by the fiat money inflation policies of foreign countries, which drove away gold by raising prices and lowering interest rates. Artificial stimulation of foreign lending in the U.S. also helped increase or sustain foreign demand for American farm exports.

The first great boom in foreign borrowing therefore coincided with the Federal Reserve inflation of latter 1921 and early 1922. The fall in bond yields during this period stimulated a surge in foreign lending, U.S. government yields falling from 5.27 per cent in June 1921 to 4.24 per cent in June, 1922 (corporate bonds fell from 7.27 per cent to 5.92 per cent in the same period). Foreign bond flotations, about $100 million per quarter-year during 1920, doubled to about $200 million per quarter in the latter part of 1921. This boom was helped by "a deluge of statements from official, industrial, and banking sources setting forth the economic necessity to the United States of foreign lending." [2]

The 1921-1922 inflation, in sum, was promoted in order to relieve the recession, stimulate production and business activity, and aid the farmers and the foreign loan market.

In the spring of 1923, the Federal Reserve substituted credit restraint for its previous expansion, but the restraint was considerably weakened by an increase in Reserve discounts, spurred by the rediscount rate being set below the market. Nevertheless, a mild recession ensued, continuing until the middle of 1924. Bond yields rose slightly, and foreign lending slumped considerably, falling below a rate of one hundred million dollars per quarter during 1923. Particularly depressed were American agricultural exports to Europe. Certainly part of this slump was caused by the Fordney-McCumber Tariff of September 1922, which turned sharply away from the fairly low Democratic tariff and toward a steeply protectionist policy.[3] Increased protection against European manufactured goods delivered a blow to European industry, and also served to keep European demand for American exports below what it would have been without governmental interference.

To supply foreign countries with the dollars needed to purchase American exports, the United States government decided, *not* sensibly to lower tariffs, but instead to promote cheap money at home, thus stimulating foreign borrowing and checking the gold inflow from abroad. Consequently, the resumption of American inflation on a grand scale in 1924 set off a foreign lending boom, which reached a peak in mid-1928. It also established American trade, not on a solid foundation of reciprocal and productive exchange, but on a feverish promotion of loans later revealed to be unsound.[4] Foreign countries were hampered in trying to sell their goods to the United States, but were encouraged to borrow dollars. But afterward, they could not sell goods to repay; they could only try to borrow more at an accelerated pace to repay the loans. Thus, in an indirect but nonetheless clear manner, American protectionist policy must shoulder some of the responsibility for our inflationist policy of the 1920's.

Who benefited, and who was injured, by the policy of protection *cum* inflation as against the rational alternative of free trade and hard money? Certainly, the bulk of the American population was injured, both as consumers of imports and as victims of inflation and poor foreign credit and later depression. Benefited were the industries protected by the tariff, the export industries uneconomically subsidized by foreign loans, and the investment bankers who floated the foreign bonds at handsome commissions.

Certainly, Professor F. W. Fetter's indictment of America's foreign economic policy in the 1920's was not overdrawn:

Producers in those lines in which foreigners were competing with us were 'taken care of' by high tariffs, promises of still higher tariffs from the Tariff Commission if 'needed,' and those interested in foreign trade were told how the Department of Commerce was going to open up huge foreign markets. Foreign loans were glorified by the same political leaders who wanted bigger and better trade restrictions, entirely oblivious to the problems involved in the repayment of such loans. . . . A tremendous volume of foreign loans made possible exports far in excess of imports . . . and Secretary Mellon and other defenders of this tariff policy pointed the finger of ridicule at those who had prophesied that the Fordney-McCumber Act would have an injurious effect upon our foreign trade.[5]

The Republican Administration, often wrongly considered to be a *"laissez-faire"* government, actually intervened actively in foreign lending throughout the 1920's. Foreign loans had been rare in the United States before the World War, and the United States government had no statutory peacetime authority to interfere with them in any way. And yet the government did intervene, though illegally. On May 25, 1921, President Harding and his cabinet held a conference with several American investment bankers, at the instigation of Secretary of Commerce Hoover, and Harding asked to be informed in advance of all public flotations of foreign bonds, so that the government "might express itself regarding them. . . ."[6] The bankers agreed. The stage had been set for this meddling at a Cabinet meeting five days before, where

The Cabinet discussed the problem of favoring exports and the desirability of the application of the proceeds of foreign loans made in our own financial markets for the purpose of exporting our commodities . . .[7]

In short, the Cabinet wished that banks floating foreign loans provide that part of the proceeds be spent in the United States. And Herbert Hoover was so enthusiastic about subsidizing foreign loans that he commented that even *bad* loans helped American exports and thus provided a cheap form of relief and employment—a "cheap" form that later brought expensive defaults and financial distress.[8]

In January, 1922, Secretary of Commerce Hoover prevailed on American investment bankers to agree that agents of the Department of Commerce would first investigate conditions in countries requesting foreign loans, whether the would-be borrowers were private or public. The applicant would also have to promise to purchase materials in the United States, and the fulfillment of this agreement would be inspected by an American commercial attaché in the borrowing country. Happily, little came of this agreement. In the meanwhile, the Harding request was repeatedly ignored, and consequently the State Department sent a circular letter to the investment bankers in March, 1922, repeating the Presidential request, admitting that it was legally unenforceable, but declaiming that "national interests" required that the State Department offer its objections to any bond issue. During April and May, Secretary Hoover protested the bankers' reluctance, and urged that banks be ordered to establish his desired rules for foreign loans, else Congress would assume control. Harding and Coolidge, however, contented themselves with a far milder form of informal intimidation.

Often the government, when challenged, denied any attempt at dictation over foreign loans. But the State Department admitted several times that it was exercising beneficial control, and admitted it had objected to a number of loans. The most noteworthy ban was on all loans to France, a punishment levied because France was still in debt to the American government. It was a ban which the bankers were often able to evade. Secretary of State Kellogg favored, but could not obtain, outright legal regulation of foreign lending.

Knowing that the State Department was intervening in foreign lending, the American public erroneously began to believe that every foreign loan had the Federal government's seal of approval and was therefore a good buy. This, of coure, stimulated reckless foreign lending all the more.

The foreign lending of the 1920's was almost all private. In

1922, however, in a harbinger of much later developments, Secretary of State Hughes urged Congress to approve a direct *governmental* loan of five million dollars to Liberia, but the Senate failed to ratify it.

HELPING BRITAIN

The great expansion of 1924 was designed, not only to stimulate loans to foreign countries, but also to check their drains of gold to the United States.[9] The drains arose, primarily, from the inflationary policies of the foreign countries. Great Britain, in particular, faced a grave economic problem. It was preparing to return to the gold standard at the pre-war par (the pound sterling equalling approximately $4.87), but this meant going back to gold at an exchange rate higher than the current free market rate. In short, Britain insisted on returning to gold at a valuation that was 10-20 per cent higher than the going exchange rate, which reflected the results of war and postwar inflation. This meant that British prices would have had to decline by about ten to twenty per cent in order to remain competitive with foreign countries, and to maintain her all-important export business. But no such decline occurred, primarily because unions did not permit wage-rates to be lowered. Real-wage rates rose, and chronic large-scale unemployment struck Great Britain. Credit was not allowed to contract, as was needed to bring about deflation, as unemployment would have grown even more menacing—an unemployment caused partly by the post-war establishment of government unemployment insurance (which permitted trade unions to hold out against any wage cuts). As a result, Great Britain tended to lose gold. Instead of repealing unemployment insurance, contracting credit, and/or going back to gold at a more realistic parity, Great Britain inflated her money supply to offset the loss of gold and turned to the United States for help. For if the United States government were to inflate *American* money, Great Britain would no longer lose gold to the United States. In short, the American public was nominated to suffer the burdens of inflation and subsequent collapse in order to maintain the British government and the British trade union movement in the style to which they insisted on becoming accustomed.[10]

The American government lost no time in rushing to the aid of Britain. The "isolationism" of U.S. foreign policy in the 1920's is almost wholly a myth, and nowhere is this more true than in economic and financial matters. The 1927 conference between the leading central bankers that led to the inflation of that year has become famous; less well known is the fact that close collaboration between Benjamin Strong, Governor of the Federal Reserve Bank of New York, and Montagu Norman, head of the Bank of England, began much earlier. On Norman's appointment as Governor during the War, Strong hastened to promise him his services. In 1920, Norman began taking annual trips to America to visit Strong, and Strong took periodic trips to visit Europe. All of these consultations were kept highly secret and were always camouflaged as "visiting with friends," "taking a vacation," and "courtesy visits." The Bank of England gave Strong a desk and a private secretary for these occasions, as did the Bank of France and the German Reichsbank. These consultations were *not* reported to the Federal Reserve Board in Washington.[11] Furthermore, the New York Bank and the Bank of England kept in close touch via weekly exchange of private cables.

As the eminent French economist Charles Rist, who represented the Bank of France at some of the important inter-Central Bank conferences, has declared:

The idea of cooperation among the central banks of different countries, to arrive at a common monetary policy, was born rather soon after the war. Before then, this cooperation had only been exceptional and sporadic.[12]

As early as 1916, Strong began private correspondent relations with the Bank of England, as well as with other European Central Banks. In the summer of 1919, Strong was already contemplating a secret conference of central bankers, and, moreover, was already worried about American interest rates being higher than the British, and thinking of arrangements with the Bank of England to remedy this condition, thus foreshadowing the later agreements to inflate in America in order to aid Britain.[13] In November, 1921 Strong offered Norman a dollar-stabilization scheme, in the course of which the Federal Reserve would lend dollars to Britain, Holland, Scandinavia, Japan, and Switzerland; but Norman turned the proposal down.[14]

In 1925, the year Britain returned to the gold standard, the United States helped greatly. As a direct measure, the New York Bank extended Britain a line of credit for gold of up to $200 million.[15] At the same time, J. P. Morgan and Co. authorized a similar credit of $100 million to the British government, a loan that would have been subsidized (if it had ever been used) by the Federal Reserve. Both loans were arranged by Strong and Norman in early January, 1925, and were warmly approved by Secretary of Treasury Mellon, Governor Crissinger, and unanimously by the Federal Reserve Board.[16] Similar lines of credit were extended to bolster the Central Banks of Belgium ($10 million in 1926), Poland ($5 million in 1927), and Italy ($15 million in 1927).

More insidious and damaging was aiding Britain by inflating in the U.S. The 1924 expansion in America was much more than coincidence with preparation for Britain's return to gold. For the pound sterling had fallen to $4.44 in mid-1922, and by mid-1924 was in even worse shape at $4.34. At that point,

matters took a decisive turn. American prices began to rise [due to the American inflation] . . . In the foreign exchange markets a return to gold at the old parity was anticipated. The sterling-dollar exchange appreciated from $4.34 to $4.78. In the spring of 1925, therefore, it was thought that the adjustment between sterling and gold prices was sufficiently close to warrant a resumption of gold payments at the old parity.[17]

That this result was brought about deliberately through credit expansion in America, is clear from a letter from Strong to Mellon in the spring of 1924, outlining the necessity of raising American price levels relative to Great Britain's and of lowering American interest rates, to enable Britain to return to gold. For higher American price levels would divert foreign trade balances from the United States to England, while lower interest rates would similarly divert capital balances. Lower interest rates, being a more immediate outcome of credit expansion, received more attention. Strong concluded this letter as follows:

the burden of this readjustment must fall more largely upon us than upon them [Great Britain]. It will be difficult politically and socially for the British Government and the Bank of England to face a price liquidation in England . . . in face of the fact that their trade is poor and they have over a million unemployed people receiving government aid.[18]

It is clear that by late 1924, the foreign exchange market saw that the United States was inflating in order to help Britain, and, anticipating success, raised the pound nearly up to its pre-war par—an appreciation caused by governmental action rather than by the fundamental economic realities. The Federal Reserve certainly kept its part of the rather one-sided bargain. Whereas throughout 1922 and 1923 the interest rate on bills in New York had been above the rate in London, the Federal Reserve managed to push these rates below those of London by mid-1924. As a result, the gold inflow into the United States, of which about 40 per cent had been coming from Great Britain, was checked for a time.[19] As we have seen, U.S. lending abroad was also greatly stimulated, thus providing Europe with longer-term funds.

Inflationary measures to aid foreign governments also spurred farm exports, since foreign countries could now expand their purchases of American farm products. Farm prices rose in the latter half of 1924, and the value of farm exports increased by over 20 per cent from 1923-1924 to 1924-1925. Yet, despite all the aid, we cannot say that the farmers particularly benefited from the foreign economic policies of the 1920's as a whole, since the protective tariff injured foreign demand for American products.

Instead of being grateful to the United States for its monetary policy, Europe carped continually during the 1920's because America wasn't inflating enough. Even in the intimate Norman-Strong partnership, it is clear that, in the early years especially, Norman was continually trying to prod Strong into a more inflationary stance. In the 1919-1920 era, before the joint inflationary policy had begun, Norman's Treasury colleague Basil Blackett urged Strong to let American prices "rise a little more"—and this in the middle of a postwar boom in America. Later, the British urged looser credit conditions in the U.S., but Strong was rather reluctant during this early period.

In February, 1922, Norman hailed the easy credit in America during the previous few months, and urged a further inflationary fall in interest rates to match the burgeoning credit expansion in Britain. At that time, Strong refused to inflate further, and Norman continued to pepper Strong during 1922 and 1923, with expressions of his displeasure at the American failure to expand credit. But in 1924, helped by the siren song of Britain's return to the "gold standard" and by a mild recession at home, Strong capitulated, so much so that by October Norman was jauntily telling Strong, "You must continue with easy money and foreign loans and we must hold on tight until we know . . . what the policy of this country is to be." [20] And yet, Norman was not fully satisfied with his American servitor. Privately, he joined the general European opinion in criticizing the United States for violating the alleged "rules of the gold standard game," by not inflating in multiple proportion to the gold flowing into its coffers.[21]

This standard argument, however, completely misconceives the role and function of the gold standard and governmental responsibility under it. The gold standard is not some sort of "game," to be played among several countries according to some mythical "rules." Gold is simply the monetary medium, and the duty of government is to leave the people free to do with the gold as they see fit. It is therefore its corollary duty not to inflate the money supply beyond the gold stock or to stimulate and encourage such inflation. If the money supply is already inflated, it is at least its responsibility not to inflate *further*. Whether money should be deflated back to the gold level is a more difficult question which we need not discuss here. If gold flows into a country, the government should welcome the opportunity to raise the gold deposit ratio, and thereby reduce the counterfeit proportion in the nation's supply of money. Countries "lose gold" (since the drain is voluntary it cannot be a true "loss") as a consequence of inflationary policies by their governments. These policies induce heavy domestic spending abroad (necessarily with gold) and discourage the nation's export trade. If European countries disliked losing gold to the United States, their governments should have contracted and not inflated their money supply. Certainly it is absurd, though convenient, to pin the blame for the consequences of a government's unsound policies upon the relatively sounder policies of *another* government.

The nobility of the American aim to help Europe return to the gold standard becomes even more questionable when we realize that Europe never *did* return to a full gold standard. Instead, it adopted a "gold bullion" standard, which prohibited gold coinage, thus restricting gold convertibility to heavy bars suitable only for large international transactions. Often it chose a "gold exchange" standard, under which a nation keeps its reserves not in gold but in a "hard" currency like dollars. It then redeems its units only in the other country's harder currency. Clearly, this system permits an international "pyramiding" of inflation on the world's given stock of gold. In both the gold bullion and the gold exchange standards, the currency is virtually fiat, since the people are *de facto* prohibited from using gold as their medium of exchange. The use of the term "gold standard" by foreign governments in the 1920's, then, was more of a deception than anything else. It was an attempt to draw to the government the prestige of being on the gold standard, while actually failing to abide by the limitations and requirements of that standard. Great Britain, in the late 1920's, was on a gold bullion standard, and most other "gold standard countries" were on the gold-exchange standard, keeping their titles to gold in London or New York. The British position, in turn, depended on American resources and lines of credit, since only America was on a true gold standard.

Thus, the close international Central Bank collaboration of the 1920's created a false era of seemingly sound prosperity, masking a dangerous world-wide inflation. As Dr. Palyi has declared, "The gold standard of the New Era was managed enough to permit the artificial lengthening and bolstering of the boom, but it was also automatic enough to make inevitable the eventual failure. . . ." [22] The pre-war standard, Palyi points out, had been autonomous; the new gold standard was based on the political cooperation of central banks, which "impatiently fostered a volume of credit flow without regard to its economic results." And Dr. Hardy justly concluded, "International cooperation to support the gold standard . . . is the maintenance of a cheap money policy without suffering the loss of gold." [23]

The fountainhead and inspiration of the financial world of the 1920's was Great Britain. It was the British government that conceived the system of inter-central bank cooperation, and that persuaded the United States to follow its lead. Britain originated the policy as a means of (temporarily) evading its own economic dilemmas, yet proclaimed it in the name of "humanitarian reconstruction." England, like the United States, also used cheap credit to lend widely to Continental Europe and thus promote its own flagging export market, hobbled by high costs imposed by excessive union wage rates.

In addition, Great Britain persuaded other European countries to adopt the gold exchange standard instead of the full gold standard, in order to promote its own "economic imperialism," i.e., to spur British exports to the Continent by inducing other countries to return to gold at overvalued exchange rates. If other countries overvalued their currencies *vis à vis* sterling, then British exports would be bolstered. (Britain showed little concern that exports from the Continent would be correspondingly hampered.) The abortive and inflationary gold exchange standard permitted countries to return to gold (at least nominally) earlier and at a higher exchange rate than they otherwise would have essayed.[24] Other countries were pressured by Great Britain to remain on the gold bullion standard, as she was, rather than proceed onward to restore a full gold-coin standard. To cooperate in international inflation, it was necessary to keep gold from domestic circulation, and to hoard it instead in Central Bank vaults. As Dr. Brown wrote:

> In some countries the reluctance to adopt the gold bullion standard was so great that some outside pressure was needed to overcome it . . . [i.e.] strong representations on the part of the Bank of England that such action would be a contribution to the general success of the stabilization effort as a whole. Without the informal pressure . . . several efforts to return in one step to the full gold standard would undoubtedly have been made.[25]

One important example of such pressure, joined in force by Benjamin Strong, occurred in the spring of 1926, when Norman induced Strong to support him in fiercely opposing a plan of Sir Basil Blackett's to establish a full gold-coin standard in India. Strong went to the length of travelling to England to testify against the measure, and was backed up by Andrew Mellon and aided by economists Professor Oliver M. W. Sprague of Harvard, Jacob Hollander of Johns Hopkins, and W. Randolph Burgess and Robert Warren of the New York Reserve Bank. The American experts warned that the ensuing gold drain to India would cause deflation in other countries (i.e., reveal their existing over-inflation), and suggested instead a gold-exchange standard and domestic "economizing" of gold (i.e., economizing for credit expansion). In addition, they urged wider banking and central banking facilities in India (i.e., more Indian inflation), and advocated continued use of a silver standard in India so as not to disrupt American silver interests by going off silver and thus lowering the world silver price.[26]

Norman was grateful to his friend Strong for helping defeat the Blackett Plan for a full Indian gold standard. To the objections of some Federal Reserve Board members to Strong's meddling in purely foreign affairs, the formidable Secretary Mellon ended the argument by saying tht he had personally asked Strong to go to England and testify.

To his great credit, Dr. Hjalmar Schacht, in addition to opposing our profligate loans to local German governments, also sharply criticized the new-model gold standard. Schacht vainly called for a return to the true gold standard of old, with capital exports financed by genuine voluntary savings, and not by fiat bank credit.[27]

A caustic but trenchant view of the financial imperialism of Great Britain in the 1920's was expressed in the following entry in the diary of Émile Moreau, Governor of the Bank of France:

. . . England having been the first European country to reestablish a stable and secure money has used that advantage to establish a basis for putting Europe under a veritable financial domination. The Financial Committee [of the League of Nations] at Geneva has been the instrument of that policy. The method consists of forcing every country in monetary difficulty to subject itself to the Committee at Geneva, which the British control. The remedies prescribed always involve the installation in the central bank of a foreign supervisor who is British or designated by the Bank of England, and the deposit of a part of the reserve of the central bank at the Bank of England, which serves both to support the pound and to fortify British influence. To guarantee against possible failure they are careful to secure the cooperation of the Federal Reserve Bank of New York. Moreover, they pass on to America the task of making some of the foreign loans if they seem too heavy, always retaining the political advantage of these operations.

England is thus completely or partially entrenched in Austria, Hungary, Belgium, Norway, and Italy. She is in the process of entrenching herself in Greece and Portugal. . . . The currencies [of Europe] will be divided into two classes. Those of the first class, the dollar and the pound sterling, based on gold, and those of the second class based on the pound and dollar—with a part of their gold reserves being held by the Bank of England and the Federal Reserve Bank of New York, the latter moneys will have lost their independence.[28]

The motives for the American inflation of 1924, then, were to aid Great Britain, the farmers, and, in passing, the investment bankers, and finally, to help reelect the Administration in the 1924 elections. President Coolidge's famous assurance to the country about low discount rates typified the political end in view. And certainly the inflation was spurred by the existence of a mild recession in 1923-1924, during which time the economy was trying to adjust to the previous inflation of 1922.

At first, the 1924 expansion accomplished what it had intended —gold inflow into the United States was replaced by a gold drain, American prices rose, foreign lending was stimulated, interest rates were lowered, and President Coolidge was triumphantly re-elected. Soon, however, with the exception of the last-named, the effects of the expansion dissipated, and prices in America began to fall once more, gold flowed in heavily again, etc. American farm product prices, which had risen from an index of 100 in 1924 to 110 the year later, dropped back again to 100 in 1926. Exports for farm and food products, which had reached a peak during 1925, also fell sharply in the following year. In sum, the American economy entered into another mild recession in the fall of 1926, continuing on into 1927. Britain was in particularly bad straits, addicted to cheap credit, yet suffering chronic unemployment and continual drains of gold. But Great Britain insisted on continuing its policy of cheap money and credit expansion—an insistence of the British government rather than its private bankers.[29]

Britain's immediate problem stemmed directly from her insistence on continuing cheap money. The Bank of England had lowered its discount rate from 5 per cent to 4½ per cent in April, 1927, in a vain attempt to stimulate British industry.[30] This further weakened the pound sterling, and Britain lost $11 million in gold during the next two months, and the Bank of France, in a strong creditor position, tried to redeem its sterling in gold.[31] Instead of tightening credit and raising interest rates sharply to meet this gold drain, as canons of sound monetary policy dictated, Great Britain turned to its old partner in inflation, the Federal Reserve System. The stage was clearly set once more, according to the logic of the American and British money managers, for another great dose of credit expansion in the United States.

Accordingly, Governor Montagu Norman, the Mephistopheles of the inflation of the 1920's, conferred with Strong and Moreau, of the Bank of France, in Paris. He tried a variety of pressures during 1927 to dissuade the Bank of France from selling its sterling balances for gold—balances which, after all, were of little use to the French.[32] Norman also tried to induce the French to do some inflating themselves, but Moreau was not a Benjamin Strong. Instead, he not only remained adamant, but urged Norman to allow Britain's loss of gold to tighten credit and raise interest rates in London (thus checking British purchase of francs). But Norman was committed to a cheap money policy.

Strong, on the contrary, leaped to Britain's aid. Trying to bolster sterling, he used American gold to ease the gold premium in Britain and also purchased some sterling bills to aid his ally. And, furthermore, Strong and Norman organized the famous inter-central bank conference at New York, in July, 1927. The conference was held *in camera*, and included Norman, Strong, and representatives from the Bank of France and the German Reichsbank: Deputy Governor Charles Rist, and Dr. Schacht respectively. Strong ran the American side with an iron hand, and even refused to permit Mr. Gates McGarrah, Chairman of the Board of the Federal Reserve Bank of New York, to attend the meeting. The Federal Reserve Board in Washington was left in the dark, and was allowed only a brief courtesy call from the distinguished guests. The conference was held at the Long Island estates of Undersecretary of the Treasury Ogden Mills and of Mrs. Ruth Pratt of the wealthy Standard Oil family.

Norman and Strong tried mightily to induce Rist and Schacht to go along with a general four-country inflation, but the latter two vigorously declined. Schacht continued his determined opposition to inflation and artificially cheap money, and expressed his alarm at the inflationary trend. Rist demurred also, and both Rist and Schacht left for home. Rist agreed, however, to buy gold from New York instead of London, thus easing the pressure on England to redeem its obligations. The New York Reserve Bank, in turn, agreed to supply France with gold at a subsidized rate: as cheap as the cost of buying it from England, despite the higher transport costs.

Remaining to weld their inflationary pact, Norman and Strong agreed to embark on a mighty inflationary push in the United States, lowering interest rates and expanding credit—an agreement which Rist maintains was concluded before the four-power conference had even begun. Strong had gaily told Rist that he

was going to give "a little *coup de whiskey* to the stock market."[33]
Strong also agreed to buy $60 million more of sterling from
the Bank of England.

The British press was delighted with this fruit of the fast
Norman-Strong friendship, and flattered Strong fulsomely. As
early as mid-1926, the influential London journal, *The Banker,*
had said of Strong that "no better friend of England" existed,
had praised the "energy and skillfullness that he has given to
the service of England," and had exulted that "his name should
be associated with that of Mr. [Walter Hines] Page as a friend
of England in her greatest need."[34]

In response to the agreement, the Federal Reserve promptly
launched a great burst of inflation and cheap credit in the latter
half of 1927. Table 8 shows that the rate of increase of bank
reserves was the greatest of the 1920's, largely because of open-
market purchases of government securities and of bankers' acceptances. Rediscount rates were also lowered. The Federal
Reserve Bank of Chicago, not under the domination of the
Bank of England, balked vigorously at lowering its rate, but
was forced to do so in September by the Federal Reserve Board.
The Chicago *Tribune* called angrily for Strong's resignation,
and charged that discount rates were being lowered in the interests of Great Britain. The regional Reserve Banks were told
by Strong that the new burst of cheap money was designed to
help the farmers rather than England, and this was the reason
proclaimed by the first bank to lower its discount rate—not
New York but Kansas City. The Kansas City Bank had
been picked by Strong as the "stalking-horse" of the new policy,
in order to give as "American" a flavor as possible to the entire
proceeding. Governor Bailey of the Kansas City Bank had no
inkling of the aid-to-Britain motive behind the new policy, and
Strong took no pains to enlighten him.[35]

Perhaps the sharpest critic of the inflationary policies within
the Coolidge Administration was Secretary Hoover, who privately
did his best to check the inflation from 1924 on, even going so
far as to denounce Strong as a "mental annex to Europe." Hoover
was overruled by Strong, Coolidge, and Mellon, with Mellon

denouncing Hoover's "alarmism" and interference. Mellon was Strong's staunchest supporter in the Administration throughout the entire period. Unfortunately for later events, Hoover—like most of Strong's academic critics—attacked only *stock-market* credit expansion rather than expansion *per se.*

The reasons for Strong's devious and secret methods, as well as the motives for his inflationary policies, have been no better described than in a private memorandum by one of Strong's staff. In the spring of 1928, Strong firmly rejected the idea of an open, formal conference of world central banks, and, in the words of his assistant:

He [Strong] was obliged to consider the viewpoint of the American public, which had decided to keep the country out of the League of Nations to avoid interferences by other nations in its domestic affairs, and which would be just as opposed to having the heads of its central banking system attend some conference or organization of the world banks of issue. . . . To illustrate how dangerous the position might become in the future as a result of the decisions reached at the present time and how inflamed public or political opinion might easily become when the results of past decisions become evident, Governor Strong cited the outcry against the speculative excesses now being indulged in on the New York market. . . . He said that very few people indeed realized that we were now paying the penalty for the decision which was reached early in 1924 to help the rest of the world back to a sound financial and monetary basis.[36]

In short, in our supposed democracy, if the people were allowed to know what had been transacted in their name and what penalties they were subsequently being forced to pay, they would rise up in their wrath. Better to keep the people in ignorance. This, of course, is the familiar attitude of the bureaucrat in power. But what of the fundamental question it raises for democracy itself: how can the people decide upon issues or judge their presumed representatives, if the latter insist on keeping vital information from them?

Strong himself, furthermore, did not realize how heavy a penalty the American public would be forced to pay in 1929. He died before the crisis came. If the public had at last been let in on the truth of Strong's actions and their consequences, perhaps, during the depression, they would have become "inflamed" against inflationary government intervention rather than against the capitalist system.

After generating the 1927 inflation, the New York Federal Reserve Bank, for the next two years, bought heavily in prime commercial bills of foreign countries, bills endorsed by foreign central banks. The purpose was to bolster foreign currencies, and to prevent an inflow of gold to the United States. The New York Bank frankly described its policy as follows:

We sought to support exchanges by our purchases and thereby not only prevent the withdrawal of further amounts of gold from Europe but also, by improving the position of the foreign exchanges, to enhance or stabilize Europe's power to buy our exports.

Those decisions were taken by the New York Reserve Bank alone, and the foreign bills were then distributed pro rata to the other Reserve Banks.[37]

While the New York Reserve Bank was the main generator of inflation and cheap credit, the Treasury also did its part. As early as March 1927, Secretary Mellon assured everyone that "an abundant supply of easy money" was available—and in January 1928, the Treasury announced that it would refund a 4¼ per cent Liberty Bond issue, falling due in September, into 3½ per cent notes.[38]

Again, the inflationary policy was temporarily successful in achieving its goals. Sterling was strengthened, the American gold inflow was sharply reversed and gold flowed outward. Farm product prices rose from 99 in 1927 to 106 the following year. Farm and food exports spurted upward, and foreign loans were stimulated to new heights, reaching a peak in mid-1928.[39] But by the summer of 1928, the pound sterling was sagging again. American farm prices fell slightly in 1929, and the value of agricultural exports also fell in the same year. Foreign lending slumped badly as both domestic and foreign funds poured into the booming American stock market. The higher interest rates caused by the boom could no longer be lower than in Europe, unless the FRS was prepared to continue inflating, perhaps at an accelerated rate. Instead, as we shall see below, it tried to curb the boom. As a result, funds were attracted to the United States, and by mid-1928, gold began to flow in again from abroad. And, by this time, England was back in its familiar mess, but now more aggravated than before.

<h3 style="text-align:center">THE CRISIS APPROACHES</h3>

By now the final phase of the great American boom was under way, led by the stock market. While a stock market loan is no more inflationary than any other type of business loan, it is equally inflationary, and therefore credit expansion in the stock market deserves censure in precisely the same way, and to the same extent, as any other quantity of inflated credit. Hence, the mischievious inflationary effect of the 1927 statements by Coolidge and Mellon who functioned as the "capeadores" of the bull market. We have also seen that the Federal Reserve Bank of New York effectively set the call rates for loans to the stock market, in cooperation with the money committee of the New York Stock Exchange, its policy being to furnish any funds necessary to enable the banks to lend readily to the market. The Bank, in short, used Wall Street banks to pour funds into the stock market. The call rate, as we have noted, stayed very far below its pre-war levels and peaks.

Alarmed at the burgeoning boom, and at the stock prices that rose about 20 per cent in the latter half of 1927, the Fed reversed its policy in the spring of 1928, and tried to halt the boom. From the end of December 1927, to the end of July 1928, the Reserve reduced total reserves by $261 million. Through the end of June, total demand deposits of all banks fell by $471 million. However, the banks managed to shift to time deposits and even to overcompensate, raising time deposits by $1.15 billion. As a result, the money supply still rose by $1.51 billion in the first half of 1928, but this was a relatively moderate rise. (This was a rise of 4.4 per cent per annum, compared to an increase of 8.1 per cent per annum in the last half of 1927, when the money supply rose by $2.70 billion.) A more stringent contraction by the Federal Reserve—one enforced, for example, by a "penalty" discount rate on Reserve loans to banks—would have ended the boom and led to a far milder depression than the one we finally attained. In fact, only in May did the contraction of reserves take hold, for until then the reduction in Federal Reserve Credit was only barely sufficient to overcome the seasonal return of money from circulation. Thus, Federal Reserve restrictions only curtailed the boom from May through July.

Yet, even so, the vigorous open market sales of securities and drawing down of acceptances hobbled the inflation. Stock prices rose only about 10 per cent from January to July.[40] By mid-1928, the gold drain was reversed and a mild inflow resumed. If the Federal Reserve had merely done nothing in the last half of 1928, reserves would have moderately contracted, due to the normal seasonal increase in money in circulation.

At this point, true tragedy struck. On the point of conquering the boom, the FRS found itself hoist by its own acceptance policy. Knowing that the Fed had pledged itself to buy all acceptances offered, the market increased its output of acceptances, and the Fed bought over three hundred million dollars of acceptances in the last half of 1928, thus feeding the boom once more. Reserves increased by $122 million, and the money supply increased by almost $1.9 billion to reach its virtual peak at the end of December 1928 At this time, total money supply had reached $73 billion, higher than at any time since the inflation had begun. Stock prices, which had actually declined by 5 per cent from May to July, now really began to skyrocket, increasing by 20 per cent from July to December. In the face of this appalling development, the Federal Reserve did nothing to neutralize its acceptance purchases. Whereas it had boldly raised rediscount rates from 3½ per cent at the beginning of 1928 to 5 per cent in July, it stubbornly refused to raise the rediscount rate any further, and the rate remained constant until the end of the boom. As a result, discounts to banks increased slightly rather than declined. Furthermore, the Federal Reserve did not sell any of its more than $200 million stock of government securities; instead it *bought* a little on net balance in the latter half of 1928.

Why was Federal Reserve policy so supine in the latter part of 1928? One reason was that Europe, as we have noted, had found the benefits from the 1927 inflation dissipated, and European opinion now clamored against any tighter money in the U.S.[41] The easing in late 1928 prevented gold inflows into the U.S. from getting very large. Great Britain was again losing gold and sterling was weak once more. The United States bowed once again to its overriding wish to see Europe avoid the inevitable consequences of its own inflationary policies. Governor Strong, ill since early 1928, had lost control of Federal Reserve policy. But while some disciples of Strong have maintained that he would have fought for tighter measuers in the latter half of the year, recent researches indicate that he felt even the modest restrictive measures pursued in 1928 to be too severe. This finding, of course, is far more consistent with Strong's previous record.[42]

Another reason for the weak Federal Reserve policy was political pressure for easy money. Inflation is always politically more popular than recession, and this, let us not forget, was a presidential election year. Furthermore, the Federal Reserve had already begun to adopt the dangerously fallacious qualitativist view that stock credit could be curbed at the same time that acceptance credit was being stimulated.[43]

The inflation of the 1920's was actually over by the end of 1928. The total money supply on December 31, 1928 was $73 billion. On June 29, 1929, it was $73.26 billion, a rise of only 0.7 per cent per annum. Thus, the monetary inflation was virtually completed by the end of 1928. From that time onward, the money supply remained level, rising only negligibly. And therefore, from that time onward, a depression to adjust the economy was inevitable. Since few Americans were familar with the "Austrian" theory of the trade cycle, few realized what was going to happen.

A great economy does not react instantaneously to change. Time, therefore, had to elapse before the end of inflation could reveal the widespread malinvestments in the economy, before the capital goods industries showed themselves to be over-extended, etc. The turning-point occurred about July, and it was in July that the great depression began.

The stock market had been the most buoyant of all the markets—this in conformity with the theory that the boom generates particular overexpansion in the capital goods industries. For the stock market is the market in the prices of titles to capital.[44] Riding on the wave of optimism generated by the boom and credit expansion, the stock market took several months after July to awaken to the realities of the downturn in business activity. But the awakening was inevitable, and in October the stock market crash made everyone realize that depression had truly arrived.

The proper monetary policy, even after a depression is underway, is to deflate or at the least to refrain from further inflation. Since the stock market continued to boom until October, the proper moderating policy would have been positive deflation. But President Coolidge continued to perform his "capeadore" role until the very end. A few days before leaving office in March he called American prosperity "absolutely sound" and stocks "cheap at current prices." [45] The new President Hoover was unfortunately one of the staunch supporters of the sudden try at "moral suasion" in the first half of 1929, which failed inevitably and disastrously. Both Hoover and Governor Roy Young of the Federal Reserve Board wanted to deny bank credit to the stock market while yet keeping it abundant to "legitimate" commerce and industry. As soon as Hoover assumed office, he began the methods of informal intimidation of private business which he had tried to pursue as Secretary of Commerce.[46] He called a meeting of leading editors and publishers to warn them about high stock prices; he sent Henry M. Robinson, a Los Angeles banker, as emissary to try to restrain the stock loans of New York banks; he tried to induce Richard Whitney, President of the New York Stock Exchange, to curb speculation. Since these methods did not attack the root of the problem, they were bound to be ineffective.

Other prominent critics of the stock market during 1928

and 1929 were Dr. Adolph C. Miller, of the Federal Reserve Board, Senator Carter Glass (Dem., Va.), and several of the "progressive" Republican senators. Thus, in January, 1928, Senator LaFollette attacked evil Wall Street speculation and the increase in brokers' loans. Senator Norbeck counselled a moral suasion policy a year before it was adopted, and Federal Reserve Board member Charles S. Hamlin persuaded Representative Dickinson of Iowa to introduce a bill to graduate bank reserve requirements in proportion to the speculative stock loans in the banks' portfolios. Senator Glass proposed a 5 per cent tax on sales of stock held less than 60 days—which, contrary to Glass' expectations, would have driven stock prices upward by discouraging stockholders from selling until two months had elapsed.[47] As it was, the federal tax law, since 1921, had imposed a specially high tax rate on capital gains from those stocks and bonds held less than two years. This induced buyers to hold on to their stocks and not sell them after purchase since the tax was on *realized*, rather than accrued, capital gains. The tax was a factor in driving up stock prices further during the boom.[48]

Why did the Federal Reserve adopt the "moral suasion" policy when it had not been used for years preceding 1929? One of the principal reasons was the death of Governor Strong toward the end of 1928. Strong's disciples at the New York Bank, recognizing the crucial importance of the quantity of money, fought for a higher discount rate during 1929. The Federal Reserve Board in Washington, and also President Hoover, on the other hand, considered credit rather in qualitative than in quantitative terms. But Professor Beckhart adds another possible point: that the "moral suasion" policy—which managed to stave off a tighter credit policy—was adopted under the influence of none other than Montagu Norman.[49] Finally, by June, moral suasion was abandoned, but discount rates were not raised, and as a result the stock market boom continued to rage, even as the economy generally was quietly but inexorably turning downward. Secretary Mellon trumpeted once again about our "unbroken and unbreakable prosperity." In August, the Federal Reserve Board finally consented to raise the rediscount rate to 6 per cent, but any tightening effect was more than offset by a simultaneous lowering of the acceptance rate, thus stimulating the acceptance market yet once more. The Federal Reserve had previously ended the acceptance menace in March by raising its acceptance buying rate above its discount rate for the first time since 1920. The net effect of this unprecedented "straddle" was to stimulate the bull market to even greater heights. The lowering of the Federal Reserve buying rate for acceptances from 5¼ per cent to 5⅛ per cent, the level of the open market, stimulated market sales of acceptances to the Federal Reserve. If not for the acceptance purchases, total reserves would have fallen from the end of June to October 23 (the day before the stock market crash) by $267 million. But the Federal Reserve purchased $297 million of acceptances during this period, raising total reserves by $21 million. The following table tells the story of this period.

TABLE 9

FACTORS DETERMINING BANK RESERVES
JULY-OCTOBER 1929
(in millions of dollars)

	July 29	October 23	Net Change
Federal Reserve Credit	1400	1374	—26
Bills discounted	1037	796	—241
Bills bought	82	379	297
U.S. Govts.	216	136	—80
All Other	65	63	—2
Treasury Currency	2019	2016	—3
Treasury Cash	204	209	—5
Treasury Deposits	36	16	20
Unexpended Capital Funds	374	393	—19
Monetary Gold Stock	4037	4099	62
Money in Circulation	4459	4465	—6
Other Deposits	28	28	0
Controlled Reserves			206
Uncontrolled Reserves			—185
Member Bank Reserves	2356	2378	22

What was the reason for this peculiarly inflationary policy favoring the acceptance market? It fitted the qualitative bias of the Administration, and it was ostensibly advanced as a step to help the American farmer. Yet, it appears that the aid-to-farmers argument was used again as a domestic smokescreen for inflationary policies. In the first place, the increase in acceptance holdings, as compared with the same season the year before, was far more heavily concentrated in *purely foreign* acceptances and less in acceptances based on American exports. Secondly, the farmers had already concluded their seasonal borrowing before August, so that they did not benefit one iota from the lower acceptance rates. In fact, as Beckhart points out, the inflationary acceptance policy was reinstituted following "closely upon another visit of Governor Norman." [50] Thus, once again, the cloven hoof of Montagu Norman exerted its baleful influence upon the American scene, and for the last time Norman was able to give an added impetus to the boom of the 1920's. Great Britain was also entering upon a depression, and yet its inflationary policies had resulted in a serious outflow of gold in June and July. Norman was then able to get a line of credit of $250 million from a New York banking consortium, but the outflow continued through September, much of it to the United States. Continuing to help England, the New York Federal Reserve Bank bought heavily in sterling bills, from August through October. The new subsidization of the acceptance market, then, permitted further aid to Britain through purchase of sterling bills.

Federal Reserve policy during the last half of 1928 and 1929 was, in brief, marked by a desire to keep credit abundant in favored markets, such as acceptances, and to tighten credit in other fields, such as the stock market (e.g., by "moral suasion"). We have seen that such a policy can only fail, and an excellent epitaph on these efforts has been penned by A. Wilfred May:

Once the credit system had become infected with cheap money, it was impossible to cut down particular outlets of this credit without cutting down all credit, because it is impossible to keep different kinds of money separated in water-tight compartments. It was impossible to make money scarce for stock-market purposes, while simultaneously keeping it cheap for commercial use. . . . When Reserve credit was created, there was no possible way that its employment could be directed into specific uses, once it had flowed through the commercial banks into the general credit stream.[51]

And so ended the great inflationary boom of the 1920's. It should be clear that the responsibility for the inflation rests upon the federal government—upon the Federal Reserve authorities primarily, and upon the Treasury and the Administration secondarily.[52] The United States government had sowed the wind —and the American people reaped the whirlwind: the great depression.

6

Theory and Inflation: Economists and the Lure of a Stable Price Level

One of the reasons that most economists of the 1920's did not recognize the existence of an inflationary problem was the widespread adoption of a stable price level as the goal and criterion for monetary policy. The extent to which the Federal Reserve authorities were guided by a desire to keep the price level stable has been a matter of considerable controversy. Far less controversial is the fact that more and more economists came to consider a stable price level as the major goal of monetary policy. The fact that general prices were more or less stable during the 1920's told most economists that there was no inflationary threat, and therefore the events of the great depression caught them completely unaware.

Actually, bank credit expansion creates its mischievous effects by distorting price relations and by raising and altering prices compared to what they would have been without the expansion. Statistically, therefore, we can only identify the increase in money supply, a simple fact. We cannot prove inflation by pointing to price increases. We can only approximate explanations of complex price movements by engaging in a comprehensive economic history of an era—a task which is beyond the scope of this study. Suffice it to say here that the stability of wholesale prices in the 1920's was the result of monetary inflation offset by increased productivity, which lowered costs of production and increased the supply of goods. But this "offset" was only *statistical;* it did not eliminate the boom-bust cycle, it only *obscured* it. The economists who emphasized the importance of a stable price level were thus especially deceived, for they should have concentrated on what was happening to the supply of money. Consequently, the economists who raised an alarm over inflation in the 1920's were largely the qualitativists. They were written off as hopelessly old-fashioned by the "newer" economists who realized the overriding importance of the quantitative in monetary affairs. The trouble did not lie with particular credit on particular markets (such as stock or real estate); the boom in the stock and real estate markets reflected Mises' trade cycle: a disproportionate boom in the prices of titles to capital goods, *caused* by the increase in money supply attendant upon bank credit expansion.[1]

The stability of the price level in the 1920's is demonstrated by the Bureau of Labor Statistics Index of Wholesale Prices, which fell to 93.4 (100 = 1926) in June 1921, rose slightly to a peak of 104.5 in November 1925, and then fell back to 95.2 by June 1929. The price level, in short, rose slightly until 1925 and fell slightly thereafter. Consumer price indices also behaved in a similar manner.[2] On the other hand, the Snyder Index of the General Price Level, which includes all types of prices (real estate, stocks, rents, and wage rates, as well as wholesale prices) rose considerably during the period, from 158 in 1922 (1913 = 100) to 179 in 1929, a rise of 13 per cent. Stability was therefore achieved only in consumer and wholesale prices, but these were and still are the fields considered especially important by most economic writers.

Within the overall aggregate of wholesale prices, foods and farm products rose over the period while metals, fuel, chemicals, and home furnishings fell considerably. That the boom was largely felt in the capital goods industries can be seen by (a) the quadrupling of stock prices over the period, and by (b) the fact that durable goods and iron and steel production each increased by about 160 per cent, while the production of non-durable goods (largely consumer goods) increased by only 60 per cent. In fact, production of such consumer items as manufactured foods and textile products increased by only 48 per cent and 36 per cent respectively, from 1921 to 1929. Another illustration of Mises' theory was that wages were bid up far more *in the capital goods industries.* Overbidding of wage rates and other costs is a distinctive feature of Mises' analysis of capital goods industries in the boom. Average hourly earnings, according to the Conference Board index, rose in selected manufacturing industries from $.52 in July 1921 to $.59 in 1929, a 12 per cent increase. Among this group, wage rates in consumer goods' industries such as boots and shoes remained constant; they rose 6 per cent in furniture, less than 3 per cent in meat packing, and 8 per cent in hardware manufacturing. On the other hand, in such capital goods' industries as machines and machine tools, wage rates rose by 12 per cent, and by 19 per cent in lumber, 22 per cent in chemicals, and 25 per cent in iron and steel.

Federal Reserve credit expansion, then, whether so intended or not, managed to keep the price level stable in the face of an increased productivity that would, in a free and unhampered market, have led to falling prices and a spread of increased living standards to everyone in the population. The inflation distorted the production structure and led to the ensuing depression-adjustment period. It also prevented the whole populace from enjoying the fruits of progress in lower prices and insured that only those enjoying higher monetary wages and incomes could benefit from the increased productivity.

There is much evidence for the charge of Phillips, McManus, and Nelson that "the end-result of what was probably the greatest price-level stabilization experiment in history proved to be, simply, the greatest depression." [3] Benjamin Strong was apparently converted to a stable-price-level philosophy during 1922. On January 11, 1925, Strong privately wrote: "that it was my belief, and I thought it was shared by all others in the Federal Reserve System, that our whole policy in the future, as in the past, would be directed toward the stability of prices so far as it was possible for us to influence prices." [4] When asked, in the Stabilization Hearings of 1927, whether the Federal Reserve Board could "stabilize the price level to a greater extent" than in the past, by open-market operations and other control devices, Governor Strong answered, "I personally think that the administration of the Federal Reserve System since the reaction of 1921 has been just as nearly directed as reasonable human wisdom could direct it toward that very object." [5]

It appears that Governor Strong had a major hand, in early 1928, in drafting the bill by Representative James G. Strong of Kansas (no relation) to compel the Federal Reserve System to promote a stable price level.[6] Governor Strong was ill by this time and out of control of the System, but he wrote the final draft of the bill along with Representative Strong. In the company of the Congressman and Professor John R. Commons, one of the leading theoreticians of a stable price level, Strong discussed the bill with members of the Federal Reserve Board. When the Board disapproved, Strong felt bound, in his public statements, to go along with them.[7] We must further note that Carl Snyder, a loyal and almost worshipful follower of Governor Strong, and head of the Statistical Department of the Federal Reserve Bank of New York, was a leading advocate of monetary and credit control by the Federal Reserve to stabilize the price level.[8]

Certainly, the leading British economists of the day firmly believed that the Federal Reserve was deliberately and success-fully stabilizing the price level. John Maynard Keynes hailed "the successful management of the dollar by the Federal Reserve Board from 1923 to 1928" as a "triumph" for currency management. D. H. Robertson concluded in 1929 that "a monetary policy con-sciously aimed at keeping the general price level approximately stable . . . has apparently been followed with some success by the Federal Reserve Board in the United States since 1922." [9] Whereas Keynes continued to hail the Reserve's policy a few years after the depression began, Robertson became critical, "Looking back . . . the great American 'stabilisation' of 1922-1929 was really a vast attempt to destabilise the value of money in terms of human effort by means of a colossal program of investment . . . which succeeded for a surprisingly long period, but which no human ingenuity could have managed to direct indefinitely on sound and balanced lines." [10]

The siren song of a stable price level had lured leading politicians, to say nothing of economists, as early as 1911. It was then that Professor Irving Fisher launched his career as head of the "stable money" movement in the United States. He quickly gained the adherence of leading statesmen and economists to a plan for an international commission to study the money and price problem. Supporters included President William Howard Taft, Secretary of War Henry Stimson, Secretary of Treasury Franklin MacVeagh, Governor Woodrow Wilson, Gifford Pinchot, seven Senators, and economists Alfred Marshall, Francis Edgeworth, and John Maynard Keynes in England. President Taft sent a special message to Congress in February, 1912, urging an appropriation for such an international conference. The message was written by Fisher, in collaboration with Assistant Secretary of State Huntington Wilson, a convert to stable money. The Senate passed the bill, but it died in the House. Woodrow Wilson expressed interest in the plan but dropped the idea in the press of other matters.

In the spring of 1918, a Committee on the Purchasing Power of Money of the American Economic Association endorsed the principle of stabilization. Though encountering banker opposition to his stable-money doctrine, led notably by A. Barton Hepburn of the Chase National Bank, Fisher began organizing the Stable Money League at the end of 1920, and established the League at the end of May, 1921—at the beginning of our inflationary era. Newton D. Baker, Secretary of War under Wilson, and Professor James Harvey Rogers of Cornell were two of the early organizers. Other prominent politicians and economists who played leading roles in the Stable Money League were Professor Jeremiah W. Jenks, its first president; Henry A. Wallace, editor of *Wallace's Farmer,* and later Secretary of Agriculture; John G. Winant, later Governor of New Hampshire; Professor John R. Commons, its second President; George Eastman of the Eastman-Kodak family; Lyman J. Gage, formerly Secretary of the Treasury;

Samuel Gompers, President of the American Federation of Labor; Senator Carter Glass of Virginia; Thomas R. Marshall, Vice-President of the United States under Wilson; Representative Oscar W. Underwood; Malcolm C. Rorty; and economists Arthur Twining Hadley, Leonard P. Ayres, William T. Foster, David Friday, Edwin W. Kemmerer, Wesley C. Mitchell, Warren M. Persons, H. Parker Willis, Allyn A. Young, and Carl Snyder.

The ideal of a stable price level is relatively innocuous during a price rise when it can aid sound money advocates in trying to check the boom; but it is highly mischievous when prices are tending to sag, and the stabilizationists call for inflation. And yet, stabilization is always a more popular rallying cry when prices are falling. The Stable Money League was founded in 1920-1921, when prices were falling during a depression. Soon, prices began to rise, and some conservatives began to see in the stable money movement a useful check against extreme inflationists. As a result, the League changed its name to the National Monetary Association in 1923, and its officers continued as before, with Professor Commons as President. By 1925, the price level had reached its peak and begun to sag, and consequently the conservatives abandoned their support of the organization, which again changed its name to the Stable Money Association. Successive Presidents of the new association were H. Parker Willis, John E. Rovensky, Executive Vice-President of the Bank of America, Professor Kemmerer, and "Uncle" Frederic W. Delano. Other eminent leaders in the Stable Money Association were Professor Willford I. King; President Nicholas Murray Butler of Columbia University; John W. Davis, Democratic candidate for President in 1924; Charles G. Dawes, Director of the Bureau of the Budget under Harding, and Vice-President under Coolidge; William Green, President of the American Federation of Labor; Charles Evans Hughes, Secretary of State until 1925; Otto H. Kahn, investment banker; Frank O. Lowden, former Republican Governor of Illinois; Elihu Root, former Secretary of State and Senator; James H. Rand, Jr.; Norman Thomas, of the Socialist Party; Paul M. Warburg; and Owen D. Young. Enlisting from abroad came Charles Rist of the Bank of France; Eduard Benes of Czechoslovakia;, Max Lazard of France; Émile Moreau of the Bank of France; Louis Rothschild of Austria; and Sir Arthur Balfour, Sir Henry Strakosch, Lord Melchett, and Sir Josiah Stamp of Great Britain. Serving as Honorary Vice-Presidents of the Association were the Presidents of the following organizations: the American Association for Labor Legislation, American Bar Association, American Farm Bureau Federation, American Farm Economic Association, American Statistical Association, Brotherhood of Railroad Trainmen, National Association of Credit Men, National Consumers' League, National Education Association, American Council on Education, United Mine Workers of America, the National Grange, the Chicago Association of Commerce, The Merchants' Association of New York, and Bankers' Associations in forty-three states and the District of Columbia.

Executive Director and operating head of the Association with such formidable backing was Norman Lombard, brought in by Fisher in 1926. The Association spread its gospel far and wide. It was helped by the publicity given to Thomas Edison and Henry Ford's proposal for a "commodity dollar" in 1922 and 1923. Other prominent stabilizationists in this period were Professors George F. Warren and Frank Pearson of Cornell, Royal Meeker, Hudson B. Hastings, Alvin Hansen, and Lionel D. Edie. In Europe, in addition to the above mentioned, advocates of stable money included: Professor Arthur C. Pigou, Ralph G. Hawtrey, J.R. Bellerby, R.A. Lehfeldt, G.M. Lewis, Sir Arthur Salter, Knut Wicksell, Gustav Cassel, Arthur Kitson, Sir Frederick Soddy, F. W. Pethick-Lawrence, Reginald McKenna, Sir Basil Blackett, and John Maynard Keynes. Keynes was particularly influential in his propaganda for a "managed currency" and a stabilized price level, as set forth in his *A Tract on Monetary Reform,* published in 1923.

Ralph Hawtrey proved to be one of the evil geniuses of the 1920's. An influential economist in a land where economists have shaped policy far more influentially than in the United States, Hawtrey, Director of Financial Studies at the British Treasury, advocated international credit control by Central Banks to achieve a stable price level as early as 1913. In 1919, Hawtrey was one of the first to call for the adoption of a gold-exchange standard by European countries, tying it in with international Central Bank cooperation. Hawtrey was one of the prime European trumpeters of the prowess of Governor Benjamin Strong. Writing in 1932, at a time when Robertson had come to realize the evils of stabilization, Hawtrey declared: "The American experiment in stabilization from 1922 to 1928 showed that an early treatment could check a tendency either to inflation or to depression . . . The American experiment was a great advance upon the practice of the nineteenth century," when the trade cycle was accepted passively.[11] When Governor Strong died, Hawtrey called the event "a disaster for the world." [12] Finally, Hawtrey was the main inspiration for the stabilization resolutions of the Genoa Conference of 1922.

It was inevitable that this host of fashionable opinion should be translated into legislative pressure, if not legislative action. Representative T. Alan Goldsborough of Maryland introduced a bill to "Stabilize the Purchasing Power of Money" in May, 1922, essentially Professor Fisher's proposal, fed to Goldsborough by former Vice-President Marshall. Witnesses for the bill were Professors Fisher, Rogers, King, and Kemmerer, but the bill was not reported out of committee. In early 1924, Goldsborough tried again, and Rep. O. B. Burtness of North Dakota introduced another stabilization bill. Neither was reported out of committee. The next major effort was a bill by Rep. James G. Strong of Kansas, introduced in January, 1926, under the urging of veteran stabilizationist George H. Shibley, who had been promoting the cause of stable prices since 1896. Rather than the earlier Fisher proposal for a "compensated dollar" to manipulate the price level, the Strong bill would have compelled the Federal Reserve System to act directly to stabilize the price level. Hearings were held from March 1926 until February 1927. Testifying for the bill were Shibley, Fisher, Lombard, Dr. William T. Foster, Rogers, Bellerby, and Commons. Commons, Rep. Strong, and Governor Strong then rewrote the bill, as indicated above, and hearings were held on the second Strong bill in the spring of 1928.

The high point of testimony for the second Strong bill was

that of Sweden's Professor Gustav Cassel, whose eminence packed the Congressional hearing room. Cassel had been promoting stabilization since 1903. The advice of this sage was that the government employ neither qualitative nor quantitative measures to check the boom, since these would lower the general price level. In a series of American lectures, Cassel also urged lower Fed reserve ratios, as well as world-wide central bank cooperation to stabilize the price level.

The Strong bill met the fate of its predecessors, and never left the committee. But the pressure exerted at the various hearings for these bills, as well as the weight of opinion and the views of Governor Strong, served to push the Federal Reserve authorities into trying to manipulate credit for purposes of price stabilization.

International pressure strengthened the drive for a stable price level. Official action began with the Genoa Conference, in the spring of 1922. This Conference was called by the League of Nations, at the initiative of Premier Lloyd George, who in turn was inspired by the dominant figure of Montagu Norman. The Financial Commission of the Conference adopted a set of resolutions which, as Fisher puts it, "have for years served as the potent armory for the advocates of stable money all over the world." [13] The resolutions urged international central bank collaboration to stabilize the world price level, and also suggested a gold exchange standard. On the Financial Commission were such stabilizationist stalwarts as Sir Basil Blackett, Professor Cassel, Dr. Vissering, and Sir Henry Strakosch.[14] The League of Nations, indeed, was quickly taken over by the stabilizationists. The Financial Committee of the League was largely inspired and run by Governor Montagu Norman, working through two close associates, Sir Otto Niemeyer and Sir Henry Strakosch. Sir Henry was, as we have indicated, a prominent stabilizationist.[15] Furthermore, Norman's chief adviser in international affairs, Sir Charles S. Addis, was also an ardent stablizationist.[16]

In 1921, a Joint Committee on Economic Crises was formed by the General Labour Conference, the International Labour Office of the League of Nations, and the Financial Committee of the League. On this Joint Committee were three leading stabilizationists: Albert Thomas, Henri Fuss, and Major J. R. Bellerby. In 1923, Thomas' report warned that a fall in the price level "almost invariably" causes unemployment. Henri Fuss of the I.L.O. propagandized for stable price levels in the *International Labour Review* in 1926. The Joint Committee met in June, 1925, to affirm the principles of the Genoa Conference. In the meanwhile, two private international organizations, the International Association for Labour Legislation and the International Association on Unemployment, held a joint International Congress on Social Policy, at Prague, in October, 1924. The Congress called for the general adoption of the principles of the Genoa Conference, by stabilizing the general price level. The International Association for Social Progress adopted a report at its Vienna meeting in September, 1928, prepared by stabilizationist Max Lazard of the investment banking house of Lazard Frères in Paris, calling for price level stability. The I.L.O. followed suit in June, 1929, terming falling prices a cause of unemployment. And, finally, the Economic Consultative Committee of the League endorsed the Genoa principles in the summer of 1928.

Just as Professors Cassel and Commons wanted no credit restraint at all in 1928 and 1929, so Representative Louis T. McFadden, powerful chairman of the House Banking and Currency Committee, exerted a similar though more powerful brand of pressure on the Federal Reserve authorities. On February 7, 1929, the day after the Federal Reserve Board's letter to the Federal Reserve Banks warning about stock market speculation, Representative McFadden himself warned the House against an adverse business reaction from this move. He pointed out that there had been no rise in the commodity price level, so how could there be any danger of inflation? The Fed, he warned skittishly, should not concern itself with the stock market or security loans, lest it produce a general slump. Tighter money would make capital financing difficult, and, coupled with the resulting loss of confidence, would precipitate a depression. In fact, McFadden declared that the Fed should be prepared to ease money rates as soon as any fall in prices or employment might appear.[17]

Other influential voices raised against any credit restriction were those of W. T. Foster and Waddill Catchings, leading stabilizationists and well known for their underconsumptionist theories. Catchings was a prominent investment banker (of Goldman, Sachs and Co.), and iron and steel magnate, and both men were close to the Hoover Administration. (As we shall see, their "plan" for curing unemployment was adopted, at one time, by Hoover.) In April, 1929, Foster and Catchings warned that any credit restriction would lower the price level and hurt business. The bull market, they assured the public—along with Fisher, Commons, and the rest—was grounded on a sure foundation of American confidence and growth.[18] And the bull speculators, of course, echoed the cry that everyone should "invest in America." Anyone who criticized the boom was considered to be unpatriotic and "selling America short."

Cassel was typical of European opinion in insisting on even greater inflationary moves by the Federal Reserve System. Sir Ralph Hawtrey, visiting at Harvard during 1928-1929, spread the gospel of price-level stabilization to his American audience.[19] Influential British Laborite Philip Snowden urged in 1927 that the United States join in a world plan for price stabilization, to prevent a prolonged price decline. The London *Statist* and the *Nation* (London) both bemoaned the Federal Reserve "deflation." Perhaps most extreme was a wildly inflationist article by the respected economist Professor Allyn A. Young, an American then teaching at the University of London. Young, in January 1929, warned about the secular downward price trend, and urged all Central Banks not to "hoard" gold, to abandon their "high gold reserve-ratio fetish," and to inflate to a fare-thee-well. "Central banks of the world," he declared, ". . . appear to be afraid of prosperity. So long as they are they will exert a retarding influence upon the growth of production." [20]

In an age of folly, Professor Young's article was perhaps the crowning *pièce de résistance*—much more censurable than the superficially more glaring errors of such economists as Irving Fisher and Charles A. Dice on the alleged "new era" prosperity of the stock market. Merely to extrapolate present stock market conditions is, after all, not nearly as reprehensible as considering deflation the main threat in the midst of a rampantly inflationary era. But such was the logical conclusion of the stabilizationist position.

We may conclude that the Federal Reserve authorities, in promulgating their inflationary policies, were motivated not only by the desire to help British inflation and to subsidize farmers, but were also guided—or rather misguided—by the fashionable economic theory of a stable price level as the goal of monetary manipulation.[21]

Part III

THE GREAT DEPRESSION: 1929-1933

7

Prelude to Depression:
Mr. Hoover and *Laissez-Faire*

If government wishes to alleviate, rather than aggravate, a depression, its only valid course is *laissez-faire*—to leave the economy alone. Only if there is no interference, direct or threatened, with prices, wage rates, and business liquidation will the necessary adjustment proceed with smooth dispatch. Any propping up of shaky positions postpones liquidation and aggravates unsound conditions. Propping up wage rates creates mass unemployment, and bolstering prices perpetuates and creates unsold surpluses. Moreover, a drastic cut in the government budget—both in taxes and expenditures—will of itself speed adjustment by changing social choice toward more saving and investment relative to consumption. For government spending, whatever the label attached to it, is solely consumption; any cut in the budget therefore raises the investment/consumption ratio in the economy and allows more rapid validation of originally wasteful and loss-yielding projects. Hence, the proper injunction to government in a depression is cut the budget and leave the economy strictly alone. Currently fashionable economic thought considers such a *dictum* hopelessly outdated; instead, it has more substantial backing now in economic law than it did during the nineteenth century.

Laissez-faire was, roughly, the traditional policy in American depressions before 1929. The *laissez-faire* precedent was set in America's first great depression, 1819, when the federal government's only act was to ease terms of payment for its own land debtors. President Van Buren also set a staunch *laissez-faire* course in the Panic of 1837. Subsequent federal governments followed a similar path, the chief sinners being state governments which periodically permitted insolvent banks to continue in operation without paying their obligations.[1] In the 1920-1921 depression, government intervened to a greater extent, but wage rates were permitted to fall, and government expenditures and taxes were reduced. And this depression was over in one year—in what Dr. Benjamin M. Anderson has called "our last natural recovery to full employment."

Laissez-faire, then, was the policy dictated both by sound theory and by historical precedent. But in 1929 the sound course was rudely brushed aside. Led by President Hoover, the government embarked on what Anderson has accurately called the "Hoover New Deal." For if we define "New Deal" as an anti-depression program marked by extensive governmental economic planning and intervention—including bolstering of wage rates and prices, expansion of credit, propping up of weak firms, and increased government spending (e.g., subsidies to unemployment and public works)—Herbert Clark Hoover must be considered the founder of the New Deal in America. Hoover, from the very start of the depression, set his course unerringly toward the violation of all the *laissez-faire* canons. As a consequence, he left office with the economy at the depths of an unprecedented depression, with no recovery in sight after three and a half years, and with unemployment at the terrible and unprecedented rate of 25 per cent of the labor force.

Hoover's role as founder of a revolutionary program of government planning to combat depression has been unjustly neglected by historians. Franklin D. Roosevelt, in large part, merely elaborated the policies laid down by his predecessor. To scoff at Hoover's tragic failure to cure the depression as a typical example of *laissez-faire* is drastically to misread the historical record. The Hoover rout must be set down as a failure of government planning and not of the free market.

To portray the interventionist efforts of the Hoover Administra-

tion to cure the depression we may quote Hoover's own summary
of his program, during his Presidential campaign in the fall of
1932:

> . . . we might have done nothing. That would have been utter ruin.
> Instead we met the situation with proposals to private business and to
> Congress of the most gigantic program of economic defense and
> counterattack ever evolved in the history of the Republic. We put it
> into action. . . . No government in Washington has hitherto considered
> that it held so broad a responsibility for leadership in such times. . . .
> For the first time in the history of depression, dividends, profits, and
> the cost of living, have been reduced before wages have suffered. . . .
> They were maintained until the cost of living had decreased and the
> profits had practically vanished. They are now the highest real wages
> in the world. . . .
> Creating new jobs and giving to the whole system a new breath
> of life; nothing has ever been devised in our history which has done
> more for . . . "the common run of men and women." . . . Some of the
> reactionary economists urged that we should allow the liquidation to
> take its course until we had found bottom. . . . We determined that
> we would not follow the advice of the bitter-end liquidationists and
> see the whole body of debtors of the United States brought to bank-
> ruptcy and the savings of our people brought to destruction.[2]

THE DEVELOPMENT OF HOOVER'S INTERVENTIONISM:
UNEMPLOYMENT

Hoover, of course, did not come upon his interventionist ideas
suddenly. It is instructive to trace their development and the
similar development in the country as a whole, if we are to understand clearly how Hoover could so easily, and with such nationwide support, reverse the policies that had ruled in all previous
depressions.

Herbert Clark Hoover was very much the "forward-looking"
politician. We have seen that Hoover pioneered in attempts to
intimidate investment bankers in placing foreign loans. Charac-ter-
istic of all Hoover's interventions was the velvet glove on the
mailed fist: i.e., the businessmen would be exhorted to adopt

"voluntary" measures that the government desired, but implicit was the threat that if business did not "volunteer" properly, compulsory controls would soon follow.

When Hoover returned to the United States after the war and a long stay abroad, he came armed with a suggested "Reconstruction Program." Such programs are familiar to the present generation, but they were new to the United States in that more innocent age. Like all such programs, it was heavy on government planning, which was envisaged as "voluntary" cooperative action under "central direction." [3] The government was supposed to correct "our marginal faults"—including undeveloped health and education, industrial "waste," the failure to conserve resources, the nasty habit of resisting unionization, and seasonal unemployment. Featured in Hoover's plan were increased inheritance taxes, public dams, and, significantly, government regulation of the stock market to eliminate "vicious speculation." Here was an early display of Hoover's hostility toward the stock market, a hostility that was to form one of the *leitmotifs* of his Administration. [4] Hoover, who to his credit has never pretended to be the stalwart of *laissez-faire* that most people now consider him, notes that some denounced his program as "radical"—as well they might have.

So "forward-looking" was Hoover and his program that Louis Brandeis, Herbert Croly of the *New Republic,* Colonel Edward M. House, Franklin D. Roosevelt, and other prominent Democrats for a while boomed Hoover for the Presidency. [5]

Hoover continued to expound interventionism in many areas during 1920. Most relevant to our concerns was the conference on labor-management relations that Hoover directed from 1919 to 1920, on appointment by President Wilson and in association with Secretary of Labor William B. Wilson, a former official of the United Mine Workers of America. The conference—which included "forward-looking" industrialists like Julius Rosenwald, Oscar Straus, and Owen D. Young, labor leaders, and economists like Frank W. Taussig—recommended wider collective bargaining, criticized "company unions," urged the abolition of child labor, and called for national old-age insurance, fewer working hours, "better housing," health insurance, and government arbitration boards for labor disputes. These recommendations reflected Hoover's views.[6]

Hoover was appointed Secretary of Commerce by President Harding in March, 1921, under pressure from the left wing of the Republican Party, led by William Allen White and Judge Nathan Miller of New York. (Hoover was one of the first of the modern breed of politician, who can find a home in either party.) We have seen that the government pursued a largely *laissez-faire* policy in the depression of 1920-1921, but this was not the doing of Herbert Hoover. On the contrary, he "set out to reconstruct America."[7] He only accepted the appointment on the condition that he would be consulted on all economic policies of the federal government. He was determined to transform the Department of Commerce into "the economic interpreter to the American people (and they badly need one)."[8] Hardly had Hoover assumed office when he began to organize an economic conference and a committee on unemployment. The committee established a branch in every state having substantial unemployment, along with sub-branches in local communities and Mayors' Emergency Committees in 31 cities.[9] The committee contributed relief to the unemployed, and also organized collaboration between the local and federal governments.

As Hoover recalls:

We developed cooperation between the federal, state, and municipal governments to increase public works. We persuaded employers to "divide" time among their employees so that as many as possible would have some incomes. We organized the industries to undertake renovation, repair, and, where possible, expand construction.[10]

Standard Oil of New Jersey announced a policy of laying off its older employees last, and it increased its repairs and production for inventory; U. S. Steel also invested $10 million in repairs immediately upon conclusion of the conference.[11] In short, the biggest businesses were the first to agree.

Happily, the depression was about over by the time these measures could take effect, but an ominous shadow had been cast

over any future depression, a shadow that would grimly material-
ize when the 1929 crash arrived. Once again, these measures bore
the characteristic Hoover stamp; the government compulsion and
planning were larded with the rhetoric of "voluntary cooperation."
He spoke of these and other suggested measures as "mobilization
of cooperative action of our manufacturers and employers, of our
public bodies and local authorities." And there came into use the
now all too familiar war analogy: "An infinite amount of misery
could be saved if we have the same spirit of spontaneous cooperation in every community for reconstruction that we had in war."

While the government did not greatly intervene in the 1920-
1921 recession, there were enough ominous seeds of the later
New Deal. In December, 1920 the War Finance Corporation was
revived as an aid to farm exports, and a $100 million Foreign
Trade Financial Corporation was established. Farm agitation
against short-selling led to the Capper Grain Futures Act, in
August, 1921, regulating trading on the grain exchanges. Further-
more, on the state level, New York passed rent laws, restricting
the eviction rights of landlords; Kansas created an Industrial
Court regulating all key industries as "public utilities"; and the
Non-Partisan League conducted socialistic experiments in North
Dakota.[12]

Perhaps the most important development of all, however, was
the President's Conference on Unemployment, called by Harding
at the instigation of the indefatigable Herbert Hoover. This was
probably the most fateful omen of anti-depression policies to
come. About 300 eminent men in industry, banking, and labor
were called together in September, 1921 to discuss the problem of
unemployment. President Harding's address to the conference
was filled with great good sense and was almost the swan song
of the Old Order's way of dealing with depressions. Harding declared that liquidation was inevitable and attacked governmental
planning and any suggestion of Treasury relief. He said, "The
excess stimulation from that source is to be reckoned a cause of
trouble rather than a source of cure." [13]

To the conference members, it was clear that Harding's words
were mere stumbling blocks to the wheels of progress, and they

were quickly disregarded. The conferees obviously preferred Hoover's opening speech, to the effect that the era of passivity was now over; in contrast to previous depressions, Hoover was convinced, the government must "do something." [14] The conference's aim was to promulgate the idea that government should be responsible for curing depressions, even if the sponsors had no clear idea of the specific things that government should do. The important steps, in the view of the dominant leaders, were to urge the necessity of government planning to combat depressions and to bolster the idea of public works as a depression-remedy. [15] The conference very strongly and repeatedly praised the expansion of public works in a depression and urged coordinated plans by all levels of government. [16] Not to be outdone by the new Administration, former President Wilson, in December, added his call for a federal public works stabilization program.

The extreme public works agitators were disappointed that the conference did not go far enough. For example, the economist William Leiserson had thought that a Federal Labor Reserve Board "would do for the labor market what the Federal Reserve Board did for the banking interests." But the wiser heads saw that they had made a great gain. As a direct result of Hoover's conference, twice as many municipal bonds for public works were floated in 1921 and 1922 as in any previous year; Federal highway grants-in-aid to the states totaled $75 million in the autumn of 1921, and American opinion was aroused on the entire subject.

It was no accident that the conference had arrived at its interventionist conclusions. As usually happens in conferences of this type, a small group of staff men, along with Herbert Hoover, actually prepared the recommendations that the illustrious front men duly ratified. [17] Secretary of the crucial Public Works Committee of the Conference was Otto Tod Mallery, for a long time the nation's leading advocate of public works programs in depressions. Mallery was a member and guiding spirit of the Pennsylvania State Industrial Board and Secretary of the Pennsylvania Emergency Public Works Commission, which had pioneered in public works planning, and Mallery's resolutions thoughtfully pointed to the examples of Pennsylvania and California as beacon

lights for the Federal government to follow.[18] Mallery was one
of the leading spirits in the American Association for Labor Legislation, an organization of eminent citizens and economists devoted to the promotion of government intervention in the fields
of labor, unemployment, and welfare. The Association had held
the first national unemployment conference in early 1914. Now,
its executive director, John B. Andrews, boasted that the Presidential Conference's recommendations followed the standard
recommendations formulated by the AALL in 1915. These standard recommendations featured public works and emergency
public relief, *at the usual hours and wage rates*—the wage rates
of the boom period were supposed to be maintained.[19] Neither
was the Conference's following of the AALL line a coincidence.
Aside from Mallery's critical role, the Conference also employed
the expert knowledge of the following economists, *all of whom
were officials of the AALL:* John B. Andrews, Henry S. Dennison,
Edwin F. Gay, Samuel A. Lewisohn, Samuel McCune Lindsay,
Wesley C. Mitchell, Ida M. Tarbell, Mary Van Kleeck, and Leo
Wolman.[20]

It seems clear that the businessmen at the conference were not
supposed to mold policy; their function was to be indoctrinated
with the Hoover-AALL line and then to spread the interventionist
gospel to other business leaders. Andrews singled out for particular praise in this regard Joseph H. Defrees, of the United
States Chamber of Commerce, who appealed to many business
organizations to cooperate with the Mayors' Emergency Committees, and generally to accept "business responsibility" to solve the
unemployment problem. President Samuel Gompers of the A F
of L also hailed the widespread acceptance by industry of its
"responsibility" for unemployment, as an outcome of this
Conference.

Hoover did his best to intervene in the recession, attempting
also to stimulate home construction and urging banks to finance
more exports. Fortunately, however, Harding and the rest of
the Cabinet were not convinced of the virtues of governmental
depression "remedies." But 8 years later, Hoover was finally to
have his chance. As Lyons concludes: "A precedent for federal

intervention in economic depression was set, rather to the horror of conservatives." [21]

It is, of course, a sociological law that a government bureau, once launched, never dies, and the Conference was true to this law. The Conference resolved itself into three research committees, run by a staff of experts, with Hoover in overall command. One project bore fruit in Leo Wolman's *Planning and Control of Public Works,* a pro-public-works study published in 1930. A second committee published a study on *Seasonal Operation in the Construction Industry,* in 1924, in cooperation with the Division of Building and Housing of the Department of Commerce. This work urged seasonal stabilization of construction, and was in part the result of a period of propaganda activity by the American Construction Council, a trade association headed by Franklin Delano Roosevelt. Its foreword was written by Herbert Hoover.[22] The most important project was a study of *Business Cycles and Unemployment,* published in 1923.

Hoover invited the National Bureau of Economic Research (headed by Wesley C. Mitchell) to make a "fact-finding" study of the problems of forecasting and control of business cycles, and then appointed a Committee on Business Cycles to draft policy recommendations for the report. Chairman of the Committee was Owen D. Young, and other members included Edward Eyre Hunt, who had been secretary of the President's Conference, Joseph Defrees, Mary Van Kleeck, Clarence Woolley, and Matthew Woll of the A F of L. Funds for the project were considerately supplied by the Carnegie Corporation. Wesley C. Mitchell, of the National Bureau and AALL, planned and directed the report, which included interventionist chapters by Mallery and Andrews on public works and unemployment benefits and by Wolman on unemployment insurance. While the National Bureau was supposed to do only fact-finding, Mitchell, in discussing his report, advocated "social experimentation." [23]

Meanwhile, Hoover had not been idle on the more direct legislative front. Senator W. S. Kenyon of Iowa, in late 1921, introduced a bill supported by Hoover, embodying recommendations of the Conference and specifically requiring a public works stabilization program. In the December, 1921 hearings, the Kenyon Bill was supported by numerous leading economists, as well as by the American Federation of Labor, the American Engineering Council (of which Hoover had just been named President), and the United States Chamber of Commerce. One of the supporters was Wesley C. Mitchell. The bill never came to a vote, however, largely due to healthy senatorial skepticism based on *laissez-faire* ideas.

The next public works stabilization bill before Congress was the Zihlman Bill in the House. This was promoted by the National Unemployment League, formed in 1922 for that purpose. Hearings were held in the House Labor Committee in February, 1923. Hoover backed the proposal, but it failed of adoption.

Finally, Hoover presented the report on Business Cycles and Unemployment to the Congress, and strongly urged a public works program in depressions. Later, in 1929, Hoover's Committee on Recent Economic Changes would also support a public works program.

In 1924, the AALL continued its agitation. It participated in a national conference proposing public works planning. The conference was called by the Federated American Engineering Societies in January. In 1923, Wisconsin and Massachusetts were persuaded to adopt a stabilizing public works program. Massachusetts was directly swayed by testimony from the ubiquitous Andrews and Mallery. These state programs were never translated into effective action, but they did indicate the developing climate. In January, 1925, Hoover had the satisfaction of seeing President Coolidge adopt his position. Addressing the Associated General Contractors of America (a group that stood to gain by a government building program), Coolidge called for public works planning to stabilize depressions. Senators George H. Pepper and James Couzens tried to pass public works planning legislation in 1925 and 1926, but they failed, along with later attempts by Senator Wesley Jones, who submitted bills that had been drafted in Hoover's Department of Commerce. The Republican Senate was the most recalcitrant, and one Pepper Bill was filibustered to death there. Even favorable reports by its Commerce Committee could not sway the Senate. By this time, not only Hoover and Coolidge, but also Secretary Mellon, the Democratic Party in 1924, and later Governor Alfred E. Smith of New York, had endorsed the public works program. In May, 1928, Senator Robert F. Wagner (D., N. Y.) introduced three bills for comprehensive public works planning, including the creation of an employment stabilization board, but the plan was not considered by Congress.[24]

After Hoover was elected President, he became more circumspect in presenting his views, but he carried on the fight with renewed vigor. His technique was to "leak" the "Hoover Plan" to trusted associates, who would obviously be presenting Hoover's views. He chose as his vehicle Governor Ralph Owen Brewster of Maine. Brewster presented a public works plan to the Conference of Governors in late 1928, and waxed eloquent about the plan as designed to "prevent depressions." [25] His use of the term "Road to Plenty" was hardly a coincidence, for Hoover had adopted the plan of Messrs. Foster and Catchings, which had recently been outlined in their famous book, *The Road to Plenty* (1928). The authors had submitted the plan to Brewster, and, after Hoover's endorsement, Brewster brought Professor William T. Foster along to the Governors' Conference as his technical advisor. Foster and Catchings, bellwethers of inflation and the bull market and leading underconsumptionists, had been closely involved in the public works agitation. Foster was director of the Pollak Foundation for Economic Research, founded by investment banker Waddill Catchings. The pair had published a series of very popular books during the 1920's, agitating for such panaceas as public works and monetary inflation.[26]

Although 7 or 8 governors were enthusiastic about the Hoover-Foster-Catchings plan, the Conference tabled the idea. A large part of the press hailed the plan in extravagant terms, as "prosperity insurance," a "prosperity reserve," or as a "pact to outlaw depression"; while more conservative organs properly ridiculed it as a chimerical and socialistic effort to outlaw the law of supply and demand. It was not surprising that William Green of the A F of L hailed the plan as the most important announcement on wages and employment in a decade, or that the A F of L's John P. Frey announced that Hoover had now accepted the old A F of L theory that depressions are caused by underconsumption and low wages.[28] The press reported that "labor is jubilant, because leaders believe that the next President has found . . . a remedy for unemployment which, at least in its philosophy and its groundwork, is identical with that of labor." [29]

The closeness of Foster and Catchings to Hoover is again demonstrated by the detailed account of their own Plan that they published in April, 1929. In an article entitled "Mr. Hoover's Plan: What It Is and What It Is Not—A New Attack on Poverty," they wrote authoritatively that Hoover should wield a stabilization public works reserve, not of $150 million, as had often been mentioned in previous years, but of the gigantic sum of $3 billion. This Plan would iron out prices and the business cycle, and stabilize business. At last, scientific economics was to be wielded as a weapon by an American President: "The Plan . . . is business guided by measurements instead of hunches. It is economics for an age of science—economics worthy of the new President." [30]

THE DEVELOPMENT OF HOOVER'S INTERVENTIONISM: LABOR RELATIONS

We cannot fully understand Hoover's disastrous interference in the labor market during the depression without tracing the development of his views and actions on the labor front during the 1920's. We have seen that his Reconstruction Program and his Economic Conference of 1920, praised collective bargaining and unionism. In 1920, Hoover arranged a meeting of leading industrialists with "advanced views" on labor relations to try (unsuccessfully) to persuade them to "establish liaison" with the American Federation of Labor.[31] From 1919 through 1923, Hoover tried to persuade private corporations to insure the uninsurable by adopting unemployment insurance, and in 1925 he praised the American Federation of Labor as having "exercised a powerful influence in stabilizing industry." He also favored the compulsory unemployment of a child labor amendment, which would have lowered the national product, and raised labor costs as well as the wages of competing adult workers. Most important of Hoover's activities in the labor field was his successful war against United States Steel and its chairman, Judge Elbert H. Gary, a war conducted as a "skillful publicity campaign" (in the words of a Hoover admirer) against "barbaric" hours of work in the steel industry.[32] The success of this battle made it much easier later on to persuade business men to go along with his labor policies during the 1929 depression. Hoover had decided that the 12-hour day in the steel industry must be eradicated and replaced by the 8-hour day. He persuaded Harding, lapsing from his usual *laissez-faire* instincts, to hold a conference of steel manufacturers in May, 1922, at which Harding and Hoover called on the magnates to eliminate the 12-hour day. An admiring biographer notes with satisfaction that Hoover made the steel leaders "squirm." [33] It was of course easy for Harding and Hoover, far removed from the necessity of meeting a payroll or organizing production, to tell other people how long and under what conditions they should work. Hoover was supported by such "enlightened" steelmen as Alexander Legge and Charles R. Hook, but bitterly opposed by other leaders like Charles M. Schwab, and of course by Judge Gary, chairman of the board of U. S. Steel and President of the American Iron and Steel Institute. The war was on.

The steel agitation, it should be pointed out, had not been begun by Hoover. It originated back in September, 1919, when Gary refused to engage in collective bargaining with a workers' union. The workers struck on that issue, and the strike was led by Communist leader William Z. Foster. By the time the strike had failed, in January, 1920, public opinion, properly regarding the strike as Bolshevik-inspired, was squarely on the side of U. S. Steel. By this time, however, the Interchurch World Movement had appointed a Commission of Inquiry into the strike; the Commission issued a report favorable to the strikers in July, 1920, and thereby initiated the eight-hour day agitation.[34] The report started a propaganda war, with the nation's leftists attempting to change the whole temper of public opinion. The Reverend A. J. Muste, the Socialist *New York Call, Labor,* and *The Nation* backed the report, while business associations strongly attacked the inquiry. The latter included the National Association of Manufacturers, the National Civic Federation, the *Wall Street Journal,* and others. Many religious papers, however, were persuaded by the prestige of the committee (a prestige in religion that somehow carried over to secular matters) to change their previous views and to line up on the anti-steel side.

It was at this critical point in the battle that Hoover entered the fray and persuaded President Harding to join him. Hoover "deliberately broke the story" of the unsuccessful private meeting with Gary, Schwab and the others to the press. He told the press that President Harding was "attempting to persuade industry to adopt a reasonable working day." [35] Thus did the government mobilize public opinion on the side of the union. Hoover managed to have the national Engineering Societies—effectively dominated by Hoover—issue a report (again outside of their competence) endorsing the 8-hour day in November, 1922. Hoover eulogized the report, wrote the introduction, and persuaded Harding to sign it.

Under the Presidential pressure, Judge Gary appointed a committee of the steel industry, headed by himself, to study the question. The committee reported on May 25, 1923, unanimously rejecting the 8-hour day demands. U.S. Steel also issued a reply to the Interchurch Report, written by Mr. Marshall Olds, and endorsed by the prominent economist, Professor Jeremiah W. Jenks. Abuse rained down on the steel industry from all sides. Forgotten were the arguments used by U.S. Steel, e.g., that the steel workers preferred the longer 12-hour day because of the increased income, and that production would suffer under an 8-hour schedule.[36]

This and other arguments were swept away by the wave of emotionalism whipped up over the issue. The forces of the Social Gospel hurled anathemas. "Social Justice" and "Social Action" committees of Protestant, Catholic, and Jewish organizations set up a clamor on issues about which they knew virtually nothing. Attaching a quantitative codicil to the qualitative moral codes of the Bible, they did not hesitate to declare that the twelve-hour day was "morally indefensible." They did not elaborate whether it had *suddenly* become "morally indefensible" or whether it, and even longer work days, had also been morally wicked throughout earlier centuries. If the latter, it was certainly strange that countless preceding generations of churchmen had overlooked the alleged sin; if the former, then a curious historical relativism was now being mingled with the presumably eternal truths of the Bible.

The American Association for Labor Legislation of course entered the fray, and threatened Federal maximum-hour legislation if the steel industry did not succumb to its imperious demands. But the most effective blow was a stern public letter of rebuke sent to Gary by President Harding on June 18, written for the President by Hoover. Faced by Harding's public requests and demands, Gary finally surrendered in July, permitting Hoover to write the notice of triumph into Harding's Independence Day address.

The Hoover-Harding victory over U.S. Steel effectively tamed industry, which, faced by this lesson, no longer had the fight to withstand a potent combination of public and governmental pressure.[37]

Nor did this exhaust Hoover's labor interventionism during the 1920's. Hoover played a major role in fostering railway unions, and in foisting upon the railroad industry the Railway Labor Act—America's first permanent incursion of the Federal government into labor-management relations. The railroad problem had begun in World War I, when the Federal government seized control of the nation's rails. Run by Secretary of the Treasury McAdoo, the government's policy was to encourage unionization. After the war was over, the railway unions tried their best to perpetuate this bastion of socialism, and advocated the Plumb Plan, which called for joint operation of the railroads by employers, unions, and the government.

The railroads were returned to private owners in 1920, but Congress gave a dangerous sop to the unions by setting up a Railroad Labor Board, with tripartite representation, to settle all labor disputes. The Board's decisions did not have the force of law, but they could exert an undue pressure on public opinion.

The unions were happy with this arrangement, until the government representatives saw the light of economic truth during the depression of 1921, and recommended reductions in wage rates. The non-operating railway unions conducted a nationwide strike in defiance of the proposed reduction in the summer of 1922. While Attorney-General Daugherty acted ably in support of person and property by obtaining a Federal injunction against union violence, the "horrified" Mr. Hoover, winning Secretary of State Hughes to his side, persuaded Harding to force Daugherty to remove the injunction. Hoover also intervened privately but insistently to try to wring pro-union concessions from the railroads.

After the unions lost their strike, they determined to rewrite the law so that they could become established with the help of federal coercion. From 1923 on, the unions fought for a compulsory arbitration law. They achieved this goal with the Railway Labor Act of 1926, which, in effect, guaranteed collective bargaining to the railway unions. The bill was drafted by union lawyers Donald Richberg and David E. Lilienthal, and also by Herbert Hoover, who originated the idea of the Railway Labor Mediation Board. Seeing the growing support for such a law and lured by the promised elimination of strikes, the bulk of the railroad industry surrendered and went along with the bill. The Railway Labor Act—the first giant step toward the collectivization of labor relations—was opposed by only a few far-sighted railroads, and by the National Association of Manufacturers.[38]

Even more mischievous than Hoover's pro-union attitude was his adoption of the new theory that high wage rates are an important cause of prosperity. The notion grew during the 1920's that America was more prosperous than other countries *because* her employers generously paid higher wage rates, thus insuring that workers had the requisite purchasing power to buy industry's products. While high real wage rates are actually the *consequence* of greater productivity and capital investment, this theory put the cart before the horse by claiming that high wage rates were the *cause* of high productivity and living standards. It followed, of course, that wage rates should be maintained, or even raised, to stave off any threatening depression.

Hoover began championing this theory during the Unemployment Conference of 1921. Employers on the manufacturing committee wanted to urge lowering wage rates as a cure for unemployment, but Hoover successfully insisted on killing this recommendation.[39] By the mid-1920's Hoover was trumpeting the "new economics" and attacking the "old economics" that resisted the new dispensation. In a speech on May 12, 1926, Secretary Hoover spread the gospel of high wage rates that was to prove so disastrous a few years later:

... not so many years ago—the employer considered it was in his interest to use the opportunities of unemployment and immigration to lower wages irrespective of other considerations. The lowest wages and longest hours were then conceived as the means to obtain lowest production costs and largest profits. ... But we are a long way on the road to new conceptions. The very essence of great production is high wages and low prices, because it depends upon a widening ... consumption, only to be obtained from the purchasing-power of high real wages and increased standards of living.[40]

Hoover was not alone in celebrating the "new economics." The National Industrial Conference Board reported that, while during the 1920-1921 depression, wage rates fell by 19 per cent in one year, the high-wage theory had taken hold from then on. More and more people adopted the theory that wage-cutting would dry up purchasing-power and thus prolong the depression, while wage rates held high would quickly cure business doldrums. This doctrine, allied with the theory that high wage rates cause prosperity, was preached by many industrialists, economists, and labor leaders throughout the 1920's.[41] The Conference Board reported that "Much was heard of the dawn of a new era in which major business depressions could have no place." And Professor Leo Wolman has stated that the prevailing theory during the 1920's was that "high and rising wages were necessary to a full flow of purchasing power and, therefore, to good business." [42]

As the final outgrowth of the famous conference of 1921, Hoover's Committee on Recent Economic Changes issued a general multi-volume report on the American economy in 1929. Once again, the basic investigations were made by the National

Bureau. The Committee did not at all foresee the great depression. Instead, it hailed the price stability of the 1920's and the higher wages. It celebrated the boom, little realizing that this was instead its swan song: "with rising wages and relatively stable prices we have become consumers of what we produce to an extent never before realized." In the early postwar period, the Committee opined, there were reactionary calls for the "liquidation" of labor back to pre-war standards. But, soon, the "leaders of industrial thought" came to see that high wages sustained purchasing power, which in turn sustained prosperity. "They began consciously to propound the principle of high wages and low costs as a policy of enlightened industrial practice. This principle has since attracted the attention of economists all over the world— its application on a broad scale is so novel." [43] This change in the industrial climate, according to the Committee, came about in a few short years, largely due to the influence of the Conference on Unemployment. By the fall of 1926, steel magnate Eugene Grace was already heralding the new dispensation in the *Saturday Evening Post*.[44]

The conclusions of the Hoover-appointed economic committee were ominous in their own right. "To maintain the dynamic equilibrium" of the 1920's, it declared, leadership must be at hand to provide more and more "deliberate public attention and control." In fact, "research and study, the orderly classification of knowledge . . . well may make complete control of the economic system a possibility." To maintain the equilibrium, "We . . . (must) develop a technique of balance," the technique to be sup> plied by economists, statisticians, and engineers, all "working in harmony together."

And so, President Herbert Hoover, on the eve of the Great Depression, stood ready to meet any storm warnings on the business horizon.[45] Hoover, the "Great Engineer," stood now armed on many fronts with the mighty weapons and blueprints of a "new economic science." Unfettered by outworn *laissez-faire* creeds, he would use his "scientific" weapons boldly, if need be, to bring the business cycle under governmental control. As we shall see, Hoover did not fail to employ promptly and vigorously his "modern" political principles, or the new "tools" provided him by "modern" economists. And, as a direct consequence, America was brought to her knees as never before. Yet, by an ironic twist of fate, the shambles that Hoover abandoned when he left office was attributed, by Democratic critics, to his devotion to the outworn tenets of *laissez-faire.*

8

The Depression Begins:
President Hoover Takes Command

And so we see that when the Great Depression struck, heralded by the stock market crash of October 24, President Hoover stood prepared for the ordeal, ready to launch an unprecedented program of government intervention for high wage rates, public works, and bolstering of unsound positions that was later to be christened the New Deal. As Hoover recalls:

> . . . the primary question at once arose as to whether the President and the Federal government should undertake to investigate and remedy the evils. . . . No President before had ever believed that there was a governmental responsibility in such cases. No matter what the urging on previous ocasions, Presidents steadfastly had maintained that the Federal government was apart from such eruptions . . . therefore, we had to pioneer a new field.[1]

As his admiring biographers, Myers and Newton, declared, "President Hoover was the first President in our history to offer Federal leadership in mobilizing the economic resources of the people." He was, of course, not the last. As Hoover later proudly proclaimed: It was a "program unparalleled in the history of depressions in any country and any time."

There was opposition within the Administration, headed, surprisingly enough, considering his interventions throughout the boom, by Secretary of Treasury Mellon. Mellon headed what

Hoover scornfully termed "the leave-it-alone liquidationists." Mellon wanted to "liquidate labor, liquidate stocks, liquidate the farmers, liquidate real estate," and so "purge the rottenness" from the economy, lower the high cost of living, and spur hard work and efficient enterprise. Mellon cited the efficient working of this process in the depression of the 1870's. While phrased somewhat luridly, this was the sound and proper course for the administration to follow. But Mellon's advice was overruled by Hoover, who was supported by Undersecretary of the Treasury Ogden Mills, Secretary of Commerce Robert Lamont, Secretary of Agriculture Hyde, and others.

THE WHITE HOUSE CONFERENCES

Hoover acted quickly and decisively. His most important act was to call a series of White House conferences with the leading financiers and industrialists of the country, to induce them to maintain wage rates and expand their investments. Such artificially induced expansion could only bring losses to business and thereby aggravate the depression. Hoover phrased the general aim of these conferences as "the coordination of business and governmental agencies in concerted action." The first conference was on November 18, with the presidents of the nation's major railroads. Attending for the government were Hoover, Mellon, and Lamont, and also participating was William Butterworth, President of the United States Chamber of Commerce. The railroad presidents promised Hoover that they would expand their construction and maintenance programs, and publicly announced this promise on November 19. Later, the railroad executives met in Chicago to establish a formal organization to carry this program into effect.

The most important White House conference was held on November 21. All the great industrial leaders of the country were there, including such men as Henry Ford, Julius Rosenwald, Walter Teagle of Standard Oil, Matthew Sloan, Owen D. Young, Edward Grace, Alfred P. Sloan, Jr., Pierre duPont, and William Butterworth. The businessmen asked Hoover to stimulate the cooperation of government and industry. Hoover pointed out to them that unemployment had already reached two to three million, that a long depression might ensue, and that wages must be kept up! Hoover

explained that immediate 'liquidation' of labor had been the industrial policy of previous depressions; that his every instinct was opposed to both the term and the policy, for labor was not a commodity: it represented human homes. . . . Moreover, from an economic viewpoint such action would deepen the depression by suddenly reducing purchasing power.

Hoover insisted that if wage rates were to be reduced eventually, they must be reduced "no more and no faster than the cost of living had previously fallen, (so that) the burden would not fall primarily on labor." In short, real wage rates must be prevented from falling. Hoover was insistent that the first shock of the depression must fall on profits and not on wages—precisely the reverse of sound policy, since profits provide the motive power for business activity. At present, then, wage rates should not be reduced at all, and industry should maintain its construction work. Industry should try to keep everyone employed, and any necessary reductions in work should be spread over all employees by reducing the work-week. (Reducing the work-week can only spread unemployment, and prevent that pressure of the unemployed upon wage rates which alone could have restored genuine full employment and equilibrium to the labor market.) If industry followed this course, "great hardship and economic and social difficulties would be avoided." The industrialists all agreed to carry out the Hoover program, and further organized cooperative efforts on its behalf in a conference in Washington on December 5.

The agreement was also announced publicly, and, in addition, the telephone industry, steel industry, and automobile industry pledged to expand their construction programs. The industrialists at the conference pledged not to cut wages, and recommended that all employers in the nation do the same. Henry Ford, in fact, bravely announced a wage *increase.* Nor was industrial cooperation left on a haphazard basis. Representatives of business were appointed to a temporary advisory committee, along with Secretary of Commerce Lamont. The group, along with representatives of various trade associations, then merged into an Executive Committee headed by Mr. Julius Barnes, chairman of the United States Chamber of Commerce, to coordinate industry collaboration on the Hoover program.

On November 22, Hoover called a conference at the White House of leading representatives of the building and construction industries, and they also pledged to maintain wage rates and expand their activity. On November 27, the President called a similar conference of the leading public utility executives, and they unanimously pledged to maintain wage rates and expand construction. The latter included representatives of the American Gas Association, the National Electric Light Association, and the Electric Railways and American Railways Associations.

In a burst of naivete, Hoover recalls that the nation's leading labor leaders, called to a White House Conference on November 21, also agreed to cooperate in the program and not press for further wage increases, this gesture being presumably a sign of their basic "patriotism." These leaders included William Green, Matthew Woll, John L. Lewis, William Hutcheson, A. F. Whitney, and Alvanley Johnston. The agreement put very little strain upon their patriotism, however, since the Hoover program was tailormade to fit the very doctrine that union leaders had been long proclaiming. There was no chance of wage *increases* in an unhampered market. The point is that unions did not have the power to enforce wage *floors* throughout industry (unions in this era being weak, constituting only about 7 per cent of the labor force, and concentrated in a few industries), and so the federal government was proposing to do it for them.

But even in an agreement so favorable to unions, the labor leaders were ready to scrap their part of the bargain at the first opportunity. William Green wrote the affiliated unions on November 27, emphasizing that the agreement concluded with Hoover was not binding, and assuring his colleagues that they were free to press for higher wage rates in their negotiations.[2]

In his annual message to Congress on December 3, Hoover

pointed out that depressions had always been marked by retrench-
ment of construction activity and reduction of wage rates, but
now things were different:

"I have instituted . . . systematic . . . cooperation with business . . .
that wages and therefore earning power shall not be reduced and that
a special effort shall be made to expand construction . . . a very large
degree of individual suffering and unemployment has been prevented."

On December 5, Hoover called together a larger conference
of industrial leaders in Washington, to adopt the Hoover program.
Hoover addressed the conference to hail their agreement, as an

advance in the whole conception of the relationship of businesses to
public welfare. You represent the business of the United States, undertaking through your own voluntary action to contribute something
very definite to the advancement of stability and progress in our
economic life. This is a far cry from the arbitrary and dog-eat-dog
attitude of . . . the business world of some thirty or forty years ago.

With all the leading industrialists thus pledged to maintain wage
rates, expand construction, and share any reduced work, it was no
wonder that the American Federation of Labor hailed the new
development. Its journal, the *American Federationist,* editorial-
ized on Jan. 1, 1930:

The President's conference has given industrial leaders a new sense
of their responsibilities. . . . Never before have they been called upon
to act together . . . in earlier recessions they have acted individually
to protect their own interests and . . . have intensified depressions.[3]

By the following March, the A F of L was hailing the new attitude toward wages, with employers now realizing—in contrast
to the 1921 depression—that it is poor business to destroy consumer purchasing power, and it greeted the fact that not one of
the big corporations had thought of lowering wages as a means
of reducing unit costs. The A F of L proclaimed that business
was now adopting the purchasing-power gospel of W. T. Foster,
and stated that the United States will "go down in history as
the creator of [an] . . . epoch in the march of civilization—high
wages." [4]

INFLATING CREDIT

If the Federal Reserve had an inflationist attitude during the boom, it was just as ready to try to cure the depression by inflating further. It stepped in immediately to expand credit and bolster shaky financial positions. In an act unprecedented in its history, the Federal Reserve moved in during the week of the crash—the final week of October—and in that brief period added almost $300 million to the reserves of the nation's banks. During that week, the Federal Reserve doubled its holdings of government securities, adding over $150 million to reserves, and it discounted about $200 million more for member banks. Instead of going through a healthy and rapid liquidation of unsound positions, the economy was fated to be continually bolstered by governmental measures that could only prolong its diseased state. This enormous expansion was generated to prevent liquidation on the stock market and to permit the New York City banks to take over the brokers' loans that the "other," non-bank, lenders were liquidating. The great bulk of the increased reserves—all "controlled"—were pumped into New York. As a result, the weekly reporting member banks expanded their deposits during the fateful last week of October by $1.8 billion (a monetary expansion of nearly 10 per cent *in one week*), of which $1.6 billion were increased deposits in New York City banks, and only $.2 billion were in banks outside of New York. The Federal Reserve also promptly and sharply lowered its rediscount rate, from 6 per cent at the beginning of the crash, to 4½ per cent by mid-November, Acceptance rates were also reduced considerably.

By mid-November, the great stock break was over, and the market, falsely stimulated by artificial credit, began to move upward again. Standard and Poor's stock-price monthly averages, which had climbed from 56 in mid-1921 to 238 in September 1929 —more than quadrupling—fell to 160 in November, a one-third drop in the course of two months. By the end of the year, stock prices had risen by several points. The stock market emergency over, bank reserves declined to their pre-crash levels. In two weeks—from November 13, when stock prices hit bottom, to November 27—member bank reserves declined by about $275 millions, or to almost exactly the level existing just before the crash. The decline did not come in securities, which *increased* in the Federal Reserve portfolio from $293 million on October 30 to $326 million a month later—a rise of $33 million. Discounts fell by about $80 million, and acceptances by another $80 million, while money in circulation embarked on its seasonal increase, rising by $70 million. Thus, from the end of October to the end of November, *controlled reserves* were reduced by $111 million (including miscellaneous factors not itemized here); uncontrolled reserves, which were more important, fell by $165 million.

By the end of 1929, total reserves at $2.36 billion were only a little over $20 million below the level of October 23 or November 27 ($2.38 billion on each date), but the distribution of factors was considerably different. Thus, while total reserves were almost the same on October 23 and December 31, security holdings had increased by $375 million, more than tripling Reserve holdings of U.S. governments. Total discounts were about $165 million less, acceptances slightly larger, money in circulation higher by over $100 million, and the gold stock down by $100 million. Of the $23 million fall in reserves from October 23 to December 31, *controlled* reserves increased by $359 million (with government securities the overriding factor), while *uncontrolled* reserves fell by $381 million. It is evident, therefore, that the failure to inflate reserves over the last quarter of 1929 was no credit of the Federal Reserve, which did its best to increase reserves, but was foiled by the decline in uncontrolled factors. The total money supply, as gauged by member bank demand deposits adjusted and time deposits, increased slightly—by about $300 million—during the final quarter of 1929.

President Hoover was proud of his experiment in cheap money, and in his speech to the business conference on December 5, he hailed the nation's good fortune in possessing the splendid Federal Reserve System, which had succeeded in saving shaky banks, had restored confidence, and had made capital more abundant by reducing interest rates. Hoover had done his part to spur the expansion by personally urging the banks to rediscount more extensively at the Federal Reserve Banks. Secretary Mellon issued one of his by now traditionally optimistic pronouncements that there was "plenty of credit available." And William Green issued a series of optimistic statements, commending the Federal Reserve's success in ending the depression. On November 22, Green said:

All the factors which make for a quick and speedy industrial and economic recovery are present and evident. The Federal Reserve System is operating, serving as a barrier against financial demoralization. Within a few months industrial conditions will become normal, confidence and stabilization in industry and finance will be restored.

PUBLIC WORKS

With Hoover's views, we would not expect him to delay in sponsoring public works and unemployment relief as aids in curing depressions. On November 23, Hoover sent a telegram to all the governors, urging cooperative expansion of all state public works programs. The governors, including Franklin D. Roosevelt of New York, heartily pledged their cooperation, and on November 24 the Department of Commerce established a definite organization to join with the states in public works programs. Hoover and Mellon also proposed to Congress an increase in the Federal Buildings program of over $400 million, and on December 3 the Department of Commerce established a Division of Public Construction to spur public works planning. Hoover himself granted more subsidies to ship construction through the federal Shipping Board and asked for a further $175 million appropriation for public works. By the end of the year, Professor J. M. Clark of Columbia University was already hailing President Hoover's "great experiment in constructive industrial statesmanship of a promising and novel sort." [5]

THE NEW DEAL FARM PROGRAM

The New Deal program of farm subsidies, characterized especially by farm price supports, arrived in the United States under the Hoover, not the Roosevelt, Administration. To understand this development, we must sketch the emergence of the farm bloc and its drive for Federal intervention in the 1920's. The first cloud no bigger than a man's hand of government grants of special privilege to farmers, came with the agricultural extension program by the U.S. Department of Agriculture, which had its beginnings at the turn of the twentieth century, and was fully established in 1914. In 1916, the United States Warehouse Act imposed regulations on agricultural warehouses.

The important drive for farm privilege came at the end of the war, when farm groups began to organize throughout the nation, originally at the behest of the county agents of the U.S.D.A., who were operating under the extension program. Soon the farm groups, led especially by the midwestern farmers, formed a pressure bloc in Congress. The bloc was cemented in the spring of 1921 under the pressure of the American Farm Bureau Federation and led in the Senate by senators from the midwest. The farm bloc first showed its power and its statist drift, in the summer of 1921, when it drove through Congress several interventionist measures—the regulation of meat packers; regulation of trading in grain futures; renovating and enlarging the War Finance Corporation, and establishing it as an aid to farmers; and an increase in the capital of the previously dormant Federal Farm Loan System.[6]

The first massive intervention in agriculture had been the Federal Farm Loan System, established by the Federal Farm Loan Act of July, 1916. This System had set up a network of Federal Land Banks, under a Federal Farm Loan Board, to lend money on long-term mortgages (under subsidized terms) to cooperative farm loan associations. The regulation of the meat packers and stockyards was the culmination of a demagogic campaign against the packers and yards that had been conducted for years. Since meat packers had few votes, it was common sport for farmers to agitate that the packers were paying them too little for livestock, while consumers denounced packers for charging them too high a price for meat. This harassment of efficient large-scale enterprise bore fruit in a Federal Trade Commission investigation and in bills before Congress during the war. Under the guise of a war emergency, Congress threatened to authorize the President to seize and operate the large stockyards himself. After threatening an anti-trust suit, Attorney-General A. Mitchell Palmer, in February, 1920, managed to force the packers to agree to a Packers' Consent Decree, which forced the packers out of all non-meat production, including stockyards, warehouses, wholesale and retail meat, etc.[7] Yet, agitation continued and culminated in the Packers and Stockyards Act of 1921, which established a detailed regulation of the activities of packers, including their pricing policy, under the direction of the Secretary of Agriculture.

The Futures' Trading Act also followed years of demagogic attacks upon grain speculators and middlemen, whose votes were also few. In this case, even an FTC investigation found no need for stringent regulation. Yet, the Futures' Trading Act placed a prohibitory tax of 20 cents a bushel on speculative transactions, including futures, puts and calls, bids and offers, except when made in certain specific markets authorized by the Secretary of Agriculture.

The War Finance Corporation, headed by Eugene Meyer, Jr., had made loans to exporters during 1919 and 1920. Suspended in May, 1920, the WFC was reactivated by Congress over the veto of President Wilson in January, 1921. It did not then do very much to finance exports, however; its major role at that point was bailing out country banks that had loaned to farmers—an operation that served as a model for the later Reconstruction Finance Corporation. The WFC worked closely with farm bloc leaders and appointed a Corn Belt Advisory Committee of these leaders to pressure midwest bankers into lending more heavily to farmers. The Act of August 1921, drafted by Chairman Meyer and Secretary of Commerce Hoover, increased the maximum authorized credits of the WFC to one billion dollars and per mitted it to lend directly to farmers' coops and foreign importers, as well as to American exporters.[8] The WFC could then supply agricultural capital. The aims of the expanded WFC were to encourage farm exports, raise farm prices, subsidize cheap credit to farmers, and subsidize farm cooperatives—which were to become the pampered pets of the government throughout this period. The new WFC superseded the Stock Growers' Finance Corporation, an organization promoted by the Federal Reserve in the spring of 1921 and financed by Eastern banks to stabilize the livestock market. The expanded WFC made loans of $39 million for exports and $297 million for agriculture, virtually ending its operations in 1925, after the creation of the Federal Intermediate Credit System.[9] The bulk of its loans had gone to farm cooperatives.

In the fall of 1921, the Interstate Commerce Commission, under Farm Bureau pressure, used its dictatorial powers over the railroad industry to order a sharp overall 10 per cent cut in freight rates—largely to aid Western grain. The Senate also directed the FTC to investigate the supposedly too low export prices that were being paid to grain farmers.

In the meanwhile, Congress established a Joint Commission on Agricultural Inquiry, which delivered a report in October 1921. It recommended that the government authorize more farm cooperatives, that it provide for intermediate-term credit to farmers, that agricultural freight rates be lowered (this was quickly adopted), that there be special agricultural attaches in foreign countries, that agricultural departments expand their research, and that more wholesale terminals be provided. An even more ominous note occurred—again belying the myth of *laissez-faire* in the 1920's—when President Harding allowed Secretary of Agriculture Henry C. Wallace to pressure him into calling a National Agricultural Conference, at the end of January, 1922. In his opening address, Harding called for increased Federal aid to cooperatives, and took the radical step of endorsing crop restrictions by co-ops to obtain higher farm prices. The conference—consisting of farm leaders, farm machinery manufacturers, meat packers, and economists such as Richard T. Ely and under the aegis of the Administration—recommended stabilization of the price level, continuation of the WFC, an agricultural representative on the Federal Reserve Board, crop insurance, more federal regulation of warehouses, agricultural tariffs, development of plants to produce cheap fertilizer at the Muscle Shoals Dam, a St. Lawrence Seaway, federal aid to farm cooperatives, and steps toward aiding farm prices in some undefined manner—although outright price fixing was rejected.

In 1922, Congress passed the Capper-Volstead Cooperative Marketing Act, which exempted cooperative marketing associations from the anti-trust laws, with the crucial requirement that no farmer have more than one vote in the co-op. The Futures Trading Act was declared unconstitutional by the courts, but the intrepid Congress passed a new law—the Grain Futures Act of 1922—with similar provisions.

In March 1922, the government made available over $1 million for the purchase of seed grain in crop failure areas. But the farm bloc wanted credits on a more regular basis. Farmers could obtain abundant bank credit for short-term loans (under six months), and they could obtain long-term mortgages from the Federal Land Banks and other institutions; they now felt a gap in the intermediate credit range. A tug-of-war ensued in Congress between two farm bloc bills: the Capper-McFadden Bill, supported by Eugene Meyer, Jr., livestock interests, and cooperative marketers, which would have extended Federal Reserve powers to farm credits; and the Lenroot-Anderson Bill, presented by the Joint Commission of Agricultural Inquiry (appointed by Harding in 1921) and backed by the three large national farmers' organizations. The latter bill would have created new institutions with capital subscribed by the Treasury, to grant intermediate (six months to three years) credits. This bill was supported by Secretaries Wallace and Hoover (and also backed by the National Agricultural Conference). The final result combined features of both bills, with perhaps more emphasis on the Lenroot-Anderson Bill. The Agricultural Credits Act of 1923 established a vast system of Federal farm credit; there were twelve Federal Intermediate Credit Banks, patterned after the Federal Reserve

Banks, and run by the Federal Farm Loan Board. Funds were supplied directly by the Treasury, and the banks were to make loans to farm associations for any agricultural purpose.

Apparently the dictation over packers and stockyards did not prove sufficient, and in 1924 the Secretary of Agriculture ordered smaller commission firms and traders to stop "discriminating against" farm cooperatives in their purchases. The Packers and Stockyards Administration of the USDA also directly helped farm cooperatives to find markets, and investigated the books of many private commission firms.

This pattern of farm intervention was the overture to the crucially important and characteristically New Deal policy of farm price support. At first, the farmers tried voluntary methods. During 1920, farm organizations centered in Kansas and Nebraska, for example, tried to hold wheat off the market and to reduce acreage in an attempt to raise the price. But such a local attempt could only fail, despite feeble efforts to organize farmers into a National Wheat Growers' Association. The withholding of wheat from the market resulted in drastic losses as wheat prices continued downward. An impudent attempt to induce the Treasury and the Federal Reserve to grant special credits to farmers to permit them to withhold wheat, collapsed.

Similar failure attended the cartellizing efforts of the American Cotton Association in the South. In fact, at the end of 1920, cotton planters reacted to falling prices by resorting to violence, including murder and destruction of the cotton and cotton gins of recalcitrants in order to reduce the quantity of cotton produced and sold. Under planter pressure, Governor Parker of Louisiana asked cotton gins to cease operations until cotton had achieved a "living price," and similar advice was given farmers by the Texas Department of Agriculture. But while sales in these states declined, prices also continued to fall. Several times, the farm organizations tried to induce the Federal Reserve Board to supply funds for withholding cotton and other farm products, but Governor W. P. G. Harding and Secretary of the Treasury Houston stoutly refused to intervene.[10]

The next year, 1921, saw determined and well-organized efforts toward a nationwide cotton cartel. The American Cotton Association, *The Cotton News,* and other groups urged an acreage reduction of up to 50 per cent for cotton, and South Carolina officially proclaimed a "Cotton Acreage Reduction Day." [11] Acreage was reduced considerably, and this, joined with a poor crop, lowered the supply greatly; but cotton prices rose less than proportionately to the fall in output, thus frustrating the cartellists once again.

Meanwhile, in corn, Henry A. Wallace, editor of *Wallace's Farmer,* preached the gospel of "sagacious sabotage," a presumably voluntary way to restrict corn production. The campaign got nowhere among the farmers in 1921, but Wallace tried again in 1922 and urged the state Farm Bureau Federations, with indifferent success, to fix systematic township and county acreage quotas for corn. Several farm journals and organizations endorsed the idea, but the major farm leaders were repelled by the idea of formal farm quotas. [12] The result was failure once more, the Corn Belt even *increasing* its acreage of corn.

The chief stumbling block in all these schemes was the noncooperating farmer, the rugged individualist who profited by expanding his production while his rival farmers cut theirs. Unlike his counterparts in industrial labor, he was not deterred by such favored epithets of frustrated cartellists as "scab" and "traitor to his fellow-farmers," hurled at him by such organs as *Wallace's Farmer.*

The next step in the drive for a farm cartel was the "Sapiro Movement," inspired by Aaron Sapiro, a high-priced young attorney for several California cooperatives. The plan was launched, under Sapiro's inspiration, by the Farm Bureau Federation in July, 1920. It aimed to amalgamate all of wheat marketing into one giant producers' cooperative. The July conference appointed a committee which produced, in the spring of 1921, a plan for a huge national grain cooperative to be called U.S. Grain Growers, Inc. [13] As almost always happens with voluntary cartels, the new organization bogged down almost immediately. Many local cooperative farm-elevators preferred dealing with existing private markets, and the private grain exchanges successfully wooed the bulk of the farmers into avoiding the new cartel. By early 1922, the grandiose scheme had proven to be a complete failure.[14]

The July 1920 conference also tried to set up numerous other national cartels—for national fruit marketing, dairy marketing, vegetable marketing, and wool marketing—and all but one were quick failures. Only a livestock marketing plan had staying power, and this because its aims were much less grandiose. Other Sapiro failures were attempts at cotton and tobacco cartels.

These failures did not end the cooperative movement, which had to turn to less flamboyant and more gradual methods; but they did show the folly of voluntary price-fixing. The next step was almost inevitable—a determined call for compulsory price-support by the federal government.

A precedent had been set by the wartime Food Administration Grain Corporation, which had fixed high prices of wheat in order to stimulate production and had itself distributed the wheat available. Furthermore, the Hoover European food relief program of 1919, widely trumpeted as a humanitarian gesture, was also a means of getting rid of "surplus" farm products and thus bolstering food prices.[15] William H. Lyon, a South Dakota attorney, now proposed that the government fix a high price for every farm product and buy up any unsold surplus. The Lyon plan won the support of Samuel Gompers, the South Dakota Assembly, many country banks, and the Republican whip in the House of Representatives. It was put forth as the Christopherson Bill in July 1921, but failed to win the support of the major farm organizations, as did other price-support bills in this and immediately following years. But the drive for compulsory price support had not begun in earnest. It reached major importance in the "Equality for Agriculture" movement, launched in the fall of 1921 by George N. Peek and General Hugh S. Johnson and backed by the powerful support of Bernard M. Baruch. The idea was that since industry was protected by tariffs, agriculture might as well join in mulcting the consumer. The government was to maintain domestic farm prices at a high level, buying the unsold surplus and selling it abroad at lower, world-market levels. Both Peek and Johnson had direct economic interests in farm subsidies as heads of the Moline Plow Company, manufacturers of agricultural machinery. They found little difficulty in interesting Secretary Wallace in their scheme, and the result was a continuing agitation over McNary-Haugen bills, embodying the plan, from 1924 through 1928. The first McNary-Haugen Bill was drawn up by Charles J. Brand, an executive of the American Fruit Growers and former head of the Bureau of Markets in the USDA. The original mass base of Peek's support was the marginal wheat farmers of the Northwest, backed by the bankers of that region. Eugene Meyer, Jr. also lent his powerful backing. In 1924, Peek established the American Council of Agriculture, with representatives from the leading farm groups, to advocate his plan. By the late 1920's the mass farm organizations were solidly behind the program.[16]

It is true that President Coolidge vetoed McNary-Haugen bills in 1927 and 1928, but it is also significant that he called upon Eugene Meyer in 1926 to head a cotton corporation to try to keep cotton prices from falling and that grants totalling $10 million were made to government-sponsored farm organizations to buy cotton at a certain price. Other countries—such as Canada, Hungary, and Poland—were also trying to keep up the price of wheat; but the threat of growing surpluses over the market had the reverse effect and drove prices lower in 1928 and 1929, inducing a farm clamor for more effective price support.

There were many other instances of Coolidge intervention in agriculture. In 1924, he supported the Norbeck-Burtness bill for government loans to northwestern farmers for livestock purchases. The bill failed to pass Congress, but Coolidge proceeded to appoint a special agricultural commission, heavily weighted with farm leaders. The commission—The President's Agricultural Conference—issued three reports during 1925. It recommended further Farm Loan Board credits, further compulsory reduction of freight rates, and large-scale subsidization of farm cooperatives through a Federal Cooperative Marketing Board. The latter provision was embodied in the Capper-Haugen bill, which was however defeated by the opposition of the farm coops, who objected to the great degree of government regulation involved.

Despite this defeat, President Coolidge was more determined than ever to aid the farm coops in any way that he could. Coolidge firmly believed that government "must encourage orderly and centralized marketing" in agriculture.[17] Herbert Hoover and Secretary of Agriculture William Jardine (a member of the President's Agricultural Conference) agreed with Coolidge. In 1925, the Congress granted additional funds for subsidizing the marketing research of farm cooperatives, and the following year, prompted by Secretary Jardine, it established a Division of Cooperative Marketing in the Bureau of Agricultural Economics in the USDA. The new Division then threw itself with enthusiasm into support of the farm coops. *This* kind of intervention was of course welcomed by the coops. In 1926, Jardine sponsored the "Jardine Plan" for a federal farm advisory council and a farmers' marketing commission to subsidize cooperatives and to aid in marketing farm surpluses. The bill failed to pass the House, which instead adopted the McNary-Haugen Bill. The next year, the Coolidge Administration brought out a revised "Jardine Plan," for a Farm Board, commodity advisory committees, and a set of stabilization corporations established by the Board, with funds to lend to cooperatives. The new plan was again sidetracked for another round in the McNary-Haugen battle.

As Secretary of Commerce, Herbert Hoover did a great deal to subsidize farmers and especially farm coops. He aided the latter in many ways—solving their research and marketing problems, helping find export markets for their produce, and making many speeches on their behalf. He also supported tariffs for agricultural produce. Furthermore, he was the man chiefly responsible for the appointment of the strongly pro-cooperative Secretary Jardine. Hoover had been one of the earliest proponents of a Federal Farm Board to aid cooperative marketing associations, and he helped write the Capper-Williams Bill of 1924 to that effect. And so it is no surprise that, as Presidential candidate, Hoover advocated support for farm cooperatives and promised the farm bloc that he would soon institute a farm-price support program. As soon as he took office, he fulfilled both promises, In June

1929, the Agricultural Marketing Act was passed, establishing the Federal Farm Board.

The new scheme was, in essence, the old "Jardine Plan." The Federal Farm Board was furnished with $500 million by the Treasury and was authorized to make all-purpose loans, up to a twenty-year period, to farm cooperatives at low interest rates. The Board could also establish stabilization corporations to control farm surpluses and bolster farm prices. Essentially, this was a Sapiro-type cartel, this time backed by the coercive arm of the federal government.[18] Hoover appointed, as chairman of the FFB, Alexander Legge, president of International Harvester Co. and long-time protegé of Bernard M. Baruch. International Harvester was one of the leading manufacturers of farm machinery, and therefore Legge, like George Peek, had a direct economic interest in farm subsidization. Other members of the FFB included the Secretary of Agriculture, Arthur M. Hyde; James C. Stone, vice-chairman and founder of the Burley Tobacco Growers' Co-operative Association; Carl Williams, a cotton grower of the Farmers' Cooperative Association; C. B. Denman of the National Livestock Producers' Association; C. C. Teague of the Fruit Growers' Exchange; William F. Schilling of the National Dairy Association; Samuel McKelvie, publisher of the *Nebraska Farmer,* representing the grain interests; and Charles S. Wilson, Professor of Agriculture at Cornell University. It is clear that the Board was dominated by representatives of the very farm cooperatives that it was organized to favor and support.[19] Thus, the Hoover Administration established a giant agricultural cartel, directed by government, and run by and for the benefit of the cartellists themselves.

As the depression struck, the FFB went into action. Its first big operation was in wheat, prices of which had been falling sharply for over a year. When first established, in August, the FFB advised farmers not to send wheat forward to market too rapidly, but rather to hold wheat in order to wait for higher prices. In September, it made additional loans to cooperatives to withhold stocks and raise prices. Yet the wheat price continued to fall sharply. On October 26, shortly after the stock market crash, the FFB announced that it would lend $150 million to wheat coops, at up to 100 per cent of the market price, to try to hold up prices by keeping wheat off the market. Soon after the stock market crash, the FFB established a Farmers' National Grain Corporation, with a capital of $10 million, to centralize cooperative marketing in wheat and other grains. The old dream of a wheat cartel had at last come true. The FFB was supposed to work largely through such "corporations," or favored farm marketing cooperatives; and the Farmers' National was selected to centralize all farmers' grain cooperatives, eliminate competition among them, and thus stabilize and raise the market price. At first, the FFB and Farmers' National loaned money to farm cooperatives to hold wheat off the market; then, after prices continued to fall, the Farmers' National itself began to buy wheat at the loan prices.

On November 25, Hoover organized one of his inimitable White House conferences with the major farm organizations, the appointed heads of the FFB, the Land Banks, etc. The farm organizations, like the unions, not surprisingly agreed with alacrity to cooperate with Hoover's program of massive subsidy to themselves.

Whenever government intervenes in the market, it aggravates rather than settles the problems it has set out to solve. This is a general economic law of government intervention. It is certainly true for the overall Hoover depression policy. Nowhere has this law been so clearly illustrated as in the American farm program since 1929. The FFB managed to hold up wheat prices for a time. Seeing this apparent success, wheat farmers naturally increased their acreage, thus aggravating the surplus problem by the spring of 1930. Furthermore, as America held wheat off the market, it lost its former share of the world's wheat trade. Yet, prices continued to fall as the months wore on, and the heavy 1930 acreage aggravated the decline. The accumulating wheat surpluses in the hands of the FFB frightened the market, and caused prices to tumble still further.

Julius Barnes, of the Chamber of Commerce and the private

grain dealers, protested in vain against the unfair competition of the Board and its pet cooperatives, since that competition was directed against the private grain traders. The latter were particularly incensed that the FFB charged the cooperatives a subsidized, lower-than-market interest rate on its loans.

In the spring of 1930, Hoover acquired from Congress an added $100 million to continue the FFB's lending and purchasing policies. But the farmers found themselves with increased surpluses, and with prices still falling. Under farm bloc pressure, Hoover then established the Grain Stabilization Corporation to replace the Farmers' National and to redouble stabilization efforts. The GSC concluded that individual wheat farmers had held off wheat in the fall, and were "profiteering" by selling wheat to the GSC. To statists, individual profits are generally heinous, so the FFB announced that from that point on, it would *only* support the prices of wheat sold by cooperatives and the GSC. Under protests of the grain trade, and the growingly evident impossibility of supporting some wheat at one price while other wheat of the same grade sold at another price, the FFB reversed its stand and decided to support all wheat once more.

The FFB programs had thus inadvertently encouraged greater wheat production, only to find by spring that prices were falling rapidly; greater surpluses threatened the market and spurred greater declines. It became clear, in the impeccable logic of government intervention, that the farmers would have to reduce their wheat production, if they were to raise prices effectively. The FFB was learning the lesson of every cartel—production must be reduced in order to raise prices. And the logic of the government's farm monopoly also drove the FFB to conclude that farmers had been "overproducing." Secretary of Agriculture Hyde accordingly lectured the farmers on the evils of "overproduction." The Secretary and the FFB urged farmers to reduce their acreage voluntarily.

The first group of farmers selected to bear the brunt of this sacrifice were the marginal Northwest growers of spring wheat— the original agitators for price supports. They were not very happy at the prospect. The farmers, after all, wanted subsidies from the government; having to reduce their production of the subsidized crop had not been included in their plans. A group of economists left Washington at the end of March to try to persuade the Northwest farmers that they would be better off if they shifted from wheat to some other crop. In the meanwhile, in this topsy-turvy world of interventionism, troubles piled up because the wheat crop was abundant. Surpluses continued to accumulate, and wheat prices continued to fall. Legge and Hyde toured the Middle West, urging farmers to reduce their wheat acreage. Governor Reed of Kansas reflected the common-sense view of the farmer when he wondered why the government on the one hand promoted reclamation projects to increase farm production and, on the other hand, urged farmers to cut production.[20] Since the indvidual farmer would lose by cutting acreage, no amount of moral exhortation could impel any substantial cut in wheat production.

As wheat piled up in useless storage, foreign countries such as Argentina and Russia increased their production, and this increase, together with the general world depression, continued to drive down wheat prices.[21] On June 30, 1930, the GSC had accumulated over 65 million bushels of wheat held off the market. Discouraged, it did little until late 1930, and then, on November 15, the GSC was authorized to purchase as much wheat as necessary to stop any further decline in wheat prices. Bravely, the GSC bought 200 million more bushels by mid-1931, but all to no avail. The forces of world supply and demand could not be flouted so easily. Wheat prices continued to fall, and wheat production continued to rise. Finally, the FFB decided to dump wheat stocks abroad, and the result was a drastic fall in market prices. By the end of the Hoover Administration, combined cotton and wheat losses by the FFB totalled over $300 million, in addition to 85 million bushels of wheat given *gratis* to the Red Cross.

The wheat program was the FFB's major effort. The Board also attempted several other programs, including a similar cartel in cotton. In the fall of 1929, the FFB made substantial loans to cotton cooperatives to stem the decline in cotton prices. These loans were added to loans from the Federal Intermediate Credit Banks. But cotton prices continued to fall, even after the American Cotton Cooperative Association was encouraged to assume management of the operation. Finally, in June 1930, the FFB established the Cotton Stabilization Corporation to try to stem the tide. The CSC took over 1.25 million bales from the coops. Under severe competition from external sources, the CSC announced that it would maintain its holding for an entire year if prices did not rise. But this proclamation, designed to firm the market, had no effect.

Again, the cartel was confronted with growing surpluses, and therefore heavier pressure on farm prices. Finally, the FFB tried to exhort the cotton farmers, too, to reduce acreage. Chairman Stone, of the FFB, urged the governors of the cotton states to ". . . immediately mobilize every interested and available agency . . . to induce immediate plowing under of every third row of cotton now growing." This action stirred up a host of indignant opposition, the New York *Times* calling it "one of the maddest things that ever came from an official body." [22] The proposal met with no success; in fact the 1931 cotton crop was considerably larger. In early 1932, the Board then tried an heroic action— along with its 1.3 million bales, it obtained an agreement from southern bankers to withhold *all* of their cotton (3.5 million bales), while it continued to finance 2.1 million bales held by the coops. This firmed prices until June 1932, when they fell drastically again. By July, the Board had bought $127 million worth of cotton, and it had lost over half of its value. The upshot was that the CSC had to give up, and it began to liquidate its cotton holdings in August 1932, completing its unloading in a year. The net loss of cotton was $16 million, in addition to 850,000 bales, worth over $78 million, donated to the Red Cross.

At the end of 1929, the FFB established a national wool cooperative—the National Wool Marketing Corporation, made up of 30 state associations. The Board also established an allied National Wool Credit Corporation to handle finances. The NWMC, unskilled in the affairs of the wool industry, turned over its selling operations to the private woolen handling firm, the

Draper Company. The NWMC made huge advances to wool growers from 1930 on, thereby concentrating a large part of the domestic wool output in the hands of the NWMC, and the FFB loaned heavily to its creature. While prices firmed at the beginning, they kept drifting inexorably downward, and the NWMC program only served to stimulate a greater production of wool. The overhanging surplus depressed prices further, and overextended the funds of the NWMC. Eventually, the NWMC had to sell its huge stock of wool at very low prices, thus aggravating the wool price problem still further. A total of $31.5 million in loans for wool were made by the FFB, of which $12.5 million were permanently lost.

In October 1929, the FFB set up the National Livestock Marketing Association, but the livestock producers disagreed and set up conflicting cooperatives, and the program was never launched on any considerable scale. The FFB also organized a dairy program, with five regional butter-marketing associations, providing aid to dairy cooperatives. An advisory committee angered the farmers by suggesting that they reduce the size of their dairy herds in order to cut the surpluses in dairy production. The farmers preferred to lobby for legislation to outlaw oleomargarine or to prevent imports of cocoanut oil from the Philippines.[23] Other FFB attempts were a National Bean Marketing Association; a National Pecan Marketing Association, established in February 1930; aid to citrus industries, as well as to figs, grapes and raisins, potatoes, apples, sugarbeets, honey, nuts, maple syrup, tobacco, poultry, eggs, and rice. However, the Board only tried fully to stabilize prices in wheat and cotton, where it failed ignominiously. Similar attempts, on a smaller scale, were made in butter, wool, and grapes, while FFB activity for the other crops was confined to subsidizing existing cooperatives. The grape stabilization program was a fiasco like the others. The California Grape Control Board lasted for two years, from 1930 to 1932, and then collapsed, with grape growers unwilling to pay stabilization fees. In the meanwhile, the Federal Prohibition Administration aggravated conditions in the industry by outlawing grape concentrates. By May, 1933, total federal loans for grapes were $25 million, with substantial losses.

In butter, the FFB granted loans to existing regional dairy cooperatives and stimulated interregional agreements between them. The most important was Land O'Lakes Creameries, Inc., in the North Central states. The Board granted a loan to Land O'Lakes in January 1930, to steady the price of butter by withholding some stock from the market. Prices firmed for a time, but then fell later as the stocks were sold. It is difficult to trace the effect of this operation because it was conducted on a rather small scale.[24] In tobacco, the FFB tried to stimulate cooperatives, which had become dormant in this industry. The Board advanced loans, but the 1931 crop was large and the price lower. The new cooperative folded in the next year.

And so the grandiose stabilization effort of the FFB failed ignominiously. Its loans encourage greater production, adding to its farm surpluses, which overhung the market, driving prices down both on direct and on psychological grounds. The FFB thus aggravated the very farm depression that it was supposed to solve. With the FFB generally acknowledged a failure, President Hoover began to pursue the inexorable logic of government intervention to the next step: recommending that productive land be withdrawn from cultivation, that crops be plowed under, and that immature farm animals be slaughtered—all to reduce the very surpluses that government's prior intervention had brought into being. It was left to the Roosevelt Administration, however, to carry out the next great logical step down the road to a wholly socialized agriculture—an agriculture socialized, we might add, on principles of irrationality and destruction.[25]

With the failure of the FFB, the leading farm organizations met in Washington, in January 1932, and called for a program of effective control of farm surpluses, outlawing of short-selling in commodities, a stable currency, and independence for the Philippines in order to stop duty free imports from that territory. But nothing was accomplished in the Congress, even though several Congressmen introduced bills for more extensive farm aid. At this point, some radical farmers decided to call a "farmers' strike" in an attempted price-support program of their own. Falling farm prices were to be combatted by withholding farm produce. The leader of this "Farm Holiday" movement was Milo Reno, head of the Iowa Farmers Union and the Farm Holiday Association. Reno, an old radical and a preacher, had been calling for such "strike" measures since 1920. Now, on May 3, a convention of 3000 Iowa farmers led by Reno voted to call a strike on July 4. Their slogan: "Stay at Home—Buy Nothing, Sell Nothing," and their song:

> "Let's call a Farmers' Holiday
> A Holiday let's hold
> We'll eat our wheat and ham and eggs
> And let them eat their gold."

This self-destructive threat to return to a barter economy was originally supposed to last a month as a warning to the rest of society. But, by the fall of 1932, the movement had become a continuing mob. Centering in Sioux City, Iowa, the movement spread, and state units were formed in North and South Dakota, Minnesota, Montana, and there was agitation in Illinois, Wisconsin, Nebraska, and Kansas; but the units did not form a very cohesive front. The farmers soon shifted from attempts to persuade their fellows to outright physical violence. As is often the case, when the strikers found that they were starving due to their own policies, while their non-striking colleagues were thriving, they attempted to force the hated "scabs" to lose *their* income as well. In August, in Sioux City, scene of the first farm strike, strikers blockaded roads, used guns to enforce their commands, stoned buildings, and forcibly stopped transportation.[26] Strikers formed their own aggressive private army, the Khaki Shirts of America. And Governor Floyd Olson of Minnesota offered to use the state militia to enforce an embargo on the "export" of all farm produce from his state, provided that all the other farm-state governors would join. Happily, his offer was refused. All this agitation failed to raise prices; in fact, more goods flowed in from non-striking (largely non-Iowa) sources, and prices continued to fall rapidly. By the end of 1932, the farmers' holiday movement had ended—with the exception of North Dakota, where a farmers' convention urged farmers to organize a council of defense, and to strike and refuse to farm for the market until prices had risen to the farms' cost of production.

Although they failed in their main objective, the farm councils managed to scale down farm mortgages, worth hundreds of thousands of dollars, and farmers also organized "penny sales," where they forcibly barred other than a bankrupt farmer's friends from attending the auction sale of his goods. The friends would buy the goods for a "penny," and then return it to the bankrupt. The low point of this criminality occurred in April, 1933, when a gang assaulted and almost hung an Iowa county judge for refusing to agree to their demand that he order no more farm foreclosures.[27] And in February 1933, Governor Olson, under threat from radical farmers of his state to march on the Minnesota capitol to demand compulsory debt moratoria, actually decreed a halt to all foreclosures.

9

1930

By early 1930, people were generally convinced that there was little to worry about. Hoover's decisive actions on so many fronts: wages, construction, public works, farm supports, etc., indicated to the public that this time swift national planning would turn the tide quickly. Farm prices then seemed to be recovering, and unemployment had not yet reached catastrophic proportions, averaging less than 9 per cent of the labor force in 1930. Such leaders as Hoover, William Green, and Charles Schwab issued buoyantly optimistic statements about early recovery, and Hoover was hailed on all sides as a great statesman. At the end of June, Hoover urged further state and city action to expand public works and thus cure unemployment, and on July 3rd Congress authorized the expenditure of a giant $915 million public works program, including a Hoover Dam on the Colorado River.

More Inflation

Dr. Anderson records that, at the end of December, 1929, the leading Federal Reserve officials wanted to pursue a *laissez-faire* policy: "the disposition was to let the money market 'sweat it out' and reach monetary ease by the wholesome process of liquidation." The Federal Reserve was prepared to let the money market find its own level, without providing artificial stimuli that could only prolong the crisis.[1] But early in 1930, the government instituted a massive easy money program. Rediscount rates of the New York Fed fell from 4½ per cent in February to 2 per cent by the end of the year. Buying rates on acceptances, and the call loan rate, fell similarly. At the end of August, Governor Roy Young of the Federal Reserve Board resigned, and was replaced by a more thoroughgoing inflationist, Eugene Meyer, Jr., who had been so active in government lending to farmers. During the entire year, 1930, total member bank reserves increased by $116 million. Controlled reserves rose by $209 million; $218 million consisted of an increase in government securities held. Gold stock increased by $309 million, and there was a net increase in member bank reserves of $116 million. Despite this increase in reserves, the total money supply (including all money-substitutes) remained almost constant during the year, falling very slightly from $73.52 billion at the end of 1929 to $73.27 billion at the end of 1930. There would have been a substantial rise, were it not for the shaky banks, which were forced to contract their operations in view of the general depression. Security issues increased, and for a while stock prices rose again, but the latter soon fell back sharply, and production and employment kept falling steadily.

A leader in the easy money policy of late 1929 and 1930 was once more the New York Federal Reserve, headed by Governor George Harrison. The Federal Reserve, in fact, began the inflationist policy on its own. Inflation would have been greater in 1930 had not the stock market boom collapsed in the spring, and if not for the wave of bank failures in late 1930.[2] The inflationists were not satisfied with events, and by late October, *Business Week* thundered denunciation of the alleged "deflationists in the saddle," supposedly inspired by the largest commercial and investment banks.[3]

THE SMOOT-HAWLEY TARIFF

In mid-1930, another chicken born in 1929 came home to roost. One of Hoover's first acts upon becoming President was to hold a special session on tariffs, beginning in the spring of

1929. Whereas we have seen that a policy of high tariffs *cum* foreign loans was bound to hurt the farmers' export markets when the loans tapered off, Hoover's answer was to raise tariffs still further, on agricultural and on manufactured products. A generation later, Hoover was still to maintain that a high tariff *helps* the farmer by building up his domestic market and lessening his "dependence" on export markets, which means, in fact, that it hurts him grievously by destroying his export markets.[4] Congress continued to work on a higher tariff, and finally reported a bill in mid-1930, which Hoover signed approvingly. In short, it was at a precarious time of depression that the Hoover Administration chose to hobble international trade, injure the American consumer, and cripple the American farmers' export markets by raising tariffs higher than their already high levels. Hoover was urged to veto the Smoot-Hawley Tariff by almost all the nation's economists, in a remarkable display of consensus, by the leading bankers, and by many other leaders. The main proponents were the Progressive bloc, the three leading farm organizations, and the American Federation of Labor.

No one had advocated higher tariffs during the 1928 campaign, and Hoover originated the drive for a higher tariff in an effort to help the farmers by raising duties on agricultural products. When the bill came to the House, however, it added tariffs on many other products. The increased duties on agriculture were not very important, since farm products were generally *export* commodities, and little was imported. Duties were raised on sugar to "do something for" the Western beet-sugar farmer; on wheat to subsidize the marginal Northwestern wheat farmers at the expense of their Canadian neighbors; on flaxseed to protect the Northwest farmers against Argentina; on cotton to protect the marginal Imperial Valley farmer against Egypt; on cattle and dairy products to injure the Canadian border trade; on hides, leather, and shoes; on wool, wool rags, and woolen textiles; on agricultural chemicals; on meat to hamper imports from Argentina; on cotton textiles to relieve this "depressed industry"; on velvets and other silks; on decorated china, surgical instruments, and other glass instruments; on pocket knives and watch movements.[5] The tariff rates were now the highest in American history.

The stock market broke sharply on the day that Hoover agreed to sign the Smoot-Hawley Bill. This bill gave the signal for protectionism to proliferate all over the world. Markets, and the international division of labor, were hampered, and American consumers were further burdened, and farm as well as other export industries were hindered by the ensuing decline of international trade.

One prominent protectionist drive was put on by the silver bloc. In February, the mining interests suggested an international monetary conference to raise and then stabilize silver prices, as well as to levy a tariff on silver. The resolution was put through the Senate in February, 1931, but the State Department could not interest foreign governments in such a conference. Main supporters of this price-raising scheme were the Western governors, at the behest of the American Silver Producers' Association, Senators such as Key Pittman of Nevada and Reed Smoot of Utah, J. H. Hammond, a mining engineer, René Leon, a New York banker, and F. H. Brownell, President of the American Smelting and Refining Co.

HOOVER IN THE SECOND HALF OF 1930

During the second half of 1930, production, prices, foreign trade, and employment continued to decline. On July 29, Hoover called for an investigation of bankruptcy laws in order to weaken them and prevent many bankruptcies—thus turning to the ancient device of attempting to revive confidence by injuring creditors and propping up unsound positions. In August, it was revealed that merchant shipping construction had swelled from 170,000 tons in July, 1929, to 487,000 tons in July, 1930—due to Federal subsidies. On September 9, Hoover took an unusual step: to relieve the unemployment problem—and also to help keep wage rates up, the President effectively banned further immigration into the United States, and did so through a mere State Department press announcement. The decree barred all but the wealthiest immigrants as "public charges," in a few months reducing immigration from Europe by 90 per cent.

Interestingly enough, Hoover's high-handed action came in defiance of previous Congressional refusal to agree to his proposal to cut immigration quotas in half, and it also came after the Senate had rejected a bill to suspend all immigration except by relatives for five years, offered by Senator Hugo Black (D., Ala.). Typical of the restrictionist, wage-raising arguments for blocking immigration was the charge of Senator Black that "foreign immigration has been utilized by the big business interests of the country as a direct weapon to break down the price of wages of the people of the land." [6] As might have been expected, William Green warmly endorsed Hoover's stand.

Reducing the labor force as a "cure" for unemployment is similar to "curing" a surplus of a certain commodity by passing a law prohibiting anyone from selling the product, and anticipated Hitler's "cure" for unemployment by forcibly sending married women back to the home. Hoover also records that he accelerated the deportation of "undesirable" aliens, again helping to ease the unemployment picture. He deported sixteen to twenty thousands aliens per year.[7] As a consequence, while the immigration law had already reduced net immigration into the United States to about 200,000 per year, Hoover's decree reduced net immigration to 35,000 in 1931, and in 1932 there was a net emigration of 77,000. In addition, Hoover's Emergency Committee on Employment organized concerted propaganda to urge young people to return to school in the fall, and thus leave the labor market.

At the end of July, Hoover organized a planning conference of leading organizations, designed to widen home ownership and bolster shaky home mortgages. The Planning Committee established by Hoover included representatives of: the National Association of Real Estate Boards, the American Federation of Labor, the American Farm Bureau Federation, the National

Farmers Union, the National Grange, the U.S. Chamber of Commerce, the American Institute of Architects, and the American Home Economic Association.

By October, Hoover apparently felt that the time had come for self-congratulation. In an address to the American Bankers' Association, he summed up his multi-faceted intervention as follows:

I determined that it was my duty, even without precedent, to call upon the business of the country for coordinated and constructive action to resist the forces of disintegration. The business community, the bankers, labor, and the government have cooperated in wider spread measures of mitigation than have ever been attempted before. Our bankers and the reserve system have carried the country through the credit . . . storm without impairment. Our leading business concerns have sustained wages, have distributed employment, have expedited heavy construction. The Government has expanded public works, assisted in credit to agriculture, and has restricted immigration. These measures have maintained a higher degree of consumption than would otherwise have been the case. They have thus prevented a large measure of unemployment. . . . Our present experience in relief should form the basis of even more amplified plans in the future.

So they did form the basis—of plans that aggravated the depression even further. To the bankers Hoover delivered his pet theory of the crash: that it was caused by credit being too scarce to commercial borrowers, it being unduly "absorbed" by speculation. He hailed the Federal Reserve System as the great instrument of promoting stability, and called for an "ample supply of credit at low rates of interest," as well as public works, as the best methods of ending the depression.

The wage agreement that Hoover had extracted at the White House Conferences unfortunately held firm for a long while, thus becoming the prime generator of unemployment. Hoover still proudly records that the wage agreement lasted in the organized trades throughout his term, while most of the non-union employers also complied. In August, William Green had praised the stabilizing effects of Hoover's program, emphasizing its success in maintaining wage rates. And in October, when Green presented Hoover to the annual Convention of the A F of L, he was exuberant:

The great influence which [Hoover] exercised upon that occasion [the White House Conferences] served to maintain wage standards— to prevent a general reduction of wages. As we emerge from this distressing period of unemployment we . . . understand and appreciate the value of the service which the President rendered the wage earners of the country.

Green had no doubt that Hoover's "great influence served to maintain wage standards and prevent a general reduction of wages."

In his address before the Convention, Hoover returned to the glorious theme of the White House Conferences:

At these White House Conferences the leaders of business and industry undertook to do their utmost to maintain the rate of wages. . . .

and to distribute work among the employees. He hailed the success of that pledge, for the

. . . great manufacturing companies, the railways, utilities, and business houses have been able to maintain the established wages. Employers have spread their employment systematically.

The spreading of employment was, in fact, a spreading of *unemployment*, and helped to maintain the existing wage scales by keeping these unemployed off the labor market. Hoover virtually admitted this when he said:

Through distribution of employment large numbers of workers have been saved from being forced into competition for new jobs.

Another evil in this work-sharing program was that employers were not permitted to discharge their least marginally-productive workers—those whose productivity was below the artificially high wage rates. Hence, costs to the employers became greater, and they suffered aggravated losses.

Hoover also commended the businessmen for their great resolution in maintaining wage scales even in the face of falling prices,[8] and pointed out that public works had "taken up the slack" and that railroads and public utilities had been induced to increase their construction by $500 million.

Also in October, Hoover launched the first of repeated attacks against his old *bête noire:* the New York Stock Exchange. He threatened Federal regulation of the Exchange despite the fact that it was wholly under the jurisdiction of New York State and that therefore such regulation would be patently unconstitutional. Hoover forced Richard Whitney, head of the Exchange, to agree "voluntarily" to withhold loans of stock for purposes of short-selling. Short selling was—and usually is—the chief object of attack by demagogues who believed that short sales were somehow fundamentally responsible for falling stock prices, thereby forgetting that for every short seller there must necessarily be a buyer, and also that short-selling accelerates the necessary depression-adjustment in stock prices. Senator Smith Brookhart of Iowa had, as early as January, 1930, introduced a bill to prohibit all short selling.

In the same month, Hoover formed a nationwide organization for the relief of distress. Colonel Arthur Woods was appointed to head the President's Emergency Committee for Employment; in the group were Fred C. Croxton, Edward Bernays, and Dr. Lillian Gilbreth.[9] As in Hoover's previous venture in 1921, the committee organized committees in each state and locality for unemployment relief. Shortly afterward, Hoover again asked for enlarged Federal public works appropriations. One public work already begun in September was the appropriately named "Hoover Dam" in Arizona, a government project to sell water and electric power. The New Deal was later happy to complete the project, as it also did with the Grand Coulee Dam on the Columbia River, and with dams in the Central Valley of California.[10]

In Hoover's second annual message in December, the President, while conceding that factory employment had fallen by 16 per cent since 1928, and manufacturing production had declined by 20 per cent, proudly pointed out that consumption and wage rates had held to their former levels, bank deposits were 5 per cent higher, and department store sales only 7 per cent less.

Unfortunately, Hoover did not attempt to relate these movements, or to realize that the declines of employment and production were the consequences of policies that bolstered consumption
and wage rates. Hoover conceded that wheat and cotton prices
were 40 per cent below 1928, and farm prices 20 per cent lower,
but he hailed the achievement of the FFB in keeping wheat prices
30 per cent higher than that of Canada, and wool prices 80
per cent higher than in Denmark. Hoover apparently never saw
that keeping prices above the world market would be self-
defeating, since few customers would buy American products at
prices artificially higher than they could obtain abroad.

In keeping with the general tone of optimism, the American
Economic Association stated at year's end that recovery in the
spring of 1931 seemed assured. More astute than these "established" economists were a few others who operated with better
theoretical tools. Thus, at the end of July, H. Parker Willis
charged, in an editorial in the New York *Journal of Commerce,*
that the current easy money policy of the Federal Reserve was
causing the increase in bank failures, "chiefly due to [their]
inability to liquidate." Willis pointed out that the country
was suffering from frozen and wasteful malinvestments in plants,
buildings and other capital, and that the depression would only
be cured when these unsound credit positions were liquidated.[11]
The economist Joseph Stagg Lawrence upheld thrift and attacked the prevalent idea that consumption led to prosperity.
He pointed out that purchases of consumer goods were being
maintained, while the main declines were taking place in producers' goods industries, such as construction, steel, and freight
traffic.[12]

One of the best counsels on the depression was set forth in an
annual report by Albert H. Wiggin, chairman of the board of
the Chase National Bank, in January, 1931. We can assume that
he was helped in making the report by Dr. Benjamin M. Anderson, economist for the bank. Wiggin called for the reduction of the
Federal capital gains tax, pointing out that the 12½ per cent tax
on realized capital gains induced people to hold onto their
stock rather than sell during the boom, and then fostered selling

during a depression, in order to take the realized stock losses. Wiggin also urged reduction in the tariff, noting that we had merely delayed the adverse effects of the protective tariff from 1924 until 1929 by heavy purchase of foreign bonds. With the decline in the foreign bond market, foreign countries no longer had the funds to purchase our exports. Only a reduction in our tariffs would permit American exports to flourish. Wiggin further pointed out that production had declined far more than consumption, thus indicating that it was not lack of "purchasing power" that was causing the depression. Finally, he noted that in the 1921 depression, costs and wages had been quickly scaled down, and unsound activities liquidated:

Past costs of production were forgotten, and goods were sold for what the market would pay . . . [but] we attempted, as a matter of collective policy, to hold the line firm following the crash of 1929. Wages were not to be reduced, buying by railroads and construction by public utilities were to be increased, prices were to be maintained, and cheap money was to be the foundation. The policy has . . . failed. . . . It is bad policy for a government, or for an industry by concerted act, to try to keep prices permanently above the level which the supply and demand situation justifies. . . . We must keep the markets open and prices free. It is not true that high wages make prosperity. Instead, prosperity makes high wages. When wages are kept higher than the market situation justifies, employment and the buying-power of labor fall off. . . . Our depression has been prolonged and not alleviated by delay in making necessary readjustments.[13]

Unfortunately, Wiggin's wise advice went unheeded.

THE PUBLIC WORKS AGITATION

While a few economists gave sound advice to little avail, scores of others helped make matters worse by agitating for a broad public works program. The Employment Stabilization Act had first been introduced into the Senate by Senator Robert Wagner of New York in 1928, under the inspiration of the veteran public works agitator, Otto Tod Mallery, as part of a comprehensive plan of government intervention to combat unemployment.[14]

The act provided for an Employment Stabilization Board, consisting of several Cabinet officers, to increase public works in order to stabilize industry, and relieve unemployment in a depression. In early 1930, Senator Wagner seized the opportunity to introduce his program again. He asserted, with due consistency, that since we now had a Federal tariff and a Federal Reserve System, why not also accept the responsibility for unemployment? No one thought to answer Wagner that his logic could be turned around to indicate repeal of both the protective tariff and the Federal Reserve. Wagner's bill authorized $150 million per annum for his program.

The California Joint Immigration Committee presented as an "alternative" to the Wagner Bill a proposal of its own to restrict immigration, thus preventing aliens from competing with high-wage, American workers, and preventing them from breaking down an artificial wage scale. This bill was supported by the American Legion of California, the California Federation of Labor, and the Native Sons of the Golden West. Hoover granted their request in September. For the Wagner bill the main witnesses in the Senate were the inevitable John B. Andrews, of the American Association for Labor Legislation, William Green, Frances Perkins, Norman Thomas, of the Socialist Party, and James A. Emery of the National Association of Manufacturers. There was, indeed, very little opposition in the Senate: Senator Hiram Johnson (R., Calif.), head of the subcommittee considering the measure, approved, as did Senator Vandenberg (R., Mich.) and President Hoover. An outpouring of the nation's economists endorsed the Wagner bill, in petitions presented to Congress by Professors Samuel Joseph of the City College of New York, and Joseph P. Chamberlain of Columbia University. Joseph's petition asserted that the bill laid the foundation for a national program to relieve unemployment, and that the principle of public works was "widely accepted" by economists as a means of stimulating construction and putting men to work.[15]

The Senate passed the Wagner Bill by an unrecorded vote. The bill ran into delays in the House despite the almost complete lack of opposition in the hearings and the pressure for the bill exerted by Andrews, Green, Perkins, Emery, Douglas, and Foster and Catchings. Representative George S. Graham (R., Pennsylvania), Chairman of the Judiciary Committee, managed to amend the substance out of the bill, and thus to deadlock the Senate-House Conference and block the bill.[16] In the meanwhile, Congress approved the various Hoover requests for additional public works appropriations, although one $150 million request was cut to $116 million.

In December, 1930, the Emergency Committee for Federal Public Works, headed by Harold S. Butenheim, editor of *American City,* appealed for large-scale borrowing of one billion dollars for public works, and the plea was endorsed by ninety-three leading economists. Among these were Thomas S. Adams, Thomas Nixon Carver, Edgar S. Furniss, Edwin R. A. Seligman, Leo Wolman, and many of the names on the Wagner Bill petitions.[17] Finally, in February, 1931, Congress passed the Employment Stabilization Act in original form and Hoover gladly signed the measure. He quickly designated the Secretary of Commerce as chairman of the Federal Employment Stabilization Board.[18] The Senate also did something in the same month destined to have far-reaching effects in the future: it passed the Wagner resolution to study the establishment of Federal unemployment insurance.

Behind the scenes, Gerard Swope, president of General Electric, urged a much larger public works plan upon Hoover. In September, 1930, Swope proposed to Hoover an immediate one billion dollar bond issue for Federal public works, to be matched by another one billion dollars similarly raised by state and local governments, under Federal guarantee. Swope's favorite argument was to point to wartime, with its bold national planning, as the ideal to be emulated. Fortunately, Hoover's own leanings in this direction were much too cautious to allow the adoption of Swope's proposal.[19]

Also urging Hoover further than he would go was Colonel Arthur Woods, head of the President's Emergency Committee for Employment, who suggested a $750 million federal-state public-works program, including a Federal Reconstruction Board for loans to states for public works.[20]

THE FISCAL BURDENS OF GOVERNMENT

In the pleasant but illusory world of "national product statistics," government expenditures on goods and services constitute *an addition to* the nation's product. Actually, since government's revenue, in contrast to all other institutions, is coerced from the taxpayers rather than paid voluntarily, it is far more realistic to regard all government expenditures as a *depredation upon,* rather than an addition to, the national product. In fact, either government expenditures or receipts, whichever is the higher, may be regarded as the burden on private national product, and subtraction of the former figure from Gross Private Product will yield an estimate of the private product left in private hands. The ratio of government depredation (government expenditures or receipts, whichever is the higher) over Gross Private Product yields the approximate percentage of government depredation of the private product of the economy.[21]

In a depression, it is particularly important that the government's fiscal burden on the economy be reduced. In the first place, it is especially important at such a time to free the economy from the heavy load of government's acquiring resources, and secondly, a lowering of the burden will tend to shift total spending so as to increase investment and lower consumption, thus providing a double impetus toward curing a depression.

How did the government react when the 1929 depression hit? Were fiscal burdens on the economy raised or lowered? Fortunately, detailed statistics are available from 1929 on, permitting us to estimate the answer to that question. In 1929, the GNP was $104.4 billion; Gross Private Product was $99.3 billion. (See our calculations in the Appendix.) Total Federal depredations on the private product equalled Federal receipts, which were $5.2 billion. (Federal expenditures were a bit lower at $4.0 billion.) State and Local depredations were $9.0 billion, the figure for expenditures, receipts being estimated at $8.8 billion. Total government depredations on the private product in 1929 were, therefore, $14.2 billion, a burden of 14.3 per cent of the gross private product (or, if we wish, 15.7 per cent of the *Net* Private Product). In 1930, GNP fell to $91.1 billion and GPP to $85.8 billion. Federal expenditures rose to $4.2 billion, while receipts fell to $4.4 billion; state and local expenditures rose to $9.7 billion, and state and local receipts to $9.1 billion. Total government depredations in 1930, therefore, remained about level at $14.1 billion. But this now constituted 16.4 per cent of the Gross Private Product, and 18.2 per cent of the net private product. The fiscal burden of government had substantially *increased* when it should have been lowered.

Given any particular tax rates, we would expect revenue to fall in a depression, as national income fell, if government simply remained passive. Government's particular responsibility, then, is to reduce its expenditures. Instead, expenditures rose by $800 million. Of this, $700 million came from state and local government (the major categories: $170 million increase in salaries to employees; $300 million increase in construction spending). The Federal government increased its expenditure by $130 million, of which $50 million was new construction. The Hoover policy of stimulating public works was already taking effect.[22]

During 1929, the Federal government had a huge surplus of $1.2 billion ($4.1 billion receipts, $2.9 billion expenditures excluding government enterprises; an estimated $5.2 billion receipts and $4.1 billion expenditures including government enterprises), and it is to the Hoover Administration's credit that as soon as the depression struck, Hoover and Mellon suggested that the top normal personal income tax rate be cut from 5 per cent to 4 per cent, and the corporate income tax be reduced from 12 per cent to 11 per cent.[23] This suggestion was speedily enacted by Congress at the end of 1929. As a partial consequence, Federal receipts fell to $4.4 billion in 1930 (or $3.3 billion excluding government enterprises). Federal expenditures, in the meanwhile, rose to $4.2 billion ($3.1 billion excluding government enterprises), still leaving a considerable surplus. The Federal fiscal burden on the private product remained approximately the same, falling from 5.2 per cent to 5.1 per cent of gross private product, and from 5.8 to 5.7 per cent of net private product. The main onus for increasing the fiscal burden of government during 1930 falls upon state and local governments, which increased their rate of depredation from 9.1 per cent to 11.3 per cent of the gross private product, from 9.9 per cent to 12.5 per cent of the net product.

10

1931—"The Tragic Year"

The year 1931, which politicians and economists were sure would bring recovery, brought instead a far deeper crisis and depression. Hence Dr. Benjamin Anderson's apt term "the tragic year." Particularly dramatic was the financial and economic crisis in Europe, which struck in that year. Europe was hit hard partly in reaction to its own previous inflation, partly from inflation induced by our foreign loans and Federal Reserve encouragement and aid, and partly from the high American tariffs which prevented them from selling us goods to pay their debts.

The foreign crisis began in the Boden-Kredit Anstalt, the most important bank in Austria and indeed in Eastern Europe, which, like its fellows, had overexpanded.[1] It had suffered serious financial trouble in 1929, but various governmental and other sources had leaped to its aid, driven by the blind expediency of the moment telling them that such a large bank must not be permitted to fail. In October, 1929, therefore, the crumbling Boden-Kredit-Anstalt merged with the older and stronger Oesterreichische-Kredit-Anstalt, with new capital provided by an international banking syndicate including J. P. Morgan and Co., and Schroeder of England, and headed by Rothschild of Vienna. The Austrian Government also guaranteed some of the Boden bank's investment. This shored up the shaky bank temporarily. The crisis came when Austria turned to its natural ally, Germany, and, in a world of growing trade barriers and restrictions, declared a customs union with Germany on March 21, 1931. The

French Government feared and hated this development, and hence the Bank of France and lesser French banks suddenly insisted on redemption of their short-term debts from Germany and Austria.

The destructive political motive of the French government cannot be condoned, but the act itself was fully justified. If Austria was in debt to France, it was the Austrian debtors' responsibility to have enough funds available to meet any liabilities that might be claimed. The guilt for the collapse must therefore rest on the bank itself and on the various governments and financiers who had tried to shore it up, and had thus aggravated its unsound position. The Kredit-Anstalt suffered a run in mid-May; and the Bank of England, the Austrian Government, Rothschild, and the Bank of International Settlements—aided by the Federal Reserve Bank of New York—again granted it many millions of dollars. None of this was sufficient. Finally, the Austrian Government, at the end of May, voted a $150 million guarantee to the bank, but the Austrian Government's credit was now worthless, and Austria soon declared national bankruptcy by going off the gold standard.

There is no need to dwell on the international difficulties that piled up in Europe in latter 1931, finally leading Germany, England, and most other European countries to renounce their obligations and go off the gold standard. The European collapse affected the United States monetarily and financially (1) by causing people to doubt the firmness of American adherence to the gold standard, and (2) through tie-ins of American banks with their collapsing European colleagues. Thus, American banks held almost $2 billion worth of German bank acceptances, and the Federal Reserve Bank of New York had participated in the unsuccessful shoring operations. The fall in European imports from the United States as a result of the depression was not the major cause of the deeper depression here. American exports in 1929 constituted less than 6 per cent of American business, so that while American agriculture was further depressed by international developments, the great bulk of the American depression was caused by strictly American problems and policies. Foreign governments contributed a small share to the American crisis, but the bulk of responsibility must be placed upon the American government itself.

Although we must confine our interest in this work to the United States, we may pause a moment, in view of its international importance, and consider the shabby actions of Great Britain in this crisis. Great Britain—the government that induced Europe to go onto the treacherous shoals of the gold bullion and gold exchange standard during the 1920's, that induced the United States government to inflate with disastrous consequences, that induced Germany to inflate through foreign investment, that tried to establish sterling as the world's premier currency—surrendered and went off the gold standard without a fight. Aided by France instead of the reverse, much stronger financially than Germany or Austria, England cynically repudiated its obligations without a struggle, while Germany and Austria had at least fought frantically to save themselves. England would not consider giving up its inflationary and cheap credit policy, even to stay on sound money. Throughout the crisis of 1931, the Bank of England kept its discount rate very low, never going above 4½ per cent, and in fact, inflated its deposits in order to offset gold losses abroad. In former financial crises, the bank rate would have gone to 10 per cent much earlier in the proceedings, and the money supply would have been contracted, not expanded. The bank accepted loans of $650 million from the Federal Reserve Banks and the Bank of France; and the Bank of France, forced against its better judgment by the French Government, kept its accounts in sterling and did not ask for redemption in gold. And then, on September 20, Britain went coolly off the gold standard, inflicting great losses on France, throwing the world into monetary chaos, and disrupting world markets. It is a final measure of the character of Governor Montagu Norman that only two days before the repudiation, he gave Doctor Vissering, head of the Netherlands Bank, unqualified assurance that Britain would remain on the gold standard and that therefore it was safe for the Netherlands to keep its accounts in sterling. If the Netherlands was tricked, it is possible that Montagu Norman's fast friends in the United States were in-

formed in advance. For in the summer of 1931, Governor Norman
visited Quebec, for "health" reasons, and saw Governor Harrison
of the New York Federal Reserve Bank. It was shortly after Norman's return to England that Great Britain went off the gold
standard.[2]

Throughout the European crisis, the Federal Reserve, particularly the New York Bank, tried its best to aid the European
governments and to prop up unsound credit positions. In mid-
July, the executive committee of the New York Bank had an
all-day conference with the leaders of J. P. Morgan and Co., and
there decided to follow the "lead" of the Bank of International
Settlements, the "club" of European central banks. It therefore
loaned money to the Reichsbank to purchase German acceptances,
and made special loans to other Central Banks to relieve frozen
assets there. The New York Federal Reserve loaned, in 1931,
$125 million to the Bank of England, $25 million to the German
Reichsbank, and smaller amounts to Hungary and Austria. As
a result, much frozen assets were shifted, to become burdens to
the United States. The Federal Reserve also renewed foreign loans
when borrowers failed to pay at maturity.[3]

THE AMERICAN MONETARY PICTURE

In the meanwhile, the depression grew ever worse in the
United States, and not because of the European situation. Production continued to plummet drastically, as did prices and
foreign trade, and unemployment skyrocketed to almost 16 per
cent of the labor force. The FRB index of manufacturing production, which had been 110 in 1929 and 90 in 1930, fell to 75
in 1931. Hardest hit, in accordance with Austrian cycle theory,
were producers' goods and higher order capital goods industries,
rather than the consumer goods' industries. Thus, from the end
of 1929 to the end of 1931, the FRB index of production of
durable manufactures fell by over 50 per cent, while the index
of nondurable production fell by less than 20 per cent. Pig iron
production fell from 131 thousand tons per day (seasonally ad-

justed) in June, 1929, to 56 thousand tons daily in December, 1930, to 33 thousand tons in December, 1931, a drop of nearly 80 per cent. On the other hand, retail department store sales only fell from an index of 118 in 1929 to 88 at the end of 1931, a drop of about 25 per cent.

The American monetary picture remained about the same until the latter half of 1931. At the end of 1930, currency and bank deposits had been $53.6 billion; on June 30, 1931, they were slightly lower, at $52.9 billion. By the end of the year, they had fallen sharply to $48.3 billion. Over the entire year, the aggregate money supply fell from $73.2 billion to $68.2 billion. The sharp deflation occurred in the final quarter, as a result of the general blow to confidence caused by Britain going off gold. From the beginning of the year until the end of September, total member bank reserves fell by $107 million. The Federal Government had tried hard to inflate, raising *controlled* reserves by $195 million—largely in bills bought and bills discounted, but *uncontrolled* reserves declined by $302 million, largely due to a huge $356 million increase of money in circulation. Normally, money in circulation declines in the first part of the year, and then increases around Christmas time. The increase in the first part of this year reflected a growing loss of confidence by Americans in their banking system—caused by the bank failures abroad and the growing number of failures at home. Americans should have lost confidence ages before, for the banking institutions were hardly worthy of their trust. The inflationary attempts of the government from January to October were thus offset by the people's attempts to convert their bank deposits into legal tender. From the end of September to the end of the year, bank reserves fell at an unprecedented rate, from $2.36 billion to $1.96 billion, a drop of $400 million in three months. The Federal Reserve tried its best to continue its favorite nostrum of inflation—pumping $268 million of new controlled reserves into the banking system (the main item: an increase of $305 million in bills discounted). But the public, at home and abroad, was now calling the turn at last. From the beginning of the depression until

September, 1931, the monetary gold stock of the country had increased from $4.0 billion to $4.7 billion, as European monetary troubles induced people to send their gold to the United States. But the British crisis made men doubt the credit of the dollar for the first time, and hence by the end of December, America's monetary gold stock had fallen to $4.2 billion. The gold drain that began in September, 1931, and was to continue until July, 1932, reduced U. S. monetary gold stock from $4.7 billion to $3.6 billion. This was a testament to the gold exchange standard that Great Britain had induced Europe to adopt in the 1920's.[4] Money in circulation also continued to increase sharply, in response to public fears about the banking structure as well as to regular seasonal demands. Money in circulation therefore rose by $400 million in these three months. Hence, the will of the public caused bank reserves to decline by $400 million in the latter half of 1931, and the money supply, as a consequence, fell by over four billion dollars in the same period.

During 1930, the Federal Reserve had steadily lowered its rediscount rates: from 4½ per cent at the beginning of the year, to 2 per cent at the end, and finally down to 1½ per cent in mid-1931. When the monetary crisis came at the end of the year, the Federal Reserve raised the rediscount rate to 3½ per cent. Acceptance buying rates were similarly raised after a steady decline. The FRS has been sharply criticized by economists for its "tight money" policy in the last quarter of 1931. Actually, its policy was still inflationary on balance, since it still increased controlled reserves. And any greater degree of inflation would have endangered the gold standard itself. Actually, the Federal Reserve should have *deflated* instead of inflated, to bolster confidence in gold, and also to speed up the adjustments needed to end the depression.

The inflationary policies of the Federal Reserve were not enough for some economists, however, including the price stabilizationist and staunch ally of the late Governor Strong, Carl Snyder, statistician at the New York Federal Reserve. As early as April, 1931, Snyder organized a petition of economists to the

Federal Reserve Board urging immediate cheap money, as well as long-range credit expansion. Among the signers were: John R. Commons, Lionel D. Edie, Virgil Jordan, Harold L. Reed, James Harvey Rogers, Walter E. Spahr, and George F. Warren.[5]

THE FISCAL BURDEN OF GOVERNMENT

How did the fiscal burden of government press upon the public during 1931? The gross national product fell from $91.1 billion in 1930, to $76.3 billion in 1931. Gross private product fell from $85.8 billion to $70.9 billion; total government depredations, on the other hand, *rose* from $14.1 to $15.2 billion. Total government receipts fell from $13.5 billion to $12.4 billion (Federal receipts fell from $4.4 to $3.4 billion), but total government expenditures rose sharply, from $13.9 billion to $15.2 billion. This time, the entire rise in expenditures came in federal, rather than state and local, spending. Federal expenditures rose from $4.2 billion in 1930 to $5.5 billion in 1931—excluding government enterprises, it rose from $3.1 billion to $4.4 billion, an enormous 42 per cent increase! In short, in the midst of a great depression when people needed desperately to be relieved of governmental burdens, the dead weight of government rose from 16.4 per cent to 21.5 per cent of the gross private product (from 18.2 per cent to 24.3 per cent of the net private product). From a modest surplus in 1930, the Federal government thus ran up a huge $2.2 billion deficit in 1931. And so President Hoover, often considered to be a staunch exponent of *laissez-faire,* had amassed by far the largest peacetime deficit yet known to American history. In one year, the fiscal burden of the Federal government had increased from 5.1 per cent to 7.8 per cent, or from 5.7 per cent to 8.8 per cent of the net private product.

Of the $1.3 billion increase in Federal expenditures in 1931, by far the largest sum, $1.0 billion, was an increase in transfer payments. New public construction also increased at the same pace as the previous year, by over $60 million; grants in aid to state and local governments rose by almost $200 million. Of the one billion dollar rise in transfer payments, $900 million was an increase in "adjusted compensation benefits," largely loans to veterans.

Public Works and Wage Rates

What of Hoover's cherished programs of public works planning and maintenance of wage rates? We have noted that Hoover established an Emergency Committee for Employment in October, 1930, headed by Colonel Arthur Woods. Woods was a trustee of the Rockefeller Foundation and of Rockefeller's General Education Board. Also on the committee were industrialists Sewell Avery, William J. Bault of Metropolitan Life, the ever ubiquitous Beardsley Ruml, and economists such as Professor Joseph H. Willits, Leo Wolman, J. Douglas Brown, W. Jett Lauck, Lewis E. Meriam, and Fred C. Croxton. The Committee strongly recommended increased expenditures for public works at all levels of government. The President's Committee was one of the major forces supporting the Wagner Employment Stabilization Act of February, 1931—its Public Works Section being especially active. And, in signing the bill, Hoover gave a large amount of the credit for the measure to none other than Otto Tod Mallery.[6] The President's Committee was the main government organ dealing with employers and urging them to maintain wage rates. Writing proudly of the Committee's work, one of its members later praised its success in inducing employers to refrain from those reductions in wage rates "which had marked similar periods" of depression.[7] It is, of course, not surprising that there were very few strikes in this period. In March, Colonel Woods proudly hailed the "new view" of industry—in accepting its "responsibility toward labor." Industry, instead of cutting wage rates, was now maintaining the purchasing-power of the workers as a measure of "enlightened self-interest." The Committee persuaded ten outstanding industrial and labor leaders to give public radio talks, explaining the brave new philosophy. The Committee was also gratified to see advances in public works construction during the year.

The Employment Stabilization Act of February merely served to whet, rather than allay, the appetites of the public works agitators.[8] During the year, Senator Wagner suggested a $2 billion public works program, and Senator LaFollette urged a gigantic $5.5 billion outlay. At the end of the year 1931, thirty-one leading economists convened in New York City at a conference sponsored by William Randolph Hearst, and recommended a $5 billion public works program. It was to be financed by a bond issue. The economists emphasized that a rise in Federal public works outlay during 1931 had been offset by a decline in state and local construction, so that overall public construction was less than in the previous year. They urged a bold program, accompanied by credit expansion, and conducted in the good old spirit of a wartime emergency. Among the signers of this document were: Professors James C. Bonbright, Phillips Bradley, Paul F. Brissenden, Thomas Nixon Carver, Paul H. Douglas, Seba Eldridge, William Trufant Foster, Arthur D. Gayer, John Ise, J. E. LeRossignol, W. N. Loucks, Robert M. MacIver, George R. Taylor, Williard L. Thorp, and Norman J. Ware.[9]

We might mention here that at the very time President Hoover was sponsoring make-work schemes, he stepped in to hamper private production in another field. In May, he ordered the cessation of the leasing of Federal forests for new lumbering, thus withdrawing forest land from production and aggravating the severe depression in the lumber trade.

On the state level, Governor Franklin D. Roosevelt of New York pioneered in public works planning, setting up a Committee on the Stabilization of Industry for the Prevention of Unemployment, with Henry Bruere chairman and Paul H. Douglas, technical adviser. The Committee recommended a state planning board for public works, and work-sharing among workers. Roosevelt also called a seven-state conference at the end of January, 1931, to urge Federal and state public works: the chief adviser was Professor Leo Wolman, and others were Professors William Leiserson and Paul H. Douglas. The next few days saw a Conference on the Permanent Prevention of Unemployment, convened by the social action departments of the Catholic, Protestant, and Jewish churches. At this conference, Edward Eyre Hunt, of the President's Emergency Committee for Employment, called for public works; William T. Foster urged an increase in the money supply, John P. Frey of the A F of L called for yet higher wages as a remedy for the depression, George Soule urged socialist planning, Professor John R. Commons and John Edgerton of the NAM quarrelled over compulsory unemployment insurance, and Senator Wagner boosted his bill for public works and stabilization.

During early 1931, California set up a State Unemployment Committee to aid localities and stimulate public works, and Pennsylvania presented a planned program of public works. Maryland speeded its public works program, Massachusetts floated a bond issue for public works, and Michigan continued highway construction during the winter—normally a slack season. Michigan insisted that contractors not cut the wage rates paid to their workers. Minnesota went so far in a make-work policy on its public work programs as to stipulate that "wherever practical, and whenever the cost is substantially the same, work should be performed by hand rather than by machines in order to provide for the employment of a greater number of persons."![10]

MAINTAINING WAGE RATES

The maintenance of wage rates in the face of steadily declining prices (wholesale prices fell by 10 per cent in 1930, by 15 per cent in 1931), meant that the *real* wage rates of the employed were sharply increasing, thereby greatly aggravating the unemployment problem as time went on. Summing up the wage question at the end of 1931, Professor Leo Wolman pointed out that business leaders, as well as government, were still under the influence of the prevailing doctrine of the 1920's: that "high and rising wages were necessary to a full flow of purchasing power and, therefore, to good business." During the depression, business leaders typically continued to say: "reducing the income of labor is not a remedy for business depression, it is a direct and contributory cause"; or "in this enlightened age when it is recognized that production is dependent upon consuming power,[11] it is my judgment that large manufacturers and producers will maintain wages and salaries as being the farsighted and in the end the most constructive thing to do." [12] Until the end of 1931, most businesses and particularly the large firms, staunchly resisted wage cuts. Some small firms in textiles and coal reduced their wage rates, but the large firms in the basic steel, public utility, and construction industries "publicly announced their adherence to a policy of high wages and their unwillingness to reduce prevailing standards." Wolman concluded that "it is indeed impossible to recall any past depression of similar intensity and duration in which the wages of prosperity were maintained as long as they have been during the depression of 1930-31." [13] He noted, however, that pressures to cut wage rates were building up almost irresistibly, and that some construction labor had been able to maintain their employment by accepting *sub rosa* wage cuts. Wage cuts responding to severe losses at the end of 1931, took place secretly, for fear of the disapproval of the Hoover Administration.[14]

Secretary of the Treasury Mellon summed up the Administration's philosophy on wage rates in May, 1931:

In this country, there has been a concerted and determined effort on the part of both government and business not only to prevent any reduction in wages but to keep the maximum number of men employed, and thereby to increase consumption.

It must be remembered that the all-important factor is purchasing power, and purchasing power . . . is dependent to a great extent on the standard of living . . . that standard of living must be maintained at all costs.[15]

The Federal government also did its part by enacting the Bacon-Davis Act, requiring a maximum eight-hour day on construction of public buildings and the payment of at least the "prevailing wage" in the locality.

It is no wonder that British economist John Maynard Keynes, in a memorandum to Prime Minister Ramsay MacDonald, reporting on a visit to America in 1931, hailed the American record of maintaining wage rates.[16]

Meanwhile, several Governors (of New York, North Carolina, South Carolina, Texas, and Wyoming) went beyond the Hoover voluntary work-sharing program to urge maximum-hour legislation.

Amid the chorus of approval on the Hoover wage program there were only a few cool, dissenting voices. John Oakwood wrote in *Barron's* that the modern industrialists and labor leaders are saying, in effect, that "they intend to keep up wage levels even if they have to close the mills." This may be fine for these leaders, but not so welcome to "employees who have been deprived of their jobs by such rigid policies." Oakwood pointed out that on the free market, selling prices determine costs and not *vice versa,* and that therefore falling prices must be reflected in falling costs, else there will be unemployment and declines in investment and production. Wage rates are a basic part of production cost. Oakwood went on to stress the essential distinction between wage rates and buying power from wages. He pointed out that an individual's buying power is really "his ability to create goods or render services that have an exchange value for other goods or services," and that the worker will always tend to receive in wages the worth of his particular productive service. True purchasing power is therefore exchange power based upon production; if a good is in great demand or in short supply, its purchasing power in terms of other goods will be high; and if *vice versa* its purchasing power will be low. During the preceding boom, credit expansion had caused a rise too high to be sustained, and the propaganda about a "new era" and a divinely-ordained American Standard of Living created the idea that this standard was some sort of vested divine right of the American worker. Hugh Bancroft, publisher of *Barron's,* wrote that it was particularly necessary for wage rates to decline in the producer goods' industries in view of the great decline in prices there, and noted that real wage rates for the employed had increased, so that the employed workers were profiteering at the expense of the unemployed. Wage cuts were necessary to the restoration of effective purchasing power.[17]

By the fall of 1931, economic reality was at last beginning to force its way through the tangle of mischievous fallacies, and the severe pressures, of the Hoover program. Wage rates, at long last, were beginning to fall. The U.S. Steel Corporation, over the opposition of its President, James A. Farrell, summoned up the courage to cut wage rates in September, whereupon William Green accused U.S. Steel of violating its 1929 pledge to the President.[18] And even Henry Ford, despite his philosophic devotion to the artificial wage maintenance policy, had to cut wages in the following year.

IMMIGRATION RESTRICTIONS

Suspension of immigration also helped to keep wage rates up, and Hoover moved diligently on this front as well. In his December, 1930, message, Hoover urged Congress to enact the suspension of immigration into law, where it would be more firmly rooted than in Presidential decree. Bills to eliminate all immigration except that of relatives of American residents were criticized by Secretary of State Stimson for not going far enough. Stimson suggested instead a general 90 per cent reduction.[19] This new bill passed the House, but failed to reach a vote in the Senate.

VOLUNTARY RELIEF

Direct relief was just about the one sphere where President Hoover seemed wholeheartedly to prefer voluntary to governmental action. The previous fall, Hoover had refused to call a special session of Congress for unemployment relief, saying this was the responsibility of voluntary agencies. In fact, the voluntaryist tradition was still so strong in this field that the Red Cross opposed a bill, in early 1931, to grant it $25 million for relief. The Red Cross declared that its own funds were adequate, and its Chairman told a House Committee that such a Congressional appropriation would "to a large extent destroy voluntary giving." Many local Red Cross leaders strongly opposed all federal aid, and even all public relief generally, and so the bill, after passing the Senate, was killed in the House.[20] Many private charity organizations, philanthropists, and social workers had the same views, and the New York *Times* hailed the "voluntary spirit" as opposed to public aid.[21] A social worker, writing of this period, has said in obvious bewilderment that:

the theory that England's depression, which began before the American disaster, had in some mysterious way [sic] been connected with their unemployment insurance system (or 'dole') had been accepted by many people in this country.[22]

State and local direct relief, however, totalled $176 million in 1931, as compared to $105 million in 1930, and $71 million in 1929. The Federal Government, while not engaging in direct relief, continued to aid the farmers. In February, it appropriated $20 million for loans to assist local agricultural credit corporations and granted $2 million for loans to various farmers.

Despite his initial voluntaryism in this field, however, Hoover appointed an Emergency Committee for Employment the previous fall. He had appointed the committee reluctantly, and warned the members that unemployment was strictly a local responsibility.[23] The chairman, Colonel Woods, however, kept urging upon Hoover a highly interventionist program, including greater public works, as well as Senator Wagner's bills for public works planning and a national employment service. Woods finally resigned in April, 1931, and was replaced by Fred Croxton. In contrast to Woods, many business leaders, understanding the role of the British governmental unemployment "dole" in creating and perpetuating unemployment, attacked any idea of governmental relief. These included Henry Ford, the leaders of the National Association of Manufacturers and the Chamber of Commerce, and also former President Coolidge.

HOOVER IN THE LAST QUARTER OF 1931

How, specifically, did President Hoover rise to the challenge of crisis in the latter part of 1931? In the first place, ominous signs began to appear that he was getting ready to weaken or abandon his devotion to the principle of voluntary relief. As early as June, 1930, the Conference of Governors had petitioned Hoover for a one billion dollar emergency federal relief appropriation. Hoover did not agree, but on February 3, he declared:

I am willing to pledge myself that if the time should ever come that the voluntary agencies of the country, together with the local and state governments, are unable to find resources with which to prevent hunger and suffering in my country, I will ask aid of every resource of the Federal Government.[24]

In mid-August, Hoover abolished the old Woods-Croxton Emergency Committee for Employment, and replaced it by a larger President's Organization on Unemployment Relief. Head of the new committee was Walter S. Gifford, President of American Telephone and Telegraph Company. Others connected with the new committee were: Newton D. Baker, Bernard M. Baruch, Fred C. Croxton, John W. Davis, Pierre duPont, John Edgerton, William Green, Will Hays, Jacob Hollander, Alexander Legge, Wesley C. Mitchell, William S. Paley, Rabbi Abba Hillel Silver, Walter Teagle, William Allen White, Matthew Woll, and Owen D. Young. While Gifford was personally opposed to governmental unemployment relief, a subcommittee of the Organization on Unemployment recommended, at the end of October, encouraging everyone to buy, spurring confidence and combatting hoarding, urging banks to lend liberally and employers to spread available work, increasing public works, and transferring surplus urban labor to the farms.[25]

As early as mid-July, Hoover returned to a favorite theme: attacking short-selling, this time the wheat market. The short-selling speculators were denounced for depressing prices and destroying confidence; their unpatriotic "intent is to take a profit from the losses of other people"—a curious charge, since for every short seller there is necessarily a long buyer speculating on a rise. When the crisis came in the fall, the Stock Exchange authorities, undoubtedly influenced by Hoover's long-standing campaign against such sales, restricted short selling. These restrictions helped drive stock prices lower than they would have been otherwise, since the short-seller's profit-taking is one of the main supports for stock prices during a decline.

As soon as the crisis struck in the fall, Hoover reverted to his favorite technique of holding conferences. On September 15, he laid plans for a Conference on Home Building and Home Ownership to be held in December, to promote the widening of home ownership and to lower interest rates on second mortgages. The resolutions of the December conference originated many of the key features of later New Deal housing policy, including heavy long-term credit at low rates of interest and government aid to blighted, low-income housing.[26]

By October, as Britain left the gold standard and gold reserves dwindled, Hoover was subjected to contradictory pressures. On the one hand, Hoover recalls with distaste that he was advised by "bitter-end liquidationists" and "reactionary economists" to let "the liquidation take its course until we found bottom." On the other hand, Governor Eugene Meyer, Jr., of the Federal Reserve Board, had been agitating since summer to re-enact a form of the old War Finance Corporation for government loans to the private economy and now urged upon Hoover a special session of Congress for this purpose. The former was the type of wise advice that Hoover, devoid of *laissez-faire* principles or sound economic knowledge, was incapable of understanding. Instead, he could only worry about the immediate hardships that would arise from foreclosures, declines in security prices, and bankruptcies. Staunchly rejecting this "reactionary" advice, and yet reluctant to launch a government lending program, Hoover resolved on a "broad program of defense and offense" by mobilizing a quasi-"voluntary" lending agency to be financed by the nation's leading bankers. The first step was to call a secret conference of forty leading New York bankers and insurance executives at Secretary Mellon's apartment on October 4. Such men as Thomas W. Lamont and George Whitney of J. P. Morgan and Co., Albert H. Wiggin of Chase National Bank, and Charles E. Mitchell of National City Bank, met with Secretary Mellon, Governor Meyer, Undersecretary Mills, and Hoover. Hoover presented his plan—to create a National Credit Corporation with capitalization of $500 million to extend credit to banks in need and to permit banks to extend credit to needy industrial firms.

The banks were to finance the capital for the NCC, and the NCC would be allowed to borrow up to one billion dollars, with Federal Reserve assistance. The idea was that the strong banks would pool their resources to bail out the weak banks; with Federal help, the NCC was to rediscount bank assets not legally eligible to be rediscounted with the Federal Reserve. Insurance companies were asked not to foreclose mortgages and, in return, they would be helped by aid from the Federal Farm Loan Banks. Although both Mills and Meyer enthusiastically backed this program, the banks and the insurance companies balked at the shoring up of unsound positions. At this point, the iron fist became evident in the velvet glove of "voluntary industry-government cooperation" in the Hoover scheme of things. If the banks did not agree, Hoover threatened, he would obtain legislation to force their cooperation. The banks then agreed to set up the NCC, and the insurance companies agreed not to press foreclosure of mortgages. In return, Hoover promised that the NCC would be temporary, for the duration of the year, and that he would soon ask Congress to recreate a new and broader War Finance Corporation for emergency loans (the old WFC had lapsed in the spring of 1929), to broaden eligibility requirements for bank rediscounts with the Federal Reserve System, and to expand the Federal Farm Loan Banks.[27]

In addition, Hoover induced Paul Bestor, head of the Federal Farm Loan Board, to promise to refuse foreclosing any mortgages unless the debtor wanted to leave his farm, and the President decided he would recommend an increased appropriation of $125 million for these land banks. Hoover also induced the Federal Reserve Board to encourage banks to lend to depositors on the latter's frozen assets in bankrupt banks.

The NCC quickly aided faltering banks in South Carolina and Louisiana, and, over a three-month period, loaned $153 million to 575 banks; but this hardly stemmed the tide of weakness and failure. Strengthening Hoover's aim to establish a government lending corporation—which was soon established as the Reconstruction Finance Corporation—was the advice of Eugene Meyer, Ogden Mills, Louis Wehle, formerly counsel of the old WFC, and

Chicago banker Melvin A. Traylor. Meyer, in particular, put pressure upon the President, to the extent of preparing his own bill for Congress. Hoover was finally completely persuaded to push for an RFC by Meyer in early December.[28]

On October 7, Hoover called another White House Conference, of the leading insurance, mortgage company, and building and loan executives. He proposed to them a grandiose program— a national system of Federal mortgage discount banks, with one central bank, like the Federal Reserve System, and with the capital subscribed by the government. The regional banks would discount mortgages and the central mortgage banks would stand behind the branches; all could issue debentures to raise more capital. This system would then stand behind all the mortgages of savings banks, insurance companies, and commercial banks. This grandiose statist and inflationist scheme was flatly rejected by the insurance companies and by most of the savings banks, although it was supported by the building and loan associations. Hoover therefore had to modify his plan, and to settle for a Home Loan Bank system, which Congress would later ratify, as a compulsory central mortgage bank for the building and loan (now "saving and loan") associations, and a voluntary bank for savings banks and insurance companies.

By early October, therefore, the forthcoming Hoover New Deal program for 1932 was already clear: the major measure, a new government corporation to make loans to business—a Reconstruction Finance Corporation to replace the stopgap, largely banker-financed National Credit Corporation; the broadening of rediscount eligibility for the Federal Reserve; the creation of a Home Loan Bank System to discount mortgages; and an expansion of the Federal Farm Loan Bank System.

On October 27, a Presidential committee of business, agricultural, and labor leaders, as well as economists, endorsed the prospective Hoover program, and called also for expansion of credit, spreading of work, and especially public works. These included Leonard P. Ayres, Fred C. Croxton, William Green, Alvanley Johnston, and Wesley C. Mitchell. On December 21, however, a highly unusual event occurred; another Presidential Committee on Public Works condemned further public works, urged a balanced budget, and readjustment to new conditions. This committee included Leonard P. Ayres, Jacob Hollander, Matthew Woll, and others.

THE SPREAD OF COLLECTIVIST IDEAS IN THE BUSINESS WORLD

Meanwhile, strange collectivist plans for ending the depression were brewing in the business world. In September, Gerard Swope, head of General Electric, far surpassed the radicalism of his old public-works proposal by presenting the Swope Plan to a convention of the National Electrical Manufacturers Association. The Plan, which garnered a great deal of publicity, amounted to a call for compulsory cartellization of American business—an imitation of fascism and an anticipation of the NRA. Every industry was to be forcibly mobilized into trade associations, under Federal control, to regulate and stabilize prices and production, and to prescribe trade practices. Overall, the Federal Government, aided by a joint administration of management and employees representing the nation's industry, would "coordinate production and consumption." [29] To its grave discredit, the U. S. Chamber of Commerce endorsed this socialistic plan in December by a large majority, as a means of employing Federal coercion to restrict production and raise prices. Leading the march for approval was the new President of the U. S. Chamber, Henry I. Harriman, of the New England Power Company. Harriman wrote, in his report of the Chamber's Committee on the Continuity of Business and Employment, that "We have left the period of extreme individualism. . . . Business prosperity and employment will be best maintained by an intelligently planned business structure." With business organized through trade associations and headed by a National Economic Council, any dissenting businessmen would be "treated like any maverick. . . . They'll be roped, and branded, and made to run with the herd." [30] The president of the National Association of Manufacturers wanted to go beyond the Swope Plan to forcibly include firms employing less than fifty workers.

Also supporting the Swope Plan were Swope's friend Owen D.

Young, Chairman of the Board of General Electric, President Nicholas Murray Butler of Columbia University, who had been thinking along the same lines, Royal W. France of Rollins College, Karl T. Compton, the leftist Stuart Chase, and Charles F. Abbott of the American Institute of Steel Construction. Abbott called the Swope Plan:

> . . . a measure of public safety. . . . We cannot have in this country much longer irresponsible, ill-informed, stubborn and non-cooperating individualism. . . . The Swope Plan, seen in its ultimate simplicity, is not one whit different in principle from the traffic cop . . . an industrial traffic officer . . . ! Constitutional liberty to do as you please is 'violated' by the traffic regulations—but . . . they become binding even upon the blustering individual who claims the right to do as he pleases.[31]

Furthermore, former Secretary of the Treasury William G. McAdoo proposed a Federal "Peace Industries Board" to adjust national production to consumption, and Senator LaFollette organized a subcommittee to investigate the possibility of a National Economic Council to stabilize the economy—and Swope was a leading witness. H. S. Person, managing director of the Taylor Society, displayed the naiveté of the technocrat when he said, in a puzzled way: "we expect the greatest enterprise of all, industry as a whole, to get along without a definite plan." [32] The historian Charles A. Beard denounced *laissez-faire* and called for a Five Year Plan of industrial cartels headed by a National Economic Council. And the popular philosopher Will Durant called for national planning by a national economic board, ruling over boards for each industry. Supreme Court Justice Louis Brandeis suggested complete state control of industry on the legal ground of public convenience and necessity.[33]

Other business leaders were thinking along similar lines. Benjamin A. Javits had developed a similar plan in 1930. Dean Wallace B. Donham, of the Harvard School of Business, had the gall to cite the Soviet Union as showing the value and necessity of a "general plan for American business." [34] Paul M. Mazur, of Lehman Brothers, referred to the "tragic lack of planning" of the capitalist system. Rudolph Spreckels, president of the Sugar Institute, urged governmental allocation to each company of its proper share of market demand. Ralph E. Flanders, of the Jones and Lamson Machine Company, called for fulfillment of the "vision" of the new stage of governmental planning of the nation's economy. And Henry S. Dennison, president of the Dennison Manufacturing Co., developed his own Five Year Plan for a national cartel of organized trade associations.

One of the most important supporters of the cartellization idea was Bernard M. Baruch, Wall St. financier. Baruch was influential not only in the Democratic Party, but in the Republican as well, as witness the high posts the Hoover Administration accorded to Baruch's proteges, Alexander Legge and Eugene Meyer, Jr. As early as 1925, Baruch, inspired by his stint as chief economic mobilizer in World War I, conceived of an economy of trusts, regulated and run by a Federal Commission, and in the spring of 1930, Baruch proposed to the Boston Chamber of Commerce a "Supreme Court of Industry." McAdoo was Baruch's oldest friend in government; and Swope's younger brother, Herbert Bayard Swope, was Baruch's closest confidant.[35]

Collectivist ideas had apparently been fermenting in parts of the business world ever since the depression began, as witness the reaction of a writer in a prominent business magazine to the White House Conferences for concerted maintenance of wage rates at the end of 1929. Hailing the conference as Hoover's "splendid adventure in economic democracy," the writer called for national economic planning through nationwide trade associations and suggested coordination of the economy by "collective reason."[36]

So far had the business world gone, that a report for the left-wing National Progressive Conference of 1931, praised the Swope plan, albeit suggesting a less "pro-business" and more egalitarian twist to the scheme of centralized planning.[37] The entire collectivist movement in business was well summed up by one of Franklin D. Roosevelt's more extreme Brain Trusters, Rexford Guy Tugwell, when he wrote of Harriman, Swope, and the rest that they "believed that more organization was needed in American industry, more planning, more attempt to estimate needs and set production goals. From this they argued that . . . investment to secure the needed investment could be encouraged. They did not stress the reverse, that other investments ought to be prohibited, but that was inherent in the argument. All this was, so far, in accord with the thought of the collectivists in Franklin's Brains Trust who tended to think of the economy in organic terms." [38]

In short, Virgil Jordan, economist for the National Industrial Conference Board, was not far from the mark when he wrote that businessmen were ready for an "economic Mussolini."

Despite all the pressure upon him, Herbert Hoover staunchly refused to endorse the Swope Plan or anything like it, and sturdily attacked the plan as fascism.[39] His speeches, however, began to be peppered with such ominous terms as "cooperation" and "elimination of waste." In the slide toward intervention, meanwhile, the Chamber of Commerce also called for public works and Federal relief, and a joint committee of the National Association of Manufacturers and the National Industrial Council urged public works and regulation of the purchasing power of the dollar.

The American Federation of Labor also adopted a radical Emergency Unemployment Program in October. As was to be expected, it hailed the Hoover policy of keeping wage rates high and cutting hours, and also advanced its own unionized version of fascism. It proposed that the government force employers to hire workers; "Industries and employers should therefore be given quotas of jobs to be furnished, according to their ability to provide work. The allocation of these quotas should be the task of a central board, representing the Government and all industrial groups." This would ensure "effective organization of the labor market." In short, the A F of L wanted to have an equal share in running a Swope Plan for industry.[40] A further typically union scheme was to compel restriction of the labor supply, thus raising wage rates for the remainder of the labor force. It is a curious "cure" for unemployment, however, to compel large groups of people to remain unemployed. Thus, the A F of L adopted as a slogan: "Keep young persons in school to avoid their competing for jobs," and urged employers to fire married women with working husbands; "Married women whose husbands have permanent positions which carry reasonable incomes should be discriminated against in the hiring of employees." It is a measure of how far we have travelled in hypocrisy that unions would not today publicly advocate these policies for such frankly ruthless reasons; instead, they would undoubtedly be cloaked in pieties about the glories of education and home life.

The A F of L also endorsed compulsory unemployment insurance at this convention, in contrast to William Green's attack on the government dole at the 1930 convention as turning the worker into a "ward of the State." The railroad union leaders bellicosely threatened Hoover with "disorder" if he did not act to provide employment and relief.

Particularly enthusiastic among union leaders for the new drive for government "planning" were John L. Lewis, of the United Mine Workers, and Sidney Hillman, of the Amalgamated Clothing Workers. Both called for a national economic council for planning to include labor and management representatives. Schlesinger is certainly correct when he says that "Lewis and Hillman, in the end, differed little from Gerard Swope and Henry I. Harriman." [41]

The AF of L also praised the Hoover Administration for carrying out the following objectives during 1930-1931: maintaining wage rates on public buildings, reduction of hours in government employ without a reduction in pay, public works planning, raising of wages for some government employees, increased appropriation for border immigration patrol (thus "relieving unemployment" by preventing Mexicans from coming here to improve their condition), appropriations for naval ships, and requiring all new naval work to be done in navy yards and arsenals instead of on private contract.

Meanwhile, the states moved in to compel cartellization and virtual socialization of the crude oil industry. The oil-producing states enacted laws to enable governmental commissions to fix the maximum amount of oil produced, and this system is basically still in effect. The state laws were enacted under the public guise of "conservation," which is a pat excuse for any compulsory monopoly or cartel in a natural resource. In 1931, new oil discoveries in East Texas drove the price of crude down from one dollar a barrel to two and one-half cents a barrel, and cartellists and conservationists set up a hue and cry. The lead was taken by Oklahoma's Governor "Alfalfa Bill" Murray, who ordered a general shutdown of the crude oil industry until the price of oil should rise to the "minimum fair price" of one dollar a barrel. When some producers proved recalcitrant, Murray sent the Oklahoma National Guard into the oil fields to enforce his decree with bayonets. Soon Texas followed suit, and the leading oil states of California, Texas, Kansas, and Oklahoma passed "conservation" and proration laws to fix production ceilings in a more orderly manner. Two emergency sessions of the Texas legislature were called to broaden the oil-regulating powers of the Texas Railroad Commission, after it had suffered unfavorable court injunctions.

The oil states also organized an Oil States Advisory Committee to decide on quotas—soon to become an interstate compact— and a "Voluntary Committee" of the Federal Oil Conservation Board aided in the effort. Some well owners found that they could evade the troops and decrees and smuggle "hot oil" out of the state, but this "loophole" of freedom was finally closed by the New Deal. To bolster the oil cartel, the Federal budget of 1932 included a tariff on imported crude oil and on petroleum products. This made the domestic cartel more effective, but it also reduced American exports of petroleum.[42] It is of course curious to find a restriction on *imports* imposed as part of a domestic resource *conservation* program, but we find the same phenomena today. If conservation were really the goal, then surely imports would have been encouraged to ease demands on domestic oil.

Let it not be thought that Hoover was idle in this movement. Even before the depression, he was considering coercive restrictions on oil production. The President cancelled permits to drill for oil in large parts of the public domain, and he and Secretary of Interior Ray Lyman Wilbur were in large part responsible for the new state "conservation" laws. Hoover and Wilbur also pressured private oil operators near the public domain into agreements to restrict oil production.[43]

As 1931 drew to a close and another Congressional session drew near, the country and indeed the world were in the midst of an authentic crisis atmosphere—a crisis of policy and of ideology. The depression, so long in effect, was now rapidly growing worse, in America and throughout the world. The stage was set for the "Hoover New Deal" of 1932.

11

The Hoover New Deal of 1932

President Hoover came to the legislative session of 1932 in an atmosphere of crisis, ready for drastic measures. In his annual message to Congress, on December 8, 1931, Hoover first reviewed his own accomplishments of the past two years:

Many undertakings have been organized and forwarded during the past year to meet the new and changing emergencies which have constantly confronted us . . . to cushion the violence of liquidation in industry and commerce, thus giving time for orderly readjustment of costs, inventories, and credits without panic and widespread bankruptcies.

Measures such as Federal and state and local public works, work-sharing, maintaining wage rates ("a large majority have maintained wages at high levels" as before), curtailment of immigration, and the National Credit Corporation, Hoover declared, have served these purposes and fostered recovery. Now, Hoover urged more drastic action, and he presented the following program:

(1) Establish a Reconstruction Finance Corporation, which would use Treasury funds to lend to banks, industries, agricultural credit agencies and local governments
(2) Broaden the eligibility requirement for discounting at the Fed
(3) Create a Home Loan Bank discount system to revive construction and employment—a measure which had been warmly endorsed by a National Housing Conference recently convened by Hoover for that purpose
(4) Expand government aid to Federal Land Banks

(5) Set up a Public Works Administration to coordinate and expand Federal public works
(6) Legalize Hoover's order restricting immigration
(7) Do something to weaken "destructive competition" (i.e., competition) in natural resource use
(8) Grant direct loans of $300 million to States for relief
(9) Reform the bankruptcy laws (i.e., weaken protection for the creditor).

Hoover also displayed anxiety to "protect railroads from unregulated competition," and to bolster the bankrupt railroad lines. In addition, he called for sharing-the-work programs to save several millions from unemployment.

THE TAX INCREASE

With a $2 billion deficit during annual year 1931, Hoover felt that he had to do something in the next year to combat it. Deficit spending is indeed an evil, but a balanced budget is not necessarily a good, particularly when the "balance" is obtained by increasing revenue and expenditures. If he wanted to balance the budget, Hoover had two choices open to him: to reduce expenditures, and thereby relieve the economy of some of the aggravated burden of government, or to increase that burden further by raising taxes. He chose the latter course. In his swan song as Secretary of Treasury, Andrew Mellon advocated, in December, 1931, drastic increases of taxes: including personal income taxes, estate taxes, sales taxes, and postal rates. Obedient to the lines charted by Mellon and Hoover, Congress passed, in the Revenue Act of 1932, one of the greatest increases in taxation ever enacted in the United States in peacetime. The range of tax increases was enormous: many wartime excise taxes were revived, sales taxes were imposed on gasoline, tires, autos, electric energy, malt, toiletries, furs, jewelry, and other articles; admission and stock transfer taxes were increased; new taxes were levied on bank checks, bond transfers, telephone, telegraph, and radio messages; and the personal income tax was raised drastically as follows: the normal rate was increased from a range of 1½ per cent - 5 per cent, to 4 per cent -

8 per cent; personal exemptions were sharply reduced, and an earned credit of 25 per cent eliminated; and surtaxes were raised enormously, from a maximum of 25 per cent to 63 per cent on the highest incomes. Furthermore, the corporate income tax was increased from 12 per cent to 13¾ per cent, and an exemption for small corporations eliminated; the estate tax was doubled, and the exemption floor halved; and the gift tax, which had been eliminated, was restored, and graduated up to 33⅓ per cent.[1] Hoover also tried his best to impose on the public a manufacturers' sales tax, but this was successfully opposed by the manufacturers. We might mention here that for Hoover the great increase in the estate tax was moral *in itself*, in addition to its alleged usefulness as a fiscal measure. The estate tax, he declared, is "one of the most economically and socially desirable—or even necessary of all taxes." He hinted darkly of the "evils of inherited economic power," of "cunning lawyers," and "obnoxious" playboys: there was no hint that he realized that a tax on inherited wealth is a tax on the property of the able or the descendants of the able, who must maintain that ability in order to preserve their fortunes; there was not the slightest understanding that a pure tax on capital such as the estate tax was the worst possible tax from the point of view of getting rid of the depression.

The raising of postal rates burdened the public further and helped swell the revenues of a compulsory governmental monopoly. The letter rates were raised from 2¢ to 3¢ despite the fact that the Post Office's own accounting system already showed a large profit on first class mail. Postage on publishers' second class mail was raised by about one-third, and parcel post rates on small parcels were increased by 25% (though rates on large parcels were lowered slightly).[2]

One of the most cogent critiques of Hoover's astoundingly wrong-headed program was delivered by the St. Louis Chamber of Commerce. Alarmed by the incessant call for higher taxes, the Chamber declared: "When governments seek to maintain the high levels of taxation they reached in good times in these days of seriously impaired income the impending specter of higher taxes constitutes one of the chief deterrents of business recovery."

The taxpayers, it insisted, should obtain a reduction of both taxes and government expenditures.[3] And the Atlanta *Constitution* called the 1932 tax act "the most vicious tax bill . . . ever saddled on the country in time of peace." [4]

EXPENDITURES VERSUS ECONOMY

Despite the drastic increase in tax rates, total Federal revenue for 1932 declined, because of the deepened depression—itself partly caused by the increase in tax rates. Total Federal receipts, excluding government enterprises, declined from $2.2 billion in 1931 to $1.9 billion in 1932; including government enterprises, Federal receipts fell from $3.4 billion to $3.0 billion. Total government receipts fell from $12.4 billion to $11.5 billion including government enterprises, from $10.3 billion to $9.5 billion excluding them. As a result, the huge Federal deficit continued despite a drop in government expenditures in 1932: Federal expenditures falling from $4.4 billion to $3.4 billion (from $5.5 billion to $4.4 billion if we include government enterprises), and aggregate government expenditures falling from $13.3 billion to $11.4 billion (from $15.2 billion to $13.2 billion if we include government enterprises). Of the $1.7 billion in total government deficit, the bulk of it—$1.4 billion—was in the Federal government account.

The decline of $1 billion in Federal expenditures over the year consisted of an $800 million decline in transfer payments (veterans' loans), and a $200 million drop in grants to state and local governments. The drop in state and local government expenditures of $900 million in 1932, consisted largely of an $800 million decline in new construction. The state and local governments, which differ from the Federal government in not being able to print new money or new bank deposits by selling bonds to a controlled banking system, found by 1932 that their financial condition was too grave to permit continued public works on such a large scale. The state and local governments were therefore forced to cut back their expenditures to near the level of their dwindling receipts.

What did all this mean for the fiscal burden of government on the economy? While the absolute amount of Federal depredations fell from $5.5 to $4.4 billion in 1932, and state and local burdens fell from $9.7 to $8.8 billion, GNP, and gross private product, declined far more drastically. GNP fell from $76.3 billion in 1931 to $58.5 billion in 1932, while GPP fell from $70.9 billion to $53.3 billion. Net private product fell from $62.7 to $45.7 billion. Hence, the percentage of Federal depredation on the gross private product *rose* from 7.8 per cent in 1931 to 8.3 per cent in 1932, and the percentage depredation of state and local governments rose from 13.7 per cent to 16.5 per cent. All in all, total fiscal burden of government on the gross private product rose from 21.5 per cent to 24.8 per cent; total burden on the net private product rose from 24.3 per cent to 28.9 per cent.

One of the most ominous projects for Federal spending during 1932 was a Congressional move for a huge $2 billion veterans bonus, to be financed by an issue of new currency. It was, indeed, the struggle over, and final defeat of, this program in the Senate in June that did most to defeat a general clamor for much larger government spending. The agitation for a veterans' bonus gave rise to a National Economy Committee, organized by Colonel Archibald R. Roosevelt, to combat the proposal. The Committee later became the National Economy League, which grew active throughout the nation by mid-1932. Chairman of the League was Admiral Richard E. Byrd, who abandoned a polar expedition to take active part, and secretary was Captain Charles M. Mills. Begun by Colonel Roosevelt and Grenville Clark, the League acquired over 60,000 members in forty-five states. The League's objective was to cut the costs of government: "We will not get back again to prosperity until high taxes are reduced." Taxation, it declared, now cripples industry, and hurts rich and poor alike. Unfortunately, the League was not willing to suggest specific areas of reduced spending—aside from veterans' aid. Captain Mills simply assumed that public works could not be reduced, since they were needed to relieve unemployment, and national defense could not be reduced—despite the fact that no country was poised to attack the United Sates.[5]

Other economizers were more stringent, and urged Hoover to

balance the budget by reducing expenditures by $2 billion, rather than by raising taxes. These included the redoubtable Rep. James M. Beck of Pennsylvania, formerly Solicitor General of the United States.[6] But Hoover rejected the pleas of numerous businessmen and bankers, many of them adherents of the Democratic Party. To one protesting businessman who urged him to reduce expenses by $2 billion, Hoover answered with the typical hysteria of the bureaucrat:

Your thesis is that the government expenses can be reduced by $2 billion—the amount of the tax decrease. This is . . . wholly impossible. It would mean we must give up the postal service, the Merchant Marine, protection of life and property and public health. We would have to turn 40,000 prisoners loose in this country; we would have to stop the maintenance of rivers and harbors; we would have to stop all construction work going on in aid of unemployment; it would mean abolishment [*sic*] of the Army and Navy. In other words it means complete chaos.

Let us waive the important question whether many of these functions are really so vital, or whether they may only be performed by the compulsory monopoly of the Federal Government. Would a $2 billion budget cut have led to these effects? Taking the *fiscal* year 1932, the Federal expenditures (including government enterprises) of $4.8 billion equalled $59.50 per person in a "real" index based on the wholesale price level of 1926. During the 1920's, the Federal Government spent a real amount of about $25 per person, and from 1890-1916, spent approximately $10 per person. This means that the Federal budget could have been cut by $2.8 billion to maintain the services provided during the 1920's, and by $4.0 billion to maintain the services provided from 1890-1916, *not* a period that lacked protection, post offices, etc.[7]

While the economizers urged Hoover to cut expenditures and taxation, radicals urged a stepped-up program of government spending. William Trufant Foster, in a speech before the Taylor Society in the spring of 1932, called for "collectively" expanding currency and credit to restore the commodity price level of 1928. Virgil Jordan, economist for *Business Week*, urged expansion of public spending: "Just as we saved our way into depression, we must squander our way out of it." *This* piece of advice was delivered before the annual banquet of the Pennsylvania Chamber of Commerce. Also calling for increased spending and "cyclical" rather than annual budget balancing were such economists as Paul H. Douglas, R. M. Haig, Simeon E. Leland, Harry A. Millis, Henry C. Simons, Sumner H. Slichter, and Jacob Viner.[8]

PUBLIC WORKS AGITATION

While expenditures were levelling out, agitators for ever-greater public works redoubled their propaganda during the spring of 1932. Virgil Jordan, economist for *Business Week,* called for expanded public works, deficits, and pump-priming. W. T. Foster, Otto Tod Mallery, and David Cushman Coyle clamored for public works. Senators LaFollette and Wagner each sponsored huge public works bills, and they were supported by numerous economists and engineers. Senator Wagner sent a questionnaire on his $1 billion public works plan to numerous economists, and drew only a few dissents in the chorus of approval.[9]

Felix Frankfurter thought that the program should go even further. Several economists, however, advised caution or expressed outright dissent, thus causing at least a welcome split in what had looked to laymen to be a solid phalanx of economists favoring a huge public works program. John Maurice Clark wrote that he was not sure, and was worried about the effect on public confidence and the weakening of bank credit that would ensue. Also worried about confidence and cautiously opposed were Professors Z. C. Dickinson, Henry B. Gardner, and Alvin H. Hansen. Firmer in opposition was Jacob Hollander of Johns Hopkins, who had signed the adverse report of the President's Committee a few months earlier. Hollander expressed concern over the credit structure and continued deficits. Edwin F. Gay of Harvard believed it imperative to economize and balance the budget.

Willford I. King, of New York University, warned that wages must fall in proportion to the decline of commodity prices, in order to eliminate unemployment. He cogently pointed out that government employment at existing high wage rates would perpetuate the unemployment problem. Unfortunately, however, King suggested monetary inflation to restore the price level to 1926 levels. M. B. Hammond, of Ohio State University, delivered an excellent critique of the Wagner bill. The proper course, he pointed out, was to economize, balance the budget, preserve the gold standard, and allow the needed price readjustments to take place:

. . . conditions will be stabilized as soon as prices in certain lines have become adjusted to price reductions which have already taken place in other lines. Large appropriations for public works would hinder such an adjustment and consequently would be unfavorable to efforts which private industry will otherwise make to resume operations.

One of the best comments on the proposal was delivered by William A. Berridge, economist for the Metropolitan Life Insurance Company. The bond issue for public works, he wrote, "would encroach seriously, and perhaps dangerously upon the supply of capital funds that private enterprise will need in order to help the country climb out of depression again." The public works projects, he added, "would undoubtedly freeze up the country's labor and capital in projects that would not contribute correspondingly to the productiveness and welfare of society in general."

Further agitation for public works was carried on by the magazine *American City*, which called for a six year program of low-interest loans to public works, and by Colonel John P. Hogan, who proposed a Productive Research Work Corporation, to be worth $1.5 billion, for loans to local governments for public works.[10]

Hogan's scheme was endorsed by the Construction League of America, and by the Associated General Contractors of America, both naturally eager for government subsidies to the construction industry. In June, the construction industry sponsored a National Committee for Trade Recovery, to promote public works. Other zealots were J. Cheever Cowden, a New York investment banker, who proposed an annual $4-5 billion public works program, Colonel Malcolm C. Rorty, who wanted $1 billion spent per year, Owen D. Young, Alfred E. Smith, and Franklin D. Roosevelt. William Randolph Hearst suggested a $5.5 billion Property Bond issue for a Federal public works program, and this was endorsed, in January, 1932, by thirty-one economists, including Thomas Nixon Carver, Paul H. Douglas, William Trufant Foster, Robert M. MacIver, and J. E. LeRossignol.[11]

By the summer of 1932, three books had appeared that would form the bellwether of the Roosevelt New Deal. These called for heavy government spending, especially on public works, as well as for central planning of the economy; they were Stuart Chase's *The New Deal*, David Cushman Coyle's *The Irrepressible Conflict; Business vs. Finance,* and George Soule's *A Planned Society*. Their public works suggestions were endorsed by the *New Republic* and the American Federation of Labor. The U.S. Conference of Mayors urged a $5 billion public works program, and the avowed Socialists Norman Thomas and Morris Hillquit topped everyone with a suggested $12 billion bond issue, one half to go for public works, and the other half for direct relief.

In the meanwhile, however, President Hoover himself was beginning to have doubts about one of his favorite policies: public works. In a conference at the end of February, Hoover admitted that his public works program, which had nearly doubled Federal construction since the start of the depression, had failed. It was very expensive, costing over $1200 per family aided, it was unavailable to the needy in remote regions and to those who were unable to perform such labor, which was, after all, unskilled made-work. Hoover now was coming to favor more Federal grants-in-aid to states *in lieu* of more Federal public works. By May, Hoover had openly reversed his earlier position, and now opposed any further extension of non-self-liquidating public works. As a result, Federal public works only increased by $60 million in 1932, to reach the $333 million mark. Experience had led the President to curtail his public works experiment, and partially to renounce views that he had championed for over a decade. Public works was not to come really to the fore again until the Roosevelt Administration.[12]

Despite this reversal, Hoover continued to insist on the merits of "self-liquidating" public works, and induced the RFC to lend abundantly for public dams, toll bridges, and slum clearance. In fact, Hoover still recalls with pride that he personally induced state and local governments to expand their public works programs by $1.5 billion during the depression. He still points out proudly that the aggregate public works of the four years of his Administration was greater than the public works in the entire previous thirty years, and he still takes credit for launching, in this period, Jones Beach, the San Francisco Bay Bridge, the Los Angeles Aqueduct, and Boulder Dam. He also signed a treaty with Canada, in July, 1932, to build a joint governmental St. Lawrence Seaway, but the Senate of that era wisely refused to approve this boondoggle and subsidy to one form of water transportation.

THE RFC

On all other aspects of the Hoover New Deal, the President blossomed rather than faltered. The most important plank in his program—the RFC—was passed hurriedly in January by the Congress.[13] The RFC was provided with government capital totalling $500 million, and was empowered to issue further debentures up to $1.5 billion. Hoover asked none other than Bernard Baruch to head the RFC, but Baruch declined. At that point, Hoover turned to name as Chairman one of his most socialistic advisers, the one who originally suggested the RFC to Hoover, Eugene Meyer, Jr., an old friend of Baruch's.[14] For the first five months of its life, the lending activities of the RFC lay shrouded in secrecy, and only determined action by the Democratic Congress finally forced the agency to make periodic public reports, beginning at the end of August. The bureaucratic excuse was that RFC loans should, like bank loans or previous NCC loans, remain confidential, lest public confidence in the aided bank or business firm be weakened. But the point is that, since the RFC was designed to lend money to unsound organizations about to fail, they *were* weak and the public *deserved* to lose confidence, and the sooner the better. Furthermore, since the taxpayers pay for government and are supposed to be its "owners," there is no excuse for governmental representatives to keep secrets from their own principals. In a democracy, secrecy is particularly culpable: for how can the people possibly make intelligent decisions if the facts are withheld from them by the government?

During the first five months of operation, from February to June, the RFC made $1 billion worth of loans, of which 80 per cent was lent to banks and railroads, and about 60 per cent to banks. The Republican claim that the RFC loans were not at all political rings pretty hollow in light of the facts. Thus, General Charles Dawes resigned as President of the RFC on June 7. Less than three weeks later, the Chicago bank which he headed, the Central Republic Bank and Trust Co., received an RFC loan of $90 million even though the bank's total deposits were only $95 million! That General Dawes resigned and then promptly asked for and received a huge loan for his own bank, certainly appears to be mulcting of the taxpayers by political collusion.[15] In addition, the RFC granted a $14 million loan to the Union Trust Company of Cleveland; chairman of the board of this bank was none other than Joseph R. Nutt, treasurer of the Republican National Committee.

The successor to Dawes as head of the RFC was the Hon. Atlee Pomerene, whose great contribution to economic wisdom was his pronouncement that he would like to compel all merchants to increase their purchases by 33 per cent. There was the road to recovery! Under Pomerene's aegis, the FRC promptly authorized a $12.3 million loan to the Guardian Trust Co., of Cleveland, of which Pomerene was a director. Another loan of $7.4 million was made to the Baltimore Trust Company, the vice-chairman of which was the influential Republican Senator Phillips L. Goldsborough. A loan of $13.0 million was granted to the Union Guardian Trust Company of Detroit, a director of which was the Secretary of Commerce, Roy D. Chapin.

Some $264 million were loaned to railroads during the five months of secrecy. The theory was that railroad securities must be protected, since many were held by savings banks and insurance companies, alleged agents of the small investor. Of the $187 million of loans that have been traced, $37 million were for the purpose of making improvements, and $150 million to repay debts. One of the first loans, for example, was a $5.75 million grant to the Missouri Pacific to repay its debt to J. P. Morgan and Co. A total of $11 million was loaned to the Van Sweringen railroads (including the Missouri Pacific) to repay bank loans. $8 million were loaned to the Baltimore and Ohio to repay a debt to Kuhn, Loeb and Company. All in all, $44 million were granted to the railroads by the RFC in order to repay bank loans. One of the main enthusiasts for this policy was Eugene Meyer, on the grounds of "promoting recovery," and, frankly, "putting more money into the banks." But this "promotion of recovery" really meant that the taxpayers were expropriated, and their money transferred by coercion to a few banks, notably J. P. Morgan and Co., and Kuhn, Loeb and Co. The extent of Meyer's humanitarianism in this affair may be gauged from the fact that his brother-in-law, George Blumenthal, was a member of J. P. Morgan and Co., and that Meyer had also served as a liaison officer between the Morgan firm and the French government. In the case of the Missouri Pacific, the RFC granted the loan despite an adverse warning by a minority of the Interstate Commerce Commission, and, as soon as the line had repaid its debt to Morgan, the Missouri Pacific was gently allowed to go into bankruptcy.[16]

John T. Flynn, in a caustic article on the RFC, pointed out correctly that such loans could only prolong the depression:

prices must come down to bring goods closer to the size of the available income . . . income itself must be freed for purchasing by the extinguishment of excessive debts. . . . Any attempt to hold up prices or to save the weaker debtors necessarily prolongs the depression.

Flynn also firmly pointed out that the best way to relieve the railroads, shaky and hobbled by debt, was to go into the "inevitable curative process" of receivership:

The quicker the correction comes, the quicker the regeneration of the road will come. . . . Instead of permitting the correction of the fatal flaw [the heavy bond load], the RFC has actually added to the bond load

of the railroads.[17]

Despite the speedy enactment of the RFC, Hoover complained that the Democratic Congress had delayed its passage by six weeks, allowing securities to be depressed for this length of time below their "true worth"—whatever that may be. Hoover's chief complaint was that Congress did not permit the RFC to lend directly to industry, to agriculture, or to government for public works. Congress, in short, did not permit the RFC to loan widely and recklessly enough.

At last, however, Hoover had his way, and Congress agreed to transform the RFC from a generally *defensive* agency aiding banks and railroads in debt, to a bold "positive" institution, making capital loans for new construction. This amendment, of July 21—the Emergency Relief and Construction Act of 1932—increased the RFC's authorized total capital from $2 billion to $3.8 billion, and permitted loans to states or cities for relief and work relief, for self-liquidating construction projects, and for financing sales of agricultural surpluses abroad, orderly marketing in agriculture, and agricultural credit corporations.[18] In a retrospective slap at General Dawes, loans were now forbidden to any bank, of which a director or officer was a member of the RFC board. In a later amendment, the RFC was ordered to allocate $25 million of its funds to the Treasury to buy the stock of the twelve newly-created Federal Home Loan Banks.

Over the entire year 1932, the RFC extended credits totaling $2.3 billion, and advanced an actual $1.6 billion in cash. Of the year's advances, 52 per cent were loaned to banks, 17 per cent to railroads (of which over half went to repay debts to banks), and 9 per cent to agriculture. In the agricultural field, the RFC established regional agricultural credit corporations, and advanced them $1.4 million, which authorizing credits of $55 million by the end of the year. The RFC was particularly active in cotton loans. And although the American Engineering Council hopefully suggested a shelf of self-liquidating public works projects totalling $1 billion (mainly water-supply and irrigation systems), the RFC only authorized $147 million, and advanced $16 million, for such projects during 1932.

GOVERNMENTAL RELIEF

If Hoover eagerly embraced the statism of the RFC, he gave ground but grudgingly on one issue where he had championed the voluntary approach: direct relief. Governor Franklin D. Roosevelt of New York led the way for state relief programs in the winter of 1931-1932, and he induced New York to establish the first state relief authority: the Temporary Emergency Relief Administration, equipped with $25 million.[19] Other states followed this lead, and Senators Costigan and LaFollette introduced a bill for a $500 million federal relief program.[20] The bill was defeated, but, with depression deepening and a Presidential election approaching, the Administration all but surrendered, passing the Emergency Relief and Construction Act of July, 1932 —the nation's first Federal relief legislation.[21] The bill did not go nearly as far as the agitators desired, extending loans for state relief rather than direct grants to states, but this was a trivial difference. The loans to the states were to be made by the RFC at 3 per cent on the basis of "need" as requested by the respective governors. The RFC was authorized to lend up to $300 million for this purpose. Grants were quickly made to Alabama, Georgia, Illinois, Montana, North Dakota, Ohio, Utah, Louisiana, and Oregon. The RFC hired a staff of social workers, headed by Fred Croxton, to administer the program.

The states, too, expanded their relief programs. While total state expenditures for emergency relief was $547 thousand in 1930-1931, they totalled $57 million in 1931-1932, and $90 million in fiscal year 1933. New York, New Jersey, and Pennsylvania led in relief expenditures, Pennsylvania financing much of its aid by a newly-imposed sales tax. All in all, total public relief in 120 of the nation's leading urban areas amounted to $33 million in 1929, $173 million in 1931, and $308 million in 1932.[22]

THE INFLATION PROGRAM

One thing Hoover was not reticent about: launching a huge inflationist program. First, the Administration cleared the path for the program by passing the Glass-Steagall Act in February, which (a) greatly broadened the assets eligible for rediscounts with the Fed, and (b) permitted the Federal Reserve to use government bonds as collateral for its notes, in addition to commercial paper.[23] The way was now cleared for a huge program of inflating reserves and engineering cheap money once again. Furthermore, Eugene Meyer, Jr. was now Governor of the Federal Reserve Board, and Ogden Mills had replaced the more conservative Andrew Mellon as Secretary of the Treasury. At the end of February, 1932, total bank reserves had fallen to $1.85 billion. At that point, the FRS launched a gigantic program of purchasing U.S. government securities. By the end of 1932, total reserves had been raised to $2.51 billion. This enormous increase of $660 million in reserves in less than a year is unprecedented in the previous history of the System. If the banks had kept loaned-up, the money supply of the nation would have increased by approximately $8 billion. Instead, the money supply fell by $3.5 billion during 1932, from $68.25 to $64.72 billion at the end of the year, and with the bank deposit component falling by $3.2 billion.

The monetary history of the year is best broken up into two parts: end of February–end of July, and end of July–end of December. In the first period, total reserves rose by $213 million. The entire securities-buying program of the Federal Reserve took place during this first period, security holdings rising from $740 million at the end of February to $1,841 million at the end of July, an enormous $1,101 million rise in five months. Total controlled reserves rose by $1,000 million. This was offset by a $290 million reduction in bank indebtedness to the Fed, a sharp $380 million fall in the total gold stock, and a $122 million rise in money in circulation, in short, a $788 million reduction in uncontrolled reserves. For open-market purchases to be pursued precisely when the gold stock was falling was pure folly, and endangered public confidence in the government's ability to maintain the dollar on the gold standard. One reason for the inflationary policy was the huge Federal deficit of $3 billion during fiscal 1932. Since the Treasury was unwilling to borrow on long-term bonds from the public, it borrowed on short-term from the member banks, and the Federal Reserve was obliged to supply the banks with sufficient reserves.

Despite this great inflationary push, it was during *this* half year that the nation's bank deposits fell by $3.1 billion; from then on they remained almost constant until the end of the year. Why this fall in money supply just when one would have expected it to rise? The answer is the emergence of the phenomenon of "excess reserves." Until the second quarter of 1932, the nation's banks had always remained loaned up, with only negligible excess reserves. Now the banks accumulated excess reserves, and Currie estimates that the proportion of excess to total bank reserves rose from 2.4 per cent in the first quarter of 1932, to 10.7 per cent in the second quarter.[24]

Why the emergence of excess reserves? In the first place, Fed purchase of governments was a purely artificial attempt to dope the inflation horse. The drop in gold demanded a *reduction* in the money supply to maintain public confidence in the dollar and in the banking system; the increase of money in circulation out of season was an ominous sign that the public was losing confidence in the banks, and a severe bank contraction was the only way to regain that confidence. In the face of this requirement for deflation, the Fed embarked on its gigantic securities-buying program. Naturally, the banks, deeply worried by the bank failures that had been and were still taking place, were reluctant to expand their deposits further, and failed to do so. A common explanation is that the demand for loans by business fell off during the depression, because business could not see many profitable opportunities ahead. But this argument overlooks the fact that banks never have to be passive, that if they really wanted to, they could buy existing securities, and increase deposits that way.

They do not have to depend upon business firms to request commercial loans, or to float new bond issues. The reason for excess reserves must be found, therefore, in the banks.

In a time of depression and financial crisis, banks will be reluctant to lend or invest, (a) to avoid endangering the confidence of their customers; and (b) to avoid the risk of lending to or investing in ventures that might default. The artificial cheap money policy in 1932 greatly lowered interest rates all-around, and therefore further discouraged the banks from making loans or investments. Just when risk was increasing, the *incentive to bear risk*—the prospective interest-return—was being lowered by governmental manipulation. And, as we noted above, we must not overlook the frightening effect of the wave of bank failures on bank policies. During the 1920's, a typical year might find 700 banks failing, with deposits totalling $170 million. In 1930, 1350 banks failed, with deposits of $837 million; in 1931, 2,293 banks collapsed, with deposits of $1,690 million; and in 1932, 1,453 banks failed, having $706 million in deposits. This enormous increase in bank failures was enough to give any bank pause—particularly when the bankers knew in their hearts that no bank (outside of the nonexisting ideal 100 per cent bank) can *ever* withstand a determined run. Consequently, the banks permitted their commercial loans to run down without increasing their investments.

Thus, the Hoover Administration pursued a giant inflationary policy from March through July 1932, raising controlled reserves by $1 billion through Fed purchase of government securities. If all other factors had remained constant, and banks fully loaned up, the money supply would have risen abruptly and wildly by over $10 billion during that period. Instead, and fortunately, the inflationary policy was reversed and turned into a rout. What defeated it? Foreigners who lost confidence in the dollar, partly as a result of the program, and drew out gold; American citizens who lost confidence in the banks and changed their deposits into Federal Reserve notes; and finally, bankers who refused to endanger themselves any further, and either used the increased resources to repay debt to the Federal Reserve or allowed them to pile up in the vaults. And so, fortunately, inflation by the government was turned into deflation by the policies of the public and the banks, and the money supply dropped by $3.5 billion. As we shall see further below, the American economy reached the depths of depression during 1932 and 1933, and yet it had begun to turn upward by mid-1932. It is not far-fetched to believe that the considerable *deflation* of July 1931-July 1932, totalling $7.5 billion of currency and deposits, or 14 per cent, was partly responsible for the mid-summer upturn.[25]

The major increase in bank reserves came in the latter half of 1932, when reserves rose from $2.05 to $2.51 billion, or by $457 million. Yet this rise was *not* caused by FRB security-buying, for the Hoover Administration had by then ceased purchasing, apparently realizing that little or nothing was being accomplished. With the *end* of Hoover's inflation, the gold stock reversed itself, and money in circulation even declined, violating its normal seasonal pattern. In this second period, controlled reserves increased by $165 million; and uncontrolled reserves rose by $293 million: chiefly gold stock, which increased by $539 million. The money supply, however, remained practically constant, currency and bank deposits totalling $45.36 billion at the end of the year. In short, in the second half of 1932, gold swarmed into the United States, and money in circulation also fell.

The public was therefore no longer a help in fighting inflation. In the face of the huge and rapid increase in gold stock, the Administration did nothing, whereas it should have sterilized the increase by tightening money and selling some of its swollen hoard of securities. In the face of the great increase in reserves, therefore, the bankers once again came to the nation's monetary rescue by piling up ever greater excess reserves, and also by reducing some indebtedness at the Fed. Currie estimates that by the fourth quarter of 1932, excess reserves had doubled, to equal 20.3 per cent of total bank reserves.

Professor Seymour Harris, writing at the depth of the depression at a time when he was a cautious moderate, conceded that the failure of the inflationist policy of the Federal Reserve might have been due to the fact "that liquidation has not proceeded far

enough." Furthermore, he added, the sound-money critics of the
Administration might be right, and it may be that the heavy open-
market purchases of securities from 1930 to 1932 "have retarded
the process of liquidation and reduction of costs, and therefore
have accentuated the depression." [26] Precisely.

If Hoover's inflationist plans were thwarted variously by foreigners, the public, and the banks, the President did not permit
himself to remain idle in the face of these obstacles. About foreigners he could do little, except to induce Congress to pass the
Glass-Steagall Act to permit more leeway for domestic expansion.
Hoover was only a moderate inflationist relative to many others,
and he did not wish to go off the gold standard. About the
public, however, Hoover could do a great deal. Seeing money-in-
circulation increase by $800 million in 1931, Hoover engineered
a coordinated hue-and-cry against "traitorous hoarding." "Hoarding," of course, meant that individuals were choosing to redeem
their own property, to ask banks to transform their deposits into
the cash which the banks had promised to have on hand for
redemption.

It is characteristic of depressions that, because of the inherently
fraudulent nature of the commercial banking system, any real
attempt by the public to redeem its own property from the banks
must cause panic among banks and government alike. And so, on
February 3, Hoover organized an anti-hoarding drive, headed by
a Citizens' Reconstruction Organization under Colonel Frank
Knox of Chicago. The hoarder is unpatriotic, ran the hue and cry;
he restricts and destroys credit (i.e., he is exposing the unsound
nature of the credit which was granted against his interests and in
destruction of his property). A group of top-level Anti-Hoarding
patriots met on February 6 to organize the drive: present were
General Dawes, Eugene Meyer, Secretaries Lamont and Mills,
A. F. Whitney, Alvanley Johnston, and industrialist Magnus
Alexander. The CRO urged hoarders to invest in short-term
Treasury securities, i.e., in unproductive rather than productive
investments. On March 6, Hoover delivered a public address on
the evils of hoarding: "the battle front today is against the hoarding of currency." Hoarding has lowered prices and incomes, and

restricted credit; it strangles our daily life. "No one will deny that if the vast sums of money hoarded in the country today could be brought into active circulation there would be a great lift to the whole of our economic progress." Hoover then commended Colonel Knox for his great battle against . . . the American people, and called on everyone to serve in protection of the American home. Perhaps Hoover is correct when he now gives credit to the Knox drive for the fact that "hoarding" never increased much during 1932: it reached a peak of $5.44 billion in July, and never rose above that until the bank crises in February, 1933. But if Hoover *is* correct, praise is not his appropriate reward. For it means that bank liquidation was postponed for another year and the final banking crisis intensified, and it also means that the public was not at last permitted to find out for itself the great truth of the nature of its banking system.

The banks also received their share of Hoover's ire for their unwillingness to expand in those troubled times. The New York *Times* reported on May 20 that Hoover was "disturbed at the apparent lack of cooperation of the commercial banks of the country in the credit expansion drive." In short, the "banks have not passed the benefits of these relief measures on to their customers." The anger of the inflationist authorities at the caution of the banks was typified by the arrogant statement of RFC chairman, Atlee Pomerene: "Now . . . and I measure my words, the bank that is 75 per cent liquid or more and refuses to make loans when proper security is offered, under present circumstances, is a parasite on the community." [27] And Hoover had certainly done his very best to spark the bank credit expansion. It was he who induced Congress to pass the Glass-Steagall Act, and he and Meyer who conducted the open-market purchases of $1 billion. After the Glass-Steagall and RFC Acts were passed, Hoover proclaimed that they would "so strengthen our whole credit structure and open the channels of credit as now to permit our banks more adequately to serve the needs" of the public. On May 19, Hoover tried to prod the banks by asking Secretary Mills to organize bankers and businessmen to use the surplus credit made available by the Federal Reserve purchases. A Committee was established

in New York City for this purpose; on it were such men as Owen
D. Young, chairman, Walter S. Gifford of A.T.&T., Charles E.
Mitchell of the National City Bank, Alfred P. Sloan, Jr., of General Motors, and Walter C. Teagle of Standard Oil. The next
day, May 20, Hoover issued a press release supporting this committee, and hoping for similar action throughout the nation. The
Young Committee tried to organize a cartel to support bond
prices, but the committee accomplished little, and the idea died.

THE INFLATION AGITATION

It is thus with considerable justification that Herbert Hoover
was to declare in later years: "after coming to the Presidency,
almost the whole of Roosevelt's credit supports were built upon
our measures." Despite his intervention and inflationism, however, Hoover considered himself sound next to some of the wildly
inflationist schemes that were filling the air during 1932. The
silver bloc, for one, stepped up its campaign for an international
conference to raise and stabilize the price of silver. They now
added proposals for bimetallic systems. Backing these efforts were
Senators King, Smoot, and Borah from the Mountain states, the
International Chamber of Commerce, and the American Federation of Labor. Senator Burton K. Wheeler (D., Mont.) introduced
a bimetallism bill with the old battle-cry of 16:1, fittingly enough
in collaboration with William Jennings Bryan, Jr. The Bimetallic
Association was formed to back such a bill in February, and it was
also defended by the left-wing National Farmers' Union. One of
the articulate leaders of the silver-subsidy bloc was René Leon,
who became adviser to the House Ways and Means Committee,
and induced the Committee to suggest the international conference. Neither of these proposals passed a house of Congress.

Meanwhile, more and more economists and politicians were
advocating credit expansion, some as a means of "reflating" the
price level back to pre-depression levels. Curiously enough, the
price-level stabilizationists, headed by Irving Fisher, whom we
have discussed above, no longer wanted mere stabilization: they,
too, wanted to reflate the price level back to pre-depression stand-

ards, and only *then* to stabilize. There is no better proof that these economists were always inflationists first, and stabilizationists second. Norman Lombard and the Stable Money Association continued to call for stabilization; before it closed down, it helped to start and was superseded by the powerful Committee for the Nation, dedicated frankly to reflation, and highly influential in finally getting the country off the gold standard in 1933-34. The Committee for the Nation was founded by veteran stabilizationist Frank A. Vanderlip, former President of the National City Bank of New York, and by James H. Rand, Jr., President of Remington Rand Company. Others cooperating in founding the Committee in late 1932 were Vincent Bendix, General Robert E. Wood of Sears-Roebuck, Magnus W. Alexander of the National Industrial Conference Board, Fred H. Sexauer, a farm leader, E. L. Cord, and Frederic H. Frazier, Chairman of the General Baking Company. When the Committee for the Nation organized formally in January, 1933, its executive secretary was Edward A. Rumely, and another of its leaders was Lessing J. Rosenwald.

Inflationist efforts in Congress during these years included: Representative Wright Patman's bill for a soldiers' bonus with fiat money (see above); Senator Walsh's plan for fiat money; Representative Burtness' (N. Dak.) plan to "stabilize the buying power of money," and another bill to "raise the commodity price level to the debt-incurring stage and to stabilize it thereafter." Burtness' bill was introduced in December, 1931, and, in the same month, Rep. Christian Ramseyer of Iowa introduced a bill to "restore and maintain the level of wholesale prices," directing the Federal Reserve to inflate prices back to 1926 levels. A similar bill was presented by Rep. Kent Keller of Illinois.

The most important inflationist bill came before the House Banking and Currency Committee in March, 1932. The Goldsborough Bill charged the Federal Reserve System with the duty of reflating to pre-depression price-levels and then stabilizing; also, the Fed was to be given power to raise or lower the gold weight of the dollar when it deemed necessary, a harking back to Irving Fisher's old scheme of the "compensated dollar." Supporting the Goldsborough Bill in the hearings were: Edward A. O'Neal,

President of the Farm Bureau Federation, which had established a Committee on Stabilization of the Unit of Value, for reflating the price level; Louis J. Taber of the National Grange; and John A. Simpson of the National Farmers' Union, all of whom doubted that the bill went far enough; Henry A. Wallace; ex-Senator Robert L. Owen; Professor Willford I. King, who also wanted the bill to go further; Alvin T. Simonds, President of the Simonds Saw and Steel Co.; Colonel Malcolm C. Rorty; W. C. Hushing of the American Federation of Labor; Professor Irving Fisher; and George H. Shibley. The House frightened the Administration and conservative opinion by passing the Goldsborough Bill on May 2 by the overwhelming margin of 289 to 60. The stabilizationists had reached their high water mark. The New York Merchants' Association strongly attacked the bill, and the *Commercial and Financial Chronicle*—throughout the 1920's a bellwether of sound money—attacked both the Goldsborough Bill and the opposing Federal Reserve authorities in its issue of May 7:

It seems useless to argue against follies such as those embodied in the Goldsborough Bill, when our legislators have lost all sense and reason, and the only hope is that the movement can be held under definite control before it is carried too far. We grieve to have to say that the Federal Reserve authorities are chargeable with a portion at least of the blame in inculcating the unsound doctrines which are finding such wide acceptance today through the Reserve policy of the large-scale purchases of United States Government Securities.

The Federal Reserve authorities strongly opposed the Goldsborough Bill (now Fletcher Bill) in the Senate. The best of these antagonists was Dr. Adolph C. Miller, who cogently charged that a reflation attempt could only aggravate the depression. Miller asserted that if the Federal Reserve had been operating under this bill during the late 1920's, the depression would now be even worse than it is. The Bill was stopped in committee by the efforts of Secretary Mills and Senator Glass.

Also agitating for inflation were Professors Commons, Edie, Friday, Kemmerer, Persons, and Rogers, Colonel Leonard P. Ayres, Father Charles Coughlin, broker Robert M. Harriss, and

Dr. Ivan Wright. Donald Richberg urged emergency loans to the unemployed. Undoubtedly the wildest of all the monetary schemes were those that envisioned Federal support for some sort of separate *barter* system among the unemployed. Here, at last, the absurd schemes of statists and inflationists reached an apogee: a virtually conscious withdrawal from the civilized monetary economy, and a step toward return to the primitive realm of barter.

It is particularly astounding that many famous economists, undoubtedly nonplussed by the depression, lent their names to barter schemes. Professor Frank D. Graham, of Princeton University, concocted an elaborate plan for an Emergency Employment Corporation, to be established by the federal government, for putting the unemployed to work in producing consumer goods, in return for scrip, based apparently on labor-hours, issued by the EEC.[28] Similar plans were suggested by Professor Willford I. King of New York University, and Howard O. Eaton of the University of Oklahoma. And finally, a whole battery of economists, headed by Professor J. Douglas Brown, director of the industrial relations section of Princeton University, and former member of the President's Emergency Committee for Employment, signed a petition for federal and state aid for establishing barter systems, where the unemployed would produce for their *own* consumption, outside of the civilized market economy.[29]

It is a sobering lesson on how the country was being governed, that of the signers, Mallery, Willits, and Wolman were members of the Hoover Emergency Committee for Employment; Willits was an adviser to the Pennsylvania state unemployment committee; Leiserson was chairman of the Ohio State Commission on Unemployment Insurance; Douglas had been technical adviser to the New York State Unemployment Relief Committee; and Graham had been an adviser of the Federal Farm Board.[30]

In the month of January, 1932, two important groups of economists gave their blessings to an expanded inflation program—though not going as far as barter or scrip. Dr. Warren M. Persons, formerly of Harvard University, organized a statement asserting that there was fairly "general agreement" in the economics profession on two steps—credit expansion by the Federal Reserve in collaboration with commercial banks, and passage of the pending RFC. Among the signers of the Persons statement were: Thomas Nixon Carver, John Maurice Clark, John R. Commons, Paul H. Douglas, Irving Fisher, David Friday, Jacob Hollander, Virgil Jordan, Edwin W. Kemmerer, Father John A. Ryan, Edwin R. A. Seligman, Frank W. Taussig, and Henry A. Wallace.[31]

One of the most important expressions of monetary and fiscal thought by economists in the depression was a conference of some of the nation's leading economists in January, 1932, at the University of Chicago, under the aegis of the Institute on Gold and Monetary Stabilization.[32] The Chicago meeting received wide notice, as well it might. Twenty-four economists there recommended the following to President Hoover: (1) what later became the Glass-Steagall Act; (2) a systematic campaign of FRB open-market purchases of securities; (3) RFC aid to banks with ineligible assets; (4) maintaining a public works program; (5) Federal unemployment relief; and (6) lowering tariffs. With the exception of the last plank, President Hoover, as we have seen, adopted every one of these inflationary and interventionist proposals. Part of the responsibility for the Hoover program and its aggravation of the depression must therefore rest on these eminent advisers who steered him so incorrectly.[33]

Unfortunately, these distinguished economists did not heed the words of two of the lecturers at the conference, who most emphatically did *not* sign the statement. One was Professor H. Parker Willis, who again proved prophetic in attacking the Federal Reserve's past and projected future inflationary policy during the depression. Willis pointed out that the cheap money policy in late 1929 and in 1931 caused a dangerous outflow of gold, and led therefore to loss of confidence in the dollar and to bank failures, which accentuated the loss of confidence. He warned that any securities-buying program might indeed raise prices but: "any such step at the present time would simply mean an aggravation of existing difficulties, due to the fact that we are already overburdened with construction work and fixed capital that are not likely soon to be employed." In short, wasteful malinvestments would only be aggravated. The gold standard would also be gravely endangered. In short, inflation and cheap money retard "progress toward the reestablishment of a solid . . . system of prices and values." Willis called courageously for a hands-off policy by the Federal Reserve.[34]

The other notable contribution to the conference was delivered by Professor Gottfried von Haberler, at that time a follower of Ludwig von Mises. Haberler here presented for perhaps the first time in America the Misesian theory of the business cycle.[35] He pointed out that the traditional monetary theory of the trade cycle emphasized stability of the price level, with an attack on falling prices as the remedy for depression. Such were the doctrines of Fisher, Cassel, and Hawtrey.

The price level, however, is a misleading guide, since credit expansion also has a fundamental influence on the structure of production. Furthermore, the price-level theories err by not distinguishing between a fall of price due to a contraction of money, and that due to a lowering of costs from increases in productivity. In 1924-1929, Haberler continued, there was a great growth in production, but wholesale commodity prices remained stable, because the volume of money increased.[36] This inflation brought on the succeeding depression. First it lengthened the period of production, because interest was lowered artificially as credit expanded. The subsequent depression, Haberler continued, is the necessary adjustment and abandonment of these longer processes, and the restoration of the old consumption/investment proportions. Consequently, shifts of capital and labor must occur before recovery can be won. The "quacks . . . preaching inflationary measures," charged Haberler, disregard the real dislocation of productive resources. Further inflation would make things worse by creating a greater artificial disproportion of consumers' and producers' goods. The worst step would be "a one-sided strengthening of the purchasing-power of the consumer, because it was precisely this disproportional increase of demand for consumers' goods which precipitated the crisis." [37]

MR. HOOVER'S WAR ON THE STOCK MARKET

During 1932, President Hoover greatly stepped up his one-man war on the stock market, particularly on short-sellers, whom he naively and absurdly persisted in blaming for the fall in stock prices. Hoover forgot that bulls and bears always exist, and that for every bear bet there must be an offsetting bull, and also forgot that speculation smooths fluctuations and facilitates movement toward equilibrium. On February 16, Hoover called in the leaders of the New York Stock Exchange and threatened governmental coercion unless it took firm action against the "bears," the short-sellers. The Exchange tried to comply, but not aggressively enough for Hoover, who declared himself unsatisfied.

Having warned the Exchange of a Congressional investigation, Hoover induced the Senate to investigate the Stock Exchange, even though he admitted that the Federal Government had no constitutional jurisdiction over a purely New York institution. The President used continual pressure to launch the investigation of what he termed "sinister" "systematic bear raids," "vicious pools . . . pounding down" security prices, "deliberately making a profit from the losses of other people." Beside such demagogic rhetoric, constitutional limitations seemed pale indeed. Secretary of Commerce Lamont protested against the investigation, as did many New York bankers, but Hoover was not to be dissuaded. In answering the New York bankers, Hoover used some unknown crystal ball to assert that present prices of securities did not represent "true values." The stock market viciously persisted in judging stocks according to their earnings, a useful criterion that Hoover seemed to find vaguely traitorous:

the pounding of prices to a basis of earnings by obvious manipulation of the market and propaganda that values should be based on earnings at the bottom of a depression is an injury to the country and to the investing public.

Instead, the public should be "willing to invest on the basis of the future of the United States."

Hoover's persistent calumniation of the "rottenness" of the

stock market finally bore fruit in the Senate investigation which led to the resignation of Albert Wiggin of the Chase National Bank, and blackmailed the stock-exchange generally—with clear-cut, negative effects on business confidence. The stock exchange was bullied into restricting short-selling, and Hoover went on to propose further controls of the stock market, in anticipation of the later SEC; including compulsory stock prospectuses, increased liability of promotors, and Congressional rules for security exchanges. It is no wonder that Hoover later had a decidedly benign attitude toward the New Deal's SEC.

THE HOME LOAN BANK SYSTEM

President Hoover, we remember, had wanted to establish a grandiose mortgage discount bank system to include all financial institutions, but the rejection of the scheme by insurance companies forced him to limit compulsory coverage to the building-and-loan associations. The Federal Home Loan Bank Act was passed in July, 1932, establishing twelve district banks ruled by a Federal Home Loan Bank Board in a manner similar to the Federal Reserve System. $125,000,000 capital was subscribed by the Treasury, and this was subsequently shifted to the RFC. Hoover complained that Congress hamstrung his program by limiting discounted mortgages to 50 per cent of value, whereas Hoover had wanted mortgages to be discounted up to 80 per cent of value. In August, Hoover set up national business and industrial committees to aid small business and to spur use of the new system. Addressing a conference of these committees on August 26, the President proclaimed the necessity of coordinating individual action with governmental activity to aid recovery, and "to give you the opportunity to organize for action."

The new Home Loan Bank System took a while to get started, opening formally on October 15, and not lending at all until December. At the beginning of 1933, total loans were only $838 thousand outstanding, but by March all the district banks were operating, and the total reached almost $94 million by the end of the year.[38]

THE BANKRUPTCY LAW

Another part of the Hoover New Deal message of 1932 that
finally bore fruit was amendment of the Federal bankruptcy law
to weaken the property rights of creditors. If there is to be a bankruptcy law at all, with the debtor summarily freed from much of
his self-incurred obligation (which in itself is highly dubious, unless creditor and debtor had contracted for such forgiveness before-
hand), then certainly minimum justice to the creditor would permit him to take over the debtor's assets. But President Hoover
thought even this excessive, and in his annual messages of
1932 and 1933 urged amendments weakening the rights of the
creditor. These important innovations were debated in Congress,
and only approved for *individuals* on March 1, 1933, and signed
by Hoover in one of his last acts as President. Congress did not
approve similar changes for corporations until the advent of the
Roosevelt New Deal.

The amendments now permitted a majority of creditors, in
amount and in number, to accept deals proferred by the insolvent
debtor for extending the time for payment without parting with
"his" assets. As a result, a minority of creditors who would want
instant redemption of their own rightful property were now
robbed of their proper claims. If there must be majority-rule
voting among creditors at all (and this seems odd since the individual creditors had no say originally on how much credit was to
be borrowed or from whom), then surely the only proper course
is to go immediately into bankruptcy, with each creditor quickly
obtaining his proper individual share of the debtor's assets. Otherwise, the minority creditor has been despoiled, and now owns
virtually nothing.

Debtor sentiment was typified by the Cleveland Trust Company's *Business Bulletin,* which called for a bill to "prevent dissenting members from successfully opposing" "orderly reor-
ganization" of corporations. President Hoover's 1933 message
called for the measure as "a matter of the most vital importance."
It was necessary, apparently, to crush "the obstruction of minority

creditors who oppose such settlements in the hope that fear of ruinous liquidation will induce the immediate settlement of their claims"—apparently a vaguely traitorous position to hold.[39] The bankruptcy changes were opposed vigorously by the nation's bankruptcy lawyers, who particularly attacked the creation of a large bureaucracy of bankruptcy administrators and examiners in the Department of Justice, as well as the unwarranted governmental interference in the relations of debtors and creditors.[40]

THE FIGHT AGAINST IMMIGRATION

Undaunted by his failure of the year before, Hoover again pressed for legal suspension of immigration in the 1932 session, and the ninety per cent reduction bill was introduced again. This time the reduction was to be permanent, not just temporary; the chief argument was economic. The AF of L, the American Legion, and various patriotic societies supported the bill, but Representative Dickstein (D., N.Y.) managed to bottle up the bill in the House Committee. On the other hand, bills by Dickstein to admit more relatives than the Administration was allowing, underwent attack by the State Department, and no action was taken in Congress, one Dickstein bill passing the House but failing in the Senate.

Thus, Hoover failed to get suspension of immigration into law, but he accomplished practically the same end by administrative fiat, and, in his fall campaign for reelection, he pointed with pride to his achievement and prepared to continue his anti-immigration policy until the depression was over.[41]

12

The Close of the Hoover Term

The fact that Hoover sought reelection in the midst of the deepest and worst depression in American history, and in the face of unprecedented unemployment did not lower his satisfaction as he looked back upon his record. After all, as he said in his acceptance speech for the Presidential renomination:

we might have done nothing. That would have been utter ruin. Instead, we met the situation with proposals to private business and to Congress of the most gigantic program of economic defense and counterattack ever evolved in the history of the Republic. We put it into action.

No one could accuse him of being slack in inaugurating the vast interventionist program:

No government in Washington has hitherto considered that it held so broad a responsibility for leadership in such times. . . . For the first time in the history of depression, dividends, profits, and the cost of living have been reduced before wages have suffered.

At St. Paul, at the end of his campaign, Hoover summarized the measures he had taken to combat the depression: higher tariffs, which had protected agriculture and prevented much unemployment; expansion of credit by the Federal Reserve, which Hoover somehow identified with "protection of the gold standard;" the Home Loan Bank system, providing long-term capital to building and loan associations and savings banks, and enabling them to expand credit and suspend foreclosures; agricultural credit banks which loaned to farmers; RFC loans to banks, states, agriculture, and public works; spreading of work to prevent unemployment; the extension of construction and public works; strengthening Federal Land Banks; and, especially, inducing employers to maintain wage rates. Wage rates "were maintained until the cost of living had decreased and the profits had practically vanished. They are now the highest real wages in the world." But was there any causal link between this fact and the highest unemployment rate in American history? This question Hoover ignored.

Hoover had, indeed, "placed humanity before money, through the sacrifice of profits and dividends before wages," but people found it difficult to subsist or prosper on "humanity." Hoover noted that he had made work for the unemployed, prevented foreclosures, saved banks, and "fought to retard falling prices." It is true that "for the first time" Hoover had prevented an "immediate attack upon wages as a basis of maintaining profits," but the result of wiping out profits and maintaining artificial wage rates was chronic, unprecedented depression. On the RFC, Hoover proclaimed, as he did for the rest of his program, "Nothing has ever been devised in our history which has done more for those whom Mr. Coolidge has aptly called the 'common run of men and women.'" Yet, after 3 years of this benevolent care, the common man was worse off than ever.

Hoover staunchly upheld a protective tariff during his campaign, and declared that his Administration had successfully kept American farm prices above world prices, aided by tariffs on agricultural products. He did not seem to see that this price-raising reduced foreign demand for American farm products. He hailed work-sharing without seeing that it perpetuated unemployment, and spoke proudly of the artificial expansion by business of construction "beyond present needs" at his request in 1929-30, without seeing the resulting malinvestment and business losses.

While claiming to defend the gold standard, Hoover greatly shook public confidence in the dollar and helped foster the ensuing monetary crisis by revealing in his opening campaign speech that the government had almost decided to go off the gold standard in the crisis of November, 1931—an assertion heatedly denied by conservative Democratic Senator Carter Glass.

The spirit of the Hoover policy was perhaps best summed up in a public statement made in May, before the campaign began, when he sounded a note that was to become all too familiar to Americans in later years—the military metaphor:

The battle to set our economic machine in motion in this emergency takes new forms and requires new tactics from time to time. We used such emergency powers to win the war; we can use them to fight the depression.

Yet if New Deal socialism was the logic of Hoover's policy, he cautiously extended the logic only so far. He warned at St. Paul of the strange and radical ideas prevalent in the Democratic Party: the schemes for currency tinkering, the pension bill, the commodity dollar, the pork-barrel bill, the plans for veterans' bonuses and over $2 billion of greenback issue, make-work schemes, and an agitation for a vast $9 billion a year public works program. It was also to Hoover's credit that he resisted the pressure of Henry Harriman, who urged Hoover to adopt the Swope Plan for economic fascism during his campaign, a plan which was soon to bear fruit in the NRA.

THE ATTACK ON PROPERTY RIGHTS:
THE FINAL CURRENCY FAILURE

As in most depressions, the property rights of creditors in debts and claims were subjected to frequent attack, in favor of debtors who wished to refuse payment of their obligations with impunity. We have noted the Federal drive to weaken the bankruptcy laws. States also joined in the attack on creditors. Many states adopted compulsory debt moratoria in early 1933, and sales at auction for debt judgments were halted by Wisconsin, Iowa, Minnesota, Nebraska, and South Dakota. Governor Clyde Herring of Iowa asked insurance and mortgage companies to stop foreclosing mortgages. Life insurance companies protested that they were being very lenient, yet in many areas the courts would not enforce foreclosures for insurance companies, enabling many borrowers arrogantly to refuse to pay. Minnesota forbade foreclosures on farms or homes for several years.[1]

Most important of the attacks on creditors' property occurred during the currency crisis that marked the end of the Hoover term. After the election, as the new Presidential term approached, people grew more and more apprehensive, and properly so, of the monetary policies of the incoming president. Dark rumors circulated about the radicalism of Roosevelt's advisers, and of their willingness to go off the gold standard. Consequently, not only did gold "hoarding" by foreigners develop momentum, but even gold hoarding by domestic citizens. For the first time in the depression, American citizens were beginning to lose confidence in the dollar itself. The loss of confidence reached its apogee in February, 1933, the month before the Roosevelt inaugural. In that one month, the monetary gold stock fell by $173 million, and money in circulation increased by the phenomenal amount of $900 million, the reflection of domestic loss of confidence. Money in circulation totalled $5.4 billion at the end of January, and $6.3 billion by the end of February. $700 million of this increase was in Federal Reserve notes, and $140 million in gold coin and gold certificates.

The Federal Reserve did its best to combat this deflationary pull on bank reserves, but its inflationary measures only served to diminish confidence in the dollar still further. Thus, in the month of February alone, Uncontrolled Reserves fell by $1,089 million. The FRS greatly inflated its Controlled Reserves: bills discounted more than doubled to increase by $308 million, bills bought multiplied tenfold to increase by $305 million, $103 million of U.S. governments were purchased. All in all, controlled reserves increased by $785 million during this month; net reserves fell by $305 million.

The impact of this fall on the money supply was very strong. Total currency and deposits fell from $45.4 billion at the end of 1932 to $41.7 billion at mid-1933. Total money supply fell from $64.72 to $61.61 billion over 1933, and all or more of this fall took place in the first half of the year.[2] A more sensitive measure of

change, net demand deposits and time deposits at weekly reporting member banks in 101 cities, totalled $16.8 billion on Febru-
ary 22, and fell to $14.1 billion by March 8. Bank failures sky-
rocketed during this period. The number of commercial bank
failures increased from 1,453 in 1932 to 4,000 in 1933 (most of
which took place in the first quarter), with deposits of failed
banks increasing from $706 million to $3.6 billion in the same
period.[3] Thus, despite the gigantic efforts of the Fed, during early
1933, to inflate the money supply, the people took matters into
their own hands, and insisted upon a rigorous deflation (gauged
by the increase of money in circulation)—and a rigorous testing
of the country's banking system in which they had placed their
trust.

   The reaction to this growing insistence of the people on claiming their rightful, legally-owned property, was a series of vigorous
attacks on property right by state after state. One by one, states
imposed "bank holidays" by fiat, thus permitting the banks to
stay in business while refusing to pay virtually all of the just
claims of their depositors (a pattern that had unfortunately become
almost traditional in America since the Panic of 1819). Nevada had
begun the parade as early as October, 1932, but only 9 out of 20
banks took advantage of the state holiday, the others remaining
open.[4] Louisiana declared a brief holiday for the hard-pressed
New Orleans banks in early February, but the bank holiday movement began in earnest with the proclamation of an 8-day holiday
on February 14, 1933, by Governor William Comstock of Michigan.[5] This action precipitated the bank runs and deflation of the
latter part of February. For if one state could, with impunity,
destroy property right in this manner, then others could—and did,
and depositors began an intense scramble to take their money out
of the banks.

   It is at times like *these* that the speciousness of apologists for
our banking system hailing fractional reserves as being as sound
as the building of bridges—on estimate that only *some* in-
habitants of the area will cross it at any one time—becomes
patently evident. For no one has a legal property ownership in the
bridge, as they do in their bank deposits. At times like these, also,
it becomes clear that bank deposits are not really money—even

on a paper, let alone a gold, standard—but mere money-*substitutes,* which serve as money ordinarily, but reveal their true identity when nationwide confidence begins to collapse.

On the request of bankers for government to save them from the consequences of their own mistakes, state after state, beginning with Indiana, declared moratoria and bank holidays. Governor Ritchie of Maryland declared a 3-day bank holiday on February 24. On February 27, the member banks of the Cleveland Clearing House Association decided arbitrarily to limit withdrawals from all their branches, and no state officials acted to stop this blatant infringement of property right. They were promptly followed by Akron and Indianapolis banks. On February 27, the Ohio, Pennsylvania, and Delaware legislatures authorized the state banking officials to restrict the right of withdrawal of deposits. The states adopted this procedure quickly and virtually without debate, the laws being rammed through on the old political excuse that the taxpaying and voting public must be kept in ignorance of the situation in order to prevent panic.[6] In such a manner do the "people's representatives" characteristically treat their supposed principals.

One of the ironic aspects of this situation was the fact that many national banks, which had worked hard to keep themselves in an at least relatively sound position, did not want to avail themselves of the special privilege of bank holiday, and had to be coerced into doing so. As Willis puts it:

in many cases, the national banks . . . had no wish to join in the holiday provisions of the localities in which they were situated. They had, in such cases, kept themselves in position to meet all claims to which they might be subject, and they desired naturally to demonstrate to depositors and customers their ability to meet and overcome the obstacles of the time, both as a service to such customers and as an evidence of their own trustworthiness. There followed what was deemed . . . the necessity or desirability of coercing . . . the sound banks of the community into acceptation of the standard thought essential for the less liquid and less well-managed institutions.[7]

By March 4, every state in the Union had declared a bank holiday, and the stage was set for President Roosevelt's dramatic and illegal closing of all the banks. The stage was set, by the way, with the full collaboration of the outgoing Administration; in late February, Congress, with the acquiescence of President Hoover, passed a law permitting national banks to cooperate with state bank holidays. And the Comptroller of the Currency obligingly issued a proposed draft of a uniform bank holiday act to aid the various state legislatures in drafting their bills.

President Roosevelt closed down all the banks throughout the nation for an entire week, from March 6 to 13, with many banks remaining closed even longer.[8] It was a final stroke of irony that Roosevelt's only semblance of legal ground for this decree was the Trading with the Enemy Act of World War I! Restrictions against so-called "hoarding" were continued afterward, and much hoarded gold returned to the banks following a Federal Reserve threat to publish a list, for full public scorn, of the leading "gold hoarders."[9] It soon became clear that, with the advent of the Roosevelt Administration, the American gold standard was doomed.

There have been a great many recriminations, particularly from the Hoover camp, about Roosevelt's "failure to cooperate," when he was President-elect, in solving the banking crisis. Certainly it is true that fear of Roosevelt's impending monetary radicalism, and Senator Glass' investigations forcing Charles E. Mitchell to resign as President of the National City Bank, contributed to the banking panic. But the important fact is that the banking system had arrived at a critical impasse. Usually, in the placid course of events, radical (in the sense of far-reaching) economic reforms, whether needed or not, meet the resistance and inertia of those who drift with the daily tide. But here, in the crisis of 1933, the banks could no longer continue as they were. Something had to be done. Essentially, there were two possible routes. One was the course taken by Roosevelt; the destruction of the property rights of bank depositors, the confiscation of gold, the taking away of the people's monetary rights, and the placing of the Federal Government in control of a vast, managed, engine of inflation. The other route would have been to seize the opportunity to awaken the American people to the true nature of their banking system, and thereby return, at one swoop, to a truly hard and sound money.

The *laissez-faire* method would have permitted the banks of the nation to close—as they probably would have done without governmental intervention. The bankrupt banks could then have been transferred to the ownership of their depositors, who would have taken charge of the invested, frozen assets of the banks. There would have been a vast, but rapid, deflation, with the money supply falling to virtually 100 per cent of the nation's gold stock. The depositors would have been "forced savers" in the existing bank assets (loans and investments). This cleansing surgical operation would have ended, once and for all, the inherently bankrupt fractional reserve system, would have henceforth grounded loans and investments on people's voluntary savings rather than artificially-extended credit, and would have brought the country to a truly sound and hard monetary base. The threat of inflation and depression would have been permanently ended, and the stage fully set for recovery from the existing crisis. But such a policy would have been dismissed as "impractical" and radical, at the very juncture when the nation set itself firmly down the "practical" and radical road to inflation, socialism, and perpetuation of the depression for almost a decade.

President Hoover, of course, did not even come close to advocating the hard money, *laissez-faire* policy. Hoover and his partisans have woven the myth that all would have been well if only Roosevelt had "cooperated" with Hoover before the inaugural, but just what *was* this projected cooperation to be? Largely, a joint agreement on partial or total national bank holidays, and on a Hoover proposal for temporary federal guarantees of bank deposits—inflationist and statist measures which Roosevelt was soon to adopt.[10,11] Furthermore, as a *pièce de résistance*, agitation for going off the gold standard kept proceeding from high up in the Hoover Administration itself; specifically from Secretary of Treasury Mills and from Undersecretary Arthur Ballantine.[12]

WAGES, HOURS, AND EMPLOYMENT
DURING THE DEPRESSION

Mr. Hoover left office in March, 1933, at the very depth of the greatest depression in American history. Production had fallen by more than one-half: industrial production had been at an index of 114 in August, 1929, and then fell to 54 by March, 1933. Unemployment was persisting at nearly 25 per cent of the labor force, and gross national product had also fallen almost in half. Hardest hit was investment, especially business construction, the latter falling from about $8.7 billion in 1929 to $1.4 billion in 1933. This is not the only indication that the depression hit hardest in the capital goods industries.

The index of *non-durable* manufacturing production fell from 94 to 66 from August, 1929, to March, 1933—a decline of 30 per cent; the index of *durable* manufactures fell from 140 to 32, in the same period, a decline of 77 per cent. Factory employment fell by 42 per cent; pig iron production decreased by an astounding 85 per cent; the value of construction contracts fell from July, 1929, by an amazing 90 per cent, and the value of building permits by 94 per cent! On the other hand, department store sales fell by less than 50 per cent over the period. Taking durable goods industries (e.g., building, roads, metals, iron and steel, lumber, railroad, etc.) Col. Leonard P. Ayres estimated that their total employment fell from 10 million in 1929 to 4 million in 1932-1933, while employment in consumer goods industries (e.g., food, farming, textiles, electricity, fuel, etc.) only fell from 15 million to 13 million in the same period.[13] Stock prices (industrials) fell by 76 per cent during the depression, wholesale prices fell by 30 per cent, and the total money supply declined by one-sixth.

What of wage rates? We saw that the Hoover policies managed to keep wage rates very high during the first two years of the depression. By 1932, however, with profits wiped out, the pressure became too great, and wage rates fell considerably. Total fall over the 1929-1933 period, however, was only 23 per cent: less than the decline in wholesale prices. Therefore, real wage rates, for the workers still remaining employed, actually *increased*. An excellent inquiry into the wage-employment problem during the depression has been conducted by Mr. Sol Shaviro, in an unpublished essay.[14] Shaviro shows that in twenty-five leading manufacturing industries, the following was the record of monetary, and real, average hourly earnings during these years:

TABLE 10
AVERAGE HOURLY EARNINGS IN
25 MANUFACTURING INDUSTRIES

(100.0 = 1929)

	Monetary	*Real*
June, 1929	100.0	100.7
December, 1929	100.0	99.8
June, 1930	100.0	102.7
December, 1930	98.1	105.3
June, 1931	96.1	111.0
December, 1931	91.5	110.1
June, 1932	83.9	108.2
December, 1932	79.1	105.7
March, 1933	77.1	108.3

We thus see that money wage rates held up almost to the prosperity-par until the latter half of 1931, while real wage rates actually increased by over 10 per cent. Only then did a monetary wage decline set in, but still without a very appreciable reduction in real wage rates from the 1931 peak. It should here be noted that, in contrast to Keynesian warnings, prices fell far *less* sharply after wage rates began to drop, than before. From July, 1929, to June, 1931, wholesale prices fell from 96.5 to 72.1, or at a rate of fall of 1.0 per month, while from June, 1931, to February, 1933, prices fell to 59.8, or at a rate of .65 per month.[15]

Shaviro points out that businessmen, particularly the large employers, were taken in by the doctrine that they should pursue an "enlightened" high-wage policy, a doctrine not only fed to them by the veiled threats of the President, but also by economists and labor leaders, on the grounds of "keeping up purchasing power" to combat the depression. The drop in wage rates had been more extensive and far more prompt in the far milder 1921 depression; in fact, even *money* wage rates rose slightly until September, 1930.[16] More wage cuts took place in smaller than in larger firms, since the smaller firms were less "enlightened," and furthermore, were not as fully in the public (and governmental) view. Furthermore, executive, and then other, salaries were generally reduced considerably more than wage rates. In fact, one reason that the eventual wage declines proved ineffective was the pseudo-humanitarian morality that governed the cuts when finally made: thus, reductions were automatically graduated in proportion to the income brackets of the workers, the higher brackets suffering greater declines. And reductions were often softened for workers with dependents. In short, instead of trying to adjust wage rates to marginal productivities, as was desperately needed, the firms allocated the "loss in income on the most just and equitable [*sic*] basis . . . [actuated by the] desire to make the burden of reduced income fall as lightly as possible on those least able to suffer the loss." In short, each man was penalized according to his ability and subsidized according to the need for which he had voluntarily assumed the responsibility (his dependents).

It was typical that executive salaries were the ones cut most promptly and severely, even though the great unemployment problem was *not* among the executives but among rank-and-file workers. As a result of this tragically wrong-headed policy, the wage cuts certainly stirred up little worker resentment, but also did little to help unemployment. In sum, management's attitude looked not for what "reduction can most easily be made, but rather how can necessary payroll economies be accomplished with the least hardship for all concerned." This policy only. *aggravated* the general hardship, as will always happen when business strays from its proper goal of maximizing profits.[17]

While real average hourly earnings rose, actual hours worked in industry fell drastically during the depression. Weekly hours averaged over 48 in 1929, and fell to less than 32 by mid-1932. In no previous depression had hours worked fallen by more than 10 per cent. This was a form of reduced employment caused by the high wage policy, a form, as we have seen, particularly recommended by the Hoover Administration. As a result of the fall in hours worked and in money wage rates, average weekly earnings fell by over 40 per cent during the depression, and real weekly earnings fell by over 30 per cent. But hardest hit were the unemployed, the percentage of whom rose to 25 per cent by 1932-1933, and reached 47 per cent in the selected manufacturing industries. The fall in manhours worked, combined with the fall in average hourly earnings, caused a truly precipitate drop in total factory payrolls—the base of that very "purchasing power" that the "enlightened" policy was supposed to sustain. Total payroll fell by over 29 per cent in 1930, a year when money wage rates (average hourly earnings) rose to a higher level than 1929, and payroll had fallen by almost 71 per cent by March, 1933. Real payroll fell by over 60 per cent in the same period.

The purchasing power theorists often declaim that the key to prosperity is national income going more to employees and less to profits: these conditions were filled to their hearts' content during the depression. For aggregate profits were *negative* during 1932 and 1933.

Although unions were not particularly important in these years, amounting to only 6 per cent of the labor force, Professor Levinson has shown that unions maintained higher wage rates for their employed workers than did comparable non-union workers.[18] This demonstrates the power of unions to maintain money wage rates during a depression, thereby aggravating the unemployment problem, and reinforcing the effects of Hoover's injunctions and "enlightened" economic theory. Wage rates of selected union workers fell only 6-12 per cent over the 1929-1932 period, while the rates of non-union workers fell by 14-36 per cent.

Levinson points out that there is a close relationship between the strength of the union and the maintenance of wage rates in each specific industry. Thus, the union in the men's clothing industry had been greatly weakened in the 1920's by moves of industry from union to non-union areas, so that it had to accept wage reductions during the depression "to protect the solvency of the organized employees"; wage rates in this industry fell by 31 per cent during the 1929-32 period.

Sharing-the-work by putting employees on reduced time was

another favorite panacea of the Hoover Administration. Yet, in 1931 the President's Emergency Committee for Employment reported that, in a sample of manufacturing, plants with under one thousand employees suffered an unemployment problem in 75 per cent of the cases, whereas 96 per cent of the plants with over five thousand workers suffered from unemployment. 88 per cent of the larger firms had engaged in work-sharing, while only 53 per cent of the smaller firms did so. In a business and industrial conference of August 26, 1932, Hoover reported that work-sharing had been used for hundreds of thousands of workers.

The Conference appointed a subcommittee headed by Walter Teagle, President of Standard Oil of New Jersey, to urge more work-spreading, in hopes of putting two million people back to work. Standard Oil set an example by hiring 3000 more workers in addition to its total of 23,000. The slogan adopted was: "job security by job sharing." In September, William J. Barrett, of the President's Organization on Unemployment Relief, delivered a comprehensive report on work-spreading. Barrett admitted that "management has undergone increased costs in providing employment for additional workers." He further revealed that the largest proportion of work-sharing occurred in the most distressed industries: i.e., the capital goods industries. This illustrates the role that work-sharing played in aggravating and perpetuating unemployment. Thus, in a sample of industries, the largest proportion of part-time workers occurred in such fields as machinery (84.9 per cent), rubber, iron and steel (79.3 per cent), metals, stone-clay-and-glass, while the smallest proportion occurred in railroads (22.3 per cent), foods (26.6 per cent), retail and wholesale, and commercial establishments (20.4 per cent). The average part-time proportion for the entire sample was 56.1 per cent.[19]

CONCLUSION:
THE LESSONS OF MR. HOOVER'S RECORD

Mr. Hoover met the challenge of the Great Depression by acting quickly and decisively, indeed almost continuously throughout his term of office, putting into effect "the greatest program of offense and defense" against depression ever attempted in America. Bravely he used every modern economic "tool," every device of progressive and "enlightened" economics, every facet of government planning, to combat the depression. For the first time, *laissez-faire* was boldly thrown overboard and every governmental weapon thrown into the breach. America had awakened, and was now ready to use the State to the hilt, unhampered by the supposed shibboleths of *laissez-faire*. President Hoover was a bold and audacious leader in this awakening. By every "progressive" tenet of our day he should have ended his term a conquering hero; instead he left America in utter and complete ruin: a ruin unprecedented in length and intensity.

What was the trouble? Economic theory demonstrates that only governmental inflation can generate a boom-and-bust cycle, and that the depression will be prolonged and aggravated by inflationist and other interventionary measures. In contrast to the myth of *laissez-faire,* we have shown in this book how government intervention generated the unsound boom of the 1920's, and how Hoover's new departure aggravated the Great Depression by massive measures of interference. The guilt for the Great Depression must, at long last, be lifted from the shoulders of the free market economy, and placed where it properly belongs: at the doors of politicians, bureaucrats, and the mass of "enlightened" economists. And in any other depression, past or future, the story will be the same.

Appendix:
Government and the National
Product, 1929-1932

In footnote 21 of Chapter 9 above, we explain how we arrive at our estimate of the degree of government depredation on the private national product. The critical assumption is the challenge to the orthodox postulate that government spending, *ipso facto*, represents a *net addition* to the national product. This is a clearly distorted view. Spending only measures value of output in the private economy because that spending is voluntary for services rendered. In government, the situation is entirely different: government acquires its money by coercion, and its spending has no necessary relation to the services that it might be providing to the private sector. There is no way, in fact, to gauge these services. Furthermore, every government-conscripted dollar deprives the citizen of expenditures he would rather have made. It is therefore far more realistic to make the *opposite* assumption, as we do here, that all government spending is a clear depredation upon, rather than an addition to, private product and private output. Any person who believes that there is *more than 50%* waste in government will have to grant that our assumption is more realistic than the standard one.

To estimate the extent of government depredation on private product, we first find private product by deducting "product" or "income" originating in government and "government enterprise"—i.e., the payment of government salaries—from Gross National Product. We now have the Gross Private Product. Government depredations upon this GPP consist of the resources that government drains from the private sector: i.e., total government expenditures or receipts, whichever is the higher. This total subtracted from the GPP yields the private product remaining in private hands, which we may call PPR. The percentage of government depredation to gross private product yields an estimate of the burden of government's fiscal operations on the private economy.[1]

If government expenditure is larger than receipts, then the deficit is a drain on private resources—whether financed by issuing new money or by borrowing private savings—and therefore the expenditure figure is chosen as a measure of government depredation of the private sector. If receipts are larger, then the surplus drains the private sector through taxes, and receipts may be considered the burden on the private sector.[2]

One significant problem created by the vagaries of the official statistics—fortunately, again, a problem not significant for our period—is that the official statistics lump together the bulk of the spending of government *enterprises* (roughly, the government agencies that charge fees) in the private, rather than the governmental, sector. There are therefore no figures available for the total spending or total receipts of government enterprises—although there *are* separate figures for the salaries paid by, the "income originating in," government enterprises. Below, we will present very rough estimates for government enterprises for these years.

Furthermore, we do not, as do the Department of Commerce accounts of government expenditures, deduct government interest *received* from interest paid by government, to arrive at a "net interest paid" figure. On the contrary, the full amount paid by government is deducted from private resources and must therefore be included; while "interest received" is a receipt from the private sector, and should be included in the estimation of government receipts.

We are presenting here the figures not only for gross product, but also for *net* product, which are also of interest. Net National Product is Gross National Product minus depreciation and other capital consumption allowances, and if we consider private *product* as net income without drain on the value of capital, then we should estimate the percentage of government depredation on *net* private product.[3]

Table I presents Gross National Product and Net National Product in current prices. (Figures in this and following tables are from *U.S. Income and Output*, Dept. of Commerce, November 1958; and *National Income, 1954 Edition*, Dept. of Commerce.)

TABLE I

NATIONAL PRODUCT
($ billions)

	Gross National Product	Net National Product
1929	104.4	95.8
1930	91.1	82.6
1931	76.3	68.1
1932	58.5	50.9

Our next step is to find the gross product of government and government enterprises, or "income originating in government and government enterprises." Table II presents these figures for Federal, and for state and local, government and government enterprises.

TABLE II

INCOME ORIGINATING IN GOVERNMENT
($ billions)

	Fed. Govt.	Fed. Govt. Ent.	State & Local Govt.	State & Local Govt. Ent.	Total Govt. and Govt. Ent.
1929	0.9	0.6	3.4	0.2	5.1
1930	0.9	0.6	3.6	0.2	5.3
1931	0.9	0.6	3.7	0.2	5.4
1932	0.9	0.5	3.6	0.2	5.2

Deducting the total figure for income originating in government and government enterprises, from GNP, we arrive at Gross Private Product (and from NNP, we arrive at Net Private Product). This is shown in Table III.

TABLE III

PRIVATE PRODUCT
($ billions)

	GNP	NNP	Total Inc. Orig. in Govt. & Govt. Ent.	Gross Private Prod.	Net Private Prod.
1929	104.4	95.8	5.1	99.3	90.7
1930	91.1	82.6	5.3	85.8	77.3
1931	76.3	68.1	5.4	70.9	62.7
1932	58.5	50.9	5.2	53.3	45.7

Table IV presents our estimates for government expenditures, not including government enterprises. As we have indicated above, "interest received," which had been deducted from "interest paid" by government to arrive at the Department of Commerce figure for government expenditures, was re-included; also, for similar reasons, "surplus of state and local government enterprises," which the Department deducted from its aggregate of state and local government spending, was re-included in our estimates.

TABLE IV

GOVERNMENT EXPENDITURES
($ billions)

	Fed. Expends.	State & Local Expends.	Total Govt. Expends.
1929	2.9	8.2	11.1
1930	3.1	8.9	12.0
1931	4.4	8.9	13.3
1932	3.4	8.0	11.4

Estimates of the expenditure of government enterprises are divisible into two parts: income originating (i.e., employee salaries), which are available from the Dept. of Commerce, and purchases from business, which are not available at all. Neither the Department of Commerce nor the Treasury has any figures available for purchases from business. The only estimates we may obtain, therefore, must be highly sketchy and arbitrary. Professor

Fabricant has prepared figures for the *fiscal* year 1932 (we have so far been dealing in calendar years) of the total purchases from business by federal and state and local governments, *including* government enterprises.[4] Fabricant estimates total Federal purchases from business, general government *and* government enterprise, as $1.02 billion for 1931-32. The average of the Department of Commerce figure of Federal government (general) purchases from business for 1931 and 1932 is $.54 billion. We may therefore estimate the expenditure by Federal *enterprises* on goods from business as $.48 billion for 1931-32.

On the state and local level, Fabricant estimates a total of $4.08 billion spent by government *and* government enterprise on business products in 1931-32; the average of 1931-1932 for general state and local government purchases from business is $3.48 billion (Dept. of Commerce). This leaves as the estimate for 1931-1932 of purchases of government enterprises, state and local, from business at $.60 billion.

Unfortunately, Fabricant presents no figures for any other years for our period on the state and local level. For Federal purchases from business, Fabricant estimates the total, for government and government enterprise, at $.88 billion for *fiscal* 1929. Now, unfortunately, we have no data for 1928; using calendar year 1929, therefore, we obtain $.36 billion as the Department of Commerce estimate for Federal government (general) purchases. Subtracting this from the Fabricant figure, we obtain a rough estimate of $.52 billion for the purchases of Federal enterprises from business during 1929.

To extrapolate these sketchy figures into estimates of federal, and state and local, government enterprises for each of these years, is certainly arbitrary, but it would just as certainly be *more* arbitrary if we simply ignored the problem altogether, and permitted government enterprises to remain partially ensconced in the private sector. We will therefore assume that, for each of our years, Federal enterprises spent $0.5 billion on the products of business, while state and local enterprises spent $0.6 billion. Our estimates for the expenditures of government enterprises are then as follows in Table V.

TABLE V

EXPENDITURES OF GOVERNMENT ENTERPRISES
($ billions)

	Income Orig. Fed.	*Purch. from Bus. Fed.*	*Income Orig. State & Local*	*Purch. from Bus. S. & L.*	*Total Expend. Govt. Enterp.*
1929	0.6	0.5	0.2	0.6	1.9
1930	0.6	0.5	0.2	0.6	1.9
1931	0.6	0.5	0.2	0.6	1.9
1932	0.5	0.5	0.2	0.6	1.8

The grand total of expenditures for government and government enterprises for these years is therefore as follows in Table VI.

TABLE VI

EXPENDITURES OF GOVERNMENT AND GOVERNMENT ENTERPRISES
($ billions)

	Federal	*State and Local*	*Total*
1929	5.2	8.8	14.0
1930	4.4	9.1	13.5
1931	3.4	9.0	12.4
1932	3.0	8.5	11.5

What were governmental receipts during these years? Here we may take the Department of Commerce data, adding to them for both federal and state and local, "interest received." As for government enterprises, we may simply and roughly assume that their receipts balanced their expenditures, and estimate them in the same way, *except* that we know from the Department of Commerce the current surplus of state and local government enterprises, which we may add to the receipt figure. Total estimated receipts of government and government enterprise are presented in Table VII.

TABLE VII

RECEIPTS OF GOVERNMENT AND GOVERNMENT ENTERPRISES
($ billions)

	Federal	State and Local	Total
1929	5.2	8.8	14.0
1930	4.4	9.1	13.5
1931	3.4	9.0	12.4
1932	3.0	8.5	11.5

It might be thought that, to arrive at the highest aggregate figure of government expenditures or receipts for any year, we simply total federal and state and local receipts, and the same for expenditures, and see which one is the higher. This is not correct, however. Whenever we have independent centers of governmental activity, the deficits and surpluses of these centers do *not* cancel each other in their impact on the private economy. Suppose hypothetically, that, in a given year the Illinois state government has a fiscal surplus of $200 million, while New York has a deficit of $200 million. If we are interested in a figure for the governmental impact of New York and Illinois states combined, we do *not* simply aggregate receipts and expenditures and compare them. For Illinois' surplus taxes drain the private sector, and New York's deficits *also* drain the private sector. The ideal step, therefore, is to take each state's and each locality's receipts or expenditures, whichever is the higher, and add up each of these *higher* figures, along with the higher figure for the Federal budget, to estimate the total fiscal impact of all level of government. With the data we have available, we can only do this for state and local on the one hand, and Federal on the other.[5]

Now, at last, in Table VIII, we are ready to estimate the fiscal "depredations of government" for Federal, and for state and local authorities (including government enterprises), and compare them to the data for private product.

TABLE VIII

GOVERNMENT AND THE PRIVATE PRODUCT
($ billions)

	Gross Private Prod.	Net Private Prod.	Fed. Depred.	State & Local Depred.	Total Govt. Depreds.
1929	99.3	90.7	5.2	9.0	14.2
1930	85.8	77.3	4.4	9.7	14.1
1931	70.9	62.7	5.5	9.7	15.2
1932	53.3	45.7	4.4	8.8	13.2

	Private Prod. Remaining (Gross)	Private Prod. Remaining (Net)
1929	85.1	76.5
1930	71.7	63.2
1931	55.7	47.5
1932	40.1	32.5

	Fed. Depreds. % of GPP	State & Local Depreds. % of GPP	Total Govt. Depreds. % of GPP
1929	5.2	9.1	14.3
1930	5.1	11.3	16.4
1931	7.8	13.7	21.5
1932	8.3	16.5	24.8

	Fed. Depreds. % of NPP	State & Local Depreds. % of NPP	Total Govt. Depreds. % of NPP
1929	5.8	9.9	15.7
1930	5.7	12.5	18.2
1931	8.8	15.5	24.3
1932	9.6	19.3	28.9

We see here, in stark relief, the record of the enormous increase in the fiscal burden of government during the depression, from 1929 to 1932. The percentage of Federal depredations on the private product rose from approximately 5 per cent to 8 per cent of the GPP, and from 6 per cent to 10 per cent of the NPP; state and local depredations rose from 9 per cent to 16 per cent of the GPP, and from 10 per cent to 19 per cent of the NPP. Total government depredations rose from 14 per cent to 25 per cent of GPP, and from 16 per cent to 29 per cent of NPP, not far from double the burden!

Notes

NOTES TO INTRODUCTION

1. The depression of 1873-1879 was a special case. It was, in the first place, a mild recession, and secondly, it was largely a price decline generated by the monetary contraction attending return to the pre-Civil War gold standard. On the mildness of this depression, particularly in manufacturing, see O.V. Wells, "The Depression of 1873-79," *Agricultural History XI* (1937), p. 240.

2. Even taken by itself, the "contraction" phase of the depression, from 1929-1933, was unusually long and unusually severe, particularly in its degree of unemployment.

3. It must be emphasized that Ludwig von Mises is in no way responsible for any of the contents of this book.

4. This is by no means to deny that the ultimate premises of economic theory, e.g., the fundamental axiom of action, or the variety of resources, are derived from experienced reality. Economic theory, however, is *a priori* to all other historical facts.

5. This "praxeological" methodology runs counter to prevailing views. Exposition of this approach, along with references to the literature, may be found in Murray N. Rothbard, "In Defense of 'Extreme A Priorism'," *Southern Economic Journal* (January, 1957), pp. 214-220; *id.*, "Praxeology: Reply to Mr. Schuller," *American Economic Review* (December, 1951), pp. 943-946; and *id.* "Toward A Reconstruction of Utility and Welfare Economics," in M. Sennholz (ed.), *On Freedom and Free Enterprise* (Princeton: D. Van Nostrand, 1956), pp. 224-262. The major methodological works of this school are: Ludwig von Mises, *Human Action* (New Haven: Yale University Press, 1949); Mises, *Theory and History* (New Haven: Yale University Press, 1957); F. A. Hayek, *The Counterrevolution of Science* (Glencoe, Ill.: The Free Press, 1952); Lionel Robbins, *The Nature and Significance of Economic Science* (London: Macmillan Co., 1935); Mises, *Epistemological Problems of Economics* (Princeton: D. Van Nostrand Co., 1960); and Mises, *The Ultimate Foundation of Economic Science* (Princeton, N.J.: D. Van Nostrand Co., 1962).

6. Similarly, if the economy had recovered, the advocates would claim success for the theory, while critics would assert that recovery came *despite* the baleful influence of governmental policy, and more painfully and slowly than would otherwise have been the case. How decide between them?

7. The only really valuable studies of the 1929 depression are: Lionel Robbins, *The Great Depression* (New York: The Macmillan Co., 1934), which deals with the United States only briefly; C. A. Phillips, T. F. McManus, and R. W. Nelson, *Banking and the Business Cycle* (New York: The Macmillan Co., 1937); and Benjamin M. Anderson, *Economics and the Public Welfare* (New York: D. Van Nostrand Co., 1949), which does not deal solely with the depression, but covers twentieth-century economic history. Otherwise, Thomas Wilson's drastically overrated *Fluctuations in Income and Employment* (3rd ed., New York: Pitman and Co., 1948) provides almost the "official" interpretation of the depression, and recently we have been confronted with John K. Galbraith's slick, superficial narrative of the pre-crash stock market, *The Great Crash 1929* (Boston: Houghton Mifflin Co., 1955). This, aside from very brief and unilluminating treatments by Slichter, Schumpeter, and Gordon is just about all. There are many tangential discussions, especially of the alleged "mature economy" of the later 1930's. Also see, on the depression and the Federal Reserve System, the recent brief article of O. K. Burrell, "The Coming Crisis in External Convertibility in U.S. Gold," *Commercial and Financial Chronicle* (April 23, 1959), pp. 5, 52-53.

NOTES TO CHAPTER 1

1. Various neo-Keynesians have advanced cycle theories. They are integated, however, not with *general* economic theory, but with holistic Keynesian systems—systems which are very *partial* indeed.
2. There is, for example, not a hint of such knowledge in Haberler's well-known discussion. See Gottfried Haberler, *Prosperity and Depression* (2nd. ed., Geneva: League of Nations, 1939).
3. *Why Wages Rise* (Irvington-on-Hudson: The Foundation for Economic Education, 1957), pp. 118-119.
4. "Under conditions of free competition . . . the market is . . . dependent upon supply and demand . . . there could [not] develop a disproportionality in the production of goods, which could draw in the whole economic system . . . such a disproportionality can arise only when, at some decisive point, the price structure does not base itself upon the play of only free competition, so that some arbitrary influence becomes possible." Siegfried Budge, *Grundzüge der Theoretische Nationalökonomie* (Jena, 1925), quoted in Simon S. Kuznets, "Monetary Business Cycle Theory in Germany," *Journal of Political Economy* (April, 1930), pp. 127-128. Kuznets himself criticizes the Austrian theory from his empiricist, anti-cause and effect-standpoint, and also erroneously considers this theory to be "static."
5. This is the "pure time preference theory" of the rate of interest; it can be found in Ludwig von Mises, *Human Action* (New Haven: Yale University Press, 1949); in Frank A. Fetter, *Economic Principles* (New York: The Century Co., 1915), and *id.*, "Interest Theories Old and New," *American Economic Review* (March, 1914), pp. 68-92.

6. "Banks," for many purposes, include also savings and loan associations, and life insurance companies, both of which create new money *via* credit expansion to business. See below for further discussion of the money and banking question.

7. On the structure of production, and its relation to investment and bank credit, see F. A. Hayek, *Prices and Production* (2nd. ed., London: Routledge and Kegan Paul, 1935): Mises, *op. cit.*; and Eugen von Böhm-Bawerk, "Positive Theory of Capital," in *Capital and Interest* (South Holland, Ill.: Libertarian Press, 1959), Vol. II.

8. "Inflation" is here defined as *an increase in the money supply not consisting of an increase in the money metal.*

9. This "Austrian" cycle theory settles the ancient economic controversy on whether or not changes in the quantity of money can affect the rate of interest. It supports the "modern" doctrine that an increase in the quantity of money lowers the rate of interest (if it first enters the loan market); on the other hand, it supports the classical view that, in the long run, quantity of money does not affect the interest rate (or can only do so if time preferences change). In fact, the depression-readjustment is the market's return to the desired free-market rate of interest.

10. It is often maintained that since business firms can find few profitable opportunities in a depression, business demand for loans falls off, and hence loans and money supply will contract. But this argument overlooks the fact that the banks, if they want to, can purchase securities, and thereby sustain the money supply by increasing their investments to compensate for dwindling loans. Contractionist pressure therefore always stems from banks and not from business borrowers.

11. Banks are "inherently bankrupt" because they issue far more warehouse receipts to cash (nowadays in the form of "deposits" redeemable in cash on demand) than they have cash available. Hence, they are always vulnerable to bank runs. These runs are not like any other business failures, because they simply consist of depositors claiming their own rightful property, which the banks do not have. "Inherent bankruptcy," then, is an essential feature of any "fractional reserve" banking system. As Frank Graham stated: "The attempt of the banks to realize the inconsistent aims of lending cash, or merely multiplied claims to cash, and still to represent that cash is available on demand is even more preposterous than . . . eating one's cake and counting on it for future consumption . . . The alleged convertibility is a delusion dependent upon the right's not being unduly exercised. . . ." Frank D. Graham, "Partial Reserve Money and the 100% Proposal," *American Economic Review* (September, 1936), p. 436.

12. In a gold standard country (such as America during the 1929 depression), Austrian economists accepted credit contraction as a perhaps necessary price to pay for remaining on gold. But few saw any remedial virtues in the deflation process itself.

13. Some readers may ask: why doesn't credit contraction lead to malinvestment, by causing overinvestment in lower-order goods and underinvestment in higher-order goods, thus reversing the consequences of

credit expansion? The answer stems from the Austrian analysis of the structure of production. There is no arbitrary choice of investing in lower or higher-order goods. Any increased investment *must* be made in the higher-order goods, must lengthen the structure of production. A decreased amount of investment in the economy simply reduces higher-order capital. Thus, credit contraction will cause *not* excess of investment in the lower orders, but simply a shorter structure than would otherwise have been established.

14. In a gold standard economy, credit contraction is limited by the total size of the gold stock.

15. In recent years, particularly in the literature on the "under-developed countries," there has been a great deal of discussion of government "investment." There can be no such investment, however. "Investment" is defined as expenditures made not for the direct satisfaction of those who make it, but for other, ultimate consumers. Machines are produced not to serve the entrepreneur, but to serve the ultimate consumers, who in turn remunerate the entrepreneurs. But government acquires its funds by seizing them from private individuals; the spending of the funds, therefore, gratifies the desires of *government officials*. Government officials have forcibly shifted production from satisfying private consumers to satisfying themselves; their spending is therefore pure consumption and can by no stretch of the term be called "investment." (Of course, to the extent that government officials do not realize this, their "consumption" is really *waste*-spending).

16. For more on the problems of fractional-reserve banking, see below.

17. See W. H. Hutt, "The Significance of Price Flexibility," in Henry Hazlitt (ed.), *The Critics of Keynesian Economics* (Princeton: D. Van Nostrand, 1960), pp. 390-392.

18. I am indebted to Mr. Rae C. Heiple II for pointing this out to me.

19. Could government increase the investment-consumption ratio by *raising* taxes in any way? It could not tax *only* consumption even if it tried; it can be shown (and Prof. Harry G. Brown has gone a long way to show) that any ostensible tax on "consumption" becomes, on the market, a tax on incomes, hurting saving as well as consumption. If we assume that the poor consume a greater proportion of their income than the rich, we might say that a tax on the poor used to subsidize the rich will raise the saving/consumption ratio and thereby help cure a depression. On the other hand, the poor do not *necessarily* have higher time preferences than the rich, and the rich might well treat government subsidies as special windfalls to be consumed. Furthermore, Harold Lubell has maintained that the effects of a *change* in income distribution on social consumption would be negligible, even though the absolute proportion of consumption is greater among the poor.

19. See Harry Gunnison Brown, "The Incidence of a General Output or a General Sales Tax," *Journal of Political Economy* (April, 1939), pp. 254-262; Harold Lubell, "Effects of Redistribution of Income on Consumers' Expenditures," *American Economic Review* (March, 1947), pp. 157-170.

20. Advocacy of any governmental policy must rest, in the final analysis,

on a system of ethical principles. We do not attempt to discuss ethics in this book. Those who *wish* to prolong a depression, for whatever reason, will, of course, enthusiastically support these government interventions, as will those whose prime aim is the accretion of power in the hands of the state.

21. For the classic treatment of hyperinflation, see Costantino Bresciani-Turroni, *The Economics of Inflation* (London: George Allen and Unwin Ltd., 1937).

22. See Mises, *op. cit.*, pp. 429-445, and *Theory of Money and Credit* (New Haven: Yale University Press, 1953).

23. When gold—formerly the banks' reserves—is transferred to a newly established Central Bank, the latter keeps only a fractional-reserve, and thus the total credit base and potential monetary supply are enlarged. See, C. A. Phillips, T. F. McManus, and R. W. Nelson, *Banking and the Business Cycle* (New York: Macmillan Co., 1937), pp. 24ff.

24. Many "state banks" were induced to join the FRS by patriotic appeals and offers of free services. Even the banks that did not join, however, are effectively controlled by the System; for, in order to obtain paper money, they must keep reserves in some member bank.

25. The average reserve requirements of all banks before 1913 was estimated at approximately 21 per cent. By mid-1917, when the FRS had fully taken shape, the average required ratio was 10 per cent. Phillips *et al.* estimate that the inherent inflationary impact of the FRS (pointed out in footnote 23) increased the expansive power of the banking system three-fold. Thus, the two factors (the inherent impact, and the deliberate lowering of reserve requirements) combined to inflate the monetary potential of the American banking system six-fold as a result of the inauguration of the FRS. See *ibid.*, pp. 23 ff.

26. The horrors of "wildcat banking" in America before the Civil War stemmed from two factors, both due to government rather than free banking: (1) Since the beginnings of banking, in 1814 and then in every ensuing panic, state governments permitted banks to continue operating, making and calling loans, etc. without having to redeem in specie. In short, banks were privileged to operate without paying their obligations. (2) Prohibitions on interstate branch banking (which still exist), coupled with poor transportation, prevented banks from promptly calling on distant banks for redemption of notes.

27. Mises, *Human Action*, p. 440.

28. A common analogy states that banks simply count on people not redeeming all their property at once, and that engineers who build bridges operate also on the principle that not everyone in a city will wish to cross the bridge at once. But the cases are entirely different. The people crossing a bridge are simply requesting a service; *they are not trying to take possession of their lawful property,* as are the bank depositors. A more fitting analogy would defend embezzlers who would never have been caught if someone hadn't fortuitously inspected the books. The crime comes when the theft or fraud is *committed,* not when it is finally revealed.

29. Perhaps a libertarian legal system would consider "general deposit

warrants" (which allow a warehouse to return any homogeneous good to the depositor) as "specific deposit warrants," which, like bills of lading, pawn tickets, dock-warrants, etc. establish ownership to specific, earmarked objects. As Jevons stated, "It used to be held as a general rule of law, that any present grant or assignment of goods not in existence is without operation." See W. Stanley Jevons, *Money and the Mechanism of Exchange* (London: Kegan Paul, 1905), pp. 207-212. For an excellent discussion of the problems of a fractional reserve money, see Amasa Walker, *The Science of Wealth* (3rd ed., Boston: Little, Brown and Co., 1867), pp. 126-232, esp. pp. 139-141.

30. Some writers make a great to-do over the legal fiction that the Federal Reserve System is "owned" by its member banks. In practice, this simply means that these banks are taxed to help pay for the support of the Federal Reserve. If the private banks really "own" the Fed., then how can its officials be appointed by the government, and the "owners" compelled to "own" the FRB by force of government statute? The Federal Reserve Banks should simply be regarded as governmental agencies.

31. See Mises, *Human Action*, pp. 576-578. Professor Hayek, in his well-known (and excellent) exposition of the Austrian theory, had early shown how the theory fully applies to credit expansion amidst unemployed factors. Hayek, *op. cit.*, pp. 96-99.

32. Haberler, *op. cit.*, Chapter 3.

33. Mises, *Human Action*, pp. 556-557. Mises also refutes the old notion that the boom is characterized by an undue conversion of "circulating capital" into "fixed capital." If that were true, then the crisis would reveal a shortage of circulating capital, and would greatly drive up the prices of, *e.g.*, industrial raw materials. Yet, these materials are precisely among the ones revealed by the crisis to be *over*-abundant, *i.e.*, resources were malinvested in "circulating" as well as in "fixed" capital in the higher stages of production.

34. For a stimulating discussion of some of these processes, see L. M. Lachmann, *Capital and Its Structure* (London: London School of Economics, 1956).

35. For the "pro-bank" position on this issue, see F. A. Hayek, *Monetary Theory and the Trade Cycle* (New York: Harcourt, Brace & Co., 1933), pp. 144-148; Fritz Machlup, *Stock Market, Credit and Capital Formation* (New York: The Macmillan Co., 1940), pp. 247-248; Haberler, *op. cit.*, pp. 64-67. On the other side, see the brief comments of Mises, *Human Action*, pp. 570, 789 n.; and Phillips *et al.*, *op. cit.*, pp. 139ff.

36. The error of the followers stems from their failure to adopt the pure time-preference theory of interest of Fetter and Mises, and their clinging to eclectic "productivity" elements in their explanation of interest. See the references mentioned in footnote 5 above.

37. Mises points out (*Human Action*, p. 789n.) that if the banks simply lowered the interest charges on their loans without expanding their credit, they would be granting gifts to debtors, and would not be generating a business cycle.

38. ". . . banks must be constantly desirous of increasing their loans, by issuing their own credit in the shape of circulation and deposits. The more they can get out, the larger the income. This is the *motive power* that ensures the constant expansion of a mixed [fractional reserve] currency to its highest possible limit. The banks will always increase their indebtedness when they can, and only contract it when they must." Walker, *op. cit.*, pp. 145ff.; also see *ibid.*, p. 159.

39. For a somewhat similar analysis of international gold flows, see F. A. Hayek, *Monetary Nationalism and International Stability* (New York: Longmans, Green & Co., 1937), pp. 24f. Also see Walker, *op. cit.*, p. 160.

NOTES TO CHAPTER 2

1. F. A. Hayek subjected J. M. Keynes's early *Treatise on Money* (now relatively forgotten amid the glow of his later *General Theory*) to a sound and searching critique, much of which applies to the later volume. Thus, Hayek pointed out that Keynes simply assumed that zero aggregate profit was just sufficient to maintain capital, whereas profits in the lower stages combined with equal losses in the higher stages would reduce the capital structure; Keynes ignored the various stages of production; ignored changes in capital value and neglected the identity between entrepreneurs and capitalists; took replacement of the capital structure for granted; neglected price differentials in the stages of production as the source of interest; and did not realize that, ultimately, the question faced by businessmen is *not* whether to invest in consumer goods or capital goods, but whether to invest in capital goods that will yield consumer goods at a *nearer or later* date. In general, Hayek found Keynes ignorant of capital theory and real-interest theory, particularly that of Böhm-Bawerk, a criticism borne out in Keynes' remarks on Mises' theory of interest. See John Maynard Keynes, *The General Theory of Employment, Interest and Money* (New York: Harcourt, Brace, and Co., 1936), pp. 192-193; F. A. Hayek, "Reflections on the Pure Theory of Money of Mr. J. M. Keynes," *Economica* (August, 1931), pp. 270-295; and *id.*, "A Rejoinder to Mr. Keynes," *Economica* (November, 1931), pp. 400-402.

2. Dennis H. Robertson, "Mr. Keynes and the Rate of Interest," in *Readings in the Theory of Income Distribution* (Philadelphia: The Blakiston Co., 1946), p. 440. Also see the article by Carl Landauer, "A Break in Keynes's Theory of Interest," *American Economic Review* (June, 1937), pp. 260-266.

3. For more on the equilibrating effects of wage reductions in a depression see the following section.

4. Some of the most damaging blows to the Keynesian system have come from friendly, but unsparing, neo-Keynesian sources; e.g., Franco Modigliani, "Liquidity Preference and the Theory of Interest and Money," in Henry Hazlitt (ed.), *The Critics of Keynesian Economics* (Princeton, N. J., D. Van Nostrand, 1960), pp. 131-184; Erik Lindahl,

"On Keynes' Economic System," *Economic Record* (May and November, 1954), pp. 19-32, 159-171. As Hutt sums up: "the apparent revolution wrought by Keynes after 1936 has been reversed by a bloodless counter-revolution conducted unwittingly by higher critics who tried very hard to be faithful. Whether some permanent benefit to our science will have made up for the destruction which the revolution left in its train, is a question which economic historians of the future will have to answer." W. H. Hutt, "The Significance of Price Flexibility," in Hazlitt, *op cit.*, p. 402.

5. *Ibid.*, p. 398.
6. See Modigliani, *loc. cit.*, and Lindahl, *loc. cit.*
7. See L. Albert Hahn, *The Economics of Illusion* (New York: Squier Publishing Co., 1949), pp. 50ff., 166ff.
8. Actually, zones of indeterminacy are apt to be wide where only two or three people live on a desert island and narrow progressively the greater the population and the more advanced the economic system. No special zone adheres to the labor contract.
9. It is immaterial to the argument whether or not the present writer believes the *mystique* to be morally absurd.
10. *Maximum* wage controls, such as prevailed in earlier centuries and in the Second World War, created artificial shortages of labor throughout the economy—the reverse of the effect of *minimum* wages.
11. See Hutt, *loc. cit.*, pp. 390ff.
12. Various empirical studies have maintained that the aggregate demand for labor is highly elastic in a depression, but the argument here does not rest upon them. See Benjamin M. Anderson, "The Road Back to Full Employment," in Paul T. Homan and Fritz Machlup (eds.), *Financing American Prosperity* (New York: Twentieth Century Fund, 1945), pp. 20-21.
13. See Hutt, *loc. cit.*, p. 400.
14. Note that, in Figure 1, the $S_L S_L$ line stops before reaching the horizontal axis. Actually, the line must stop at the wage yielding the minimum subsistence income. Below that wage rate, no one will work, and therefore, the supply curve of labor will really be horizontal, on the free market, at the minimum subsistence point. Certainly it will not be possible for speculative withholding to reduce wage rates to the subsistence level, for three reasons: (a) this speculative withholding almost always results in *hoarding,* which reduces prices all-round and which will therefore reduce the equilibrium *money* wage rate without reducing the equilibrium *real* wage rate—the relevant rate for the subsistence level; (b) entrepreneurs will realize that their speculation has overshot the mark long before the subsistence level is reached; and (c) this is especially true in an advanced capitalist economy, where the rates are far above subsistence.
15. On the other hand, wage rates maintained above the free-market level will discourage investment and thereby tend to increase hoarding at the expense of saving-investment. This decline in the investment/consumption ratio aggravates the depression further. Freely declining wage rates

would permit investments to return to previous proportions, thus adding another important impetus to recovery. See Frederic Benham, *British Monetary Policy* (London: P. S. King and Son, 1932), p. 77.

16. It has often been maintained that a falling price level injures business firms because it aggravates the burden of fixed monetary debt. However, the *creditors* of a firm are just as much its owners as are the equity shareholders. The equity shareholders have less equity in the business to the extent of its debts. Bond-holders (long-term creditors) are just different types of owners, very much as preferred and common stock holders exercise their ownership rights differently. Creditors save money and invest it in an enterprise, just as do stockholders. Therefore, no change in price level by itself helps or hampers a business; creditor-owners and debtor-owners may simply divide their gains (or losses) in different proportions. These are mere intra-owner controversies.

NOTES TO CHAPTER 3

1. See the discussion by Scott in Wesley C. Mitchell, *Business Cycles, The Problem and its Setting* (New York: National Bureau of Economic Research, 1927), pp. 75ff.
2. See C. A. Phillips, T. F. McManus, and R. W. Nelson, *Banking and the Business Cycle* (New York: Macmillan Co., 1937), pp. 59-64.
3. In the Keynesian theory, "aggregate equilibrium" is reached by two routes: profits and losses, and "unintended" investment or disinvestment in inventory. But there *is* no *unintended* investment, since prices could always be cut low enough to sell inventory if so desired.
4. We often come across the argument that the money supply must be increased "in order to keep up with the increased supply of goods." But goods and money are not at all commensurate, and the entire injunction is therefore meaningless. There is no way that money can be matched with goods.
5. For a brilliant critique of underconsumptionism by an Austrian, see F. A. Hayek, "The 'Paradox' of Saving," in *Profits, Interest and Investment* (London: Routledge and Kegan Paul, 1939), pp. 199-263. Hayek points out the grave and neglected weaknesses in the capital, interest, and production-structure theory of the underconsumptionists Foster and Catchings. Also see Phillips, *et al., op. cit.*, pp. 69-76.
6. The Keynesian approach stresses *underspending* rather than under-consumption alone; on "hoarding," the Keynesian dichotomization of saving and investment, and the Keynesian view of wages and unemployment, see above.
7. Either that, or such an expansion must have occurred in *some* previous decade, after which the firm—*or whole economy*—lapsed into a sluggish stationary state.
8. See his brilliant critique of the acceleration principle in W. H. Hutt, "Coordination and the Price System" (unpublished, but available from the Foundation for Economic Education, Irvington-on-Hudson, New York, 1955), pp. 73-117.

9. This is not merely the problem of a time lag necessary to produce the new machines; it is the far broader question of the great range of choice of the time period in which to make the investment. But this reminds us of another fallacy made by the accelerationists: that production of the new machines is virtually instantaneous.

10. The accelerationists habitually confuse consumption with production of consumer goods, and talk about one when the other is relevant.

11. The "Cobweb Theorem" is another doctrine built on the assumption that all entrepreneurs are dolts, who blindly react rather than speculate and succeed in predicting the future.

12. Anglo-American economics suffers badly from this deficiency. The Marshallian system rested on a partial theory of the "industry," while modern economics fragments itself further to discuss the isolated firm. To remedy this defect, Keynesians and later econometric systems discuss the economy in terms of a few holistic aggregates. Only the Misesian and Walrasian systems are truly general, being based themselves on interrelated individual exchanges. The Walrasian scheme is unrealistic, consisting solely of a mathematical analysis of an unrealizable (though important) equilibrium system.

13. Another defect of the accelerationist explanation of the cycle is its stress on *durable* capital equipment as the preeminently fluctuating activity. Actually, as we have shown above, the boom is *not* characterized by an undue stress on *durable* capital; in fact, such non-durable items as industrial raw materials fluctuate as strongly as fixed capital goods. The fluctuation takes place in producers' goods industries (the Austrian emphasis) and not just *durable* producers' goods (the Accelerationist emphasis).

14. See Hutt, *op. cit.,* p. 109.

15. The acceleration principle also claims to explain the alleged tendency of the downturn in capital goods to *lead* downturns in consumer goods activity. However, it could only do so, even on its own terms, under the very special—and almost never realized—assumption that the sale of consumer goods describes a sine-shaped curve over the business cycle. Other possible curves give rise to no leads at all.

On the acceleration principle, also see L. Albert Hahn, *Common Sense Economics* (New York: Abelard-Schuman, 1956), pp. 139-143; Mises, *Human Action* (New Haven: Yale University Press, 1949), pp. 581-583; and S. S. Kuznets, "Relation Between Capital Goods and Finished Products in the Business Cycle," in *Economic Essays in Honor of Wesley C. Mitchell* (New York: Columbia University Press, 1935), pp. 209-267.

16. Alvin H. Hansen, "Economic Progress and Declining Population Growth," in *Readings in Business Cycle Theory* (Philadelphia: The Blakiston Co., 1944), pp. 366-384.

17. For an example, see George Terborgh, *The Bogey of Economic Maturity* (Chicago: Machinery and Allied Products Institute, 1945).

18. Curiously, these same worriers did not call upon the federal government to abandon its conservation policies, which led it to close millions of

acres of public domain permanently. Nowadays, outer space will presumably provide "frontier" enough.

19. *Saving,* not monetary expansion. A backward country, for example, could not industrialize itself by issuing unlimited quantities of paper money or bank deposits. That could only bring on runaway inflation.

20. The economic fortunes of a small country producing one product for the market will of course be dominated by the course of events in that industry.

21. Schumpeter's pure theory was presented in his famous *Theory of Economic Development* (Cambridge: Harvard University Press, 1934)—first published in 1911. It later appeared as the "first approximation" in an elaborated approach that really amounted to a confession of failure, and which introduced an abundance of new fallacies into the argument. The later version constituted his *Business Cycles* (New York: McGraw-Hill, 1939, 2 vols.).

22. To be sure, the Schumpeterian "Pure Model" explicitly postulates perfect knowledge and therefore absence of error by entrepreneurs. But this is a flagrantly self-contradictory assumption within Schumpeter's own model, since the *very reason* for depression in the Pure Model is the fact that risks increase, old firms are suddenly driven to the wall, etc., and no one innovates again until the situation clears.

23. Schumpeter wisely saw that voluntary savings could only cause simple economic growth and could not give rise to business cycles.

24. See Carolyn Shaw Solo, "Innovation in the Capitalist Process: A Critique of the Schumpeterian Theory," *Quarterly Journal of Economics* (August, 1951), pp. 417-428.

25. This refutes Clemence and Doody's defense of Schumpeter against Kuznets' criticism that the cluster of innovations assumes a cluster of entrepreneurial ability. Clemence and Doody identified such ability solely with the making of innovations and the setting up of new firms. See Richard V. Clemence and Francis S. Doody, *The Schumpeterian System* (Cambridge: Addison Wesley Press, 1950), pp. 52ff; S. S. Kuznets, "Schumpeter's *Business Cycles,*" *American Economic Review* (June, 1940), pp. 262-263.

26. Schumpeter also discusses a "secondary wave" super-imposed on his pure model. This wave takes into account general inflation, price speculation, etc., but there is nothing particularly Schumpeterian about this discussion, and if we discard both the pure model and the multi-cycle approach, the Schumpeterian theory is finished.

27. Thus, during the late 1920's, when banks, influenced by qualitative credit doctrines, tried to shut off the flow of credit to the stock market specifically, the market was able to borrow from the swollen funds of non-bankers, funds swollen by years of bank credit inflation.

On the fallacies of the qualitative credit theorists, and of their views on the stock market, see the excellent study by Fritz Machlup, who at that time was a leading Austrian School theorist, *The Stock Market, Credit and Capital Formation* (New York: Macmillan Co., 1940).

28. On all this, see *ibid, passim.* An individual broker might borrow in

order to pay another broker, but in the aggregate, inter-broker transactions cancel out, and total brokers' loans reflect only broker-customer
relations.

29. Real estate values will often behave similarly, real estate conveying units
of title of capital in land.
30. See Schumpeter, *Business Cycles, Vol. I.,* Chap. 4.
31. V. Lewis Bassie, "Recent Developments in Short-Term Forecasting," in
Short-Term Forecasting, Studies in Income and Wealth, Vol. XVII
(Princeton: National Bureau of Economic Research, 1955), pp. 11-12.
Also see *ibid.,* pp. 20-21.

NOTES TO CHAPTER 4

1. See Lin Lin, "Are Time Deposits Money?," *American Economic Review*
(March, 1937), pp. 76-86. Lin points out that demand and time deposits
are interchangeable at par and in cash, and are so regarded by the
public. Also see Gordon W. McKinley, "The Federal Home Loan Bank
System and the Control of Credit," *The Journal of Finance* (Sept.,
1957), pp. 319-332, and McKinley, "Reply," *Journal of Finance* (December, 1958), p. 545.
2. Governor George L. Harrison, head of the Federal Reserve Bank of
New York, testified in 1931 that any bank suffering a run must pay
both its demand and savings deposits on demand. Any request for a
thirty-day notice would probably cause the state or the Comptroller of
Currency to close the bank immediately. Harrison concluded: ". . . in
effect and in substance these [time] accounts are demanded deposits."
Charles E. Mitchell, head of the National City Bank of New York, agreed
that "no commercial bank could afford to invoke the right to delay
payment on these deposits." And, in fact, the heavy bank runs of 1931-
1933 took place in time deposits as well as demand deposits. Senate
Banking and Currency Committee, *Hearings on Operations of National
and Federal Reserve Banking Systems, Part I* (Washington, 1931),
pp. 36, 321-322, and Lin Lin, *loc cit.*
3. Time deposits, furthermore, are often used directly to make payments.
Individuals may obtain *cashier's checks* from the bank, and use them
directly as money. Even D. R. French, who tried to deny that time
deposits are money, admitted that some firms used time deposits for
"large special payments, such as taxes, after notification to the bank."
D. R. French, "The Significance of Time Deposits in the Expansion of
Bank Credit, 1922-1928," *Journal of Political Economy* (December,
1931), p. 763. Also see Senate Banking-Currency Committee, Hearings,
op. cit., pp. 321-322; Committee on Bank Reserves, "Member Bank
Reserves" in Federal Reserve Board, *19th Annual Report, 1932*
(Washington, 1933), pp. 27ff; Lin Lin, *loc. cit.,* and *Business Week*
(November 16, 1957).
4. See Lin Lin, "Professor Graham on Reserve Money and the One
Hundred Per Cent Proposal," *American Economic Review* (March, 1937),
pp. 112-113.

5. As Frank Graham pointed out, the attempt to maintain time deposits as both a fully liquid asset *and* an interest-bearing investment is trying to eat one's cake and have it too. This applies to demand deposits, savings-and-loan shares, and cash surrender values of life insurance companies as well. See Frank D. Graham, "One Hundred Per Cent Reserves: Comment," *American Economic Review* (June, 1941), p. 339.

6. See McKinley, *loc. cit.*, pp. 323-324. On those economists who do and do not include time deposits as money, see Richard T. Selden, "Monetary Velocity in the United States," in Milton Friedman (ed.), *Studies in the Quantity Theory of Money* (Chicago: University of Chicago Press, 1956), pp. 179-257.

7. In his latest exposition of the subject, McKinley approaches recognition of the cash surrender value of life insurance policies as part of the money supply, in the broader sense. Gordon W. McKinley, "Effects of Federal Reserve Policy on Nonmonetary Financial Institutions," in Herbert V. Prochnow (ed.), *The Federal Reserve System* (New York: Harper & Bros., 1960), pp. 217n., 222.

   In the present day, government savings bonds would have to be included in the money supply. On the other hand, pension funds are *not* part of the money supply, being simply saved and invested and not redeemable on demand, and neither are mutual funds—even the modern "open-end" variety of funds are redeemable not at *par*, but at market value of the stock.

8. Data for savings-and-loan shares and life-insurance reserves, are reliable only for the end-of-the-year: mid-year data are estimated by the author by interpolation. Strictly, the country's money supply is equal to the above data *minus* the amount of cash and demand deposits held by the savings and loan and life insurance companies. The latter figures are not available, but their absence does not unduly alter the results.

9. On the reluctance of banks during this era to lend to consumers, see Clyde W. Phelps, *The Role of the Sales Finance Companies in the American Economy* (Baltimore: Commercial Credit Co., 1952).

10. As McKinley says: "Just as the ultimate source of reserve for commercial banks consists of the deposit liabilities of the Federal Reserve Banks, so the ultimate source of the reserves of non-bank institutions consist of the deposit liabilities of the commercial banks. The money supply [is] . . . two inverted pyramids one on top of the other. The Federal Reserve stands at the base of the lower pyramid, and . . . by controlling the volume of their own deposit liabilities, the FRB's influence not only the deposit liabilities of the commercial banks but also the deposit liabilities of all those institutions which use the deposit liabilities of the commercial banks as cash reserves." McKinley, "The Federal Home Loan Bank," p. 326. Also see Donald Shelby, "Some Implications of the Growth of Financial Intermediaries," *Journal of Finance* (Dec., 1958), pp. 527-541.

11. It might be asked, despairingly: if the supposedly "savings" institutions (savings banks, insurance companies, saving and loan associations, etc.) are to be subject to a one hundred per cent requirement, what savings

would a libertarian society permit? The answer is: genuine savings, e.g., the issue of shares in an investing firm, or the sale of bonds or other debentures or term notes to savers, which would fall due at a certain date in the future. These genuinely saved funds would in turn be invested in business enterprise.

12. Federal Reserve System, *Banking and Monetary Statistics* (Washington, D.C.: Federal Reserve Board, 1943), pp. 370-371. The excess listed for 1929 averages about forty million dollars, or about two per cent of total reserve balances.

13. *Banking and Monetary Statistics* (Washington, D.C.: Federal Reserve Board, 1943), pp. 34 and 75. The deposits reckoned are "demand deposits adjusted" plus U.S. Govt. deposits. A shift from member to non-member bank deposits would tend to reduce effective reserve requirements and increase excess reserves and the money supply, since non-member banks use deposits at member banks as the basis for *their* reserves. See Lauchlin Currie, *The Supply and Control of Money in the United States* (2nd. ed.) (Cambridge, Mass.: Harvard University Press, 1935), p. 74.

14. On time deposits in the 1920's see Benjamin M. Anderson, *Economics and the Public Welfare* (New York: D. Van Nostrand, 1949), pp. 128-131; C. A. Phillips, T. F. McManus, and R. W. Nelson, *Banking and the Business Cycle* (New York: Macmillan Co., 1937), pp. 98-101.

15. The well-known category of "Federal Reserve Credit" consists of Federal Reserve Assets Purchased and Bills Discounted.

16. For the Pittman Act, see Edwin W. Kemmerer, *The ABC of the Federal Reserve System* (9th ed., Princeton: Princeton University Press, 1932), pp. 258-262.

17. H. Parker Willis, "Conclusions," in H. Parker Willis, *et al.*, "Report of an Inquiry into Contemporary Banking in the United States," (type-written ms., New York, 1925), Vol. VII, pp. 16-18.

18. See Seymour E. Harris, *Twenty Years of Federal Reserve Policy* (Cambridge: Harvard University Press, 1933), I, 3-10, 39-48.

19. *Ibid.*, pp. 108ff.

20. Federal Reserve *Annual Report, 1923*, p. 10; cited in Harris, *op. cit.*, p. 109.

21. See Phillips, *op. cit.*, pp. 93-94.

22. Harris, *op. cit.*, p. 91.

23. Oliver M. W. Sprague, "Immediate Advances in the Discount Rate Unlikely," *The Annalist* (1926), p. 493.

24. See H. Parker Willis, "Politics and the Federal Reserve System," *Banker's Magazine* (January, 1925), pp. 13-20; Willis, "Will the Racing Stock Market Become A Juggernaut?" *The Annalist* (November 24, 1924), pp. 541-542; and *The Annalist* (November 10, 1924), p. 477.

25. The War Finance Corporation had been dormant until 1921, when Congress expanded its authorized lending power and reorganized it to grant capital loans to farm cooperatives. In addition, the Federal Land Bank system, set up in 1916 to make mortgage loans to farm associations, resumed lending, and more Treasury funds for capital were authorized. And finally, the farm bloc pushed through the Agricultural Credits Act

of 1923, which established twelve governmental Federal Intermediate Credit Banks to lend to farm associations. See Theodore Saloutos and John D. Hicks, *Agricultural Discontent in the Middle West, 1900-1939* (Madison, Wis.: University of Wisconsin Press, 1951), pp. 324-340.

26. See Harris, *op. cit.*, p. 209.

27. Charles E. Mitchell, then head of the National City Bank of New York, has been pilloried for years for allegedly defying the FRB and frustrating the policy of moral suasion, by stepping in to lend to the stock market during the looming market crisis at the end of March. But it now appears that Mitchell and the other leading New York banks acted only upon approval of the Governor of the New York Federal Reserve Bank and of the entire Federal Reserve Board, which thus clearly did not even maintain the courage of its own convictions. See Anderson, *op. cit.*, p. 206.

28. See Charles O. Hardy, *Credit Policies of the Federal Reserve System* (Washington: The Brookings Institution, 1932), pp. 122-138. Dr. Lawrence E. Clark, a follower of H. Parker Willis, charged that Mr. Gates McGarrah, Chairman of the New York Federal Reserve Bank at the time, opposed moral suasion because he himself was engaged in stock market speculation and in bank borrowing for that purpose. If this were the reason, however, McGarrah would hardly have been—as he was —the main force in urging an increase in the rediscount rate. Instead, he would have been against any check on the inflation. See Lawrence E. Clark, *Central Banking Under the Federal Reserve System* (New York: The Macmillan Company, 1935), p. 267n.

29. The moral suasion policy was searchingly criticized by former FRB Chairman W. P. G. Harding. The policy continued on, however, probably at the insistence of Secretary of the Treasury Mellon, who strongly opposed any increase in the rediscount rate. See Anderson, *op. cit.*, p. 210.

30. See Clark, *op. cit.*, p. 382. The call rate rarely went above 8 per cent in 1928, or above 10 per cent in 1929. See Adolph C. Miller, "Responsibility for Federal Reserve Policies: 1927-1929," *American Economic Review* (September, 1935).

31. Ralph W. Robey, "The Capeadores of Wall Street," *Atlantic Monthly* (September, 1928).

32. Acceptances are sold by borrowers to acceptance dealers or "acceptance banks," who in turn sell the bills to ultimate investors—in this case, the Federal Reserve System.

33. Thus, on June 30, 1927, over 26 per cent of the nation's total of bankers' acceptances outstanding was held by the FRS for its own account, and another 20 per cent was held for its foreign accounts (foreign central banks). Thus 46 per cent of all bankers' acceptances were held by the Federal Reserve, and the same proportion held true in June, 1929. See Hardy, *op. cit.*, p. 258.

34. See Senate Banking and Currency Committee, *Hearings On Operation of National and Federal Reserve Banking Systems* (Washington, 1931), *Appendix, Part 6*, p. 884.

35. See Harris, *op. cit.,* p. 324n.
36. About half of the acceptances in the Federal Reserve System were *held* in the Federal Reserve Bank of New York; more important, almost all the *purchases* of acceptances were made by the New York Bank, and then distributed at definite proportions to the other Reserve Banks. See Clark, *op. cit.,* p. 168.
37. See a presidential address by Warburg before the American Acceptance Council, January 19, 1923, in Paul M. Warburg, *The Federal Reserve System* (New York: The Macmillan Co., 1930), II, 822. Of course, Warburg would have preferred an even larger subsidy. Even Warburg's perceptive warning on the developing inflation in March 1929, was marred by his simultaneous deploring of our "inability to develop a country-wide bill market." *Commercial and Financial Chronicle* (March 9, 1929), pp. 1443-1444; also see Harris, *op. cit.,* p. 324.
38. See Lester V. Chandler, *Benjamin Strong, Central Banker* (Washington, D.C.: The Brookings Institution, 1958), p. 39 and *passim*. It was only on the insistence of Warburg and Henry Davison of J. P. Morgan and Co., that Strong had accepted this post.
39. See H. Parker Willis, "The Banking Problem in the United States," in Willis, *et al., Report of an Inquiry into Contemporary Banking in the United States, op. cit.,* I, 31-37.
40. See A. S. J. Baster, "The International Acceptance Market," *American Economic Review* (June, 1937), p. 298.
41. See Charles Cortez Abbott, *The New York Bond Market, 1920-1930* (Cambridge: Harvard University Press, 1937), pp. 124ff.
42. See Hardy, *op. cit.,* pp. 256-257. Also *Hearings, Operation of Banking Systems, Appendix, Part C, op. cit.,* pp. 852ff.
43. Sterling bills were also purchased by the Fed to help Great Britain, e.g., $16 million in late 1929 and $10 million in the summer of 1927. See Hardy, *op. cit.,* pp. 100ff.
44. The boom in loans to Germany began with the 1924 "Dawes loan," part of the Dawes Plan reparations, with $110 million loaned to Germany by an investment banking syndicate headed by J. P. Morgan and Co.
45. Schacht personally visited New York in late 1925 to press this course on the banks, and he, Gilbert, and German Treasury officials sent a cable to the New York banks in the same vein. The securities affiliate of the Chase National Bank did comply with these requests. See Anderson, *op. cit.,* pp. 150ff. See also Garet Garrett, *A Bubble That Broke the World* (Boston: Little Brown and Co., 1932), pp. 23-24, and Lionel Robbins, *The Great Depression* (New York: Macmillan Co., 1934), p. 64.
46. "In late 1925 the agents of fourteen different American investment banking houses were in Germany soliciting loans from the German states and municipalities." Anderson, *op. cit.,* p. 152. Also see Robert L. Sammons, "Capital Movements," in Hal B. Lary and Associates, *The United States in the World Economy* (Washington, D.C.: U.S. Govt. Printing Office, 1943), pp. 95-100; and Garrett, *op. cit.,* pp. 20, 24.

47. See Clark, *op. cit.*, p. 333. As early as 1924, the FRB had suggested that American acceptance credits finance the export of cotton to Germany.
48. See H. Parker Willis, *The Theory and Practice of Central Banking* (New York: Harper and Bros., 1936), pp. 210-212, 223.
49. *Hearings, Operation of Banking Systems*, pp. 852ff.
50. Clark, *op. cit.*, pp. 242-248; 376-378; Hardy, *op. cit.*, p. 248.
51. *Hearings, Operation of Banking Systems, Appendix, Part 6, op. cit.*, pp. 847, 922-923.
52. Yet not *wholly* unexpected, for we find Governor Strong writing in April, 1922 that one of his major reasons for open-market purchases was "to establish a level of interest rates . . . which would facilitate foreign borrowing in this country . . . and facilitate business improvement." Benjamin Strong to Under-Secretary of the Treasury S. Parker Gilbert, April 18, 1922. Chandler, *op. cit.*, pp. 210-211.
53. Harold L. Reed, *Federal Reserve Policy, 1921-1930* (New York: McGraw-Hill, 1930), pp. 20, and 14-41. Governor Miller agreed "that though prices were moving upward, so was production and trade, and sooner or later production would overtake the rise of prices . . ." *Ibid.*, pp.40-41.
54. See Chandler, *op. cit.*, p. 233, and pp. 222-233. Also see Hardy, *op. cit.*, pp. 38-40; Anderson, *op. cit.*, pp. 82-85, 144-147.
55. See H. Parker Willis, "What Caused the Panic of 1929?," *North American Review* (1930), p. 178; and Charles O. Hardy, *Credit Policies of the Federal Reserve System* (Washington, D.C.: The Brookings Institution, 1932), p. 287. Tax exemption on income from government bonds also spurred the banks' purchases. See Esther Rogoff Taus, *Central Banking Functions of the United States Treasury, 1789-1941* (New York: Columbia University Press, 1943), pp. 182ff.

NOTES TO CHAPTER 5

1. Seymour E. Harris, *Twenty Years of Federal Reserve Policy* (Cambridge, Mass.: Harvard University Press, 1933), I, 94.
2. Robert L. Sammons, "Capital Movements," in Hal B. Lary and Associates, *The United States in the World Economy* (Washington, D.C.: Government Printing Office, 1943), p. 94.
3. See Abraham Berglund, "The Tariff Act of 1922," *American Economic Review* (March, 1923), pp. 14-33.
4. See Benjamin H. Beckhart, "The Basis of Money Market Funds," in Beckhart, *et al.*, *The New York Money Market* (New York: Columbia University Press, 1931), II, 70.
5. Frank W. Fetter, "Tariff Policy and Foreign Trade," in J. G. Smith, ed., *Facing the Facts* (New York: G. P. Putnam's Sons, 1932), p. 83. Also see George E. Putnam, "What Shall We Do About Depressions?," *Journal of Business* (April, 1938), pp. 130-142, and Winthrop W. Aldrich, *The Causes of the Present Depression and Possible Remedies* (New York, 1933), pp. 7-8.

6. Jacob Viner, "Political Aspects of International Finance," *Journal of Business* (April, 1928), p. 170. Also see Herbert Hoover, *Memoirs*, (New York: The Macmillan Co., 1952), II, 80-86.

7. Viner, "Political Aspects of International Finance, Part II," *Journal of Business* (July, 1928), p. 359.

8. Harris Gaylord Warren, *Herbert Hoover and the Great Depression* (New York: Oxford University Press, 1959), p. 27.

9. As we have indicated above, a third motive for the 1924 credit expansion was to promote recovery in agriculture and business from the mild 1923 recession.

10. See Lionel Robbins, *The Great Depression* (New York: Macmillan Co., 1934), pp. 77-87; Sir William Beveridge, *Unemployment, A Problem of Industry* (London: The Macmillan Company, 1930), Chapter XVI; and Frederic Benham, *British Monetary Policy* (London: P. S. King and Son, 1932).

11. Lawrence E. Clark, *Central Banking Under the Federal Reserve System* (New York: Macmillan Co., 1935), pp. 310ff.

12. Charles Rist, "Notice Biographique," *Revue d' Économie Politique* (November-December, 1955), p. 1005. (Translation mine.)

13. Lester V. Chandler, *Benjamin Strong, Central Banker* (Washington, D.C.: The Brookings Institution, 1958), pp. 147-149.

14. Sir Henry Clay, *Lord Norman* (London: Macmillan and Co., 1957), pp. 140-141.

15. Former Assistant Secretary of the Treasury Oscar T. Crosby perceptively attacked this credit at the time as setting a dangerous precedent for inter-governmental lending. *Commercial and Financial Chronicle* (May 9, 1925), pp. 2357ff.

16. The Morgan credit was apparently instigated by Strong. See Chandler, *op. cit.*, pp. 284ff., 308ff., 312ff. Relations between the New York Fed and the House of Morgan were very close throughout this period. Strong had worked closely with the Morgan interests before assuming his post at the Federal Reserve. It is therefore significant that "J. P. Morgan and Company have been the fiscal agents in this country of foreign governments and have had 'close working agreements' with the Federal Reserve Bank of New York." Clark, *op. cit.*, p. 329. In particular, the Morgans were agents of the Bank of England. Also see Rist, *loc. cit.* To their credit, however, Morgans refused to go along with a Strong-Norman scheme to lend money to the Belgian government in order to prop up the Belgian exchange rate at an overvalued level, and thus subsidize inflationary Belgian policies.

17. Robbins, *op. cit.*, p. 80.

18. Strong to Mellon, May 27, 1924. Quoted in Chandler, *op. cit.*, pp. 283-284. Also see *ibid.*, pp. 293ff.

19. See Benjamin H. Beckhart, "Federal Reserve Policy and the Money Market, 1923-1931," in *op. cit.*, IV, 45.

20. Norman to Strong, October 16, 1924. Chandler, *op. cit.*, p. 302.

21. Norman to Hjalmar Schacht, December 28, 1926. Clay, *op. cit.*, p. 224.

22. Melchior Palyi, "The Meaning of the Gold Standard," *Journal of Business* (July, 1941), pp. 300-301. Also see Aldrich, *op. cit.*, pp. 10-11.
23. Palyi, *loc. cit.*, p. 304; Hardy, *op. cit.*, pp. 113-117.
24. "The ease with which the gold exchange standard can be instituted, especially with borrowed money, has led a good many nations during the past decade to 'stabilize' . . . at too high a rate." H. Parker Willis, "The Breakdown of the Gold Exchange Standard and its Financial Imperialism," *The Annalist* (October 16, 1931), pp. 626f. On the gold exchange standard, see also William Adams Brown, Jr., *The International Gold Standard Reinterpreted, 1914-1934* (New York: National Bureau of Economic Research, 1940), II, 732-749.
25. Brown, *op. cit.*, I, 355.
26. This is not to endorse the entire Blackett Plan, which also envisioned a £100 million gold loan to India by the U.S. and British governments. See Chandler, *op.cit.*, pp. 356ff.
27. See Beckhart, "The Basis of Money Market Funds," *loc. cit.*, p. 61.
28. Entry of February 6, 1928. Chandler, *op. cit.*, pp. 379-380. Norman did not insist on League of Nations control, however, when he and Strong agreed, in December 1927, to finance the stabilization of the Italian lira, by jointly extending a $75 million credit to the Bank of Italy ($30 million from the New York Bank), along with a $25 million credit by Morgan's and an equal loan by other private bankers in London. The Federal Reserve Board, as well as Secretary Mellon, approved of these subsidies. *Ibid.*, p. 388.
29. See Benjamin M. Anderson, *Economics and the Public Welfare* (New York: D. Van Nostrand Co., 1949), p. 167.
30. During the fall of 1925, Norman had similarly reduced Bank Rate. At that time, Strong had been critical, and was also led by the American boom to raise discount rates at home. By December, Britain's Bank Rate was raised again to its previous level.
31. Much of its sterling balances were accumulated as the result of a heavy British credit expansion in 1926.
32. The Bank of France had acquired these balances in a struggle to stabilize the franc at too *low* a rate, but without yet declaring gold convertibility. The latter step was finally taken in June, 1928.
33. Rist, *loc. cit.*, pp. 1006ff.
34. See Clark, *op. cit.*, p. 315. Paul Warburg's tribute to Strong was even more lavish. Warburg heralded Strong as the pathfinder and pioneer in "welding the central banks together into an intimate group." He concluded that "the members of the American Acceptance Council would cherish his memory." Paul M. Warburg, *The Federal Reserve System* (New York: Macmillan Co., 1930), II, 870.
   In the autumn of 1926, a leading banker admitted that bad consequences would follow the cheap money policy, but said: "that cannot be helped. It is the price we must pay for helping Europe." H. Parker Willis, "The Failure of the Federal Reserve," *North American Review* (1929), p. 553.

35. See Anderson, *Economics and the Public Welfare, op. cit.,* pp. 182-183; Beckhart, "Federal Reserve Policy and the Money Market," *loc. cit.,* pp. 67ff.; and Clark, *op. cit.,* p. 314.
36. O. Ernest Moore to Sir Arthur Salter, May 25, 1928. Quoted in Chandler, *op. cit.,* pp. 280-281.
37. Clark, *op. cit.,* p. 198. We have seen that sterling bills were bought in considerable amount in 1927 and 1929.
38. See Harold L. Reed, *Federal Reserve Policy, 1921-1930* (New York: McGraw-Hill, 1930), p. 32.
39. Clark points out that the cheap credit particularly succeeded in aiding the financial, investment banking, and speculative interests with whom Strong and his associates were personally affiliated. Clark, *op. cit.,* p. 344.
40. Anderson *(op. cit.)* is surely wrong when he infers that the stock market had by this time run away, and that the authorities could do little further. More vigor would have ended the boom then and there.
41. See Harris, *op. cit.,* II, 436ff.; Charles Cortez Abbott, *The New York Bond Market, 1920-1930* (Cambridge, Mass.: Harvard University Press, 1937), pp. 117-130.
42. See Strong to Walter W. Stewart, August 3, 1928. Chandler, *op. cit.,* pp. 459-465. For a contrary view, see Carl Snyder, *Capitalism, the Creator* (New York: The Macmillan Co., 1940), pp. 227-228.

    Dr. Stewart, we might note, had shifted easily from being head of the Division of Research of the Federal Reserve System, to a post of Economic Advisor to the Bank of England a few years later, from which he had written to Strong warning of too tight restriction on American bank credit.
43. See *Review of Economic Statistics* (1929), p. 13.
44. Real estate is the other large market in titles to capital. On the real estate boom of the 1920's, see Homer Hoyt, "The Effect of Cyclical Fluctuations upon Real Estate Finance," *Journal of Finance* (April, 1947), p. 57.
45. Significantly, the leading "bull" speculator of the era, William C. Durant, who failed ignominiously in the crash, hailed Coolidge and Mellon as the leading spirits of the cheap money program. *Commercial and Financial Chronicle* (April 20, 1929), pp, 2557ff.
46. Herbert Hoover, *Memoirs of Herbert Hoover* (New York: Macmillan Co., 1952), III, 16ff.
47. See Joseph Stagg Lawrence, *Wall Street and Washington* (Princeton: University Press, 1929), pp. 7ff., and *passim.*
48. See Irving Fisher, *The Stock Market Crash—And After* (New York: The Macmillan Co., 1930), pp. 37ff.
49. "The policy of 'moral suasion' . . . was inaugurated following a visit to this country of Mr. Montagu Norman." Beckhart, "Federal Reserve Policy and the Money Market," *loc. cit.,* p. 127.
50. *Ibid.,* pp. 142ff.
51. A. Wilfred May, "Inflation in Securities," in H. Parker Willis and John M. Chapman (eds.), *The Economics of Inflation* (New York:

Columbia University Press, 1935), pp. 292-293. Also see Hardy, *op. cit.,* pp. 124-177; and Oskar Morgenstern "Developments in the Federal Reserve System," *Harvard Business Review* (October, 1930), pp. 2-3.

52. For an excellent contemporary discussion of the Federal Reserve, and of its removal of the natural checks on commercial bank inflation, see Ralph W. Robey, "The Progress of Inflation and 'Freezing' of Assets in the National Banks," *The Annalist* (February 27, 1931), pp. 427-429. Also see C. A. Phillips, T. F. McManus, and R. W. Nelson, *Banking and the Business Cycle* (New York: Macmillan Co., 1937), pp. 140-142; and C. Reinold Noyes, "The Gold Inflation in the United States," *American Economic Review* (June, 1930), pp. 191-197.

NOTES TO CHAPTER 6

1. The qualitative aspect of credit is important to the extent that bank loans must be to *business,* and not to government or to consumers, to put the trade cycle mechanism into motion.

2. The NICB Consumer price index rose from 102.3 (1923 = 100) in 1921 to 104.3 in 1926, then fell to 100.1 in 1929; the BLS consumer good index fell from 127.7 (1935-1939 = 100) in 1921 to 122.5 in 1929. *Historical Statistics, op. cit.,* pp. 226-236, 344.

3. Phillips *et al., op. cit.,* pp. 176ff.

4. Chandler, *op. cit.,* p. 312. In this view, Strong was, of course, warmly supported by Montagu Norman. *Ibid.,* p. 315.

5. Also see Chandler, *op. cit.,* pp. 199ff. And Charles Rist recalls that, in his private conversations, "Strong was convinced that he was able to fix the price level, by his interest and credit policy." Rist, *loc. cit.,* p. 1029.

6. Strong thus overcame his previous marked skepticism toward any legislative mandate for price stabilization. Before this, he had preferred to leave the matter strictly to Fed discretion. See Chandler, *op. cit.,* pp. 202ff.

7. See the account in Irving Fisher, *Stabilised Money* (London: George Allen and Unwin, 1935), pp. 170-171. Commons wrote of Governor Strong: "I admired him both for his open-minded help to us on the bill and his reservation that he must go along with his associates."

8. See Fisher's eulogy of Snyder, *ibid.,* pp. 64-67; and Carl Snyder, "The Stabilization of Gold: A Plan," *American Economic Review* (June, 1923), pp. 276-285; Snyder, *Capitalism the Creator, op. cit.,* pp. 226-228.

9. D. H. Robertson, "The Trade Cycle," *Encyclopaedia Britannica,* 14th Ed. (1929), Vol. 22, p. 354.

10. D. H. Robertson, "How Do We Want Gold to Behave?," in *The International Gold Problem* (London: Humphrey Milford, 1932), p. 45; quoted in Phillips, *et al., op. cit.,* pp. 186-187.

11. Ralph G. Hawtrey, *The Art of Central Banking* (London: Longmans, Green and Co., 1932), p. 300.

12. Leading stabilizationist Norman Lombard also hailed Strong's alleged achievement: "By applying the principles expounded in this book . . .

he [Strong] maintained in the United States a fairly stable price level and a consequent condition of widespread economic well-being from 1922 to 1928." Norman Lombard, *Monetary Statesmanship* (New York: Harpers, 1934), p. 32n. On the influence of stable price ideas on Federal Reserve policy, see also David A. Friedman, "Study of Price Theories Behind Federal Reserve Credit Policy, 1921-29" (unpublished M. A. essay, Columbia University, 1938).

13. Fisher, *Stabilised Money, op. cit.*, p. 282. Our account of the growth of the stable money movement rests heavily upon Fisher's work.

14. While Hawtrey was the main inspiration for the resolutions, he criticized them for not going far enough.

15. See Paul Einzig, *Montagu Norman* (London: Kegan Paul, 1932), pp. 67, 78.

16. See Clay, *op. cit.*, p. 138.

17. Cited in Lawrence, *op. cit.*, pp. 437-443.

18. *Commercial and Financial Chronicle* (April, 1929), pp. 2204-2206. Also see Beckhart, "Federal Reserve Policy," *loc. cit.*, pp. 99ff.

19. See Joseph Dorfman, *The Economic Mind in American Civilization* (New York: Viking Press, 1959), IV, 178.

20. Allyn A. Young, "Downward Price Trend Probable, Due to Hoarding of Gold by Central Banks," *The Annalist* (January 18, 1929), pp. 96-97. Also see, "Our Reserve Bank Policy as Europe Thinks It Sees It," *The Annalist* (September 2, 1927), pp. 374-375.

21. Also see Harris, *op. cit.*, I, 192ff., and Aldrich, *op. cit.*, pp. 20-21.

NOTES TO CHAPTER 7

1. For an appreciation of the importance of this fact for American monetary history, see Vera C. Smith, *The Rationale of Central Banking* (London: P. S. King & Son, 1936).

2. From his acceptance speech on August 11, and his campaign speech at Des Moines on October 4. For full account of the Hoover speeches and anti-depression program, see William Starr Myers and Walter H. Newton, *The Hoover Administration* (New York: 1936), Part I; Myers, ed. *The State Papers of Herbert Hoover*, Vol. I and II (New York: 1934). Also see Herbert Hoover, *Memoirs of Herbert Hoover* (New York: Macmillan Co., 1937), Vol. III.

3. See Joseph Dorfman, *The Economic Mind in American Civilization* (New York: Viking Press, 1959), IV, 27.

4. Hoover, *Memoirs, op. cit.*, II, 29. Hoover's evasive rhetoric is typical: "I insisted that these improvements could be effected without government control, but the government should cooperate by research, intellectual leadership [*sic*], and prohibitions upon the abuse of power."

5. Cf. Arthur M. Schlesinger, Jr. *The Crisis of the Old Order, 1919-1933* (Boston: Houghton Mifflin Co., 1957), pp. 81ff.; Harris Gaylord Warren, *Herbert Hoover and the Great Depression* (New York: Oxford University Press, 1959), pp. 24ff.

6. Hoover records that the "extreme right" was hostile to these proposals —and understandably so—and notably the Boston Chamber of Commerce. Also see Eugene Lyons, *Our Unknown Ex-President* (New York: Doubleday and Co., 1948), pp. 213-214.

7. Hoover to Wesley C. Mitchell, July 29, 1921. Lucy Sprague Mitchell, *Two Lives* (New York: Simon and Schuster, 1953), p. 364.

8. Warren, *op. cit.*, p. 26.

9. See Hoover, *Memoirs, Vol. II, op. cit.*; and Lloyd M. Graves, *The Great Depression and Beyond* (New York: The Brookmire Economic Service, 1932), p. 84.

10. Hoover, *Memoirs, Vol. II, op. cit.*, pp. 41-42.

11. See Joseph H. McMullen, "The President's Unemployment Conference of 1921 and its Results" (unpublished M. A. essay, Columbia University, 1922), p. 33.

12. See Graves, *op. cit.*

13. See E. Jay Howenstine, Jr., "Public Works Policy in the Twenties," *Social Research* (December, 1946), pp. 479-500.

14. See Lyons, *op. cit.*, p. 230.

15. In reality, public works only prolong the depression, aggravate the malinvestment problem, and intensify the shortage of savings by wasting more capital. They also prolong unemployment by bolstering wage rates. See Mises, *Human Action, op. cit.*, pp. 792-794.

16. The payment of charity wages as high as market rates began in the depression of 1893; public works as a depression remedy started on a municipal scale in the recession of 1914-1915. The secretary of Mayor John Purroy Mitchell's New York Committee on Unemployment urged public works in 1916, and Nathan J. Stone, chief statistician of the U.S. Tariff Board, urged a national public works and employment reserve in 1915. Immediately after the war, Governor Alfred E. Smith of New York and Governor Frank O. Lowden of Illinois urged a national p·:blic works stabilization program. See Raphael Margolin, "Public Works as a Remedy for Unemployment in the United States" (unpublished M. A. essay, Columbia University, 1928).

17. See McMullen, *op. cit.*, p. 16.

18. Pennsylvania had established the first public works stabilization program in 1917, largely inspired by Mallery; it was later repealed. Mallery had also been made head of a new Division of Development of Public Works by States and Cities During the Transition Period, in the Wilson Administration. See Dorfman, *op. cit.*, IV, 7.

19. See John B. Andrews, "The President's Unemployment Conference— Success or Failure?," *American Labor Legislation Review* (December, 1921), pp. 307-310. Also see "Unemployment Survey," in *ibid.* (June, 1921), pp. 211-212.

20. *American Labor Legislation Review* (March, 1922), p. 79. Other officials of the AALL included: Jane Addams, Thomas L. Chadbourne, Professor John R. Commons, Professor Irving Fisher, Adolph Lewisohn, Lillian Wald, Felix M. Warburg, Woodrow Wilson, and Rabbi Stephen S. Wise.

21. Lyons, *op. cit.*, p. 230.
22. The American Construction Council was formed in response to the hounding of the New York construction industry by state and Federal authorities during the depression of 1920-1921. The governments charged the industry with "price-fixing" and "excessive profits." Hoover and Roosevelt together formed the Council in the summer of 1922, to stabilize and organize the industry. The aim was to cartellize construction, impose various codes of operation and "ethics," and to plan the entire industry. Franklin Roosevelt, as President of the Council, took repeated opportunity to denounce profit-seeking and rugged individualism. The "codes of fair practice" were Hoover's idea. See Daniel R. Fusfeld, *The Economic Thought of Franklin D. Roosevelt and the Origins of the New Deal* (New York: Columbia University Press, 1956), pp. 102ff.
23. Wesley C. Mitchell, "Unemployment and Business Fluctuations," *American Labor Legislation Review* (March, 1923), pp. 15-22.
24. The following economists, businessmen and other leaders, had by now served as officers of the American Association for Labor Legislation, in addition to those named above: Ray Stannard Baker, Bernard M. Baruch, Mrs. Mary Beard, Joseph P. Chamberlain, Morris Llewellyn Cooke, Fred C. Croxton, Paul H. Douglas, Morris L. Ernst, Herbert Feis, S. Fels, Walton H. Hamilton, William Hard, Ernest M. Hopkins, Royal W. Meeker, Broadus Mitchell, William F. Ogburn, Thomas I. Parkinson, Mrs. George D. Pratt, Roscoe Pound, Mrs. Raymond Robins, Julius Rosenwald, John A. Ryan, Nahum I. Stone, Gerard Swope, Mrs. Frank A. Vanderlip, Joseph H. Willits, and John G. Winant.
25. Ralph Owen Brewster, "Footprints on the Road to Plenty—A Three Billion Dollar Fund to Stabilize Business," *Commercial and Financial Chronicle* (November 28, 1928), p. 2527.
26. The Foster-Catchings plan called for an organized public works program of $3 billion to iron out the business cycle and stabilize the price level. Individual initiative, the authors decided, may be well and good, but in a situation of this sort "we must have collective leadership." William T. Foster and Waddill Catchings, *The Road to Plenty* (Boston: Houghton Mifflin Company, 1928), p. 187. For a brilliant critique of the underconsumptionist theories of Foster and Catchings, see F. A. Hayek, "The 'Paradox' of Savings," in *Profit, Interest and Investment* (London: Routledge and Kegan Paul, 1939), pp. 199-263.
28. See Dorfman, IV, *op. cit.*, pp. 349-350.
29. "Hoover's Plan to Keep the Dinner-Pail Full," *Literary Digest* (December 8, 1928), pp. 5-7.
30. William T. Foster and Waddill Catchings, "Mr. Hoover's Plan: What It Is and What It Is Not—The New Attack on Poverty," *Review of Reviews* (April, 1929), pp. 77-78. For a laudatory survey of Hoover's pro-public works views in the 1920's, by an official of the AALL, see George H. Trafton, "Hoover and Unemployment," *American Labor Legislation Review* (September, 1929), pp. 267ff; and *id.*, "Hoover's Unemployment Policy," *ibid.* (December, 1929), pp. 373ff.

31. Irving Bernstein, *The Lean Years: A History of the American Worker, 1920-1933* (Boston: Houghton Mifflin Co., 1960), p. 147. As early as 1909, Hoover had called unions "proper antidotes for unlimited capitalistic organizations," *Ibid.,* p. 250.

32. Warren, *op. cit.,* p. 28.

33. Lyons, *op. cit.,* p. 231.

34. See Marshall Olds, *Analysis of the Interchurch World Movement Report on the Steel Strike* (New York: G. P. Putnam and Sons, 1922), pp. 417ff.

35. Lyons, *op. cit.,* p. 231.

36. Also forgotten was the fact that *wages* were involved in the struggle, as well as hours. The workers wanted shorter hours with a "living wage," or as the Inquiry Report put it, "a minimum comfort wage"—in short, they wanted higher hourly wage rates. See Samuel Yellen, *American Labor Struggles* (New York: S. A. Russell, 1956 ed.) pp. 255ff.

37. On the twelve-hour day episode, see Frederick W. MacKenzie, "Steel Abandons the 12-Hour Day," *American Labor Legislation Review* (September, 1923), pp. 179ff.: Hoover, *Memoirs, op. cit.,* II, 103-104; and Robert M. Miller, "American Protestantism and the Twelve-Hour Day," *Southwestern Social Science Quarterly* (September, 1956), pp. 137-148. In the same year, Governor Pinchot of Pennsylvania forced the anthracite coal mines of that state to adopt the eight-hour day.

38. For a pro-union account of the affair, see Donald R. Richberg, *Labor Union Monopoly* (Chicago; Henry Regnery Co., 1957), pp. 3-28; also see Hoover, *Vol. II, op. cit.*

39. See McMullen, *op. cit.,* p. 17.

40. Hoover, *Memoirs, Vol. II, op. cit.,* p. 108.

41. One of these industrialists was the same Charles M. Schwab, head of Bethlehem Steel, who had bitterly fought Hoover in the eight-hour day dispute. Thus, in early 1929, Schwab opined that the way to keep prosperity permanent was to "pay labor the highest possible wages." *Commercial and Financial Chronicle, Vol. 128* (Jan. 5, 1929), p. 23.

42. National Industrial Conference Board, *Salary and Wage Policy in the Depression* (New York: the Conference Board, 1932), p. 3; Leo Wolman, *Wages in Relation to Economic Recovery* (Chicago: University of Chicago Press, 1931), p. 1.

43. Committee on Recent Economic Changes, *Recent Economic Changes in the United States* (New York: McGraw-Hill, 1929), I, xi.

44. See *Ibid., Vol. II,* Henry Dennison, "Management," p. 523.

45. Another important foretaste of the later NRA was Hoover's use of the Department of Commerce during the 1920's to help trade associations form "codes," endorsed by the FTC, to curtail competition in the name of eliminating "unfair" trade practices.

NOTES TO CHAPTER 8

1. Hoover, *Memoirs, op. cit.,* III, 29ff. For the sake of simplicity, any quotations from, or references based upon, the *Memoirs,* Myers and Newton's *The Hoover Administration,* Wilbur and Hyde's *The Hoover Policies,* or Hoover's *State Papers,* will not be footnoted from this point on.
2. Bernstein, *op. cit.,* p. 253.
3. In addition to the above sources on the Hoover conferences, see Robert P. Lamont, "The White House Conferences," *The Journal of Business* (July, 1930), p. 269.
4. *The American Federationist, Vol. 37* (March, 1930), p. 344.
5. "Public Works and Unemployment," *American Economic Review, Papers and Proceedings* (May, 1930), pp. 15ff.
6. See Theodore Saloutos and John D. Hicks, *Agricultural Discontents in the Middle West, 1900-1939* (Madison, Wisc.: University of Wisconsin Press, 1951), pp. 321-448; and Murray R. Benedict, *Farm Policies of the United States, 1790-1950* (New York: Twentieth Century Fund, 1953), pp. 145-275, for accounts of the farm bloc and farm programs in the 1920's and during the depression. Also see Alice M. Christensen, "Agricultural Pressure and Governmental Response in the United States, 1919-1929," *Agricultural History,* XI (1937) pp. 33-42, and V. N. Valgren, "The Agricultural Credits Act of 1923," *American Economic Review* (September, 1923), pp. 442-460.
7. Part of the pressure for this attack on the meat-packers came from wholesale grocers, who raised the familiar cry of "unfair competition" against efficient rivals. See Benedict, *op. cit.,* p. 150n. For similar instances, see Charles F. Phillips, *Competition? Yes But . . .* (Irvington-on-Hudson, N.Y.: Foundation for Economic Education, 1955).
8. President Wilson had suspended and then vainly vetoed renewal of the WFC at the behest of Secretary of Treasury David Houston, who was opposed in principle to any continuation of war intervention in the peacetime economy. Even after Congress overrode the veto, Houston was able to keep a checkrein on WFC activities. When Harding became President, he reappointed Eugene Meyer as head of the WFC and, under Meyer's inspiration, supported the subsequent expansion. See Gerald D. Nash, "Herbert Hoover and the Origins of the RFC," *Mississippi Valley Historical Review* (December, 1959), pp. 459-460.
9. Joseph Dorfman, *The Economic Mind in American Civilization* (New York: Viking Press, 1959), IV, 40.
10. See James H. Shideler, *Farm Crisis 1919-1923* (Berkeley: University of California Press, 1957), pp. 50-51, 55-56.
11. It may surprise many to learn that much of the cartel agitation came *not* from cotton farmers. It came from the merchants and bankers with large inventories of cotton on hand, and who would not suffer from reductions in acreage. *Ibid.,* p. 85.

12. The Iowa Farm Bureau Federation resolved in January, 1922 to present the facts on reduction of corn acreage to its membership, but added that "we entrust each farmer to adjust his acreage in accordance with his own judgment." *Ibid.*, p. 87.
13. See Benedict, *op. cit.*, pp. 186*n* and 194ff.
14. In 1924, Gray Silver, powerful Washington lobbyist for the farm bloc, attempted another national grain cooperative, setting up the Grain Marketing Company. The GMC aimed at becoming a holding company of the major private grain marketing firms, but farmers failed to support the plan, and the company died a year later.
15. See Shideler, *op. cit.*, p. 21.
16. By 1924, in addition to Peek, Johnson, the two Henry Wallaces—father and son, and Bernard Baruch, in support of McNary-Haugen there were the Illinois Agricultural Association, most Western farm journals, the American Farm Bureau Federation, the National Grange, the National Board of Farm Organizations, the American Wheat Growers' Association, and the prominent banker Otto H. Kahn.
17. See Saloutos and Hicks, *op. cit.*, pp. 286-291; and John D. Black, *Agricultural Reform in the United States* (New York: McGraw-Hill Co., 1929), pp. 337, 351ff.
18. Behind the scenes, Bernard Baruch had also been advocating a Federal Farm Board to raise farm prices by organizing agriculture under government aegis, starting with wheat and cotton. Also active in urging Commerce and the National Industrial Conference Board. The Commission on Agriculture, jointly established by the U.S. Chamber of Commerce and the National Industrial Conference Board. The Commission was sure that *"laissez-faire* is of the past." See Dorfman, Vol. IV, *op. cit.*, pp. 79-80.
19. "Hoover chose the Board members from men proposed by farm organizations, as requested by the Administration." See Edgar E. Robinson, "The Hoover Leadership, 1929-1933" (unpublished), pp. 128ff.
    After the first year of operations, Legge retired and Stone became chairman. Teague and McKelvie were replaced by two former high officials in the American Farm Bureau Federation, Frank Evans and the aggressive Sam H. Thompson.
20. This was to become a permanent question for logical people, with no sign yet that anyone is willing to answer. From the point of view of the general public, of course, the policies are contradictory and irrational. From the point of view of the government bureaucracy, however, *both* measures add to its power and swell its number.
21. The FFB forced the Chicago Board of Trade to prohibit short selling by foreign governments, notably by Russia.
22. Harris Gaylord Warren, *Herbert Hoover and the Great Depression* (New York: Oxford University Press, 1959), p. 175.
23. To their great credit, some organizations bitterly opposed the FFB throughout these years. These included the Nebraska Farmers' Union, which attacked the FFB as a great exploitative bureaucracy, the Corn Belt Committee, and the Minnesota Farm Bureau.

24. Murray R. Benedict and Oscar C. Stine, *The Agricultural Commodity Programs* (New York: The Twentieth Century Fund, 1956), pp. 235-236.

25. At the end of 1931, Secretary of Agriculture Hyde was advocating the replacement of our traditional "planless" agriculture by a program of government purchase and reforestation of submarginal lands. "Hyde, however, had rejected as incompatible with American liberty the proposal of Senator Arthur H. Vandenberg (R., Michigan) to compel farmers to curtail their production." Gilbert N. Fite, "Farmer Opinion and the Agricultural Adjustment Act, 1933," *Mississippi Valley Historical Review* (March, 1962), p. 663.

26. There were also "milk strikes" in some areas, with milk trucks seized on the roads, and their contents dumped upon the ground. Wisconsin and California, in 1932, pioneered in setting up state milk controls, amounting to compulsory milk cartellization on a state-wide level. See Benedict and Stine. *op. cit.*, p. 444.

27. See Fred A. Shannon, *American Farmers' Movements* (Princeton, N.J.: D. Van Nostrand Co., 1957), pp. 88-91, 178-182.

NOTES TO CHAPTER 9

1. Benjamin M. Anderson, *Economics and the Public Welfare* (New York: D. Van Nostrand, 1949), pp. 222-223.

2. The New York Federal Reserve also continued to lead in collaborating with foreign central banks, often against the wishes of the Administration. Thus, the Bank for International Settlements, an attempt at an inter-central banks' central bank, instigated by Montagu Norman, treated the New York Bank as America's central bank. Chairman of the B.I.S.'s first organizing committee was Jackson E. Reynolds, a director of the New York Federal Reserve, and its first President was Gates W. McGarrah, who resigned as Governor of the New York Reserve Bank in February, 1930, to assume the post. J. P. Morgan and Co. supplied much of the American capital in the new Bank. In November, Governor Harrison made a "regular business trip" abroad to confer with other central bankers, and discuss loans to foreign governments. In 1931, the New York Federal Reserve extended loans to the BIS. Yet there was no legislative sanction for our participation in the Bank.

3. *Business Week* (October 22, 1930). Dr. Virgil Jordan was the chief economist for *Business Week*—then as now, a leading spokesman for "enlightened" business opinion.

4. Herbert Hoover, *Memoirs of Herbert Hoover* (New York: Macmillan Co., 1952), II, 291ff. See John H. Fahey, "Tariff Barriers and Business Depressions," *Proceedings of the Academy of Political Science* (June, 1931), pp. 41ff.

5. See Frank W. Taussig, "The Tariff Act of 1930," *Quarterly Journal of Economics* (November, 1930), pp. 1-21; and *id.*, "The Tariff, 1929-1930," *ibid.* (February, 1930), pp. 175-204.

6. Robert A. Divine, *American Immigration Policy, 1924-1952* (New Haven: Yale University Press, 1957), p. 78.
7. The labor union movement applauded the program, with William Green urging increased Congressional appropriations for the Federal border patrol to keep out immigrants. In California, Filipino field hands were beaten and shot to keep them from employment in the agricultural valleys. Irving Bernstein, *The Lean Years: A History of the American Worker, 1920-1933* (Boston: Houghton Mifflin Co., 1960), p. 305.
8. In the same month, October, however, Hoover's aide Edward Eyre Hunt, writing to Colonel Woods, was critical of whatever wage cuts had occurred. Bernstein, *op. cit.*, p. 259.
9. Bernays' major contribution was insistence on the public-relations superiority of the word "employment," rather than "unemployment," in the name of the organization. Bernstein, *op. cit.*, pp. 302-303.
10. Hoover's interest in governmental dams by no means began with the depression, as witness his proud launching of the Boulder Dam in December, 1928. That private business is not always a reliable champion of free private enterprise, is shown by the approval of the dam by such utility companies as the Southern California Edison Company, which hoped to benefit by purchasing cheap, subsidized government power. In addition, private power companies saw Boulder Dam as a risky, submarginal project plagued by grave engineering difficulties, and were content to have the taxpayers assume the risk.

    On the other hand, it must be admitted that Hoover staunchly resisted Congressional attempts during 1931 and 1932 to launch into socialized electric power production and distribution at Muscle Shoals, a project strongly opposed by private power companies and later enlarged by the New Deal into the TVA. See Harris Gaylord Warren, *Herbert Hoover and the Great Depression* (New York: Oxford University Press, 1959), pp. 64, 77-80.
11. *Commercial and Financial Chronicle* Vol. *131* (August 2, 1930), pp. 690-691.
12. Joseph Stagg Lawrence, "The Attack on Thrift," *Journal of the American Bankers' Association* (January, 1931), pp. 597ff.
13. *Commercial and Financial Chronicle, Vol. 132* (January 17, 1931), pp. 428-429.
14. See U.S. Senate, Committee on Banking and Currency, *History of the Employment Stabilization Act of 1931* (Washington, 1945); Joseph E. Reeve, *Monetary Reform Movements* (Washington: American Council on Public Affairs, 1943), pp. 1ff.; U.S. Senate, Committee on Judiciary, 71st Congress, 2nd Session, *Hearings on S. 3059* (Washington, 1930).
15. The economists and others who signed these petitions included the following:

Edith Abbott
Asher Achinstein
Emily Green Balch
Bruce Bliven

Sophinisba P. Breckenridge
Paul F. Brissenden
William Adams Brown, Jr.
Edward C. Carter

Ralph Cassady, Jr.
Waddill Catchings
Zechariah Chafee, Jr.
Joseph P. Chamberlain
John Bates Clark
John Maurice Clark
Victor S. Clark
Joanna C. Colcord
John R. Commons
Morris L. Cooke
Morris A. Copeland
Malcolm Cowley
Donald Cowling
Jerome Davis
Davis F. Dewey
Paul H. Douglas
Stephen P. Duggan
Seba Eldridge
Henry Pratt Fairchild
John M. Ferguson
Frank A. Fetter
Edward A. Filene
Irving Fisher
Elisha M. Friedman
A. Anton Friedrich
S. Colum Gilfillan
Meredith B. Givens
Carter Goodrich
Henry F. Grady
Robert L. Hale
Walton Hamilton
Mason B. Hammond
Charles O. Hardy
Sidney Hillman
Arthur N. Holcombe
Paul T. Homan
B. W. Huebsch
Alvin S. Johnson
H. V. Kaltenborn

Edwin W. Kemmerer
Willford I. King
Alfred Knopf
Hazel Kyrk
Harry W. Laidler
Corliss Lamont
Kenneth S. Latourette
William Leiserson
J. E. LeRossignol
Roswell C. McCrea
Otto Tod Mallery
Harry A. Millis
Broadus Mitchell
Harold G. Moulton
Paul M. O'Leary
Thomas I. Parkinson
S. Howard Patterson
Harold L. Reed
Father John A. Ryan
Francis B. Sayre
G. T. Schwenning
Henry R. Seager
Thorsten Sellin
Mary K. Simkhovitch
Nahum I. Stone
Frank Tannenbaum
Frank W. Taussig
Ordway Tead
Willard Thorp
Mary Van Kleeck
Oswald G. Villard
Lillian Wald
J. P. Warbasse
Colston E. Warne
Gordon S. Watkins
William O. Weyforth
Joseph H. Willits
Chase Going Woodhouse
Matthew Woll

Also involved in the agitation, by virtue of their being officers and members of the American Association for Labor Legislation during this period, were the following economists and other intellectual leaders:

Willard E. Atkins
C. C. Burlingham
Stuart Chase
Dorothy W. Douglas
Richard T. Ely

Felix Frankfurter
Arthur D. Gayer
Harold M. Groves
Luther Gulick
Mrs. Thomas W. Lamont

Eduard C. Lindeman
William N. Loucks
Wesley C. Mitchell
Jessica Peixotto
Donald Richberg
Bernard L. Shientag

Sumner H. Slichter
Edwin S. Smith
George Soule
William F. Willoughby
Edwin E. Witte

16. Bernstein, *op. cit.*, p. 304.
17. See Joseph Dorfman, *The Economic Mind in American Civilization* (New York: Viking Press, 1959), V, 674-675.
18. The following month, five Progressive Senators called a conference to agitate for a gigantic five billion dollar public works program; the conference was addressed by Detroit's progressive Mayor, Frank Murphy, Professor Leo Wolman, and Father John A. Ryan. Senator LaFollette and William Randolph Hearst also called for a similar measure.
19. See David Loth, *Swope of GE* (New York: Simon and Schuster, 1958), pp. 198-200.
20. Bernstein, *op. cit.*, p. 304.
21. Generally, government expenditures are compared with Gross National Product, in weighing the fiscal extent of government activity in the economy. But since government expenditure is more depredation than production, it is first necessary to deduct "product originating in government and in government enterprises" from GNP to arrive at Gross Private Product. It might be thought that total government expenditures should not be deducted from GPP, because this involves double counting of government expenditures on bureaucrats' salaries ("product originating in government"). But this is *not* double counting, for the great bulk of money spent on bureaucratic salaries is gathered by means of taxation of the *private* sector, and, therefore, it too involves depredation upon the private economy. Our method involves a slight amount of overcounting of depredation, however, insofar as funds for government spending come from taxation of the *bureaucrats* themselves, and are therefore not deducted from private product. This amount, particularly in the 1929-1932 period, may safely be ignored, however, as there is no accurate way of estimating it and no better way of estimating government depredation on the private sector.

　　If government expenditures and receipts are just balanced, then obviously each is a measure of depredation, as funds are acquired by taxation and channelled into expenditures. If expenditures are larger, then the deficit is either financed by issuing new money or by borrowing private savings. In either case, the deficit constitutes a drain of resources from the private sector. If there is a surplus of receipts over expenditures then the surplus taxes are drains on the private sector. For a more extended discussion, and a tabulation of estimates of these figures for the 1929-1932 period, see the Appendix.
22. While the data in the Appendix below list the rise in Federal expenditure to be $200 million, this is the effect of rounding. The actual increase was $133 million.
23. See Sidney Ratner, *American Taxation* (New York: W. W. Norton and Co., 1942), p. 443.

NOTES TO CHAPTER 10

1. Benjamin McAlester Anderson, *Economics and the Public Welfare* (Princeton, N.J.: D. Van Nostrand Co., 1949), pp. 232ff.
2. The secret relations between Governor Norman and the head of the Federal Reserve Bank of New York continued during the depression. In August, 1932, Norman landed at Boston, and travelled to New York under the alias of "Professor Clarence Skinner." We do not know what transpired at this conference with Reserve Bank leaders, but the Bank of England congratulated Norman upon his return for having "sowed a seed." See Lawrence E. Clark, *Central Banking Under the Federal Reserve System* (New York: Macmillan Co., 1935), p. 312.
3. Clark plausibly maintains that the true motive of the New York Federal Reserve for these salvage operations was to bail out favored New York banks holding large quantities of frozen foreign assets, e.g., German acceptances. *Ibid.*, pp. 343f.
4. See Winthrop W. Aldrich, *The Causes of the Present Depression and Possible Remedies* (New York, 1933), p. 12.
5. Joseph Dorfman, *The Economic Mind in American Civilization* (New York: Viking Press, 1959), V, 675.
6. See Irving Bernstein, *The Lean Years: A History of the American Worker, 1920-1933* (Boston: Houghton Mifflin Co., 1960) and Dorfman, Vol, V, *op. cit.*, p. 7n. However, Hoover did veto a Woods-supported bill, passed in March, to strengthen the U.S. Employment Service. See Harris Gaylord Warren, *Herbert Hoover and the Great Depression* (New York: Oxford University Press, 1959), pp. 24ff.
7. E. P. Hayes, *Activities of the President's Emergency Committee for Employment, October 17, 1930-August 19, 1931* (printed by the author, 1936).
8. The director of the new Federal Employment Stabilization Board, D. H. Sawyer, was critical of the time lag inherent in public works programs, and preferred to leave public works to the localities. In addition, J. S. Taylor, head of the Division of Public Construction, opposed public works in principle. Bernstein, *op. cit.*, pp. 273-274.
9. *Congressional Record, Vol. 75* (January 11, 1932), pp. 1655-1657.
10. *Monthly Labor Review, Vol. 32* (1931), pp. 834ff.
11. The truth is precisely the opposite; consuming power is wholly dependent upon production.
12. Leo Wolman, *Wages in Relation to Economic Recovery* (Chicago: University of Chicago Press, 1931).
13. Secretary of Commerce Lamont declared in April, 1931, that "I have canvassed the principal industries, and I find no movement to reduce the rate of wages. On the contrary, there is a desire to support the situation in every way." Quoted in Edward Angly, comp., *Oh Yeah?* (New York: Viking Press, 1931), p. 26.

14. National Industrial Conference Board, *Salary and Wage Policy in the Depression* (New York: The Conference Board, 1933), p. 6.
15. Angly, *op. cit.*, p. 22.
16. We might also note that Keynes found the attitude of the Federal Reserve authorities "thoroughly satisfactory," i.e., satisfactorily inflationist. Roy F. Harrod, *The Life of John Maynard Keynes* (New York: Harcourt, Brace and Co., 1951), pp. 437-448.
17. See John Oakwood, "Wage Cuts and Economic Realities," *Barron's* (June 29, 1931); Oakwood, "How High Wages Destroy Buying Power," *Barron's* (February 29, 1932); Hugh Bancroft, "Wage Cuts a Cure for Depression," *Barron's* (October 19,1931); and Bancroft, "Fighting Economic Law—Wage Scales and Purchasing Power," *Barron's* (January 25, 1932). Also see George Putnam, "Is Wage Maintenance a Fallacy?," *Journal of the American Bankers' Association* (January, 1932), pp. 429ff.
18. See Fred R. Fairchild, "Government Saves Us From Depression," *Yale Review* (Summer, 1932), pp. 667ff.; and Dorfman, *op. cit.*, V, 620.
19. Stimson also added a racist note, fearing that permitting relatives would allow the bringing in of too many of the "southern" as against the "northern" and "Nordic" races. See Robert A. Divine, *American Immigration Policy, 1924-1952* (New Haven: Yale University Press, 1957), p. 78.
20. On the vigorous attempts of the President's Emergency Committee for Employment to pressure the Red Cross into giving relief to coal miners, see Bernstein, *op. cit.*, pp. 308ff.
21. By June, however, the American Association of Public Welfare Relief was calling for a federal relief program.
22. Edith Abbott, *Public Assistance* (Chicago: University of Chicago Press, 1940), I, 657-658, and 509-670. Even voluntary relief, if given indiscriminately, will prolong unemployment by preventing downward pressure on wage rates from clearing the labor market.
23. See Arthur M. Schlesinger, Jr., *The Crisis of the Old Order, 1919-1933* (Boston: Houghton Mifflin Co., 1957), pp. 169, 507.
24. Daniel R. Fusfeld, *The Economic Thought of Franklin D. Roosevelt and the Origins of the New Deal* (New York: Columbia University Press, 1956), p. 267.
25. *Monthly Labor Review, Vol. 33* (1931), pp. 1341-1342.
26. See Paul F. Wendt, *The Role of the Federal Government in Housing* (Washington, D.C.: American Enterprise Association, 1956), pp. 8-9.
27. Nash maintains that it was *Meyer* who made the promise to the bankers after Hoover and Mellon had left. Meyer and Senator Joseph Robinson, Democratic Senate leader, urged a special session to enact a new WFC, but Hoover still held back. At this point, Meyer secretly put a staff together, headed by Walter Wyatt, counsel of the FRB, to draft what was later to become the RFC. Gerald D. Nash, "Herbert Hoover and the Origins of the RFC," *Mississippi Valley Historical Review* (December, 1959), pp. 461ff.
28. Nash, *loc. cit.*, and Warren, *op. cit.*, pp.140ff.
29. See *Monthly Labor Review, Vol. 33* (1931), pp. 1049-1057.

30. Quoted in Schlesinger, *op. cit.*, pp. 182-183.
31. J. George Frederick, *Readings in Economic Planning* (New York: The Business Bourse, 1932), pp. 332ff. Frederick was a leading Swope disciple.
32. Frederick, *op. cit.*
33. See Fusfeld, *op. cit.*, pp. 311ff.; David Loth, *Swope of GE* (New York: Simon and Schuster, 1958), pp. 201ff.; Schlesinger, *op. cit.*, p. 200.
34. Wallace B. Donham, *Business Adrift* (1931), cited in Schlesinger, *op. cit.*, p. 181. Nicholas Murray Butler also considered the Soviet Union to have the "vast advantage" of "a plan." See Dorfman, *op. cit.*, IV, 631-632.
35. Later, the Swope idea took form in the NRA, with Swope himself helping to write the final draft, and staying in Washington to help run it. Swope thus became perhaps the leading industrialist among the "Brain Trust." Henry I. Harriman, another contributor to the drafting of the NRA, also turned up as a leader in the agricultural Brain Trust of the New Deal. Another Baruch disciple, and a friend of Swope's, General Hugh S. Johnson, was chosen head of the NRA (with old colleague George Peek as head of the AAA). When Johnson was relieved, Baruch himself was offered the post. See Margaret Coit, *Mr. Baruch* (Boston: Moughton Mifflin Co., 1957), pp. 220-221, 440-442; Loth, *op. cit.*, pp. 223ff.
36. Theodore M. Knappen, "Business Rallies to the Standard of Permanent Prosperity," *The Magazine of Wall Street* (December 14, 1929), p. 265.
37. The report, "Long-Range Planning for the Regularization of Industry," was prepared by Professor John Maurice Clark of Columbia University, and concurred in by George Soule, Edwin S. Smith, and J. Russell Smith. See Dorfman, *Vol. V, op. cit.*, pp. 758-761.
38. Rexford Guy Tugwell, *The Democratic Roosevelt* (New York: Doubleday and Co., 1957), p. 283.
39. Hoover relates that Henry I. Harriman warned him that if he persisted in opposing the Swope Plan, the business world would support Roosevelt for President, because the latter had agreed to enact the plan. He also reports that leading businessmen carried out this threat.
40. *Monthly Labor Review, Vol. 33* (1931), pp. 1049-1057.
41. Schlesinger. *op. cit.*, p. 186.
42. See George W. Stocking, "Stabilization of the Oil Industry: Its Economic and Legal Aspects," *American Economic Review, Papers and Proceedings* (May, 1933), pp. 59-70.
43. If the coal industry was not as successful as the oil in becoming cartellized, it was not for lack of trying. C. E. Bockus, president of the National Coal Association, wrote in an article, "The Menace of Overproduction," of the need of the coal industry "to secure, by cooperative action, the continuous adjustment of the production of bituminous coal to the existing demand for it, thereby discouraging wasteful methods of production and consumption. . . . The European method of meeting this situation is through the establishment of cartels. . . ." Quoted in Ralph J. Watkins, *A Planned Economy Through Coordinated Control of Basic Industries* (mimeographed manuscript, submitted to American Philanthropic Association, October, 1931), pp. 54ff.

Hoover also reduced production in other fields by adding over two million acres to the virtually useless national forests during his regime, as well as increasing the area of the totally useless national parks and monuments by forty per cent. If Congress had not balked, he would have permanently sequestered much more usable land. See Harris Gaylord Warren, *Herbert Hoover and the Great Depression* (New York: Oxford University Press, 1959), pp. 64, 77-80.

NOTES TO CHAPTER 11

1. See Sidney Ratner, *American Taxation* (New York: W. W. Norton and Co., 1942), pp. 447-449.
2. See Jane Kennedy, "Development of Postal Rates: 1845-1955," *Land Economics* (May, 1957), pp. 93-112; and Kennedy, "Structure and Policy in Postal Rates," *Journal of Political Economy* (June, 1957), pp. 185-208. Hoover also deliberately used a system of airmail subsidies effectively to bring the air transport industry under government dictation. To Hoover, this was a device for "orderly development" of the airline industry. See Harris Gaylord Warren, *Herbert Hoover and the Great Depression* (New York: Oxford University Press, 1959), p. 70.
3. *Congressional Record, Vol. 75* (January 12, 1932), p. 1763. Also see Russell C. Leffingwell, "Causes of Depression," *Proceedings of the Academy of Political Science* (June, 1931), p. 1.
4. Randolph Paul, *Taxation in the United States* (Boston: Little Brown and Co., 1954), p. 162.
5. It was undoubtedly this vagueness that drew declarations of support for the League from such disparate figures as: President Hoover, Governor Franklin D. Roosevelt, William Green, farm leader Louis Taber, Calvin Coolidge, chairman of the Advisory Council of the League, Alfred E. Smith, Newton D. Baker, Elihu Root, and General Pershing. See Bank of the Manhattan Company, *Chapters in Business and Finance* (New York, 1932), pp. 59-68. Also see National Economy League, *Brief in Support of Petition of May 4, 1932*. On this Committee and on the similar National Action Committee, see Warren, *op. cit.*, p. 162.
6. See James M. Beck, *Our Wonderland of Bureaucracy* (New York: The Macmillan Co., 1932); Mauritz A. Hallgren, *Seeds of Revolt* (New York: Alfred A. Knopf, 1933), pp. 274ff.
7. Cf. M. Slade Kendrick, *A Century and a Half of Federal Expenditures* (New York: National Bureau of Economic Research, 1955), pp. 77ff.
8. See Lewis H. Kimmel, *Federal Budget and Fiscal Policy, 1789-1958* (Washington: The Brookings Institution, 1959), pp. 155ff.
9. *Congressional Record* (May 16, 1932), pp. 10309-10339. Among the supporters were such economists as:

Edwin W. Borchard   Richard T. Ely
Paul W. Brissenden   Ralph C. Epstein
Morris L. Cooke   Irving Fisher

Felix Frankfurter	E. R. A. Seligman
Walton Hamilton	Sumner H. Slichter
Horace M. Kallen	George Soule
Frank H. Knight	Frank W. Taussig
William M. Leiserson	Ordway Tead
W. N. Loucks	Gordon S. Watkins
Broadus Mitchell	Myron W. Watkins
Harold G. Moulton	W. F. Willcox
E. M. Patterson	E. E. Witte
Selig Perlman	

10. See Joseph E. Reeve, *Monetary Reform Movements* (Washington, D.C.: American Council on Public Affairs, 1943), p. 19.
11. On the economists' petition, see Joseph Dorfman, *The Economic Mind in American Civilization* (New York: Viking Press, 1959), V, 675.
12. See Vladimir D. Kazakévich, "Inflation and Public Works," in H. Parker Willis and John M. Chapman, *The Economics of Inflation* (New York: Columbia University Press, 1935), pp. 344-349.
13. Dr. Anderson's account of the 1932 measures is unaccountably weak, since he does an about-face to favor the Hoover program—including the NCC, the RFC, and the Glass-Steagall Act—after opposing similarly statist and inflationary measures of earlier Hoover years. See Anderson, *Economics and the Public Welfare, op. cit.,* pp. 266-278.
14. Senator Robinson had obtained Hoover's promise to name Meyer as head of RFC in return for Democratic support in Congress. Gerald D. Nash, "Herbert Hoover and the Origins of the RFC," *Mississippi Valley Historical Review* (December, 1959), pp. 461ff.
15. See John T. Flynn, "Inside the RFC," *Harper's Magazine, Vol. 166* (1933), pp. 161-169. The Hoover group maintains, however, that General Dawes didn't want the RFC loan, which was rather insisted upon by Democratic bankers in Chicago, and by the Democratic members of the Board of the RFC.
16. The Missouri Pacific had apparently falsified its balance sheet prior to asking for the RFC loan, to claim more cash on hand than it really had. Ferdinand Lundberg, *America's Sixty Families* (New York: The Citadel Press, 1946), p. 233.
17. Flynn, *loc. cit.* Another consequence of RFC loans to railroads was an approach toward direct socialization from the creditor interest of the RFC in bankrupt roads, and the consequent placing of government directors on the reorganized railroads. Dewing maintains that "the government through the power of its loans was in a position to dominate the policy of the reorganized road." Arthur Stone Dewing, *The Financial Policy of Corporations* (5th edition, New York: Ronald Press, 1953), II, 1263.
18. J. Franklin Ebersole, "One Year of the Reconstruction Finance Corporation," *Quarterly Journal of Economics* (May, 1933), pp. 464-487.
19. See Edith Abbott, *Public Assistance* (Chicago: University of Chicago Press, 1940).
20. Costigan and LaFollette obtained the material for their bill from the

newly-formed Social Work Conference on Federal Action on Unemployment, headed by Linton B. Swift of the Family Welfare Association. The new organization symbolized the recent shift among professional social workers in favor of federal relief. The May, 1932 meeting of the National Conference of Social Work reversed the 1931 opposition' to federal relief. Irving Bernstein, *The Lean Years: A History of the American Worker, 1920-1933* (Boston: Houghton Mifflin Co., 1960), pp. 462ff.

21. Particularly influential in inducing Hoover's surrender was a plea for federal relief, at the beginning of June, by leading industrialists of Chicago. Having been refused further relief funds by the Illinois legislature, these Chicagoans turned to the federal government. They included the chief executives of Armour, Wilson, Cudahy, International Harvester, Santa Fe R. R., Marshall Field, Colgate-Palmolive-Peet, Inland Steel, Bendix, U.S. Gypsum, A. B. Dick, Illinois Bell Telephone, and the First National Bank. Bernstein, *op. cit.,* p. 467.

22. See A. E. Geddes, *Trends in Relief Expenditures, 1910-1935* (Washington: U.S. Government Printing Office, 1937), p. 31.

23. The defenders of the Glass-Steagall Act might protest that the Act fitted the quantitativist policy of considering *total quantity* rather than *quality* of assets, and therefore that an "Austrian" economist should defend the measure. But the point is that *any further* permission for government to lend to banks, whether quantitative or qualitative, is an inflationary addition to the *quantity* of money, and therefore to be criticized by the "Austrian" economist.

24. Lauchlin Currie, *The Supply and Control of Money in the United States* (2nd. ed., Cambridge Mass.: Harvard University Press, 1935), p. 116.

25. To keep our perspective on the monetary contraction of the 1929-1932 period, which has often been pointed at with alarm, we should remember that the total money supply fell from $73.3 billion in June 1929, to $64.7 billion at the end of 1932, a fall of only 11.6 per cent, or 3.3 per cent per annum. Compare this rate to the inflationary rise of 7.7 per cent per annum during the boom of the 1920's.

26. Seymour E. Harris, *Twenty Years of Federal Reserve Policy* (Cambridge, Mass.: Harvard University Press, 1933), II, 700.
Dorfman, *op. cit., Vol. V,* pp. 720-721.

28. See Frank D. Graham, *The Abolition of Unemployment* (1932), and Dorfman, *op. cit., Vol. V,* pp. 720-721.

29. It is instructive to record the names and affiliations of the more prominent signers of this monumental inanity. They were:
Willard E. Atkins, New York University
Frank Aydelotte, President of Swarthmore College
C. Canby Balderston, University of Pennsylvania
George E. Barnett, Johns Hopkins, President of the American Economic Association
John Bates Clark, Columbia University
Miss Joanna C. Colcord, the Russell Sage Foundation
Morris A. Copeland, University of Michigan

Paul H. Douglas, University of Chicago
Howard O. Eaton, University of Oklahoma
Frank Albert Fetter, Princeton University
Frank Whitson Fetter, Princeton University
Irving Fisher, Yale University
Frank Whitson Fetter, Princeton University
Walton H. Hamilton, Yale University
Paul U. Kellogg, editor of *Survey Graphic*
Willford I. King, New York University
William M. Leiserson, Antioch College
Richard A. Lester, Princeton University
Harley Leist Lutz, Princeton University
James D. Magee, New York University
Otto Tod Mallery
Broadus Mitchell, Johns Hopkins University
Sumner H. Slichter, Harvard University
Charles T. Tippetts, University of Buffalo
Jacob Viner, University of Chicago
Charles R. Whittlesey, Princeton University
Joseph H. Willits, Dean of Wharton School, University of Pennsylvania
Leo Wolman, Columbia University

30. *New York Times* (January 16, 1933), p. 23. The barter movement had previously been tried voluntarily on local levels, and had, of course, failed ignominiously, a fact which almost always spurs ideologues to urge that the same scheme be imposed coercively by the federal government. The barter movement as local cooperative had begun with the Unemployed Citizens' League of Seattle in July, 1931, and soon spread to more than half the states. They all failed quickly. Similar local "scrip exchanges" failed rapidly, after each issuance of the supposedly miraculous scrip. The most prominent scrip exchange was the Emergency Exchange Association of New York, flamboyantly organized by Stuart Chase and other intellectuals and professional men. See Dorfman, *op. cit.*, V, 624-625, 677.

31. Dorfman, *op. cit.*, V, 675-676.

32. See Quincy Wright (ed.), *Gold and Monetary Stabilization* (Chicago: University of Chicago Press, 1932).

33. The group of economists included:

James W. Angell	Harold G. Moulton
Garfield V. Cox	Ernest M. Patterson
Aaron Director	C. A. Phillips
Irving Fisher	Henry Schultz
Harold D. Gideonse	Henry C. Simons
Alvin H. Hansen	Charles S. Tippetts
Charles O. Hardy	Jacob Viner
Frank H. Knight	C. W. Wright
Arthur W. Marget	Ivan Wright
Harry A. Millis	Theodore O. Yntema
Lloyd W. Mints	

34. H. Parker Willis, "Federal Reserve Policy in Depression," in Wright, ed., *op. cit.*, pp. 77-108.
35. Gottfried von Haberler, "Money and the Business Cycle," in *ibid.*, pp. 43-74.
36. Speaking at the same conference, Professor John H. Williams admitted that, for the 1920's: "It can be argued that but for credit expansion prices would have fallen, and that they should have done so. It was on such grounds that the Austrian economists predicted the depression." John H. Williams, "Monetary Stabilization and the Gold Standard," in *ibid.*, p. 149. Williams did not sign the general statement either.
37. Another expression of sound money sentiment, though hardly as penetrating as Haberler's, came later in the year, in September. A group of economists issued a statement, attacking inflation or any abandonment of the gold standard, calling for a balanced budget through lower taxes and expenditures rather than through higher taxes, attacking government propping up of unsound corporate positions which should liquidate quickly, and attacking the Hoover experiments in farm price supports. They pointed out that inflation's benefits are only illusory and that it simply and disruptively benefits one group at the expense of another, and therefore could not help cure the depression. They also urged tariff reduction, and cutting the salaries of government employees, whose pay had unfortunately remained the same while the income of taxpayers had declined. Deviating from soundness, however, were their proposals for a Federal system of employment exchanges, hints of favoring unemployment insurance, and acceptance of a continuing RFC, relief programs, and temporary expedients to check deflation. Among the signers were financial economists W. W. Cumberland, Lionel D. Edie, Leland Rex Robinson, Alexander Sachs, Rufus S. Tucker, and Robert B. Warren, and such academic economists as Theodore E. Gregory of the London School of Economics, Edwin W. Kemmerer of Princeton, Dean Roswell C. McCrea of Columbia School of Business, and Dean A. Wellington Taylor of NYU School of Business Administration. "Prosperity Essentials," *Barrons'*, September 26, 1932.
38. See J. E. McDonough, "The Federal Home Loan Bank System," *American Economic Review* (December, 1934), pp. 668-685.
39. The 1933 amendments similarly weakened the property rights of railroad creditors. On the bankruptcy changes, see Charles C. Rohlfing, Edward W. Carter, Bradford W. West, and John G. Hervey, *Business and Government* (Chicago: The Foundation Press, 1934), pp. 402-430.
40. On the opposition, see Warren, *op. cit.*, p. 69.
41. Robert A. Divine, *American Immigration Policy, 1924-1952* (New Haven, Conn.: Yale University Press, 1957), pp. 84-89.

NOTES TO CHAPTER 12

1. Theodore Saloutos and John D. Hicks, *Agricultural Discontent in the Middle West, 1900-1939* (Madison, Wisc.: University of Wisconsin Press, 1951), p. 448.

2. Total monetary contraction from June, 1929 to the end of 1933 was 16.0 per cent, or 3.6 per cent per annum.

3. An apt commentary on whether time deposits are money is this statement by two St. Louis bankers: "Actually all of us were treating our savings and time deposits as demand deposits and we still do . . . we still pay our savings depositors on demand. It is significant that the heavy runs on banks were engineered by savings and time depositors. When the trouble was at its height in January, 1933, practically every bank in St. Louis faced heavy withdrawals from . . . savings depositors and had a minimum of difficulty with the checking depositors. This was true throughout most of the country." F. R. von Windegger and W. L. Gregory, in Irving Fisher, *100% Money* (New York: Adelphi Press, 1935), pp. 150-151.

4. See Jesse H. Jones and Edward Angly, *Fifty Billion Dollars* (New York: Macmillan Co., 1951), pp. 17ff.

5. Detroit had especially overexpanded during the boom, and frantic efforts by Hoover and his Administration, along with Detroit industrialists and New York banks, to save the leading Detroit banks, had foundered on the devotion to private enterprise and true private responsibility of Henry Ford and of Michigan's Senator Couzens, both of whom refused to agree to subsidize unsound banking. See Jones and Angly, *op. cit.*, pp. 58-65. Also see Lawrence E. Clark, *Central Banking Under the Federal Reserve System* (New York: Macmillan Co., 1935), pp. 226ff.; Benjamin M. Anderson, *Economics and the Public Welfare,* (New York: D. Van Nostrand Co., 1949), pp. 285ff. Dr. Anderson, supposedly an advocate of *laissez-faire,* sound money, and property right, went so far in the other direction as to chide the states for not going further in declaring bank holidays. He declared that bank moratoria should have applied to one hundred per cent, not just ninety-five per cent, of bank deposits, and he also attacked the Clearing House for failing to issue large quantities of paper money during the crisis.

6. See H. Parker Willis, "A Crisis in American Banking," in Willis and John M. Chapman, eds., *The Banking Situation* (New York: Columbia University Press, 1934), pp. 9ff. The holiday laws either (a) forbade banks to redeem the funds of depositors, or (b) permitted the banks to choose the proportion of claims that they would pay, or (c) designated the proportion of claims the depositors might redeem.

7. Willis, *loc. cit.*, p. 11. In New York, the pressure for bank closing came from the upstate, rather than from the Wall Street, banks.

8. See Jones and Angly, *op. cit.* Michigan's Governor Comstock, who had begun the furore, naturally extended his holiday beyond the original eight-day period.

9. Lest it be thought that Hoover would never have contemplated going this far, Jesse Jones reports that Hoover, during the banking crisis, was seriously contemplating invoking a forgotten wartime law making hoarding a criminal offense! Jones and Angly, *op. cit.*, p. 18.

10. There was a recurring tendency on the part of Hoover and his colleagues to blame the whole depression on a plot by Hoover's political enemies.

Hoover attributed part of the currency crisis to Communists spreading distrust of the American monetary system (it is remarkable that Communists were needed for distrust to arise!); and Simeon D. Fess, Chairman of the Republican National Committee, said quite seriously in the fall of 1930: "Persons high in Republican circles are beginning to believe that there is some concerted effort on foot to utilize the stock market as a method of discrediting the Administration. Every time an Administration official gives out an optimistic statement about business conditions, the market immediately drops." Edward Angly (comp.) *Oh Yeah?* (New York: Viking Press, 1931), p. 27.

11. Another Hoover contribution to these times was a secret attempt to stop the press from printing the full truth about the banking crisis, and about views hostile to his Administration. See Kent Cooper, *Kent Cooper and the Associated Press* (New York: Random House, 1959), p. 157.

12. In fact, Ballantine recently wrote, rather proudly: "the going off [gold] cannot be laid to Franklin Roosevelt. It had been determined to be necessary by Ogden Mills, Secretary of the Treasury, and myself as his Undersecretary, long before Franklin Roosevelt took office." *New York Herald-Tribune* (May 5, 1958), p. 18.

13. Leonard P. Ayres, *The Chief Cause of This and Other Depressions* (Cleveland: Cleveland Trust Co., 1935), pp. 26ff.

14. Sol Shaviro, "Wages and Payroll in the Depression, 1929-1933," (Unpublished M. A. essay, Columbia University, 1947).

15. See C. A. Phillips, T. F. McManus, and R. W. Nelson, *Banking and the Business Cycle* (New York: Macmillan Co., 1937), pp. 231-232.

16. "Maintenance of higher wage rates caused many firms to discharge workers rather than appear as slackers by cutting wages, although they might have been able to continue operations if they had made such reductions." Dale Yoder and George R. Davies, *Depression and Recovery* (New York: McGraw-Hill Co., 1934), p. 89.

17. National Industrial Conference Board, *Salary and Wage Policy in the Depression* (New York: The Conference Board, 1933), pp. 31-38.

18. Harold M. Levinson, "Unionism, Wage Trends, and Income Distribution: 1914-1947," *Michigan Business Studies* (June, 1951), pp. 34-47. Hoover and Secretary Lamont tried to induce the nation's industrialists to be more favorable to unions, by urging them, during 1930 and 1931, to meet at a formal conference with leaders of organized labor. See James O. Morris, "The AF of L in the 1920's: A Strategy of Defense," *Industrial and Labor Relations Review* (July, 1958), pp. 577-578.

19. *Monthly Labor Review, Vol. 35* (1932), pp. 489ff., 790ff.

NOTES TO APPENDIX

1. It is conventionally argued, e.g., by Professor Due, that we should not include government *transfer payments*, e.g., relief payments, in any such expenditures deducted because transfer payments are *not* included in the original GNP figure. But the important consideration is that

taxes (or deficits) to finance transfer payments *do* act as a drain on the national product, and therefore must be subtracted from GPP to yield PPR. Due claims that, in gauging the relative size of governmental and private activity, transfer payments should not be included because they "merely shift purchasing power" from one set of private hands to another, without the government's using up resources. But this "mere shift" is just as much a burden upon the private *producers,* just as much a shift from voluntary production to state-created privilege, as any other governmental expenditure. It is a government-induced using of resources. John F. Due, *Government Finance* (Homewood, Ill.: Richard D. Irwin, 1954), pp. 64, 76-77.

2. A surplus slightly overestimates the extent of depredation if it is used to deflate the money supply, and government expenditures slightly overstate the extent of depredation by counting in the amount of government taxes levied on government bureaucrats themselves. The amount of distortion is slight, however, particularly for the 1929-1932 period, and is less than the distortion of using GNP instead of GPP, and thus counting governmental payment of salaries as equivalent to the "product" of government.

3. Of course, official figures are not always accurate estimates of true depreciation. For a cogent discussion of the advantages and disadvantages of using *net* or *gross* measures of the governmental burden on the economy, see *The Tax Burden In Relation To National Income and Product* (New York: The Tax Foundation, 1957).

4. Solomon Fabricant and Robert E. Lipsey, *The Trend of Government Activity in the United States Since 1900* (New York: National Bureau of Economic Research, 1952), pp. 222-234.

5. Because, in our figures, state and local governments are already lumped together, our estimates will, from this standpoint, considerably *underestimate* the fiscal burden of government on the private sector.

Index